SHADOW COLD WAR

THE NEW COLD WAR HISTORY
Odd Arne Westad, *editor*

*This series focuses on new interpretations of the Cold War era
made possible by the opening of Soviet, East European, Chinese,
and other archives. Books in the series based on multilingual and
multiarchival research incorporate interdisciplinary insights and
new conceptual frameworks that place historical scholarship in a
broad, international context.*

SHADOW COLD WAR

The Sino-Soviet Competition for the Third World

Jeremy Friedman

The University of North Carolina Press *Chapel Hill*

Published with the assistance of the Anniversary Fund of the University of North Carolina Press

Set in Minion by Westchester Publishing Services

The paper in this book meets the guidelines for permanence and durability of the Committee on Production Guidelines for Book Longevity of the Council on Library Resources. The University of North Carolina Press has been a member of the Green Press Initiative since 2003.

Cover images: Grunge China flag, depositphoto.com, © Engin Korkmaz; hammer and sickle, depositphotos.com, © wawritto.

Complete cataloging information for this title is available from the Library of Congress.
ISBN 978-1-4696-2376-4 (cloth: alk. paper)
ISBN 978-1-4696-4552-0 (pbk.: alk. paper)
ISBN 978-1-4696-2377-1 (ebook)

Portions of chapters 1–3 were previously published in a different form in "Soviet Policy in the Developing World and the Chinese Challenge in the 1960s," *Cold War History* 10.2 (Spring 2010): 247–72, and "Free at Last, Now What: The Soviet and Chinese Attempts to Offer a Roadmap for the Post-colonial World," *Modern China Studies* 22.1 (Winter 2015): 254–87. Used with permission.

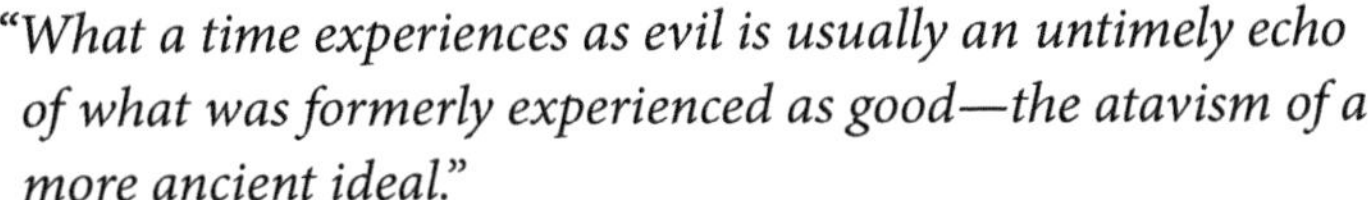

"What a time experiences as evil is usually an untimely echo of what was formerly experienced as good—the atavism of a more ancient ideal."

—Friedrich Nietzsche, *Beyond Good and Evil*

Contents

Acknowledgments

The publication of this book entailed the use of many resources beyond my own, financial and logistical as well as intellectual. I have to thank first and foremost International Security Studies (ISS) and the Brady-Johnson Program in Grand Strategy at Yale University for their financial support and for giving me a professional and intellectual home these past few years. I have also benefited from two research fellowships from the Social Science Research Council (SSRC) as well as from the Institute for European, Russian and Eurasian Studies (IERES) at the Elliot School of International Affairs at the George Washington University. I would particularly like to thank Kathleen Galo, Elizabeth Vastakis, and Igor Biryukov at ISS; Cynthia Buckley, Denise Mishiwiec, and Sam Zief at SSRC; and Hope Harrison, Henry Hale, Gregg Brazinsky, and Harris Mylonas at IERES.

The support of these organizations allowed me to travel widely and frequently for research, and I owe a debt of gratitude to many archivists and librarians, particularly the staff at the Russian State Archive of Contemporary History (RGANI), and the Archive of the Foreign Policy of the Russian Federation (AVPRF) as well as the Archive of the Chilean Ministry of Foreign Relations (AMREC), the South African Department of Foreign Affairs Archive (SADFAA), and the staff at the Bundesarchiv in Berlin. In particular, archivist Hao Weihua at the Chinese Foreign Ministry Archive (CFMA) helped me immeasurably, as did archivist Steve De Agrela at the South African National Defense Forces Archive (SANDFA), from whom I learned much about everything from wars in southern Africa to the finer points of Hindi grammar during lunch at the small building on Visagie Street. I would also like to thank the Wingrin family for giving me a home in Pretoria.

Intellectually, this work is a product of numerous influences and interactions. Stephen Kotkin helped shaped this work in a multitude of ways, keeping my eye on the mechanics of history while encouraging me to be bold and ambitious, and I am forever grateful to him. Daniel Rodgers, Kevin Kruse, and Gilbert Rozman provided useful commentary and perspectives. Since coming to Yale, I have learned much about both form and content from John Gaddis, Adam Tooze, Paul Kennedy, Scott Boorman, and Paul Solman. Ryan Irwin and Amanda Behm have been invaluable as interlocutors and editors, and their support has enabled me to get through some of the more difficult periods of completing this project. Odd Arne Westad has been a mentor, an intellectual role model, and an advocate, and without him this book might never have been conceived, let alone completed. Chen Jian has always been willing to engage with my work, and his passion for history and the importance of what we study is an inspiration. Others who have been instrumental are almost too many to list. Vladimir Shubin at the Institute of Africa in Moscow took a chance on a cocky kid and introduced me to all sorts of former members of the Soviet Central Committee's International Department. Amir Weiner helped start me on this road as an undergraduate at Stanford, making sure that a doctorate in history was in my future. Mark Kramer, James Hershberg, Paul Bushkovitch, Sergey Radchenko, Artemy Kalinovsky, Pey-yi Chu, Jeffrey Byrne, Jeremi Suri, Michelle Reeves, Kate Geoghegan, Sulmaan Khan, Chris Miller, Joe Parrott, and Anand Toprani all provided useful feedback and a welcoming intellectual community. I am grateful for the book's anonymous reviewers who forced me to sharpen the arguments, and for the efforts of the University of North Carolina Press, especially Charles Grench, in seeing the project through. I would also like to thank the editors at *Cold War History* and *Modern China Studies* who gave me permission to incorporate aspects of my earlier work into this book.

I would like to thank my erstwhile roommate Jack Tannous for his companionship, brilliance, and wit through the long years of researching and writing. Amanda Grady has been in my corner every step of the way through the publishing process, and her enthusiasm and support have kept me afloat more than once. This book is hers too.

Finally, I would like to thank my parents for countless rides to the airport and shipments of clothes, books, and medicines—and even one kosher salami via diplomatic pouch. They are the ones who have seen this book evolve from its true beginnings as an eighth-grade term paper, and it is they who might finally make my brother read it.

INTRODUCTION
A Tale of Two Revolutions

"If you want to become another Tarzan, a white man coming among black men, leading them and protecting them . . . it can't be done."[1] So said Egypt's charismatic young leader, the tribune of Pan-Arabism, Gamal Abdel Nasser to another young revolutionary, Che Guevara, on the eve of the latter's journey to the jungles of Kivu Province in the former Belgian Congo to spearhead revolution in the heart of Africa. When Guevara first met Nasser in 1959 in the course of his initial first postrevolutionary tour of Africa, he asked him how many refugees had been created in Egypt's own revolution. Nasser had replied only a few, which Guevara declared meant "that nothing much happened in your revolution . . . I measure the depth of the social transformation by the number of people who are affected by it and feel they have no place in the new society."[2] Though the former upper-middle-class medical student from Buenos Aires and the young, nationalist officer from Alexandria met each other as icons of revolution, their concepts of revolution were fundamentally different. For Nasser, revolution meant the unification of the Egyptian, and Arab, people to restore their sovereignty and dignity against foreign oppressors. For Guevara, revolution was first and foremost about violently rectifying the inequities within each society. For the former, the line of revolutionary division circled the world like a second equator between oppressed and oppressor nations. For the latter, it ran through the center of every country, though, of course, the ruling groups in some countries were more powerful than the ruling groups in others.

This book will examine the clash of these two revolutionary programs, the anti-imperialist revolution and the anticapitalist one, at the nexus of the Cold War and decolonization via the conflict known as the Sino-Soviet split. Though the split has generally been presented as a clash of interests or egos, this book will argue, instead, that it should be seen also as the geopolitical mechanism by which the demands, ideas, and interests of the newly decolonized states challenged and ultimately came to shape the revolutionary agenda of the global Left centered around the international communist movement. While the ruling parties of both the Soviet Union and the People's Republic of China (PRC) believed that one unified world revolutionary process existed that would overturn the inextricably linked systems of capitalism and imperialism—a revolutionary process they each sought to lead—those parties perceived that revolutionary process through the prism of their own histories and political traditions, a divide that would lead them to see the priorities of revolution differently. For the Soviets, the cause of replacing capitalism with socialism would always remain their top priority, and anti-imperialism mattered insofar as it served that greater purpose. For the Chinese, on the other hand, having had more direct experience with the trials and tribulations of imperialism, anti-imperialism remained the guiding focus of the revolutionary process, and socialism was seen as a tool with which to shift the global balance of power through economic development and autarchy. The conflict between Moscow and Beijing thus played out globally as a conflict between these competing revolutionary agendas. To rebuff the Chinese challenge to its supposed position as the leader of the world revolution, the Soviets would be forced ultimately to adapt their revolutionary agenda to account for the interests of the Global South at the expense of the global working class, a shift that would have profound consequences for revolutionary movements and political rhetoric the world over.

These two revolutions were not strangers. Lenin had famously connected them by declaring that imperialism was the highest stage of capitalism, and, by the time that Nasser and Che met, it had become accepted dogma for many revolutionaries that these two phenomena formed a single system of oppression that would, therefore, be overthrown by a single revolutionary process. This approach was formally embraced at the Second Comintern Congress in July 1920 and in the creation of the League against Imperialism at the 1927 Brussels Anti-Imperialism conference.[3] In the years between World War I and World War II, the Soviet Union and the Comintern did attempt to support the anticolonial struggle. However, their primary focus remained on the revolution within the industrialized world. As the world sank into depression and politics radicalized across the ideological spectrum in the 1930s, the prospect of working-class revolution in the industrialized nations, where traditional Marxism had always envisioned it, seemed very real indeed. With breadlines, mass unemployment, and violent, racist, authoritarian politics the order of the day in much of Europe and North America, the explosive economic growth of Stalin's USSR seemed to provide a tempting alternative. By the 1960s, though, the global revolutionary battleground had shifted. The West, to the shock not only of Moscow, but of many in Washington and London as well, had failed to return to depression after the war, and the prospects for Marxist revolution in the developed world began to recede. Instead, revolutionary energies exploded in the developing world. The grievances that motivated these revolutionary outbreaks were often expressed in terms of identity—racial, ethnic, or national— more than class, while in the industrialized world the insurrectionary ferment of the now largely sated working class was replaced by the alienation of students and racial minorities.

Nevertheless, the two revolutions still had common ground. While the nationalist, anti-imperialist revolutions might have been framed in terms of national, ethnic, or racial identity, much of the impetus for revolutionary activity still came from material deprivation. The new leaders of the 1960s knew that millennial hopes for economic growth and material prosperity lay behind the enthusiasm with which their peoples greeted independence and that failure on this score would be catastrophic. In a sense then, both Nasser's revolution and Che's revolution met in the 1960s on the grounds of modernization. Modernization is a notoriously tricky concept, and one that was often invoked during the Cold War to describe a universal process that both capitalist and communist countries would undergo, perhaps leading to a sort of convergence. In this case, I am using modernity in a relative, not an absolute sense. The struggle for modernization was a struggle of those peoples who had been left behind economically, oppressed politically, and repressed culturally to attain not only living standards that approximated those of the most industrialized countries, but also a certain dignity and influence in the international arena that they had been denied. The quest for this sort of modernity often focused on alternative paths from those well-trodden by the industrialized countries, paths that seemed quicker, easier, and maybe even superior. The goal was, as the old Stalinist phrase had it, to "catch up and overtake." In this way, both the Cold War and the process of decolonization fit within a larger twentieth-century narrative of modernization, which took the form of an international and domestic competition to find the development model that would provide a solution to both international and domestic inequality and bring the benefits of the technological revolutions of the previous three centuries to the majority of the world's population.

This ubiquitous desire for modernization was often accompanied by a belief that revolution confined to the boundaries of an individual state was insufficient. Since the late nineteenth century, advances in transportation and communication, combined with the extension of European imperialist influence to all corners of the globe, had given rise to a growing sense that radical change in one country or part of the world necessitated change on a global scale, both because of the growing awareness of parallel political structures and economic regimes and because of the consciousness that imperialism was too formidable to be confronted alone.[4] Even the liberal nationalists of Erez Manela's "Wilsonian Moment" thought that the satisfaction of their own national aspirations required nothing less than the transformation of the whole system of international relations.[5] Once former colonies gained their independence but found that their material circumstances had not changed, this push for global revolution would take on economic overtones. As Kwame Nkrumah, the tribune of Pan-Africanism, wrote in his book *Neo-Colonialism: The Last Stage of Imperialism*, which was essentially an updating of Lenin's argument for the postcolonial age, "The danger is now not civil war within individual states provoked by intolerable conditions within those states, but international war provoked ultimately by the misery of the majority of mankind who daily grow poorer and poorer."[6] This belief in the possibility and necessity of global revolution led ambitious political leaders to construct theories and policies with an eye toward their international resonances, believing that they had a unique role to play in the transformation of the international order. In many, but not all, cases these leaders were influenced by Marxism of some sort. Candidates for the mantle of the leader of world revolution included figures as diverse as Che Guevara, Ho Chi Minh, Nkrumah, Ahmed Sukarno, Gamal Abdel Nasser, and even Nicolae Ceaușescu. Though their ideologies and philosophies varied greatly, they all fundamentally agreed that revolution had to be a global phenomenon in order to solve the problems of inequality and oppression that characterized the imperialist world order.

For the leaders of the Soviet Union and People's Republic of China, formally committed to an ideology that predicted world revolution, establishing their leadership of that world revolutionary process was both an ideological necessity and a grand strategic imperative. The latter was the case because neither Imperial Russia nor Republican China enjoyed the economic and political conditions that seemed necessary to build a socialist utopia on its own, and both Bolsheviks in Russia and the Chinese Communist Party found themselves surrounded by hostile forces upon taking power. Though the imperatives of more narrow Soviet political interest would at times override those of world revolution, the claim to be the leader of the world revolution remained central to the role the USSR attempted to play on the world stage and to the support that it commanded around the globe. Emerging victorious after World War II, with expanded global influence and a phalanx of satellites in Eastern Europe, the Soviet Union could claim more strongly than ever that history was on its side. It soon found itself in a direct confrontation with the United States, first in Europe and then in the rest of the world, over ideology and influence. In time, though, the revolutionary battleground shifted, away from the booming West toward the decolonizing South, and with this shift the degree of unity that Moscow had managed to achieve within the Communist movement at the end of the war began to crumble.

Decolonization changed the terms of the anticipated world revolution. It put the question of revolutionary war squarely on the table in a way that it had not been arguably since the Red Army was stopped outside Warsaw in 1920. It changed the economic questions from ones about how to reorganize an industrial economy along socialist lines to others about how to rescue nations from abject poverty and construct an industrial economy from the ground up. Finally, it put race and nation, rather than class, at the center of revolutionary discourse in many places. By itself, this placed the Soviet leadership, in competition with the West for influence in the decolonizing world, in a difficult spot. However, despite the best efforts of some, the postcolonial states never managed to form a united front that could have offered an alternative to the USSR as the leader of the world revolutionary process. It took the People's Republic of China, a power of similar ambition and immense size, to crystallize the threat that decolonization posed to Soviet revolutionary leadership into one that could actually present a true alternative. The PRC, a nonwhite, non-European, primarily agrarian nation which had suffered tremendously from the depredations of imperialism, managed to rally others in its challenge to the Soviet agenda and revolutionary model, and, for a while, it threatened Soviet influence in Asia, Africa, and to some degree in Latin America as well. In part, the Chinese leadership felt compelled to mount this challenge in order to build its own global constituency to protect it from American aggression and Soviet betrayal. As a result, the Soviets now were waging a two-front struggle against the United States on one side and China on the other. While much has been written about the first of these struggles, much less has been written about the second, and that which has been written has focused on the bilateral Sino-Soviet relationship rather than the competition between these two nations for influence around the world.[7] Viewed from the perspective of the global competition between the USSR and the PRC, it becomes clear that the divide between the Soviets and the Chinese ran deeper than personal rivalries or domestic politics. It reflected a much more profound tension between two different revolutionary agendas, agendas that were not the sole province or concern of either Moscow or Beijing.

Revolutionary Origins and Trajectories

In his introduction to a book on the rise and fall of the Sino-Soviet alliance, Odd Arne Westad makes an important point about the nature of the role of ideology in the Sino-Soviet split: "The fact that ideology was crucial to both sides, while there was never a *common* ideology [italics his], is essential to understanding the rise and fall of the Sino-Soviet alliance."[8] To many readers this will sound strange. After all, the leaders of both the USSR and the PRC called themselves Marxist-Leninist, they appealed primarily to the same textual canon, and Soviet Communists were instrumental in constructing and guiding the Chinese Communist Party from the day it was created until mid-1960. Where could these differing ideologies have come from? Part of the answer is supplied in a quote from the memoirs of Karen Brutents, a member of the International Department of the Central Committee of the Communist Party of the Soviet Union (CPSU) for almost thirty years and its deputy director for almost half of that time. Writing about the Sino-Soviet split and the sympathy that the PRC engendered among many Asian parties as the "strongest blow against the communist movement," Brutents goes beyond the bilateral framework and asserts that "the Chinese assertion (*vystuplenie*) demonstrated not only the force which the national (or nationalist) factor had scored, but also that the disagreement within the communist movement was connected to the differences between the situations of backward, agrarian and industrially-developed countries."[9] In true Marxist fashion, Brutents points to "objective" factors underlying the split beyond the "subjective" factors, such as ego-clashes and cultural animosities. This view has a number of advantages. Besides explaining the global resonance of the split, it also allows us to put the split in the greater historical context of both the Russian and the Chinese revolutions.

The CPSU and the Chinese Communist Party (CCP) both claimed to be "Marxist-Leninist" parties and they consequently battled for what they believed to be the mantle of leadership of a single global revolution. However, they were in fact two very different parties confronting different problems and pursuing different agendas. Lenin's fateful conflation of imperialism with capitalism, and the consequent identification of the anti-imperialist struggle with the anticapitalist one, had obscured what were, in fact, two different revolutionary struggles. The revolutionaries who made the Russian Revolution and constructed the Soviet Union were primarily products of the anticapitalist revolution. The imperatives of the Russian Revolution, before even the introduction of Marxism, were overcoming social inequality and domestic political tyranny. These factors had been prominent from the days of the Decembrists in the 1820s through the era of the Populists in the 1870s and beyond.[10] When Marxism was introduced to Russia, the intellectuals attracted to it came under the sway of more powerful and prominent European socialist parties where the anticapitalist struggle, at the height of the Industrial Revolution, was in full swing. Many of the key figures of the Bolshevik Revolution—Lenin, Trotsky, Zinoviev, and others—spent most of the decade before 1917 in European exile, in constant contact with their French and German comrades and viewing Russia from a distance. Consequently, the overriding imperative in their minds was to conduct a victorious class struggle, establish the dictatorship of the proletariat, and socialize the means of production. The enemies of the Russian Revolution, though there were certainly many around the world in the ruling circles of international monopoly capitalism, were still, first and foremost, domestic. The struggle of the Bolshevik Party, and its very legitimacy, was tied to its ability to replace the economic order of the Tsarist regime with something more egalitarian and more productive, even if it meant reliance on thousands of foreign experts. Unlike the Chinese Revolution with its nationalist emphasis and rhetoric, Lenin made demolishing Russian nationalism one of the regime's early political objectives. He famously wrote in response to Rosa Luxembourg, "Fight against all nationalisms and, first of all, against Great Russian nationalism."[11] The Russian Revolution, directed as it was at the leveling of inequalities and the building of socialism within Russia more than the defeat of foreign enemies, was fundamentally anticapitalist.

Since Russia was, however, the "weakest link in the capitalist chain," the leaders of the Bolshevik Party believed that the survival and success of the world's first socialist revolution depended upon its being immediately followed by socialist revolutions in the more developed capitalist countries, above all Germany.[12] When this revolution failed to take place, either through local uprisings or by means of the bayonets of the Red Army, Lenin and the newly created Communist International (Comintern) adopted a new strategy: the promotion of nationalist revolution in the colonial world in order to weaken, and ultimately destroy, the reigning political and economic order in the European metropoles. As Trotsky expressed it, "The road to India may prove at the given moment to be more readily passable and shorter for us than the road to Soviet Hungary."[13] Lenin's theory of imperialism as a global system therefore proved a necessary corollary to the possibility of socialist revolution in Russia. However, the center of this theory of imperialism remained the struggle of the working class in the advanced countries against the international networks of finance capital that relied upon the imperialist order. The colonial world played an ancillary role, as Lenin and the Comintern envisioned the role of these regions as aiding the struggle of the workers in the West rather than confronting, and then overturning, the world order themselves. As Karl Radek told the Baku Congress of the Peoples of the East in 1920, the Soviet task was to "unite with the peoples of the East and hasten the victory of West-European proletariat."[14] Given the priority of the struggle in the West, it is no surprise that the newly created Executive Committee of the Communist International in 1919 contained no representatives from the East.[15] In the "Theses on the Eastern Question," adopted in 1922 at the Fourth Comintern Congress, the priorities of the Comintern in the colonial world were made explicit: "The demand for a close alliance with the proletarian Soviet republic is the keynote of the anti-imperialist united front."[16] Though the Comintern would become extensively involved in revolutionary adventures in Asia, and to a lesser degree in Africa and Latin America, these efforts would remain subordinate, on the level of both theory and practice, to events in the industrialized world. Anti-imperialism, as understood by the early Soviet government and the Communist International, was clearly meant to serve the purposes of anticapitalism.

The Chinese Revolution had a very different provenance from the Russian one. China had been thrown into revolutionary ferment by the depredations of Western powers beginning with the First Opium War in 1839 and the impetus for change had come from the humiliation and exploitation suffered at the hands of foreigners. There were many grievances against the emperor and the social structure, as had often been the case in Chinese history, but what ultimately discredited these entities was their failure to defend China and their obvious inadequacy compared to the leading powers of the age. Rebecca Karl, in her study of Chinese intellectuals and nationalism at the turn of the twentieth century, writes that Chinese nationalism at this stage already began to take on a global perspective in which the sufferings of China were tied to those of other peoples around the world oppressed by imperialism. Chen Duxiu, writing in 1904, long before he would become a Marxist-Leninist and the first leader of the CCP, remarked that "the more I considered [China's problems], the more I thought, and then the more I grieved: the reason that our China is unlike foreign countries and indeed is bullied by these countries must have a good explanation. So I went to investigate [the histories of] other countries, and guess what? China is not the only country in this world being bullied by foreign countries! Look at Poland, Egypt, the Jews, India, Burma, Vietnam, and so on: they have all been destroyed and turned into dependencies."[17] While anti-imperialism was already present therefore in the minds of Chinese intellectuals, Marxism was nearly nonexistent in China before the popular movement that began on May 4, 1919. This movement arose spontaneously among students in Beijing objecting to the decision of the victorious Allied powers at the Versailles conference to award former German possessions in the Shandong Peninsula to Japan. That led to the growing attraction of Marxism in China because, as Maurice Meisner writes, "the Western ideas and ideologies that became most prominent after the May Fourth Incident were ones critical of the existing order in the West."[18] The Chinese Communist Party was founded two years later, its membership centered on two professors, Li Dazhao and Chen Duxiu, and their students who had been sparked to action by the nationalist sentiment of the May Fourth Movement. Though the new CCP soon came under the guidance of the Comintern, it found success only after it abandoned the Comintern strategy of urban uprisings and working-class support, appealing instead to the peasantry and, in the famous argument of Chalmers Johnson, mobilizing nationalist anti-Japanese sentiment. As Michael Hunt wrote, for Mao, imperialism was not some "bloodless abstraction," as it was in the Comintern's revolutionary theory, but rather the "bedrock" of his "personal experience."[19] The role of the CCP in fighting against Japan, though Mao hoped to gain from the destruction of the Nationalists, stood in contrast to the defeatism of Lenin and the Bolsheviks during World War I, when the latter believed that the defeat of Russia by more advanced countries was best for the success of the revolution.[20]

The attraction of Marxism in China, however, was not simply its anti-Western character. The shock of defeat and humiliation at the hands of foreigners had not only ignited nationalist sentiment, but it had also led slowly and fitfully to a recognition that fundamental social, political, and economic changes would be necessary if China were to survive, let alone compete, in the modern world. This notion that the preservation of the Chinese state required the transformation of Chinese society produced the Self-Strengthening Movement and later the reforms of the Hundred Days in 1898; however, as time went on and defeat after defeat piled on, it became clear that the proposed changes were not fundamental enough. The first decades of the twentieth century saw a flowering of movements and organizations seeking to transform the culture, but none attained the coherence and, by the late 1920s and 1930s, impressive track record of Communism.[21] Development, not only economic but social and cultural as well, was therefore at the center of the appeal of Marxism in China because it offered a way to build a China that could stand up for itself in the world. Marxists shared with other Chinese nationalists and reformists the diagnosis that the causes of China's humiliation were ultimately internal weakness and corrosion, and China would regain its rightful place in the world only after it had restored its own vitality. While debates raged, both within and without Communist circles in the period between the fall of the Qing in 1912 and the victory of the CCP in 1949, about the values and structures that China should adopt to restore its rightful place in the world, one principle was held in common: anti-imperialism, and Chinese resurgence, must begin at home.

In the wake of the Chinese Communist victory of 1949, the Chinese construction of socialism took on a decidedly different tactical approach from the Soviet one, a fact which was all the more striking given the extensive presence of Soviet experts and aid in the PRC at the time. Describing his notion of a "people's democratic dictatorship," Mao asserted that the new government would rest on a coalition of four classes: the proletariat, the peasantry, the petty bourgeoisie, and the national bourgeoisie.[22] This approach reflected two elements: a nationalist desire to incorporate as much of the nation as possible in the effort to build "New China" and a consequent shift in the notion of class from one built strictly on one's relation to the means of production to a more malleable one based on loyalty to the political system and its ideology. While the Chinese Communist victory in the civil war had been aided by the mobilization of the sense of grievance of many groups—poor peasants, women, workers—once in power the imperatives of national growth and reconstruction—imperatives that had propelled the Chinese revolution since the third quarter of the nineteenth century—led the CCP to use "class" in such a way that would allow it to increase its power and harness the capabilities of its people rather than excising too many large, predetermined groups from the Chinese body politic. This entailed a departure from the Stalinist orthodoxy that the class struggle intensified as the achievement of socialism approached. Mao argued instead that "Contradictions in socialist society are fundamentally different from those in the old societies, such as capitalist society. In capitalist society contradictions find expression in acute antagonisms and conflicts, in sharp class struggle. . . . The case is quite different in socialist society; on the contrary, they are not antagonistic and can be ceaselessly resolved by the socialist system itself."[23] One of the ways to do this was to make class identity malleable, something that could be changed with political education rather than permanently embedded. While it would be an exaggeration to assert, as Soviet China expert Fedor Burlatskii did, that this approach "allows for arbitrariness in identifying a person's class affiliation,"[24] it did enable the regime to "define class more on the basis of political attitudes than according to objective Marxian economic and social criteria."[25] In the development of Chinese socialism, then, "class" would become something one could change or prove by demonstrating loyalty to Mao, a phenomenon that would reach its tragic apex in the battles between Red Guards and Radical Red Guards during the Cultural Revolution. However, at other times, it would enable the regime to be more flexible in making use of the talents and energies of its population to grow the Chinese state and economy.

This flexibility was evident in the way the regime undertook several major initiatives at the outset. The initial land reform, launched by the Agrarian Reform law of June 28, 1950, sought to preserve the "rich-peasant economy."[26] While CCP land reform efforts during the civil war had entailed massive violence against landlords, and even this new land reform policy would be far more violent in practice than in theory,[27] the intent remained to avoid the economic damage inflicted by Stalinist collectivization. In his major address opening the land reform campaign in June 1950, Liu Shaoqi argued that the Communist victory made it logical that the rich peasants would accept Communist authority, and so land reform could be completed with less violence. As Ezra Vogel observes, "Having studied Soviet affairs very closely, Liu was well aware of the difficulties resulting from the liquidation of the Kulaks."[28] Mao did not share Liu's positive view of peasant land ownership, and he pushed a more rapid path to collectivization, but even he, when faced with determined peasant resistance, stopped short of the full-scale "war" on the peasantry that Stalin had joined.[29] Instead, at the height of peasant protest against the grain-procurement program in 1955, "the state emphasized the use of persuasion and education to handle the unrest."[30] According to Alexander Pantsov and Steven Levine, "on the whole, socialism came rather peacefully to the Chinese countryside."[31] That is not to say that the transition to socialism was carried out bloodlessly or harmoniously in China, but that the search for enemies focused more on dissidence and disobedience, especially within the party, than on eliminating whole groups based on their class background.[32] As Vogel writes, "In the Chinese view, the Russian effort to counter 'rightist resistance' relied too heavily on force and too little on 'thought preparation.'"[33] Violence in the socialization of the countryside in China was most certainly abundant, and it should not be minimized. However, the key distinction here is the way in which violence was employed and where it was directed. Violence was used with an eye toward creating the most obedient and effective economic and political machine rather than as a means of breaking entire classes of people who did not fit into the Marxist schema.

In building a socialist commercial and industrial base, the new PRC government relied on the cooperation of the bourgeoisie, though, of course, from a position of coercive power. As Mao wrote in 1950, "existing industry and commerce should be properly readjusted, and relations between labor and capital should be effectively and suitably improved; thus under the leadership of the socialist state sector all sectors of the economy will function satisfactorily with a due division of labor to promote the rehabilitation and development of the whole economy."[34] This process itself was brutal enough, but the terror unleashed against the "capitalist class" in 1952 ultimately classified the majority as "basically law-abiding" or "semi law-abiding" and let them off with fines in order to make use of them.[35] A series of agreements made with businessmen in 1955 eased the transition into a socialist economy, and the government couched this transition in nationalist terms: "The state requests that businessmen continue their work and shoulder responsibilities, expressing love for their great and glorious fatherland and warm and sincere support for socialist transformation."[36] Socialism was seen as the best way to create a new, powerful, independent China and, as such, it was imperative that as many of the Chinese people as possible participate. Perhaps the simplest indication of the different natures of the respective revolutions is the difference in the terms that Russians and Chinese use, to this day, to describe their own revolutions. In Russian, the period before 1917 is naturally referred to as *dorevoliutsionnyi*, literally "prerevolutionary." In Chinese, however, the period before 1949 is not called *geming qian* (革命前), "before the revolution," but rather *jiefang qian* (解放前), "before the liberation." Though similar means were adopted by both sides, at least until the late 1970s, the underlying aims of the two revolutions were different, a fact that would impact not only the domestic conduct of the revolution, but also understandings of global processes and historical trends and, ultimately, the respective abilities of each side to reform.

Revolutions Together

Nevertheless, the influence of the Leninist conception of imperialism was very real, and both the CPSU and the CCP leaders considered the anticapitalist and anti-imperialist revolutions to be one and the same. That is why, when the global revolutionary battleground shifted from the capitalist world in the 1930s to the developing world in the 1960s, releasing centrifugal forces within the international Communist movement, both the Soviets and the Chinese saw it as their task to reestablish the unity of revolutionary forces around the world by promoting their respective models of revolution. The two revolutions were misperceived as one. Nevertheless, the different backgrounds of the Soviet and Chinese Revolutions led them to emphasize different policies based on different priorities, such as "peaceful coexistence" and economic competition in the Soviet case as opposed to militant anti-imperialism and "self-reliance" in the Chinese case. Initially, the Chinese approach commanded significant sympathy in the developing world, as Brutents noted, and the Soviet Union was faced with the real prospect of losing its status as the leader of the world revolution. China's appeal rested on its own experience with imperialist oppression, cultural and racial factors, and its success in building a powerful new state on the basis of a backward, agrarian country. To defeat the Chinese challenge and attempt to recover its leadership in a world transfigured by decolonization, the Soviet leaders had to adopt the Chinese revolutionary agenda to a significant degree. They shifted from peaceful coexistence to militant anti-imperialism, from emphasis on class struggle to a greater attention to national, ethnic, and racial issues, and from an emphasis on domestic economic reform oriented toward socializing the means of production to a model based more on economic growth and restructuring the international terms of trade. The result was that the anti-imperialist agenda often took precedence over the anticapitalist one, a major shift for left-wing forces around the globe, even as many of them continued to see the two revolutions as one.

The mass wave of decolonization that followed World War II was not the first time that the anticapitalist and anti-imperialist revolutions had been combined. However, the Comintern and Soviet engagement with the anti-imperialist revolution in the interwar period reflected both the Euro-centrist agenda of the Bolshevik leadership and the limited resources and reach of the young state. The Comintern turned its attention to the colonial world at its Second Congress in 1920 where Lenin and Indian Communist M. N. Roy clashed over whether Communist parties in developing states should ally themselves with other nationalist forces (Lenin's position) or maintain their independent action (Roy's stance). The congress was followed later that year by the Congress of the Toilers of the East in Baku and the next year by the establishment of the University of the Toilers of the East. Despite this opening, the scope of Comintern activity in the developing world was quite limited, focused primarily on China and, to a lesser degree, India, Persia, and Turkey. The Chinese episode marked the most famous failure of the Comintern, as the latter's policy of directing the CCP to ally itself with the Guomindang (GMD) resulted in the massacre of most of the members of the former by the latter under the leadership of Jiang Jieshi (Chiang Kaishek) in 1927. The bitter experiences of the CCP, especially Mao Zedong, who often found himself at odds with the Comintern-oriented party leadership, undoubtedly played a major role in later CCP inclinations to doubt both the wisdom and the commitment of Moscow's policy in the developing world.[37] The disaster in China led the Comintern at the Sixth Congress in 1928 to change course, abandoning the idea of national fronts in favor of a narrow communist struggle, a decision that effectively ended its serious involvement in the anticolonial struggle. Demonstrating how limited the reach of the Comintern had been before 1928, the Sixth Congress marked the first time that Latin America had attained substantial representation, and the Comintern leaders thus declared their "discovery of America."[38] Ironically, it was at this Sixth Congress, which resulted in lessened Comintern involvement in the anticolonial struggle, that the Comintern first put forth a program for revolutionaries in developing countries to follow upon attainment of power.[39] This platform, however, gave a more detailed blueprint for the socialist revolution than it did for the so-called democratic-bourgeois revolution. The legacy of the Comintern therefore offered little that would prove valuable to the USSR when the dam of decolonization burst.

The real work of developing a useful model for the postcolonial world would have to wait until the Khrushchev era when the opportunity presented itself and the Soviet state had the resources to do something about it. In the meantime, even as the decolonization process began in earnest after 1945, Stalin did not believe that the newly independent states were really independent or that they represented an important change in the world balance of power. In a letter to Molotov in December 1946 concerning the UN's creation of a Trusteeship Council, Stalin wrote: "These leaders [of the colonies], as you well know, in their majority are corrupt and care not so much for the independence of their territories as for the preservation of their privileges with regard to the population of these territories. The time is not yet ripe for us to clash over the fate of these territories and to quarrel over their future with the rest of the world, including their corrupt leaders themselves."[40] When the Communist Information Bureau (Cominform) was founded as a kind of replacement for the Comintern in 1947, not a single representative of one of the Communist parties of Asia, Africa, or Latin America was present, not even from the CCP. Instead, in contrast to the tension that would arise between Khrushchev's aggressive policy toward the developing world and his advocacy of peaceful coexistence, Mikhail Suslov declared at a Cominform meeting in 1949 that "the Communist and Workers' Parties must use every means in the struggle to ensure stable and prolonged peace; they must subordinate all their activities to this paramount task of the day."[41] This left very little room for support of anticolonial movements.

The CCP, on the other hand, led by Mao, took greater notice of the role of the colonial world in the global revolutionary process from an earlier stage. The ambiguities of the U.S.-Soviet relationship at the end of World War II, in particular the ways that both Moscow and Washington related to the burgeoning Chinese civil war, with Moscow cutting deals with the GMD while Washington failed to offer Jiang Jieshi unqualified support, led the CCP leadership to abandon its view that a direct confrontation between the USA and USSR was imminent. Instead, in late 1946, Mao and the CCP began to promote the concept of the "intermediate zone," which allegedly encompassed those parts of Asia, Africa, and Europe that stood between the USA and USSR and would be the focus of American imperialism for the immediate future.[42] For the time being, however, Mao's application of this concept focused greatly on the potential for leftist ascendancy within the Western camp, particular in Western Europe and even among the American public, and therefore it did not quite yet put the notion of an Afro-Asian anti-imperialist front at the center.[43] The difference between the CCP's vision and that of Moscow, though, was that the CCP saw the role of Asia as a battleground almost, if not equally, as important as Europe at this early stage, and this view would profoundly affect Beijing's post-1949 view of its own role and importance in the global revolutionary struggle.

Institutions of Revolution

In the wake of decolonization, Moscow would begin to realize the necessity of competing with the West and taking advantage of the available geopolitical opportunities. Khrushchev would therefore have to initiate a sea change in Soviet policy to raise the Soviet profile and increase its influence in the developing world. It would take not only a massive dedication of resources, but also a theoretical reconfiguration of the Soviet model of the global revolutionary process. The necessity for this theoretical reconfiguration, and the expertise that the new policy required, would have a tremendous effect on the institutional structure of the Soviet foreign policy apparatus. While the CPSU never fully achieved the ideal of collective leadership under Khrushchev, there was still more room for different voices from below to be heard than there had been under Stalin. Under Brezhnev, policymaking increasingly became the responsibility of the entire Politburo. Different figures within the Politburo had different institutional bases of power and the ascendance or decline of each member had a corresponding effect on the influence of the institution he represented. For example, when asked about Brezhnev's influence in charting the general direction of Soviet foreign policy, Karen Brutents retorted, "Brezhnev? Brezhnev read whatever we put in front of him!"[44] Brutents explained that generally Andropov, director of the KGB, Foreign Minister Gromyko, and often Boris Ponomarev, long-time head of the International Department, would convene before Politburo meetings in the late 1970s to work out a united position and that position would hold sway. While Brutents, writing from the perspective of the International Department, wrote that it, along with the KGB and Foreign Ministry, was the primary voice in foreign policy, the importance of the Ministry of Defense, though difficult to establish for reasons of archival access, cannot be discounted.[45] Key conversations in the Soviet foreign policy–making process often took place within the KGB, the International Department, and the Foreign Ministry. Nikolai Leonov, head of the Information-Analytical Administration of the KGB in the 1970s, describes such policy briefs prepared for Andropov and meetings in Andropov's office in his memoirs.[46] Brutents describes similar meetings within the International Department.[47] Since, as both Leonov and Brutents wrote, Foreign Minister Gromyko often could not be bothered with the affairs of the "Third World," responsibility for Soviet policy in the developing world would often fall upon the shoulders of the International Department and the KGB.[48] In particular, it often fell to working groups composed of Brutents and others within the International Department, as well as academic experts, to draft Brezhnev's speeches and other documents that outlined Soviet policy in the developing world.[49]

Who were these academic experts and where did they come from? When Khrushchev decided upon a more active policy in the developing world in response to decolonization in the late 1950s, the woeful lack of available Soviet expertise quickly became apparent. The response, as will be detailed in chapter 1, was to create a series of academic institutes and journals that would produce the expertise and information necessary to support this policy. Since the International Department itself was quite small, numbering roughly 300 individuals at its peak in the late 1980s and probably many fewer in the early 1960s,[50] it could not on its own do the work necessary to keep the leadership informed. Consequently, the International Department often relied on either collaboration with or out-sourcing to the various academic institutes, some of whose leaders commanded significant influence themselves within the Central Committee.[51] For example Babadjan Gafurov, appointed to head the Institute of Oriental Studies by Khrushchev in 1956, was the former first secretary of the Tadjik Communist Party.[52] A considerable amount of overlap and movement of personnel also could be found between the International Department, the academic institutes, the Foreign Ministry, and the so-called nongovernmental organizations. These organizations, such as the Soviet Committee for Solidarity with the Countries of Asia and Africa (SCSCAA) and the Soviet Peace Committee, were of course created by Central Committee resolutions,[53] and they contained high-ranking members of the academic community with political ties, such as the afore-mentioned Gafurov. While top Soviet leaders rarely traveled abroad and had little time to meet with representatives of liberation movements or leaders of political parties from the developing world, these tasks were taken up by SCSCAA and the International Department. Consequently, while ultimate decision-making power rested with the Politburo, the col-lection and analysis of information, the formation of policy recommen-dations, and the conduct of face-to-face meetings and implementation of policy were carried out by a group that came to be called the *mezhdun-arodniki* ("Internationalists"), consisting of the various members of the International Department, academic institutes, and "nongovernmental organizations." The *mezhdunarodniki* would accordingly play the key role in creating and adapting the new Soviet model for the developing world.

The picture of the decision-making apparatus in the PRC was quite different. Unlike the USSR, where the International Department essen-tially became the successor to the Comintern and Cominform after the latter's dissolution in 1956, its Chinese equivalent, the *Zhonglianbu* (中联部), or "Liaison Department," was much more limited in its func-tions. It dealt primarily, in these early years before the Cultural Revolu-tion, with contacts with other Communist/workers' parties, especially within the Socialist Bloc.[54] Consequently, the Foreign Ministry played the dominant role in interfacing with political actors in the developing world as well as collecting and analyzing information and making policy recommendations. Beijing's resources were much more limited than Moscow's and its institutions, such as the People's Liberation Army, were less developed, and so it had fewer tools for gaining direct access to the rest of the world. Though the PRC, like the USSR, began to set up aca-demic institutes during this time, the shorter scholarly tradition and scarcer resources meant that the primary task of these institutes was to make foreign scholarship available to the party. By the late 1950s, the Chinese Peace and Solidarity Committees, like their Soviet equivalents, began to play a significant role in the foreign policy process. They became the main tools for interacting with nongovernmental actors such as liberation movements. On the domestic side, the Peace Committee and the Institute of Foreign Affairs were responsible for receiving nonstate actors from abroad, and they, once again like their Soviet equivalents, became largely responsible for advising, arming, and training members of liberation movements in the PRC. Before the Cultural Revolution, the diplomats of the Chinese Foreign Ministry abroad seem to have played an important role not only in carrying out policy directions from the center, but also in gathering intelligence and occasionally even offering their own original assessments and suggestions, which sometimes affected policy back in Beijing. With the advent of the Cultural Revolution in late 1966, the Foreign Ministry was thrown into chaos and, besides Mao, Zhou, and perhaps a few other top leaders at times, it is hard to see who, if anyone, had a strong voice in Chinese foreign policy decision making during that time.[55]

Ideology and Policy

The attention devoted to the mechanisms of foreign policy decision making, and, in particular, the role of the *mezhdunarodniki*, is closely tied to a central debate of the historiography on Soviet and Chinese policy in the developing world, namely the role of ideology. While scholars writing during the Cold War lacked the archival access necessary to connect ideological pronouncements with policy outcomes,[56] post–Cold War scholarship, particularly on the "Third World," has focused more on the power dynamics of relationships between smaller states and superpowers than on the role of revolutionary ideology within the policy-making process or in the international arena.[57] The story of the Cold War in the developing world is a story of power dynamics, but it is not solely a story of power dynamics. The defining characteristic of the Cold War was that it was a clash of ideologies, a battle for the future political and economic development of humanity. The very nature of this struggle meant that it was not merely something that leaders such as Nasser or Nkrumah could manipulate to their advantage, but one in which they had a stake as well, and their own opinions reflected that fact. The nature of an ideological battle is such that anyone with an idea or an ideology of their own, and sufficient means to broadcast it, can make themselves heard. On issues such as the proper way to conduct land reform or the role of nationalism in the revolution, leaders of developing countries were able to make themselves heard in the global discussion and this meant that their relationships with Moscow, Beijing, and Washington went beyond mere struggles over aid and influence. None of this is to diminish either the role of power politics or the vast power asymmetry between the superpowers and the newly emerging states of the developing world. It is rather to say that there is another dimension to this story that needs to be explored to gain a full appreciation of the impact of the Cold War–decolonization confluence.

The question of the role of ideology in foreign policy, and particularly in the foreign policy of communist states, is not new. The issue of ideology versus *realpolitik* was central to the work of many scholars during the Cold War and, while the opening of archives has reignited the debate, its impact has been ambiguous. Mari Olsen, writing about Soviet and Chinese competition in Vietnam, claims: "During the Cold War, ideology was seen as a tool of limited relevance in helping us understand Soviet policies. Access to new sources has modified that view, *and the impact of ideology now seems to be the major new finding after more than ten years* with at least limited access to archives in the former Soviet Union, Eastern Europe, and China"(italics mine).[58] In contrast, Robert Ross, in his introduction to a volume on Sino-American relations, asserts: "Much of the literature on U.S.-China relations posits that each side was motivated either by its own ideologically informed interests or by ideological assumptions about its counterpart. The more recent Western literature on the U.S.-China conflict, however, tends to stress the importance of pragmatism."[59] It seems then that both sides have agreed that while the debate between ideology and realism raged during the Cold War, with the other side in the ascendant, post–Cold War research has subsequently ended the debate and proved their side correct, whichever side that may be.

The difficulty of making headway in the debate can be attributed to a number of problems that are presented by the nature of the question. To claim that foreign policy was affected by ideological considerations, it seems necessary first to define what ideology is, how it operates, what the tenets of the particular ideology supposedly being applied in this case are, and how those tenets would or should translate into political practice. A second problem is the issue of consistency. To what degree must the tenets of the ideology remain consistent for the ideology to be seen as a driving force? What does "consistent" even mean in the context of ideology, given constantly changing international circumstances? Ultimately, this problem revolves around whether perceived changes in ideology are merely opportunistic *post facto* justifications of policies motivated by other factors or genuine reassessments based on new events. Finally, perhaps the most intractable is the problem of documentation. Reliance on texts is unavoidable in history, but the very nature of a regime explicitly dedicated to a particular ideological program produces documents that will always frame issues in the terms of that ideology. Historians are then left to sift through the multiplicity of documents, including government proclamations, mass media, diplomatic conversations, government deliberations, and personal memoirs and correspondence, trying, often in vain, to determine which texts represent the "genuine" thoughts and motivations of the historical actors and which are merely justifications or propaganda. It is tempting to believe that more archival access is the solution, as access to increasingly secret and important documents must provide a window into the "true" nature of the regime, but that hope seems bound to be illusory.

I would argue instead that best way to conceive of the role of ideology in foreign policy is neither as a stable set of axioms against which to test policy nor as a nebulous set of goals with which to guide it, but rather as a prism through which information about the world is received and deciphered. As Sun Ki-Chai explains in his book *Choosing and Identity: A General Model of Preference and Belief Formation*, the realist view of state activity "posit[s] either that all actors possess all relevant facts about the environment around them or that beliefs are a product of features of the environment that are directly observable to each actor and the logical/statistical inferences that can be made from them."[60] The idea, therefore, is that any rational political actor, given the same set of circumstances, would behave more or less in the same way. This model breaks down, however, if we find instead that reality is often ambiguous and that observation itself is affected by ideological beliefs that are not common to all.[61] One example of this was outlined by Peter Gourevitch in his book *Politics in Hard Times*, when he argued that "there is considerable ambiguity about economic reality, and ambiguity permits different interpretations. Different understandings or models of a situation shape to different ends calculations of the costs and benefits of action, its opportunities and disadvantages, and hence of behavior."[62] This ambiguity includes not only economics, but also individuals, political parties, and other social groups. Someone who could be seen as an "anti-imperialist nationalist" by one might be seen as a "nebulous petty-bourgeois idealist" by another. Consequently, ideology was the tool used by policymakers in Moscow, Beijing, and other places to make sense of the world. Which regimes could be relied upon to remain loyal to the Socialist bloc and which might defect? When a series of military coups overthrow left-leaning regimes in the developing world in the mid-1960s, as will be seen in chapter 4, the question for many Soviet scholars became how to predict which regimes were on solid ground and which were vulnerable to coups. The answers to these questions, answers essential to the conduct of foreign policy at the highest levels, rested upon the interpretation of the world available, which, if one were a Marxist-Leninist, would revolve around class origins and the consequent interests and strengths of various social groups or political leaders. In this way, ideology was not merely adaptable, but it guided the adaptation of policy as well. Ideological conceptions also influenced what sorts of solutions to a given problem were seen as not only effective, but also available and legitimate. As an example, though this goes beyond the temporal scope of this particular work, such considerations might have affected the way the various superpowers viewed the power of Islamic fundamentalism. Though both the United States, in Iran, and the USSR, in Afghanistan, became targets of Islamic fundamentalists, the United States seemed more willing to view them as potential allies when possible, even though, to an objective observer, it might seem that the USSR had an equally compelling interest in just such an alliance against the United States.[63] This view of ideology makes the role of the *mezhdunarodniki* even more essential because it was they who were primarily charged with the task of analyzing and interpreting the world for the leadership in terms of Marxist-Leninist ideology and in suggesting courses of action. They were, in a certain sense, the institutional incarnation of the role of ideology in the state foreign policy–making process.

The United States, whose impact is felt throughout the book, is treated sparingly for two reasons. The first is that far more scholarship is available on its role in the Third World than on the Soviets or Chinese, and this book seeks to help bridge that gap. On a deeper level, however, the attention given to the United States is limited because this book is about policy and ideological debates on the Left, among those who already took the role of Washington as the leader of the imperialist powers to be axiomatic. While Moscow and Beijing paid much attention to monitoring and predicting the effects on U.S. policy of such factors as domestic political and economic circumstances, personalities, and alliance politics, fundamentally, in the equation of revolution, the U. S. government was seen as more of a constant than a variable. As Khrushchev told Castro when the latter complained about the measures the United States was taking against his country, the Americans were just capitalists defending their class interests—"What do you want them to do, send presents?"[64]

The book is divided into five chapters. In total, they cover the narrative of the evolution of Soviet and Chinese policy in the developing world from the Twentieth CPSU Congress in 1956 and the subsequent beginning of the wave of decolonization in sub-Saharan Africa through the death of Mao Zedong, a momentous event for the conduct of Chinese foreign policy, in September 1976. Chapter 1 details the efforts of both Moscow and Beijing to react to the sudden opportunities presented by decolonization between 1958 and 1960, including the establishment of institutes and journals and the expansion of aid programs. It also explains the beginnings of Chinese suspicions of Soviet intentions and policies, especially in the wake of Moscow's decision to support India in its border conflict with the PRC in 1959. Chapter 2 discusses the heyday of Khrushchev's effort to build socialism in the developing world from 1961 through 1963 as well as the growing challenge presented by Chinese accusations that the USSR was betraying the anti-imperialist struggle, accusations that became particularly forceful following the Cuban Missile Crisis. Chapter 3 examines the height of the Sino-Soviet rivalry for leadership of the revolution in the developing world from 1963 to 1965, using brief examinations of events in the United Arab Republic (UAR), Algeria, and Indonesia to illustrate how the Soviets ultimately rebuffed the Chinese challenge by adapting their policies, chiefly by embracing militant anti-imperialism. Chapter 4 looks at Soviet foreign policy in the late 1960s during the period of Chinese eclipse due to the Cultural Revolution, and its success, or lack thereof, in reestablishing a united revolutionary front under its own leadership. Chapter 5 follows the Chinese reemergence on the world stage in the 1970s, particularly following the PRC's entry into the UN in 1971, and its attempt to put itself at the head of a rising Third World movement, as well as Soviet attempts, once again successful, to defeat this attempt and present the USSR as the main champion of the revolution. The book concludes by examining the enigmatic nature of the Soviet triumph. While China after the death of Mao conceded the battle in the developing world, thereby allowing it to focus on its own domestic economic development, the Soviets struggled under the burden of their foreign commitments. The burden in question was not merely financial but ideological and political as well. Adopting the struggles of the Third World as its own made the prospect of leading a true global working-class revolution ever more remote for the erstwhile Kremlin revolutionaries. In the end, it was a shallow victory indeed, not only for Soviet power, but also for opponents of the capitalist system around the world.

CHAPTER ONE

Divergent Agendas

Peaceful Coexistence versus Anti-Imperialism, 1956–1960

At the Twentieth Congress of the Communist Party of the Soviet Union (CPSU) in February 1956, Nikita Khrushchev declared that "international relations have gone beyond the bounds of relations of states populated primarily by peoples of the white race, and have begun to adopt the character of truly global relations."[1] At the same congress, Khrushchev formally announced the Soviet Union's new foreign policy of "Peaceful Coexistence." Arguing that the possibility of thermonuclear war had made military confrontation with the capitalist world too dangerous to contemplate, and that the increasingly strong position of the socialist camp in the post–World War II years allowed for it to overtake the capitalist world in peaceful economic competition, Khrushchev dispensed with the traditional Leninist notion that war between capitalism and socialism was ultimately inevitable. As a practical demonstration of the significance of the break with past Soviet foreign policy, Khrushchev disbanded the Cominform in April, both to establish a more open and egalitarian model of interaction between Communist parties and to combat the suspicion among new states of the USSR's interference in their domestic affairs.[2] While the Twentieth Congress is most famous for Khrushchev's secret speech denouncing Stalin, the two points above are fundamental elements of de-Stalinization as well. Stalin's foreign policy had been focused on conflict in Europe between the Soviet Union and the Western bloc, and it had largely ignored the colonial and postcolonial world, with the exception of China and Korea. After missteps in China in the 1920s, the Comintern's policy in Africa and Asia had largely become a function of Soviet foreign policy vis-à-vis the fascist threat, and in the postwar years, Stalin did not value the revolutionary movements of East Asia very highly, even negotiating a deal

with Chiang Kai-shek and the Nationalist Chinese government to preserve Soviet privileges in China rather than unequivocally supporting
the Chinese Communist Party. A textbook on the international communist movement used in the CPSU's party school explained: "The ar-
bitrary policy of *diktat* associated with the cult of personality infringed
Marxist-Leninist principles on relations between Communist parties and
did serious harm to the whole Communist movement. It held back creative developments in the immediate problems of the international
working-class movement and the national liberation movement."[3]
Khrushchev was now signaling to the world that the scope, and perhaps
the priorities, of Soviet foreign policy had changed in a way as would befit
a confident new superpower rather than an isolated socialist fortress.

The concepts that underlay the change in foreign policy, however, were
not new. Rather, Soviet foreign policy resurrected the concept of the "noncapitalist path of development," a notion introduced by Lenin in the long-
since practically abandoned resolution of the Second Comintern Congress
of the summer of 1920.[4] The "noncapitalist path," a term that would be the
subject of intense debate and analysis during the course of Communist
engagement with the postcolonial world, initially meant simply a way of
avoiding having to traverse the capitalist stage of development to reach
socialism. This path, Lenin said, would be possible only with the aid and
protection of established socialist countries. However, while conceptu-
ally the new Soviet foreign policy had its roots in the Leninist past, in
practice it would be very much a function of the new role that the USSR
would need to play on the world stage. The Comintern resolution had
dealt primarily with communist participation in anticolonial nationalist
movements, but the Soviet Union was now a recognized world power, a
founding member of the United Nations, and a permanent member of
the Security Council, and so the focus of its new policy, at least initially,
would be to strengthen relations with the governments of the newly
formed states and aid development of their societies. With the hopes for
socialist revolution in the postcolonial world very low, the goal of the new
Soviet policy was simply to find a way to weaken the connection between
the newly independent countries and their former colonial masters,
allowing for a more flexible and dynamic global arena.

While the Soviet Union was seeking to fill its role as the socialist superpower and an established part of the international order, the People's
Republic of China (PRC) had much more modest ambitions. In the early
1950s, China had been the Soviet Union's chief lieutenant in Asia, fight-

ing the UN forces in Korea and aiding the struggle of Ho Chi Minh's Viet Minh against the French in Vietnam, but its role thus far had been strictly regional, and it lacked the capacity to play a global role.[5] Though the Geneva Conference of 1954 and Bandung Conference of 1955 had introduced the PRC on the world stage, they served largely only to break the cloak of fearful isolation in which China found itself among its Asian neighbors due to its radical posture. According to one scholar, the goal of the Bandung meeting was in large part an attempt by Asian countries to gain a commitment by China to peaceful interaction with its neighbors.[6] On a global level, however, China was still excluded from the United Nations, not recognized by many countries, and, most importantly, economically weak and only in the initial stages of socialist development. In the first few years after Khrushchev's speech, Beijing would generally defer to Moscow in public international fora, supporting its policies, including peaceful coexistence, and advertising Moscow's aid to developing countries in lieu of its own rather meager efforts.[7]

This deference shown by Beijing toward Moscow, however, did not imply complete agreement or the lack of a vision of its own place in the revolutionary firmament. China's own revolutionary self-conception and its potential implications for policy were revealed in an article written by Lu Dingyi, a top theorist of the Chinese Communist Party (CCP) in *Shijie ZhiShi* (World Knowledge) in June 1951. In the wake of Chinese decisions to aid both Kim Il Sung and Ho Chi Minh the previous year, Lu wrote that while the October Revolution was a "classic example of revolution in the imperialist countries," the Chinese Revolution presented a similar model for the "colonial and semi-colonial countries." Furthermore, he asserted, the Chinese Revolution "remains a new contribution to the general treasure-house of Marxism-Leninism."[8] In particular, this new contribution related to the support of armed struggle in the context of anticolonial national liberation movements. The Korean and Vietnamese interventions then ultimately had potential significance for the Chinese global revolutionary posture outside the bounds of the Sino-Soviet alliance. While Chinese foreign policy in the wake of those interventions during 1954–55 seemed to imply the adoption of a policy akin to peaceful coexistence, and despite the Chinese failure to openly contradict the Soviet policy at the Twentieth Congress, the Chinese leadership did, in fact, express dissatisfaction with the new policy. In the wake of the Moscow conference of 1957, a gathering of world Communist Parties seeking to replace the Cominform as the venue for international communist discussion and cooperation, the Chinese delivered a secret memorandum to the Soviets emphasizing their disagreement with the doctrine of peaceful coexistence.[9] Publicly, however, there was as yet no open split over the issue, as Shen Zhihua argues, because the Chinese were not yet sure how the rhetoric of peaceful coexistence would manifest itself in Soviet practice. Consequently, it would be presumptuous to read the later divide over approaches to foreign policy as having been evident from the time of the Twentieth Congress itself.[10]

As the process of decolonization, primarily in Africa, accelerated in the period from 1958 to 1960, however, Sino-Soviet divisions over foreign policy would become increasingly manifest. The Soviet strategy in foreign policy toward the newly emerging states focused on detaching them politically from their former colonial masters and opening them up to Soviet influence, which largely meant Soviet economic assistance and direction. This approach was in keeping with the broader Soviet policy of promoting peace to gain sympathy in Europe and lower the perception of Moscow as a threat around the world while asserting the practical superiority of the socialist system. For the Chinese, however, the increasingly radical rhetoric emerging from the developing world along with the rapid pace of decolonization contrasted sharply with the Soviet practice of peaceful coexistence. Beijing concluded that the Soviet Union had failed to adequately evaluate the revolutionary significance of movements in the developing world or, worse, that it was willfully prioritizing its own standing within Europe and vis-à-vis the West over the revolutionary aspirations of the peoples of Asia and Africa. China's perceptions of the gap in revolutionary imagination between the so-called national liberation movements of Asia and Africa and the Soviet Union's implementation of peaceful coexistence reached a crucial turning point in late 1959 and early 1960. Moscow's failure to support the Chinese in the way that they felt they had a right to expect in the border conflict with India, along with its continuing support for Indian "neutralism" and "nonalignment," demonstrated that the failure of the Soviet Union to follow a sufficiently anti-imperialist policy now posed a direct threat to China's security. Peaceful coexistence implied geographic priorities that the PRC, and many others in the developing world, did not share. By 1960 then, Beijing felt it had no choice but to begin attacking Moscow's line in the hopes of forcing it into adopting a more consistent and forceful anti-imperialist position.

In the months following the Twentieth Congress of 1956, little substantive change occurred in either Soviet or Chinese policy toward the developing world. The former was occupied for much of 1956 with events in Poland and Hungary while the latter was caught up with issues of domestic policy, primarily the aftermath of the socialist high tide and the subsequent "Hundred Flowers" movement. Though Soviet engagement with Asia and Africa had already begun in the fall of 1955 with an arms deal with Egypt and a visit by Khrushchev to India, Burma, and Afghanistan, the combination of domestic political upheaval and instability in the Eastern bloc kept the Kremlin busy. By 1958, however, a number of events combined to put the decolonizing world squarely on the agenda of the socialist powers. First, in March 1957, Ghana became the first majority-ruled sub-Saharan African country to attain independence since Liberia over a century earlier. Its new prime minister (later president), Kwame Nkrumah, a promoter of Pan-Africanism, saw Ghana as the bridgehead of a liberated, and perhaps united, Africa. "The independence of Ghana is meaningless unless it is linked with the total liberation of Africa," announced Nkrumah at Ghana's independence celebration.[11] Nkrumah immediately attempted to put this doctrine into practice, making Accra the center of sub-Saharan African political life, convening a Conference of Independent African States there in April 1958, followed by an All-African People's Conference that December. Second, at the end of December 1957, the first conference of the Afro-Asian People's Solidarity Organization (AAPSO) was held in Cairo. This conference emerged out of the Asian solidarity committee set up at a conference in New Delhi in May 1955, and it was intended to be a nongovernmental conference that would allow for more action and less diplomatic restriction than that evidenced at the rather proper Bandung Conference of April 1955. By the end of 1958, two new events had given tremendous impetus to socialist attentions: the revolutionary overthrow of the Iraqi monarchy and the rejection by Guinean voters of President Charles De Gaulle's new plan for a French Union, leading to the independence of Guinea.

The evidence of the impact of these events on Soviet policy toward the developing world is clear. Soviet aid to the developing world had begun in 1954 with aid agreements with India and Afghanistan, and, starting in September 1955, with military aid to Egypt as well. Nevertheless, the year

1958 represented a sea change in Soviet aid policy. The total amount of Soviet economic and technical aid pledged to developing countries nearly doubled from 1957 to 1958, and by 1961 sums had reached nearly triple the 1958 figure at almost 2.5 billion rubles, or roughly $2.64 billion.[12] The number of countries receiving aid also expanded rapidly from five in 1956 to twelve in 1958 and twenty by the beginning of 1961.[13] Early on, Soviet aid was largely focused on Afghanistan, India, and the United Arab Republic (UAR), but by 1961, major recipients of Soviet aid included Iraq, Guinea, Ghana, Indonesia, Ceylon, Cuba, and Ethiopia, and new agreements had just been signed with Mali and Pakistan. According to Chinese sources, in the year 1960 Soviet loan guarantees to "nationalist" (nonsocialist developing) countries eclipsed loan guarantees to socialist countries by over 50 percent.[14] The Soviet Union directed its aid in large part at visible projects that would establish it in the eyes of the world as the real friend of the peoples of Asia and Africa once the West had shown its true face. When the United States and the United Kingdom turned down Nasser's proposal for a dam on the Nile in the wake of his nationalization of the Suez Canal, the Soviets stepped in to construct what would become the Aswan High Dam. Similarly, when France cut off all aid to Guinea as a penalty for choosing independence, Moscow stepped into the breach. As Khrushchev declared at the United Nations General Assembly in September 1959, the socialist world, despite not being morally culpable in the sin of colonialism, nevertheless saw aiding the development of the newly independent states as its socialist duty.[15]

However, competing with the West for influence, in particular with the former imperialist powers, in the newly emerging nations of Asia and Africa would not be as simple as writing a check. Western countries had decades, if not centuries, of experience in dealing with the peoples of these regions, had imposed their languages on them, and had educated and, to a significant degree, created their elites. The Soviet Union found itself devoid of both scholars who understood the culture and history of the new states of Asia and Africa and experts who could be sent out to provide the needed technological and economic assistance that newly independent countries required. According to the Central Committee's Commission on Travel Abroad, from 1955 through 1957, the Soviet Union sent only forty-eight specialists to underdeveloped countries through the United Nations, as compared with 924 from the United States, 1,143 from the United Kingdom, and 683 from France.[16] This dearth of experts "does not accord with the role and significance of the

USSR in international affairs and scale of our dues in the UN fund for technical assistance," according to the committee. Not only were few Soviets being sent overseas, but even the ones that went were often unable to fulfill their tasks. Most of those sent to other countries had no previous experience abroad or in international organizations. They had little familiarity with the social and political conditions of the places to which they were sent, and a full two-thirds of the reserve of 352 experts ready for dispatch abroad, created by a Central Committee resolution of January 7, 1959, spoke no foreign languages. In conclusion, the report demanded that "in the interests of strengthening our position in underdeveloped countries, it is necessary to create a powerful reserve of specialists, with which we would have the ability to exert influence on these countries in the directions we need. We also consider it necessary to organize many-sided preparation of candidates for expertise, included in the reserve, accounting for the particularities of various geographic regions—Africa, Southeast Asia, the Middle and Near East, and also the countries of Latin America."[17]

Scholarship and knowledge of these regions was nearly absent even at the highest levels of policymaking. According to Karen Brutents, when he was asked to join the newly formed Africa sector of the International Department of the Central Committee in May 1961, only two or three Africanists could be found in the entire Soviet Union. (It is likely that Brutents was exaggerating somewhat because the Institute of Africa, established in 1960, had already begun operating by then.) The head of the sector was an expert on Greece and Albania who spoke neither English nor French nor any African languages. Brutents himself was put in charge of the formerly British colonies of West Africa, with which he was wholly unfamiliar.[18] An entire scholarly apparatus would need to be created to support Soviet efforts in the developing world.

The difficulties faced by the Soviet Union, however, paled in comparison with those faced by China. With a state less than ten years old, an underdeveloped scholarly apparatus, and a regime about to embark on the Great Leap Forward, China was in an especially weak position to attempt to project influence in the newly decolonized states. However, despite its more limited means, China did begin to make an effort to cope with the changing global scene. Though in more modest amounts than the USSR, China granted credits to the UAR, Nepal, and Cambodia in 1956, to Ceylon in 1957, and, in 1958, to Indonesia, Yemen, Burma and, at the end of the year, the Provisional Government of Algeria.[19] Institutionally, the PRC made adjustments as well. Unlike the Soviet Union, where the activity of the Foreign Ministry was largely confined to relations with Europe and North America while the rest of the globe was covered by the International Department, the KGB, and the Ministry of Defense, in the PRC, the Foreign Ministry was the primary domestic conduit of information about the world to the Central Committee at this time. The Chinese equivalent of the International Department, the *Zhonglianbu,* or Liaison Department, due to the historically insular nature of the Chinese Communist Party, had as yet few contacts outside established Communist Parties, leaving it dependent upon Chinese embassies abroad, precisely the opposite of the situation on the Soviet side.[20] Consequently, the addition of new divisions to the Foreign Ministry, one for West Asia and Africa in September 1956[21] and a second Asia division to cover North Korea, Mongolia, North Vietnam, Cambodia, Laos, South Korea, and South Vietnam in October 1958,[22] represented important steps in the expansion of Chinese interest in Africa and Asia.

Offering aid primarily to its neighboring states and expanding the Foreign Ministry, however, were steps that reflected a desire to continue China's post–Korean War policy of peacefully expanding its diplomatic footprint in Asia in order to elevate its global status and increase economic opportunities. The first AAPSO Conference in Cairo from December 26, 1957, to January 1, 1958, though, would provide a new perspective on the newly emerging states of Africa and Asia, one that suggested both dangers and opportunities. The directions of the Chinese Foreign Ministry to its delegation in advance of the conference reflect careful adherence to the Soviet line. These guidelines included preserving peace and supporting the Moscow Peace Declaration of 1957 as well as meticulous instructions on exactly what language could be supported on the issue of Israel, given that the Soviet Union had voted in favor of the UN partition plan and consequently considered the existence of Israel legitimate.[23] The militant tone of the conference concerned the Soviets, who worried that the gathering presented a different face of the developing world than Bandung and the principles of Pancha Shila, one which had the potential to alienate European supporters of the peace movement that had been the international focus of the socialist camp since the Twentieth Congress of the CPSU in February 1956.[24] In a conversation with Kovalenko, the deputy head of the Southeast Asian division of the Soviet Foreign Ministry, Liao Chengzhi, the deputy head of the Liaison Department, said that the Chinese also thought that the conference might alienate

Europeans since ultimately anticolonialism would contradict their material interests. Liao said that the conference reflected the radical coloring of Arab nationalism, which was acceptable in this case since it was directed against imperialism. In order not to frighten China's neighbors, the PRC would tread carefully in terms of its propaganda use of the conference.[25]

Internally, China's evaluation of the conference was not as cautious. The Chinese Foreign Ministry sent out a report to all of its personnel abroad saying that the militant anti-imperialism of this conference reflected the increasing prominence of Africa versus Asia in the anticolonial movement and that, as Mao proclaimed the year before, "The east wind prevails over the west wind." On the other hand, the anti-imperialism of the "nationalist" countries still had limits, and any solidarity between socialist and "nationalist" countries would be limited in a corresponding manner.[26] Ultimately, explained Liu Ningyi, the head of the Chinese delegation at the conference, to the ambassadors of socialist countries assembled in Beijing, many nationalist governments were afraid of their own people. As a result they were reluctant to openly call on their people to rise up in an anti-imperialist struggle for fear that they too would be overthrown in revolution.[27] In his report to the Foreign Ministry, he admitted that this had produced a final resolution that was unfavorably softened from the opening statement. China was also disappointed, although not surprised, that some countries sought only to criticize the colonial powers themselves rather than the United States.[28] Nevertheless, the final Chinese verdict on the conference was that they had underestimated the level of anti-imperialist fervor in Africa and Asia and that this new situation would require greater Chinese support, study, and attention, particularly toward Africa, which China had neglected thus far.[29]

For both China and the Soviet Union then, the conference constituted a signal that the developing world offered more than the mere chance to lure new states away from former imperial masters through economic cooperation under the banners of "peace" and "neutrality." Rather, the forces proclaiming anti-imperialism and a desire for socialist revolution were real and represented opportunities for influence. Exploiting these opportunities, however, would require a new theoretical framework. In the context of states dominated by ideological systems, it was only possible for the formation of policy to proceed, and decisions to be made, once the new environment of the nascent postcolonial world had been made intelligible ideologically. This necessity presented something of a problem, however, for the Marxist-Leninist system. The newly emerging states of the developing world were largely unindustrialized and precapitalist, far from the setting envisioned for a Marxist-style proletarian revolution. In the context of the Cold War, however, to direct them on a long slog through capitalist development, one which would inevitably entail continued close ties with their former colonial masters, would have meant the loss of potential influence over the greater part of the world's population. Consequently, both the Soviet Union and China attempted to rise to the challenge of creating a theoretical revolutionary framework for the newly independent states.

At this early stage, though, theoretical tools would first need to be created and introduced before being developed into the full-fledged revolutionary theories that would follow only in the 1960s. For now, the task was simply to create room in the Marxist framework for a gray area between capitalism/imperialism and socialism. In the Soviet Union, this first required a more flexible approach to the concepts of the state, the working class, and the transition to socialism. The orthodox Marxist view held that the state was merely the tool of the ruling class, used for maintaining its dominant position. At the Twenty-First Congress of the CPSU in 1959, Khrushchev pronounced that states which have recently been liberated from colonial or semicolonial dependence, while not being socialist, could not nevertheless be automatically counted with the imperialist world; rather, some had chosen to follow their own path and skip the capitalist stage of development.[30] He called on Soviet Orientalists to study the possibilities of development along the "noncapitalist path," a term newly introduced into political usage after a long period of dormancy. This meant focusing on questions of agrarian reform, class differentiation among the peasantry, and the development of the working class and its role in the peasant movement. In particular, he called on Soviet Sinologists to study the experience of building socialism in China, specifically because of its use of methods "in many cases not resembling the methods employed in other socialist countries."[31] A new journal was created, *Problemy Vostokovedeniia*, in the wake of Khrushchev's speech, whose self-proclaimed mission was the treatment of "contemporary questions of history, economics, politics, culture, literature and languages of the people of the countries of Asia and Africa. In its pages will be systematically published materials on the life and struggle of the workers of people's democratic countries of the East for the construction of socialism."[32]

The possibility of development along a "noncapitalist path" meant that Soviet aid policy would have to be adjusted accordingly. Soviet aid would not be directed merely toward strengthening relations with developing countries or supporting friendly regimes; rather, it would be directed toward leading states along its own path of development. On the eve of an Afro-Asian economic conference in Cairo in December 1958, Soviet Orientalists gathered to discuss Soviet aid policy toward the developing world, subsequently presenting their proposal to Secretary N. A. Mukhitdinov of the Central Committee. Their proposal called for expanding assistance to strengthen the "political and economic influence of the USSR."[33] This effort would entail supporting state-led industrialization, although the possibility of cooperation with "progressive" parts of the national bourgeoisie was not to be excluded. In addition, they proposed greater concentration on agricultural assistance through the Ministry of Agriculture as well as greater stress given to training cadres by the Ministry of Higher Education and the Academy of Sciences. Central to both proposals was the involvement of the newly renamed and revamped State Committee on External Economic Ties (GKES), whose original function of coordinating economic aid to the countries of Eastern Europe was replaced with a focus on the "underdeveloped capitalist countries" in June 1957, with the "capitalist" dropped in January 1958.[34] The speech of the Soviet delegation at the Cairo conference reflected the Orientalists' proposal on many points, including the focus on state-led industrialization, advocating accumulation of capital through mass mobilization and liquidation of private capital.[35]

The form of Soviet economic engagement largely followed the contours of the proposal laid out above as trade was primarily directed through the state sector, except where it was impossible, such as in the UAR where trade in cotton, its major export, was still in private hands. Nevertheless, Soviet pressure had an increasing effect on the structure of trade, leading some governments to set up state agencies for the purpose of trade with the USSR.[36] Soviet aid was concentrated on the construction of large industrial enterprises. Electricity accounted for 23 percent of Soviet aid projects, metallurgy 21 percent, and machine building 9.5 percent by 1961.[37] Already in the fall of 1959, *Kommunist*, the organ of the CPSU, pointed to the flagship projects of the Soviet aid program, the Aswan High Dam and the Bhilai metallurgical plant in India, in claiming that socialist countries directed their aid toward the fastest possible industrialization, the true key to economic independence, unlike capitalist countries that sought to maintain dependence. The structural significance of Soviet aid was unmistakable; thanks to it, "the proportional weight of large enterprises, located under the control of the state, and the role of state sector, are growing."[38]

A different focus, however, was evident in the Chinese theoretical evaluation of the developing world in 1958. Rather than concentrate primarily on analysis of the choices of political and economic development of the newly independent states, the Chinese Foreign Ministry pursued the recommendation of its delegation to the first AAPSO conference and studied the revolutionary situation in Africa, taking the maturity and militancy of the anti-imperialist struggle rather than the sociopolitical structures of economic development as its revolutionary barometer. Among the independent states of North Africa and the Middle East, Chinese evaluation concentrated on the supposed level of "anti-imperialism" of the various regimes.

To explain and evaluate the situation in Asia and Africa, however, the Chinese government, demonstrating the influence of Marxist-Leninism, broke down the class structures of the societies in question. In December 1958, two reports were submitted by the Foreign Ministry to the Central Committee. The first, on the situation in the French-controlled regions of Africa, was submitted by the Chinese embassy in Switzerland, since at the time the PRC did not have relations either with France or with any nation in sub-Saharan Africa. The report examined the class structures of Algeria, French West and Equatorial Africa, and Madagascar, with reference to each class's role in the anti-imperialist struggle. The authors of the report connected success in driving out colonialism with the consolidation of an anti-imperialist movement led by a powerful and conscious working class, one led by its own party, namely a Communist Party. Consequently, only Algeria, which the report claimed had a working class numbering some 1.6 million that included mining, transportation, and agricultural workers, was on the path to imminent victory. With the working class in the lead and, according to the report, demographically dominant among the 200,000 members of the national liberation army, the peasantry, radicalized by French seizures of the best land, the national bourgeoisie, which though small had suffered in competition with French firms, and the intellectuals, some of whom had been radicalized by their education, could play their part in the "national liberation struggle." In sub-Saharan Africa the situation was more complicated. Before the arrival of the French, none of these areas had achieved a "modern class structure" and even now development was uneven, with remnants of feudalism, slavery, and even primitive communism coexisting with colonial industry. Consequently, the working class was small and divided, and it still largely retained a peasant mentality. The peasants therefore formed the backbone of the "national independence" movement, but they could not be counted on to remain united and determined, especially as in many areas scarcity of land had not yet reached a critical point. With the national bourgeoisie also in its infancy, it was the feudal and tribal aristocracies that played a large role in the leadership of the national independence struggle, and so the movements had not yet firmly united behind a program of complete political and economic independence. Given the presence of these factors, the report concluded that linear progress toward liberation could not yet be expected, and victory could still be a while away. The report did add an optimistic note: the existence of the socialist camp and the rising tide of the global "national independence movement" could not but accelerate the development of events in sub-Saharan Africa, and once the working class became united, conscious of its class identity, and put forth its own leaders, total liberation would come.[39]

The second report, submitted by the two-year-old West Asia and Africa Division of the Foreign Ministry, dealt primarily with the political situation in the independent countries of the Middle East and North Africa, as well as Ghana and Guinea.[40] It overlapped with a yearly report on the region produced by the Central Committee's own research department, submitted in January 1959.[41] Both reports attempted to provide a political analysis of the region, specifically with regard to the level of anti-imperialism displayed by the key regimes, especially Nasser's in Egypt, Nkrumah's in Ghana, and the new regime of 'Abd al-Karim Qasim in Iraq, along with the rivalries for power and influence in the Arab world between Nasser and Qasim and in Africa between Nasser and Nkrumah. The lengthier Central Committee report supported its evaluation with a classification of the regimes in the region into three categories. First were those regimes dominated by a "feudal class or comprador bourgeoisie," including Western-allied states such as Turkey, Iran, and Jordan, which the report insisted were facing rising internal instability and economic difficulties. Second were countries that united multiple classes in their ruling group, such as Lebanon, Libya, and Saudi Arabia, that pursued an independent foreign policy. The final group was made up of countries whose regimes were dominated by the national bourgeoisie, ranging from the UAR, which leaned to the right and was anticommunist domestically but pursued a foreign policy of neutralism, anti-imperialism, and friendly relations with socialist countries, to Ghana and Guinea, where the nationalist bourgeoisie worked together with progressives of the worker and peasant classes. The report went on to give a more detailed analysis of each individual country, examining recent developments pointing to shifts in the class composition of the ruling groups or potential for destabilization and change. Both Nasser and Nkrumah were treated extensively, since their power and influence made them unavoidable interlocutors for gaining influence in Africa. Nasser was said to personally have rightist leanings, which would be kept in check by the rising tide of Arab nationalism, while Nkrumah's party was described as promoting the interests of Ghana's merchants and capitalists under the banner of Pan-Africanism.[42] Consequently, this report, along with another sent from the Foreign Ministry to all Chinese representatives abroad the same month, counseled supporting Nasser's and Nkrumah's anti-imperialist policies whenever possible, not involving themselves in power struggles or rivalries between them or with other leaders, while at the same time avoiding endorsement of Nasser's anticommunism or Nkrumah's advocacy of nonviolence.[43] The Central Committee report argued that, as long as the East wind prevails over the West wind, both leaders would be prevented from moving too far to the right.[44]

This method of class-based evaluation of the nature and potential for success of so-called national independence movements, along with the dynamics of anti-imperialist policies in the region, would soon become essential as aid requests began to arrive from such parties throughout Africa. The Union of the Peoples of Cameroon (UPC) made contact with the Chinese embassy in Cairo in August 1958, appealing to the PRC for aid in claiming that China was already popular in Africa and that its revolution seemed most appropriate to the character of African revolutions due to its semi-colonial nature and legacy of a broad class coalition, making reference to the influence of Mao Zedong's writing.[45] Similarly, the Senegalese African Independence Party approached the Chinese embassies in Morocco and Czechoslovakia asking for aid.[46] In all cases, the Chinese embassies forwarded the requests to the Foreign Ministry with no idea of how to respond. Beijing had not yet developed a policy for relating to such groups or aid requests and it did not yet have either the information or the clarity of an agenda with which to evaluate these groups and their potential role in Chinese foreign policy. It would take a significant shock to Chinese foreign policy in late 1959, consisting of a border dispute with India and the subsequent Soviet response, to force China to reassess the practical implications of its ideology for foreign policy in the developing world.

For now, however, China was content to follow the direction of Soviet foreign policy in its promotion of peace and avoidance of open involvement in colonial issues. The Chinese Foreign Ministry's report on Asia and Africa to its representatives abroad still instructed them to emphasize that "the socialist camp, led by the Soviet Union, stands on the side of the African people."[47] In a meeting between the Soviet and Chinese State Committees on Cultural Ties from April 21 to May 4, 1959, the Chinese discussed with their Soviet counterparts cooperation on propaganda in the developing world. The Chinese side even suggested that the Soviets take the lead in propaganda efforts in places such as India and Japan, where Moscow had better connections. As the Chinese representative said, "We, the PRC and the Soviet Union, are one orchestra, even though we play different instruments."[48]

Nevertheless, under the surface, a fundamental difference of approach to the issues raised by the new role played by Africa and Asia on the world stage was evident between Beijing and Moscow. The Soviet Union's basic focus was on lowering international tension and reducing the perceived threat of communism both in the West and in the newly emerging states.[49] That is not to say, of course, that the USSR was committed to peace at all costs, but rather that it found the image of promoting peace to be useful for its larger strategic goals. This stance would not only raise the USSR's international prestige, but it would also allow it to find more open doors and willing audiences for its economic advice and aid. The Soviets could then use such opportunities to promote their own political-economic approach: focus on state-controlled industrialization, long-term economic planning, construction of large enterprises of heavy industry, and nationalization of banks, transportation, and trade. According to Soviet thinking, this would inevitably lead to the growth of working-class political power and organizations and ultimately produce governments more friendly to the Soviet Union, not to mention the ascendancy that such development would give the ideology of socialism around the world. In other words, the revolution the Soviet Union was promoting was focused on replacing the capitalist economic system with a socialist one.

China's priority, on the other hand, was clearly directed toward promoting anti-imperialism. China's concern was not with peace or international détente, despite its adherence to that agenda in public. In fact, the Soviets would soon be concerned that China was openly saying that the point of advocating disarmament was not to actually achieve it but rather to paint the imperialists in a negative light, exposing and therefore undermining the Soviet strategy.[50] Rather, China's priority was to unite as much of the world as possible in a broad, anti-imperialist coalition for the sake of confrontation with the West in general and the United States in particular. Socioeconomic formations had a role to play in this anti-imperialist vision of revolution as well. Chinese policymakers were meticulously analyzing class origins of individual leaders, class compositions of movements and regimes, and economic processes in order to better understand and predict which leaders, movements, and states could be expected to be reliably anti-imperialist and which would ultimately sacrifice anti-imperialism to other agendas, whether those were personal aggrandizement, Western aid, or preservation of power. For the moment, China was as yet unsure how the Soviet doctrine of peaceful coexistence would play out in practice and, as such, was unwilling to go it alone in foreign policy while it was at such a weak and vulnerable stage. The course of events in 1959, in particular the Sino-Indian conflict, would change that viewpoint, and, by early 1960, the tension between the Soviet Union and China, between anticapitalist and anti-imperialist revolution, would begin to manifest itself openly.

A Shaky Alliance

For the Chinese, the events of 1959 could be traced back to an old problem: Marshal Tito of Yugoslavia. While the Soviet Union had been performing a delicate dance in its relations with Yugoslavia already before the Twentieth Congress, alternately embracing and scolding the Yugoslavs in an attempt to find a *modus vivendi*, Beijing had never wavered from its belief that Yugoslav revisionism constituted a fundamental threat to the socialist camp and the project of world revolution.[51] As a Chinese official said in a speech to the Soviet State Committee on Cultural Ties, "The struggle with Yugoslav revisionism is one of the most important tasks of our foreign political propaganda at the current stage."[52] Worrisomely for the Chinese, as Brzezinski wrote, "the Yugoslav program did articulate a conception of the world and of relations among Communist states that in the years to come became increasingly acceptable even to the Soviet leaders themselves."[53] In the aftermath of the twin crises of the fall of

1956, the Hungarian Revolution and the Suez Crisis, Tito had increasingly reached out to the two most influential leaders of Africa and Asia, Nasser and Nehru, in the hopes of creating a "third force" capable of standing up to both superpower blocs in the interests of nonalignment. The three leaders had already met at Brione, Yugoslavia, in June 1956, and personal visits and consultations increased significantly over the next five years, ultimately leading to the first Non-Aligned Movement summit in Belgrade in September 1961.

China viewed Tito's meddling in Africa and Asia with a great deal of concern. Chinese relations with India had been positive since Zhou Enlai's first visit to India in June 1954, and in 1958, *Shijie Zhishi* was still able to publish an article praising India's foreign policy and its contribution to world peace.[54] However, alarm bells sounded after Tito's visit to India in January 1959. China worried that Yugoslavia was trying to harm India's relations with both the USSR and the PRC and was seeking to get India to join a "group of neutral countries," telling India that if small, neutral countries did not band together, the superpowers would always be able to pressure them. While China was encouraged that India continued to refuse to convene Tito's proposed nonaligned conference, a report from the Chinese Foreign Ministry division on the Soviet Union and Eastern Europe concluded that "Yugoslav revisionism still has a rather large market in India."[55]

In the AAPSO secretariat, located in Cairo and headed by Yusuf al-Sibai, an Egyptian as general secretary who had been selected by Nasser himself,[56] China found itself increasingly confronted with the unwelcome political agendas of both the UAR and India. While initially the two nations seemed to be battling for influence in the Afro-Asian solidarity movement, China increasingly began to see cooperation between the two as unfavorable to itself. Both countries were pushing African decolonization through nonviolent means through the United Nations, a stance that China found doubly troubling, not only because it would reduce the possibility for a broad militant international front against imperialism, but because it asserted the validity of a world organization from which the PRC was excluded. China countered by using its African "friends" on the secretariat, including Cameroon and Uganda, to combat Egyptian and Indian influence.[57] Egypt counterattacked by calling for a change in the nature of the solidarity movement at an executive council session in February 1959, arguing that its "anti-imperialist" nature meant that it should be limited to "nationalist" countries to the exclusion of Communist ones.[58] For the time being, the Chinese secretary in Cairo, Yang Shuo, worked closely with his Soviet counterpart to combat this Egyptian and, to a lesser degree, Indian agenda.[59]

Events occurred in March that would sabotage this cooperation, however. Unrest in Tibet precipitated military action by the People's Liberation Army (PLA) and the flight of the Dalai Lama to India. This action led to Chinese rhetorical attacks on India in April and May, and eventually to clashes over disputed regions of the border between the two on August 7 and 25. Beijing failed to inform Moscow about them until September 6, nine days after the Indian ambassador had done so.[60] While the PRC expected that its military alliance with the Soviet Union, not to mention solidarity with a fellow socialist country in a conflict with a nonsocialist one, should produce Soviet support, the Soviet government did not believe China's claims of Indian aggression, thought that China had violated the alliance treaty by lack of consultation, and, in the pages of *Pravda*, effectively declared neutrality.[61] The failure of the USSR to support China in its border conflict had a dramatic impact upon Chinese perceptions of Soviet foreign policy. In August, the Chinese foreign minister Chen Yi had expressed support for Khrushchev's visit to the United States, seeing it as a sign of imperialist weakness and a victory for Communist foreign policy.[62] Now, Beijing attacked the visit as a form of appeasement. On the basis of Khrushchev's meeting with Eisenhower and the Soviet refusal back in July to deliver a prototype of a nuclear weapon to China in fulfillment of an agreement it had signed, China concluded that the Soviet Union had chosen détente with the West and its relations with India over its duties of proletarian internationalism to a brother socialist state. Visiting Beijing for the tenth anniversary of the PRC immediately following his return from Washington, Khrushchev did not help matters by encouraging the Chinese to "unite" with India in "opposing imperialism."[63] In return, he was met with harsh, accusatory tones, and the border conflict flared up again in October.

On the Soviet side, Mikhail Suslov launched a broad attack on Chinese foreign policy in a report to a Soviet party plenum in December, rejecting Mao's "paper tiger" theory of imperialism and calling the Sino-Indian border conflict "a disruption of the Soviet pursuit of peace." Ominously, he compared the cult of personality that had grown up around Mao Zedong in China to that which had surrounded Stalin.[64] Not to be outdone by the Chinese on the matter of betrayal and conspiracy theories, Khrushchev later wrote that Mao started the border war on the eve of his visit to the United States "out of some sick fantasy" in order to "dictate to the Soviet Union" its foreign policy.[65] Distrust now permeated the thinking of both sides: the Chinese doubted the commitment of the Soviets to proletarian internationalism and anti-imperialism and the Soviets saw the Chinese as dangerously undermining peaceful coexistence. For the time being, however, both sides would try to maintain what remained of their international cooperation.

Back in Cairo, the coverage in the Egyptian press and the machinations of the Indian secretary pushing for a resolution condemning Chinese aggression led China to feel that it faced an Indo-Egyptian onslaught.[66] Initially, the Chinese thought that the UAR's support for India on this issue was given in an attempt to curry favor with the United States. After the renewal of armed clashes in October, the Indian secretary began telling others that the Soviet Union actually supported India, not China, and that it condemned Chinese actions. India pushed for a resolution in the AAPSO secretariat supporting Khrushchev's statement on the Sino-Indian border issue of October 31 in the Supreme Soviet and calling on him to mediate. The Chinese ambassador, speaking in the absence of the Chinese AAPSO secretary, countered with the improbable argument that any resolution on Khrushchev's speech would have to comment on all of it and not just the paragraph dealing with the border issue. The Soviet secretary Rashidov managed to save face by arguing that, since the Chinese secretary himself was not present at Cairo at the time, any resolution would have to await his return.[67] That is where matters would stay until the second AAPSO conference the following April.

The Indian border conflict, nevertheless, opened a deep fissure in the Sino-Soviet relationship that would widen significantly over the following year. It was not, however, a matter of security that disturbed the Chinese, since the clashes were minor and China was in the stronger position militarily. Rather, the Soviet stance of neutrality coupled with Khrushchev's enthusiastic embrace of Eisenhower in the wake of his visit to the United States led China to believe that the Soviets prioritized peace and détente over the anti-imperialist struggle. India, which China now regarded as an enemy, presented an important case of the tension between the anticapitalist and anti-imperialist approaches to revolution. For the Soviet Union, India was an important ally. Its international stance had won it great prestige around the world, and its promotion of peace, disarmament, and nonalignment dovetailed with the Soviet agenda. Furthermore, India was attempting to pursue rapid, state-led industrialization.

For China, however, India represented a threat to the possibility of a broad anti-imperialist alliance and its "pacifism" or "neutralism," combined with the efforts along similar lines of Tito and Nasser, set a dangerous example for the rest of Africa and Asia. The significance of the Soviet-Indian relationship then, for both Moscow and Beijing, far exceeded the importance of a few remote, snowy Himalayan passes.

On the Road to Open Competition

By the time of the second AAPSO conference, held in Conakry, Guinea, in April 1960, the agendas of the USSR and the PRC in Africa and Asia had clearly diverged. The Soviet Union's commitment to peaceful coexistence as the solution not only to the fear of nuclear war in the developed world, but also to the economic difficulties in the developing world had only increased. The USSR promoted the idea that disarmament would free up greater resources for economic aid, and therefore Moscow expected that Asians and Africans would support its agenda of peace and disarmament. The fact that Africans, especially, seemed to perceive their interests differently did not deter Moscow. A second meeting of the All-African People's Congress was held in Tunis in January 1960 as a successor to the one convened a year earlier in Accra, and it did not even include references to peace and disarmament in its resolutions. Instead, it explicitly endorsed the armed struggle in Algeria.[68] At a meeting of the presidium of the Soviet Committee of Solidarity with the Countries of Asia and Africa (SCSCAA) in preparation for the conference, E. M. Zhukov remarked that "it has become clear to us, that not everyone abroad understands the significance of reduction of tension in the international situation for the success of the struggle of the peoples of Asia and Africa. There are incorrect inclinations such as that détente disrupts solidarity and obstructs the unification of the peoples of Asia and Africa, because it enables the consolidation of the great powers."[69] Vice Chairman Anatoly Safronov informed his fellow members that "representatives of a whole range of especially African countries are turning to us with requests for the most varied forms of aid from moral to material, all the way to arms. We accordingly explain in discussion that we cannot help with any arms, and even the forms of material aid are extremely complicated."[70] The Soviet delegation went to Conakry with the goal of getting those gathered to place their faith in the doctrine of peaceful coexistence.

The Chinese delegation, on the other hand, went to Conakry to combat what it saw as a potential Indo-Egyptian hijacking of the solidarity movement in favor of "neutrality." They fought the Indo-Egyptian push for inviting South Vietnam and South Korea, and they had Al-Sibai add "anticolonialism" and "anti-imperialism" to the three slogans promoted by the secretariat of "independence, equality, and peace."[71] When the Chinese saw the initial draft of Al-Sibai's speech at the conference, they were livid. The report of Zhu Ziqi, the new Chinese representative at AAPSO headquarters in Cairo, after breaking down the speech point by point, concluded that "from the above, one can clearly see that after the failure of their [India and Egypt] attempt to make neutrality the policy of the solidarity movement, they still conspire to boost the policy of so-called opposition to blocs and nonalignment, under the cover of anti-imperialism engage in antisocialism, as well as stealthily spreading the seeds of anti-Sinicism, in order to weaken and shift anti-imperialism, and they are rather preparing to completely lean towards imperialism, in Afro-Asia, especially in Africa, to create chaos and confusion, in order to change the general character of the solidarity movement, replace it with reactionary content and have it led by the right-wing of the bourgeoisie."[72] It was supposedly Soviet vacillation on the issue of anti-imperialism, however, that had opened up space for India and Egypt to exploit, due to the Soviet policy characterized by the Chinese as "struggle superficially and concede stealthily, or struggle a little and concede a lot" (明争暗让或小争大让).[73] Zhu said that the speech may have been put out under the name of the UAR, but its main content was written by India, and "the Soviet comrades acted as the advisor on certain questions."[74]

When Zhu talked to his Soviet counterpart, however, the latter refrained from expressing an opinion on the speech and counseled patience and discretion on the part of the Chinese. On March 19, the Soviets introduced a proposed two-page addition to Al-Sibai's speech on the issues of peaceful coexistence and disarmament as well as a list of other pet Soviet issues, writing that this was in fact what the peoples of Africa and Asia cared about most. It seems that this was the point at which the Chinese came to regard the Soviet Union, rather than India or Egypt, as their primary antagonist at the conference. Apparently unaware of the true Chinese position, the Soviets asked the Chinese to support this proposal and Zhu Ziqi deceitfully agreed, writing at the same time to Beijing that this "directly waters down and shifts the anti-imperialist struggle."[75]

He said that for months the Soviets had completely abandoned anti-imperialism in favor of disarmament. Given that the Soviets were now the main opponent, the Chinese adopted a new policy with regard to India and Egypt known as *"yida yila"* (一打一拉), or "attack and attract."[76] As for the rest of the delegations, the Chinese arrived in Conakry early in order to meet with as many of them as possible before the conference started on April 11. The delegation of the Algerian FLN, the very incarnation of the anti-imperialist struggle at the moment, told the Chinese that "the Algerian and African people deeply understand that *only* China truly supports and aids the Algerian people's liberation struggle[77] (italics mine).

The conference itself turned out to be quite a high-level affair, as is evident from the roster of attendees. The Egyptian delegation was led by Anwar Sadat, minister of state in Nasser's government, while India's delegation was led by Nehru's wife. Among the African leaders were Patrice Lumumba and Joseph Kasavubu, soon to be the prime minister and president of the Congo, respectively, as well as Kenyan leaders Tom Mboya and Oginga Odinga.[78] After it was over, Liu Ningyi, vice chairman of the Chinese Committee for Afro-Asian Solidarity, wrote back to Beijing expressing elation in saying that the majority of the conference understood that with colonialism and imperialism "there is no peaceful coexistence, anti-imperialism cannot be neutral."[79] The conference refused to endorse peace and disarmament, supported the Algerian armed struggle, and passed resolutions according to Chinese specifications. India and Egypt, after their initial speeches, quickly appraised the atmosphere of the conference and abandoned all talk of neutrality. Meanwhile, the Soviets found themselves in the unusual position of being directly confronted by the opposition of a number of African delegations and were forced to ask the Chinese for help.[80] For both countries, however, this would only open the door to even deeper involvement in African affairs. As the official report of the Chinese Peace Committee (which was closely associated with the Afro-Asian Solidarity Committee) concluded, "We believe that by strengthening our work in Africa, broadening friendly exchanges with Africa, using great force to support African nationalist movements, and publicizing Mao Zedong thought in Africa, this will produce a very deep influence on the healthy development of the African nationalist revolutionary movement."[81]

In the aftermath of the conference, delegations of both countries took the opportunity to prolong their stays and meet with officials in both

Guinea and Ghana as well as with representatives of parties and movements from other countries present in Conakry. The Chinese delegation saw its purpose at the conference largely in making connections with Africans interested in China and inviting as many of them as possible to China.[82] In the meantime, they met with Sekou Touré, president of Guinea, who told them that many of the ruling party's members had matured within the French Communist Party and believed in Marxist principles. He claimed that he was building a "People's Democracy," the term currently applied by Moscow to Eastern European states, even though he could not proclaim this publicly for political reasons.[83] At the end of June, Moscow sent a delegation to Ghana to discuss potential aid and economic cooperation, in the course of which the members met with both Nkrumah and Touré, reporting their evaluations to the Central Committee. Despite agreeing to a minimal amount of aid in order to maintain friendly relations with what was undoubtedly one of the most influential new African leaders, the delegation returned disillusioned with Nkrumah, considering him to still be very much under the control of the British and his talk of socialism to be empty. This impression came, in no small part, from Touré himself, who impressed the Soviets much more. The delegation ended up recommending a course toward increasing Soviet influence in Ghana in order to undermine Nkrumah from the left, calling for support of "progressive" elements and for extending invitations to more Ghanaian officials to visit the USSR as well as more Ghanaian technical cadres to train there. Finally, they advocated increasing the embassy staff in Accra and strengthening propaganda efforts in the country.[84]

The report's recommendations dovetailed with a broader Soviet policy direction in 1960 to focus more on influence over personnel in the newly emerging states. Competition with the Western powers on aid projects and the battles over which path of development to follow within each country had led Soviet officials in the relevant institutions to conclude that money and factories would be meaningless without the training and education of cadres, both in the narrow technical sense as well as more broadly in state-led development, planning, and socialism. The centerpiece of this effort was the creation of the People's Friendship University in February 1960, which would subsequently be named after assassinated Congolese prime minister Patrice Lumumba. The governing council of the university would consist of SCSCAA, who would have the dominant say on student admissions, and the All-Union Central Union of Trade Unions.[85] In the first year People's Friendship University enrolled

550 students from developing countries, as part of a total of some 2,671 in the USSR by the spring of 1961.[86]

In addition to bringing students to the USSR, the Soviet Union greatly expanded its scholarly and propaganda apparatus in order to influence publics abroad. A Central Committee resolution of January 29, 1960, led to the doubling of Soviet radio programming abroad by late 1961, with broadcasts from Moscow in 39 languages, including Swahili, Amharic, Tamil, Urdu, Hindi, Bengali, Burmese, and others.[87] The Soviet press agency TASS produced a daily bulletin to compete with Western news agencies in providing wire stories for local papers. *Mezhdunarodnaia Kniga* distributed everything from Marxist-Leninist classics to the latest Soviet monographs on economic development, while *Soveksportfilm* distributed Soviet films abroad. The existing journals *Sovremmenyi Vostok* (Contemporary East) and *Problemy Vostokovedeniia* (Problems of Oriental Studies) were given makeovers and renamed *Aziia i Afrika Segodnia* (Asia and Africa Today) and *Narody Azii i Afriki* (Peoples of Asia and Africa), respectively. These journals were closely associated with newly created institutes in the Academy of Sciences, such as the Institute of Africa and the Institute of Latin America. New divisions of the International Department and KGB were created as well to deal with these regions. The editorial boards of the journals demonstrated the fluid relations between Soviet governmental organizations, party organizations, academic organizations, and so-called nongovernmental organizations, such as SCSCAA and the Soviet Peace Committee. *Aziia i Afrika Segodnia*, while published by the Institute of the Peoples of Asia and later the Institute of Africa as well, was seen as the quasi-organ of SCSCAA, which was constantly pushing for a greater focus on current events and for translation of the journal into English and French for distribution abroad. This effort finally came to fruition in 1976 when Karen Brutents, deputy head of the International Department, became an editor of the journal.[88] Similarly, when the journal *Latinskaia Amerika* was created in 1969, its editorial board included Nikolai Leonov, head of the Latin American division of the KGB. As these and many other career paths demonstrate, the lines among state, party, and academe were very fluid, producing an environment in which ideas and information were shared and in which debates over policy often crossed institutional boundaries.

By this time, Soviet efforts to influence people in the developing world came to greatly concern the Chinese, who were worried about the content of that influence. The Chinese embassy in Moscow produced a series of reports throughout the year on the increasing Soviet interest in Africa, which expressed a concern more with what they were not saying than what they were. Chinese officials reported on the founding of the Soviet-African People's Friendship Society, the Institute of Africa, and the journal *Problemy Vostokovedeniia*.[89] A Chinese embassy official relayed the content of a conversation with the deputy head of the Soviet State Committee on Cultural Ties regarding Africa policy, writing that he only emphasized publicizing daily Soviet life and socialist construction as well as peaceful coexistence, without saying anything about encouraging Africans to rise up against imperialism, concluding that "this is also a reflection of the Soviet Union's entire policy."[90] The embassy reported worriedly on the Soviet press coverage of the founding of the new People's Friendship University, saying it spoke only of "friendship" and "humanism" but indicated that the Soviets would not actively promote revolution. To add insult to injury, the Soviet press pointed to the university as a product of disarmament, claiming it would be funded with money saved from arms expenditures.[91] Clearly the situation had changed dramatically from 1958 in Beijing's eyes, and Soviet influence was no longer seen as a positive factor in the developing world.

Despite the havoc wrought by the Great Leap Forward and generally inferior Chinese resources, the Chinese leadership nevertheless felt the need to attempt to compete with and counteract Soviet influence. Luckily, the Chinese did not have to look far for opportunities. Responding to supposed requests from student groups in Algeria, Venezuela, Chad, Congo, Gabon, Argentina, and others, the Central Committee of the Communist Youth League sent a letter to the Liaison Department, the State Committee on Cultural Ties, and others advocating setting up a system for recruiting and educating students from Africa as well as Latin America.[92] Thus far, only a few students had come to China for study, and no formal infrastructure had been set up devoted to their needs. However, now "attracting them to our country to study abroad will expand our country's influence and help the revolutionary forces in these countries to grow. At the same time, this is also an important measure in the struggle for the youth of the intermediate regions with imperialism."[93] Officials now advocated actively recruiting students, although the numbers being discussed were still modest by Soviet standards, roughly 100 per year. The content of the program and its ambitions were not modest, however. The Youth League hoped that a kernel of 100 well-prepared students per year would have a dramatic impact on the revolutionary situations in their countries, especially as the planned curriculum was to include special classes on the experience of the Chinese revolutionary struggle.[94]

In addition to requests from student organizations to send students to study in China, the Chinese were increasingly getting requests, primarily from political parties in Africa, both those in states that had already attained independence and those that had not, for all sorts of training of cadres, including military training.[95] In August 1960, Deng Xiaoping raised the issue in a top-secret letter to the Central Committee.[96] Deng wrote that the newly independent states were desperate for expertise and that, as of yet, they were "ideologically and politically immature." At the same time, he feared that Marxist thought would not be disseminated broadly enough. Right now most of those asking to come were left wing or center left in their political orientation, primarily intellectuals with some workers and peasants, although he thought their political level was rather low and their practical revolutionary experience rather poor. However, they displayed great interest in China and had high hopes that "from China's revolutionary experience they will study the basic theories and methods of struggle of nationalist revolution." Accordingly, Deng laid out the following proposals. He did not advocate actively trying to persuade reluctant countries to send people to China, but he did counsel accepting those who wanted to come with warmth and enthusiasm. The basic content of their studies would be the thought of Mao Zedong and China's revolutionary experience. They would learn about raising national consciousness, recognizing the nature of the imperialist camp centered on the United States, relying on the masses of peasants and workers, and persevering through a long, potentially violent, struggle. They would promote the Chinese approach of assembling the widest possible class coalition both in terms of each country's domestic struggle and in terms of a broad international anti-imperialist front as well. A select few were to be educated in Marxist theory in depth in an effort to form the nuclei of Marxist parties. The training was to be carried on by Chinese trade union, youth, and women's organizations in tandem, and it would take six months at most.

In efforts to secure influence, the Chinese were not to be outdone by the Soviets. They actively pursued agreements with local political parties, book distributors, and publishing houses in Africa to disseminate material, and, by the spring of 1960, the Chinese already had such connections in Senegal, Nigeria, Congo, Kenya, Uganda, Tanganyika, and others. They had individual subscribers to Chinese publications such as the glossy journals *People's China* and *People's Illustrated* in Algeria, Angola, Mozambique, and other countries that had not yet attained independence. Potential distribution of Chinese publications was always brought up when any African visitor came to China, such as the general secretary of Zanzibar's Nationalist Party in February 1960.[97] A Xinhua delegation toured Latin America in the summer of 1959 in the wake of the Cuban Revolution, visiting Chile, Uruguay, and Brazil in addition to Cuba. They left behind a Xinhua correspondent to set up a permanent base in Havana, giving China its first propaganda foothold in Latin America.[98] The lack of expertise in China on these regions hampered Chinese diplomatic and propaganda efforts. Mao admitted to a visiting delegation from Asia and Africa on April 27, 1961, that "We don't have a clear understanding of African history, geography, and the present situation."[99] On July 4 of that year, the Institute of West Asian and African Studies was founded under the aegis of the Liaison Department and the Chinese Academy of Sciences.[100] Similarly, an Institute of Latin American Studies, also tied to the Liaison Department, was founded in the early 1960s as well.[101] However, given the low level of existing expertise in China, the primary task of these institutes, at least in their original incarnations before being shut down due to the Cultural Revolution in 1966, was to translate foreign works on Asia, Africa, and Latin America for the consumption of party officials and policymakers, not to produce their own original research.

With ideological battle lines drawn and propaganda efforts underway, Sino-Soviet divisions exploded into the open in the spring and summer of 1960. In response to a confrontation over foreign policy at a meeting of the Political Consultative Committee of the Warsaw Pact on February 4, 1960, Khrushchev went on a tirade, calling Mao a "pair of worn out galoshes standing discarded in a corner."[102] In response, Mao had a group of propaganda workers write a series of three polemics to be published on the occasion of Lenin's ninetieth birthday. "Long Live Leninism" duly shocked the Soviets, but they refused to reply openly on the eve of the Paris summit between Khrushchev and Eisenhower scheduled for May.[103] The downing of a U-2 spy plane right before the summit seemed to confirm the Chinese view of the war-mongering Americans and put the Soviets on the defensive. Beijing saw this as an opportune time to press its ideological agenda within a broader institutional setting. At a meeting of the World Federation of Trade Unions (WFTU) in

Beijing in early June the Chinese used every opportunity for ideological influence over their guests, including a long dinner at which Liu Shaoqi and Deng Xiaoping harangued attendees about the differences between the CPSU and the CCP. A number of Eastern European delegates, returning via Moscow, remarked to the Soviets that "the Chinese are trying to take the international Communist and workers' movement under their control."[104] In a meeting before the Romanian Party Congress in Bucharest at the beginning of July, the Soviets confronted the Chinese directly. A Soviet delegation led by Frol Kozlov, Otto Kuusinen, Boris Ponomarev, Yuri Andropov, and others asked a Chinese delegation led by Peng Zhen and Kang Sheng, "Are you looking for allies for yourselves in a struggle against the CPSU?"[105] Both sides argued extensively at the conference, airing disagreements on the issues of peaceful coexistence, the inevitability of world war, the danger of local conflict, and the implications of all of this for the national liberation struggle in the developing world. Frol Kozlov, narrating all of this in his speech at a CPSU party plenum soon after the Bucharest congress, argued that China was damaging the profile of communism in Africa and Asia, specifically by trying to drag the USSR into conflict with India, contradicting the advice of the Indian Communist Party, and causing harm to the cause of communism in that country, as well as poisoning other "nationalist" regimes against the socialist camp, especially Indonesia and Burma. Kozlov concluded his speech with a detailed elaboration of all that the USSR had done for China in terms of economic aid. Moscow would do it no longer, however. Khrushchev had suddenly decided to retaliate by removing all Soviet specialists from the PRC, and Moscow notified Beijing of this action two days after the conclusion of the plenum.[106]

With the substance of Sino-Soviet ideological disagreement now a matter of public knowledge, the Chinese had solid grounds on which to evaluate the political nature of their continuous stream of African visitors, at least 520 people from forty-one countries between 1949 and June 1960 according to an incomplete count of the Propaganda Department.[107] For each conversation with a visiting delegation, in each evaluation of a potential aid request, or in each new encounter with a representative of a new party abroad, Chinese diplomats would evaluate their interlocutors on the basis of a sort of checklist to determine their relative worth and reliability in the broader anti-imperialist struggle. Typical topics on which they would be evaluated included their stance on the issues of peace and disarmament, the possibility of peaceful coexistence with imperialism and the inevitability of war, and willingness to resort to armed struggle as well as their positions regarding "illusions" about the potential utility of the United Nations, willingness to rely on one's own forces (自力更生) or dependence on foreign aid, reliance on mass struggle, and appreciation of the value and relevance of the Chinese revolutionary experience and Mao Zedong thought for the revolution in the developing world. When the secretary of the Committee of African Organizations, Dennis Phombeah, visited China in June 1960, the subsequent report on his visit criticized him for believing that imperialism had changed and would grant all African countries independence peacefully within three to five years and for maintaining "illusions" about Julius Nyerere and his notion of "nonracism" as well as British offers of autonomy and "racial partnership." He was taken to task for arguing that East Africa had no traditional class structure, for relying too much on the leadership of intellectuals and neglecting the mass base, and for his failure to see the attempt of the United States to co-opt Africa's nationalist leaders.[108] Two members of the Congolese African Solidarity Party were condemned for failing to understand that the United Nations was a tool of imperialism, incorrectly evaluating the current international relation of forces, and relying too much on foreign aid to the exclusion of their own forces and of the use of mass struggle.[109] Such evaluations usually meant little or no aid would be forthcoming.

However, China was also only too eager to use these visits to shape the political views of impressionable young students and activists. When a group of ten African students, who were currently studying in Czechoslovakia, came for one month of study in August 1960, their arrival was welcomed as a useful opportunity despite the fact that their political development was described as "uneven" and their understanding of domestic and international issues as "confused." On the bright side, they were described as anti-imperialist, firmly pro-independence, and eager to learn about China's revolutionary experience as well as its current socialist construction.[110] The goals for the treatment of the delegation as laid out by the secretariat of the Communist Youth League included "actively influenc[ing] their politics and thought in order to encourage their will and confidence for total anti-imperialist struggle, introduc[ing] the basic concepts of Marxism-Leninism according to their intellectual level, establish[ing] the thought of the leadership of the proletariat, encourag[ing] their revolutionary-ness (革命化)."[111] To inoculate them against what they might learn back in Prague, those responsible for caring for the students were told that "in order to help them recognize the current beneficial situation and distinguish enemies, obvious or not, raise their level of recognition of revisionist thought and their ability to distinguish it."[112] Upon their debriefing by the Chinese embassy in Prague, the students seemed to demonstrate that the Youth League had accomplished its mission. One student remarked that "even though China was not the earliest socialist country, the people's socialist consciousness is the highest" and that other socialist countries should study it. Another declared that "only through armed struggle can true national independence be won."[113] Beijing was learning to turn anger, idealism, and ideological orthodoxy into a powerful concoction for producing pro-Chinese feeling.

Greater attention to the ideological predilections of visitors also meant that the Chinese were open to bestowing greater rewards. The visit in August 1960 of two leading representatives of liberation movements from Portugal's African colonies, Viriato da Cruz of the Popular Movement for the Liberation of Angola (MPLA) and Amilcar Cabral of the African Independence Party of Guinea and Cape Verde (PAIGC), constituted a case in point. Though visits to Moscow and East Berlin produced little in terms of aid,[114] Cruz received a much more enthusiastic reception on his visit to Beijing. While initially hesitant because of the MPLA's previous public promotion of peaceful methods of struggle, the Chinese Foreign Ministry soon reported: "They are very friendly towards us, admire our achievements in construction, strongly condemn Portugal's violent, oppressive rule, and criticize U.S. imperialism's support for Portugal's oppression of colonial peoples. They are pushing for total, immediate independence and are preparing armed struggle, and want to study the experience of armed struggle."[115] Satisfied that their visitors sided with them against the Soviets on issues of war and peace, disarmament, revisionism, and others, the Chinese agreed to meet their aid requests, giving each party $20,000 in the midst of the Great Leap Famine, as well as agreeing to accept ten people for military training. Beijing agreed to provide arms as well, pending discussions with President Sekou Touré of Guinea, who was currently hosting both organizations in Conakry.[116]

The experience of the MPLA and PAIGC delegations to the socialist world in 1960 would seem to indicate that there was, in fact, something to the claim that the Chinese were more willing to support armed anti-imperialist struggle than the USSR or its Eastern European allies. The MPLA, in particular, was still small and obscure in 1960, Angola had not yet seen major eruptions of revolutionary violence and was not then at the center of international attention in Africa, and so Cruz's brave talk about Marxism and guerrilla warfare failed to elicit much of a response in Moscow. The Chinese, however, took him much more seriously, providing both economic and military aid as well as treating the delegation with the respect accorded high-level foreign dignitaries. In the wake of the visit, Cruz's sympathy with the Chinese positions on important international questions, which does not seem to have even been much remarked upon in Moscow or East Berlin, would grow to a full-scale pro-Chinese orientation.

Despite these grand plans for winning friends and influencing people in the newly emerging states, however, both the USSR and the PRC encountered practical difficulties in undertaking the task of educating foreign students. African students at one school in Beijing skipped class to meet their friends and refused to stand when the teacher entered the room. They complained about the food quality, the lack of closet space in the dorms, morning showers, and spending money as well as the fact that they were segregated from the European students, who were allowed to attend Peking University. They went on strike until their demands were met. The Education Department tried to meet their material demands, but as far as the allegation of discrimination, the Africans were told that because China was a socialist country that had also suffered imperialist discrimination "therefore it is completely impossible for it to produce racial discrimination, on the contrary, the Chinese people and African people have a deep friendship through their joint struggle against imperialism and colonialism."[117] Just to be safe, though, the school suggested encouraging Chinese students to act in friendly ways toward the Africans and to organize more activities so that they would not complain about racial discrimination to African dignitaries arriving for the October 1 Independence Day celebrations.

Meanwhile, race was fundamentally coloring perceptions of the USSR, especially in Africa. M. Tursun-Zade, the chairman of SCSCAA, in reviewing the difficulties that the Soviets had encountered at the second AAPSO conference in Conakry, concluded that "they right now relate to all whites with suspicion, and they know very little about the Soviet Union."[118] Confirming this perception, African students in the USSR were subject to numerous acts of racial intolerance, as evidenced by a KGB report detailing an incident in which a Guinean soldier training in Poti, Georgia, was attacked in an incident over a girl, leading the Guinean contingent there to complain of "racial discrimination" and to ask to be transferred.[119] In Tbilisi, one student announced when an African student entered the dining hall that he could "no longer eat." This was not limited to Georgia. A member of SCSCAA declared that such incidents were just as common in Moscow or Tashkent.[120] Race would prove to be an Achilles' heel for the Soviets in the battle for influence in Asia and Africa, one that the Chinese would readily exploit.

In any event, in the second half of 1960, China perceived that events in Africa were definitely going its way. The West Asian/African Division of the Foreign Ministry summed up the situation in July as follows: "The anti-imperialist national independence struggle is becoming even more fierce and deep; calls for using violence and arms to conduct struggle are increasing daily. Under the direct influence of the Algerian national liberation war, the ideology of armed struggle is being accepted by more and more nationalists."[121] In addition to Algeria, armed struggle was now going on in the former Belgian Congo and in Cameroon, and armed clashes were occurring in Angola, Mauretania, Chad, and Kenya. Meanwhile, "Marxism and the works of Mao Zedong are being publicized more widely every day."[122] "Contradictions" were becoming increasingly evident not only between Africans and imperialism, but even within the ruling groups of African countries and between the countries. The report saw the potential for armed conflict everywhere.[123] By the end of the year, the Chinese Foreign Ministry believed that the Congo crisis had fundamentally altered the nature of the independence struggle. "The Congolese and Cameroonian peoples conducting armed struggle after achieving independence are struggling between real and fake independence. This shows the consciousness of the African people has been raised tremendously. . . . African people cannot be limited to the independence that imperialism is ready to agree to, i.e., fake independence, they need to struggle to achieve the independence that imperialism opposes, real independence; they also cannot only be limited to political independence, they will endeavor to attain economic independence."[124] At the same time, the political horizon of Africa had been transformed by the involvement of socialist countries. "Under the influence of socialist countries, a group of vanguardists has already appeared in Africa, they have begun to recognize socialism and accept Marxism-Leninism, Mao Zedong thought. There are some African youths in the UK who read many of Chairman Mao's works and can discuss 'the theory of contradiction,' 'paper tigers' and 'armed struggle' and think that China's path is Africa's path."[125] The report offered a detailed prescription for

Chinese activity in Africa in 1961, one that represented increased attention, based on the Chinese leadership's ideological proclivities, to political nuance and the different situations in each country.

The year 1960, however, would end with the last real attempt to unify the Communist bloc to meet with a significant degree of success. Months of tentative contacts in the wake of the Bucharest fiasco, facilitated by the intense mediation efforts of Ho Chi Minh, paved the way for a temporary truce to be achieved at the Moscow meeting of the international Communist and workers movement in November, attended by eighty-one parties. As the conference began, Khrushchev and Deng Xiaoping were still firing angry salvoes at one another. It became clear, however, that the majority stood opposed to the CCP, and, with the authorization from Mao back in Beijing for a tactical retreat provided certain Chinese demands were met, Peng Zhen and Frol Kozlov managed to find common ground at the last minute and salvage a respectable solution.[126] Neither side, though, was willing to declare "peace in our time."

On issues related to the developing world, the meeting did represent a significant step toward the Chinese position, one that would allow Beijing to claim victory, though the Soviets denied that their position had changed at all. Summing up the results of the meeting at a party plenum in January, Mikhail Suslov talked about the approach embodied in the conference document toward the newly liberated countries. "The overriding tasks of national rebirth in these countries can only be successfully solved under the conditions of decisive struggle with imperialism and the remnants of feudalism, through the path of unification in a united national front of all patriotic forces of the nation. Within this the basic form of the national front is supposed to be the union of the working class and peasantry, as the most important force in the conquest and defense of national independence, realization of deep democratic transformation and the enabling of social progress."[127] The documents produced at the meeting introduced the concept of "National Democracy" as the new official doctrine of the Communist movement for the development of the newly independent states. "National Democracy," unlike the old concept of "People's Democracy" that had been applied originally to the countries of Eastern Europe, did not entail the dictatorship of the proletariat, but, under benevolent conditions and with the proper political line buttressed by the activism of all progressive forces led by Communists, it could serve as a "transitional stage" to the non-capitalist path of development for the liberated colonies.[128] This was the new ideological basis on which the Communist movement would attempt to deal with a world increasingly filled with underdeveloped states seeking to build their national futures, and it became the point of departure for Soviet and Chinese theoreticians and policymakers.

In the wake of the conference, the Chinese Foreign Ministry sent a top-secret directive to its personnel abroad. The report rather pessimistically said that the meeting might reduce tension temporarily, but it was certainly not as good as if the theoretical debates had actually been solved, let alone if they had never arisen in the first place.[129] The Foreign Ministry did believe that progress had been achieved relative to the 1957 Moscow statement regarding the strength of its anti-imperialist stance, the nature of the current epoch, support for national liberation struggles, the class composition of the united national front, the difference between revolutionary war and counterrevolutionary war, and the advocacy of a broad international front against imperialism, as well as other issues.[130] On a practical level, it called for all Chinese personnel abroad, including students, to study the Moscow document and use it in all political discussions, emphasize Sino-Soviet solidarity and the solidarity of the socialist camp, and avoid any discussion of issues that might lead to disagreement. It specifically ordered Chinese abroad to stop using terms such as "revisionist" and "right-wing opportunist."[131] A report from the Chinese embassy in Moscow, however, expressed disappointment with Soviet foreign policy in the wake of the Moscow meeting. A certain change in tone had been perceived, but the Soviets were still generally promoting peaceful coexistence and disarmament, still perpetuating "illusions" about the utility of the United Nations, and, in particular, seemingly harboring unjustified hopes for the incoming Kennedy administration.[132] Evidently, the truce would be short indeed.

As 1960—the "Year of Africa" as proclaimed by the United Nations— came to a close, the divergent agendas of anticapitalist revolution and anti-imperialist revolution became increasingly evident. The Soviet Union had moved over the course of the late 1950s from a desire to use diplomatic engagement and economic aid to pry former colonies away from their colonial masters toward a committed ideological struggle to shape their economic and political future by molding their development. Peaceful coexistence meant that the struggle between capitalism and communism would be fought on the grounds of economic competition, but by the end of 1960, that no longer meant only competition between the economies of the North Atlantic Treaty Organization (NATO) and the Warsaw

Pact. Economic competition now meant competition for influence over the economic direction of the newly liberated states, and soon it would mean comparisons of the results achieved in those states. Saddled with an ideology developed in nineteenth-century industrial Europe and a model of development that had been achieved in a former great power at an unthinkable human cost, the Soviet Union would need to devote its newly developed scholarly and political resources to solving the challenge of creating a development model for the new states that could compete not only with the capitalist model offered by the West, but with the example offered by China as well.

For the Chinese, the year 1960 ended on an unmistakable high note in foreign policy. The Congo crisis had brought the anti-imperialist revolutionary fervor of Africa to an all-time high. The foreign policy priorities of Beijing, derived from its ideological orientation toward anti-imperialism, combined with the need for allies against American power, had proven to be more popular in the new revolutionary battleground of the decolonized states than the Soviet program of "peaceful coexistence" and economic competition. Despite the superiority of Soviet resources, the greater appeal of the Chinese worldview had made Beijing ascendant. However, from this point there seemed to be nowhere to go but down. Once the majority of African countries had achieved independence or were clearly on the path to doing so, militant revolutionary struggle would begin to recede from their agenda in favor of the new tasks of national construction and economic development. On the surface, China seemed to have little to offer in this area. The year 1960 also marked the low point in China's domestic development, as its Great Leap Forward program collapsed in famine and misery. For China to build its own power base in the developing world independent of the Soviet Union, it would need to compete with the Soviets for economic and political influence in the new states. Given the Chinese disadvantage in economic and intellectual capital, this was quite a tall order.

CHAPTER TWO

New Frontiers

Development and Struggle, 1961–1963

"Communists are revolutionaries, and it would be bad if they did not notice (*podmechali*) newly arising possibilities, did not find new ways and forms which better than anything lead to the achievement of the set goals," pronounced Nikita Khrushchev to a gathering of Communist Party and academic officials on January 6, 1961.[1] Khrushchev went on to talk about the new possibilities that were arising in Asia, Africa, and Latin America, invoking the theory of the state national democracy contained in the Moscow Declaration of a month earlier. The audience that found his words most interesting, however, was on the other side of the world. President-elect John F. Kennedy, only two weeks before his own inauguration, told his advisers to study Khrushchev's speech, telling them "You've got to understand it, this is our clue to the Soviet Union."[2] As a member of the Senate Foreign Relations Committee, Kennedy had emphasized the importance of the emerging Third World in the global Cold War struggle, famously criticizing the Eisenhower administration's support of the French war in Algeria in 1957. His inaugural promise to "pay any price, bear any burden" was soon made concrete with an ambitious new agenda directed toward promoting development in the underdeveloped world. Modernization theorists inside and outside the administration pointed to a dangerous window at the beginning of the transition from "traditional" toward "modern" societies during which penetration by communism was possible, and, consequently, they sought to shrink that window by accelerating the modernization process.[3] In March, Kennedy spoke to Congress, outlining his approach to the development of Asia, Africa, and Latin America, establishing the Agency for International Development (AID), ordering the creation of the Peace Corps, and creating the Alliance for Progress as the administrative structure for American aid to Latin America. A new era was dawning in which the struggle between capitalism and communism in the developing nations of the Global South would not be merely about foreign policy stances and military alliances; rather, it would entail a competition between alternative models of development.

The decolonization struggle, however, was far from over at the beginning of 1961. Just three days before Kennedy's inauguration, Patrice Lumumba, the young former prime minister of newly independent Congo, was killed while in the custody of Moises Tshombe, leader of the renegade province of Katanga. Though news of his death did not reach the outside world immediately, rumors of CIA involvement in Lumumba's murder would come to color perceptions of American policies in Africa at least as much as any of Kennedy's projects. Lumumba's death came at an important juncture in the decolonization process in Africa. While almost all of the northern and western parts of the continent were independent by the end of 1960, the focus of attention had now shifted toward the east and south, where, unlike the surprisingly quick and peaceful process of liberation in West Africa, nationalist movements found themselves confronting more determined foes who were less inclined to compromise. The presence of significant numbers of white settlers, largely absent in West Africa, complicated British efforts at decolonization in Kenya, Tanganyika, Northern Rhodesia, Southern Rhodesia, and Nyasaland. Farther south, the struggle was already turning violent. Northern Angola erupted in February 1961, and the Portuguese responded by sending large numbers of troops to conduct a scorched-earth campaign. Portuguese Guinea and Mozambique soon followed suit as Portugal clung ever more tightly to its colonial empire. The Sharpeville massacre of March 21, 1960, had exacerbated the situation in the Union of South Africa, leading to the banning of the Pan-African Congress and African National Congress. The increasing international condemnation led a year later to South Africa's exit from the British Commonwealth and its declaration as a republic. Meanwhile, the Algerian war continued apace. Across the Atlantic, Fidel Castro's regime in Cuba was moving ever farther to the left, with Castro officially labeling the revolution "socialist" in April and calling himself a Marxist-Leninist in December. Finally, the Southeast Asian cauldron was beginning to reach its boiling point, though, at the moment, the primary object of contestation between West and East was Laos, neutralized by the first Geneva Conference in 1954, rather than South Vietnam. The heyday of militant anti-imperialism, and with it the potential for Chinese ascendance across the developing world, had not yet exhausted itself.

At the beginning of 1961, though, China found itself in very difficult circumstances. Its Great Leap Forward policy, introduced in 1958, combined with a series of weather-related problems, led to a massive famine in which tens of millions died. By the beginning of 1961, it had become clear that a change of course was necessary. The Ninth Plenum of the Eighth Central Committee, which was held January 14–18, 1961, confirmed a number of shifts which had begun to be floated among the leadership from the time of a meeting in Beidahe in July and August 1960. The basis of these changes was the official end of the Great Leap Forward and a shift away from the policy of rapid industrialization to one of "agriculture as base."[4] Mao himself shouldered some of the blame for the failed policy, and he retreated to the "second line," removing himself from the day-to-day administration of affairs and even making some sort of self-criticism at a Communist Party of China (CCP) Central Work Conference in Beijing in June 1961, which was nevertheless not circulated among the lower levels of the party.[5] With the reins of leadership seemingly passed to Liu Shaoqi, who was inclined to adopt a more conciliatory line toward the USSR[6] and a necessary focus on domestic priorities, the PRC was neither able nor willing to compete fully with the overseas development agendas now put forward by the United States and the Soviet Union.

For the time being then, the Soviet Union would set the ambitious new agenda for the "socialist camp"—a term still used by both the USSR and the People's Republic of China (PRC) at the time—in the newly independent states. That agenda now consisted not merely of aiding the economies of newly independent states in order to foster economic and political independence from their former colonial masters but also of attempting to actually demonstrate the viability of socialism, built with Soviet aid and guidance, in the developing world. Called the "noncapitalist path of development," a term whose relationship to socialism proper constituted an object of debate among Soviet theorists,[7] the USSR would invest financial, academic, and political resources in the attempt to promote a model of development that would chart the way to modernity, that is socialist modernity, for millions of newly liberated people. In foreign policy, the USSR continued its promotion of "peaceful coexistence," advocating disarmament and peaceful decolonization, though Soviet practice often contradicted its rhetoric. To a certain degree, Soviet officials dealing specifically with colonial issues did adopt a more militant tone partly in order to placate the Chinese and also partly because of the growing realization that the Soviet rhetoric of peace was producing dissatisfaction, in Africa in particular. In the wake of the truce established by the Moscow meeting of 1960 and weakened by domestic difficulties, the Chinese did not vehemently contest the Soviet agenda during the first half of 1961. However, the Chinese did not share the belief that socialism could or should be constructed in the newly liberated states at the current stage and they did not promote the noncapitalist path of development, soon dropping the term "state of national democracy," introduced in the Moscow Declaration, from their political vocabulary entirely. While the Soviets sought to transform states internally to promote the growth of socialism, the Chinese remained focused on foreign policy above all, seeking to build a broad, anti-imperialist front. In the wake of the Twenty-Second CPSU Congress in October 1961, which the Chinese leadership perceived as a direct attack, China began once again to combat Soviet policy in the developing world, this time more openly than before. The clash between the competing agendas of peaceful coexistence and anti-imperialism would reach a climax in the wake of the Cuban Missile Crisis, ultimately leading to a reevaluation of policy in both Moscow and Beijing.

Calm before the Storm

In the immediate aftermath of the Moscow meeting of November 1960, both the Soviet and the Chinese leaderships attempted to preserve the tentative truce that had been achieved. A report sent by the Chinese Foreign Ministry to all its embassies abroad reflected the sober pragmatism with which China viewed the outcome of the meeting, calling it a victory for Marxism-Leninism but one that would have been better if the major theoretical debates had actually been solved, or had never occurred in the first place.[8] At the same time, while Chinese evaluations of the situation in Africa pointed to the rise in support for the concept of armed struggle, the advent of newly independent regimes also dictated a somewhat more cautious policy than in the earlier era of complete colonial domination. A report from the Chinese embassy in London, evaluating the situation in Africa in 1961, pointed to a number of difficulties facing the anti-imperialist struggle, including remnants of feudalism and tribalism leading to intra-African conflicts; the weakness of African governments led by representatives of the "national bourgeoisie"; illusions about the United States and United Nations; competition for African leadership among Nkrumah, Nasser, Touré, and others; the continued promotion of nonviolence by some leaders such as Nkrumah in Ghana and Nyerere in Tanganyika; and the ongoing dearth of communist organizations.[9] Coupled with Chinese domestic difficulties and the continued Soviet need for Chinese facilitation in Asia and Africa, the stage was set for one last attempt at a united policy.

This renewed effort at cooperation was in evidence at an extraordinary executive council session of the AAPSO called in January 1961, convened to deal with the ongoing crisis in the Congo. The Chinese delegation arrived in Moscow for consultations on the eve of the meeting to a friendly Soviet reception. The Soviet delegation told the Chinese directly that the Central Committee of the Communist Party of the Soviet Union (CPSU) had ordered them to cooperate with the Chinese.[10] The Soviets laid out their agenda for the meeting, with an emphasis on concrete action to aid the struggles in Congo and Algeria, and they claimed that the Soviet and Chinese positions on the United Nations, one of the major points of difference in 1960, were now, in effect, identical. While the content of the proposed Soviet resolution was still not militant enough for the Chinese, and they recognized the remaining tension in the meeting, they reported to Beijing that there had been significant changes in the Soviets' tone and in the atmosphere in relations.[11] In the end, the cooperation of the USSR and the PRC produced a series of resolutions more militant than those passed by the AAPSO in the past, due to the new willingness of the Soviets to include direct condemnations of the United States and the United Nations. The Soviets allowed the Chinese to insert their corrections into the documents they had prepared for the meeting in Moscow, and Moscow even proposed the PRC as one of the vice chairmen of the newly founded Aid to Congo Committee. The Chinese pronounced themselves satisfied with the Soviets' conduct.[12]

The Soviet approach to the meeting, however, revealed a fundamental dilemma of Soviet policy. While emphasizing immediate concrete aid to Congo and Algeria, the Soviets sought to de-emphasize the importance of militant public resolutions in support of both of those causes.[13] This reflected a desire, on the one hand, to satisfy the Chinese and reassure left-wing Africans that the USSR would be there to support their anti-imperialist struggle while, on the other hand, maintaining a public façade of peace for a Western audience and not openly undermining the authority of the United Nations. An example of the Soviet attempt to square this circle was Moscow's promise to provide advanced weaponry, including naval weapons and Mig-19s, to Indonesia in February 1961, just as the conflict between Indonesia and the Netherlands over West Irian was heating up. Included in the agreement was a specific provision that the Indonesian government would take all measures to keep this action secret.[14] This reflected a Soviet effort to honor their commitment to peaceful coexistence in the breach even when concrete politics got in the way. Despite their cooperation with the Chinese, the Soviets found their doctrine of peaceful coexistence meeting with severe criticism by Africans at AAPSO meetings in 1961. SCSCAA members reported that Africans misunderstood coexistence to mean that the colonized must "coexist" with their colonizers, that the Soviets were against any sort of war, and that the total disarmament advocated by Moscow would apply to all African countries and liberation movements.[15] At a meeting of the AAPSO secretariat in January, the Algerian representative complained that because the imperialists were convinced that the Soviets wanted to avoid war at all costs, they had no fear of invading.[16] SCSCAA representatives tried to explain that the Soviet Union was not against local wars such as the struggle of the Algerian National Liberation Front (FLN), but they determined that Soviet propaganda on this issue was wholly insufficient.

The issue of "neocolonialism" became a particular point of contention in 1961. Due to the increasing number of independent states, attention shifted from battles with direct political and military control to the various ways in which Western countries attempted to maintain or, in the case of the United States, create economic influence in Asia, Africa, and Latin America. Consequently, neocolonialism was added to colonialism and imperialism, most prominently by President Sukarno of Indonesia, who coined the term "Nekolim" (neocolonialism, colonialism, and imperialism), but also by many others, a development encouraged by the Chinese in the hopes that neocolonialism would serve as a tool for mobilizing anti-American sentiment. The Soviets, however, were reluctant to allow the term to be employed in resolutions. In the AAPSO council and subsequent executive committee meetings in Bandung, Indonesia, in April, the Soviet representatives consistently opposed use of the term "neocolonialism," a stance that the Chinese attributed to a desire to avoid offending the United States.[17] This seems to be a case in which the focus by the Chinese on their own agenda led them to misinterpret Soviet motivations. In a SCSCAA Presidium session following the Bandung meeting, I. Potekhin, the senior Africanist in the USSR, director of the Institute of Africa and a member of the Solidarity Committee, argued that the use of the term "neocolonialism" necessarily implied some form of "neo-imperialism," and he feared that such a term might be applied to the Soviet Union itself. "There is no such thing as neocolonialism, there is only the regular old colonialism, which has only changed the methods and forms of realizing its old colonial policy," declared Potekhin.[18] This disagreement over neocolonialism, however, was no mere matter of semantics. It pointed to a much deeper division between the Soviet Union, on the one hand, and China and many African and Asian states, on the other, regarding the current relationship between the newly independent states and the Western powers. While Moscow seemed to see the days of traditional anti-imperial struggle coming to an end soon, to be replaced by a focus on domestic economic matters, many in the PRC and in Africa and Asia saw the international arena as the focus of revolutionary energies for the foreseeable future. This would contribute to the demise of the nascent Sino-Soviet rapprochement within a matter of months.

As long as Sino-Soviet cooperation lasted, however, the two countries together managed to dominate the AAPSO, overwhelming the Egyptians who had controlled it largely by playing the two Communist powers against each other. The speech of AAPSO General Secretary Yusuf al-Sibai at the Bandung meeting was significantly more militant than any which had preceded it at earlier conferences, particularly in terms of the support given for struggles in Congo, Laos, and Algeria, and the condemnation of the United Nations as an imperialist tool. Even the Chinese were satisfied with the speech.[19] Before the conference, the Chinese and Soviets had worked out a compromise line regarding the United Nations and the Soviets, who even agreed to condemn Yugoslavia directly for the first time in years.[20] A leading member of SCSCAA even told the Chinese that the USSR still believed that it would be best if China took the lead on socialist activity in Africa and Asia, to which Zhu Ziqi, the leader of the Chinese delegation, courteously replied that it would be just as fitting to count on the great USSR.[21] In the conference post-mortem during a SCSCAA Presidium meeting, the committee chairman Tursun-Zade said that the Soviet delegation had worked closely with the Chinese on all questions.[22] This newfound cooperation was not only a one-way street, however. On the eve of the Bandung meeting, the Liaison Department of the CCP edited the proposed content of the Chinese delegation's speech, significantly moderating it. The Liaison Department emphasized the need to "raise the banner of peace," moderate the categorical language on the United Nations to focus on the role of the United States rather than the institution per se, and support the Soviet proposal for a new Geneva conference on Laos.[23] The fact that the changes were ordered from Beijing clearly indicates that compromise with the Soviets to maintain a united anti-imperialist front was considered an imperative at the highest level of decision making in the PRC.

By the end of the conference, however, Chinese dissatisfaction with the Soviet line was beginning to grow again. The temporary shift toward a more militant tone by the USSR had ended and now the Soviets were once again promoting disarmament, with their new line being that disarmament would allow money to be saved, which could then be used to provide economic aid for the development of backward countries. Moscow increasingly emphasized the anticolonial resolution they had pushed through at the Fifteenth United Nations General Assembly in the fall of 1960, implicitly promoting peaceful negotiation under the aegis of the UN as the chief method of gaining independence for the remaining colonies. The Chinese tried to prevent this Soviet shift by quoting lines from the text of the Moscow Declaration regarding support for the "national liberation movements," but the Soviet delegation at the Bandung Conference replied that they could not go back to Moscow if the conference statement did not include support for disarmament and peaceful coexistence.[24] They tried to get the Japanese to introduce a disarmament resolution instead, but the Chinese delegation convinced the Japanese otherwise. The Chinese worried that if they did not increase their presence within the AAPSO, the Soviet position might gain traction.[25] Once again, Soviet and Chinese views of the imperatives of socialist policy vis-à-vis the developing world were diverging.

The most intense point of disagreement as the year went on centered on the First Non-Aligned Conference in Belgrade in September 1961. As would be expected regarding a conference whose primary sponsors included Tito and Nehru and which seemed to be based on a form of neutralism, the Chinese were vehemently opposed. Meanwhile, the Soviets took a more pragmatic tack. The Chinese embassy in Moscow reported that the Soviet press in the wake of the conference supported the conference's conclusions and claimed that the greeting sent by Khrushchev had a major impact on the course of the conference.[26] *Pravda* argued that the conference showed that the participating countries acknowledged a difference between nonalignment and neutrality, an understanding that on questions of war and peace one cannot be neutral, and that only struggle against colonial forces can clear the road for peace. The positive outcome was not a matter of fortune. The Soviets had spent months preparing for the conference, preventing European neutrals such as Sweden and Finland from being invited, making sure that neither Tito nor Nehru attempted to create a "third force," and using friendly countries to introduce items of Soviet policy onto the conference agenda, as the deputy Soviet foreign minister explained to the ambassadors of socialist countries in Moscow.[27] Despite intense disagreement over the conference, however, the Soviets and Chinese maintained close coordination and consultation in the lead up to the event.

Consequently, despite the evident divergence between the Chinese promotion of a broad, militant, anti-imperialist front and the Soviet agenda of peaceful coexistence and disarmament as the year 1961 progressed, there was no clear attempt on either side to assume an openly combative posture toward the other before the Twenty-Second CPSU Congress in October. A number of contemporary and subsequent observers, writing in the aftermath of the open Sino-Soviet break in the mid-1960s, have claimed that the Chinese promotion of militant anti-imperialism as far back as 1958–1959 represented a concerted attempt to wrest leadership of a Third World bloc from the Soviets, either due to a personal struggle for leadership of the international communist movement between Mao and Khrushchev or for some other reason.[28] The increased militancy of the AAPSO in 1961 is seen as evidence of the ascendancy of the Chinese line.[29] However, the evidence seems to indicate that, until the Twenty-Second Congress, the primary Chinese goal was not to compete for influence with the Soviet Union but rather to influence and mobilize Afro-Asian anti-imperialist opinion in order to exert pressure on the USSR to change its own policy. In other words, underlying ideological divisions were pushing apart two states, the USSR and the PRC, which were otherwise trying to work together, rather than the more conventional picture of states creating imaginary ideological divisions to justify political conflicts. This supports the argument that the primary motivating factor behind China's suspicion of the Soviet policy of peaceful coexistence was its concern that the Soviets would ultimately come to an arrangement with the West, which would leave China and the rest of Africa and Asia out in the cold, a concern that was crystallized in September 1959 when the Soviet Union failed to support China in its border clash with India. The remark of the Chinese Foreign Ministry in its internal memorandum to Chinese embassies in December 1960 that the Moscow meeting had reduced the tension in the Sino-Soviet relationship, which had been building for fifteen months, affirms the notion of the Sino-Indian border conflict as the key moment.[30] It was only the Twenty-Second Congress, which China would see as a declaration of war against itself, that would fundamentally alter the dynamic of Sino-Soviet relations in the developing world. Subsequently, the internal dynamics of Chinese domestic politics would play no small part in fueling the drive of Beijing toward outright competition with the Soviets, as will be explained later in the chapter.

Nevertheless, despite the desire in both Moscow and Beijing to work together and present a united front to the world, the fundamentally different revolutionary visions of the two governments expressed themselves in different foreign policy agendas that lay underneath the surface attempt to maintain cordiality. In 1961, the Soviet focus shifted decisively toward development, attempting to promote a socialist model as the key element in its struggle against capitalism. This change was reflected in the new Soviet talking point that disarmament was a core Afro-Asian interest because it would free more funds for economic aid, and it was also reflected in the Soviet lack of concern with neocolonialism. In fact, though Khrushchev was definitely wary of Kennedy's aid offensive in the developing world, he was not necessarily categorically opposed to developing countries accepting aid from capitalist countries, as long as it helped the construction of heavy industry and did not entail political and military dependence.[31] Meanwhile, for the Chinese, the requirements of the anti-imperialist struggle remained supreme. Anticapitalism, to the degree that it concerned particular internal structures within developing countries as opposed to international anti-imperialism, was a much lower priority for the Chinese, whose revolutionary agenda and understanding differed profoundly from those of Moscow.

The Trials and Tribulations of the Noncapitalist Path of Development

Socialism was on the minds and lips of many leaders of newly independent states in Asia and Africa in the early 1960s. Capitalism was largely discredited due to its association with the imperialist powers that had so recently been expelled. In addition, the long slog of capitalist development, and its attendant social and political dislocations, seemed not only undesirable but unnecessary when compared to the apparently miraculous leaps of development achieved in a comparatively short period of time by the socialist countries. Given the near absence of domestic infrastructure and industrial development, the abandonment of businesses and factories by fleeing Europeans, and a still-extant system of some form of communal agriculture, particularly in West Africa, the course of state planning, nationalization, and cooperativization seemed not only more natural but more suited to the circumstances of many newly independent states. As the planning minister of Mali, Seydou Badian Kouyate so succinctly expressed it, "You cannot be a capitalist when you have no capital."[32] Above all, the mammoth tasks of raising the living standards of dreadfully poor populations who viewed independence largely as a promise to be fulfilled in material terms imposed itself upon the agendas of the new leaders. "We consider our goal to be socialism not only because it seems to us appropriate and useful, but because we have no other path to solving our economic problems," declared Indian prime minister Jawaharlal Nehru.[33]

This desire for socialism, however, expressed itself in multifaceted ways. Almost all leaders of newly independent states rhetorically supported socialism in some form ranging from Nasser's "Arab socialism" to Nkrumah's "African socialism," even including such ostensibly pro-Western leaders as Tunisia's Habib Bourguiba and Senegal's Léopold Senghor. While the Soviet Union saw the general promotion of socialism as proof positive that people's consciousness had been raised and that the desire for socialism was nearly universal, the invocation of "nonscientific" socialism by leaders seen to be pro-Western was perceived as dangerous demagoguery.[34] "African socialism," in particular, due to the theoretical nature of its claims, presented a problem for the Soviet program. As elaborated in its various versions by Nkrumah, Nyerere, Senghor, and others, the notion of African socialism purported to relate to the intrinsic spiritual and communal values and heritage of Africans, which were said to be inimical to capitalism. On a practical level, this expressed itself in terms of a supposed "natural" tendency toward one-party rule and an inclination toward communal methods of work and property division.[35] The most troubling element for Soviet theorists, however, was the claim of supporters of the idea of African socialism that Africa had no classes, and consequently no class struggle. "The dissemination of the idea of such 'supraclass' (*nadklassovyi*) socialism is objectively directed towards the deflection of the masses from the struggle for the fundamental solution of basic social problems in order to not allow the growth of class self-consciousness of the laborers (*trudiash-chikhsia*)."[36] The task confronting Soviet policy was therefore clear: to prevent the dissipation of the drive toward socialism through misdirected or demagogic local political forces by presenting its own viable model to be followed in the developing world that would lead to the eventual embrace of "scientific" socialism.

The solution to this problem was to be found in the related concepts of the "state of national democracy" and the "noncapitalist path of development." As mentioned in chapter 1, these concepts were introduced into the text of the 1960 Moscow Declaration as part of the official program of the international communist movement regarding "national liberation movements." The "state of national democracy" was meant to be ruled by a "wide national front," encompassing workers, peasants, the "democratic intelligentsia," and the "national bourgeoisie." This "state of national democracy" led by a "wide national front," a formulation suspiciously similar to Mao's explanation of the initial period of the PRC, would "under fortunate circumstances, and the correct political line and militant activism of all progressive forces headed by the communists . . . be for the former colonial countries a transitional form to the noncapitalist path of development."[37] These concepts would be included in a more fully elaborated form in the new CPSU program adopted at the Twenty-Second Congress in October 1961. Whereas the Twentieth Congress had merely introduced the idea that the newly independent states could potentially pursue an independent foreign policy, and the Twenty-First Congress had mentioned the possibility of skipping the capitalist path, the program of the Twenty-Second Congress declared in no uncertain terms that socioeconomic transformation was essential. "The national-liberation revolution does not end with the conquest of political independence. This independence will be shaky (*shatkoi*) and will be transformed into a fiction if the revolution does not lead to deep changes in social and economic life, if it does not solve the vital tasks of national rebirth."[38] This focus would shift the objectives of Soviet aid policy from simply weaning former colonies from dependence on the former metropoles to transforming the economic and social structures of the recipient states.

Expanding and defending the concepts of "national democracy" and the "noncapitalist path of development" was not a simple task within a traditional Marxist-Leninist framework, however. Marxism-Leninism, after all, was an ideology of working-class revolution in the advanced industrial world, of which Russia itself had been at best a marginal member in 1917. Marx's writings had not envisioned solutions to the revolutionary tasks posed by decolonization. To put into practice a plan for constructing socialism in the developing world then, Soviet theorists had to come up with a conception of the state and class structure that would help them figure out who their allies were and build a roadmap to socialism in the developing countries. The countries in question often had little that could be labeled a "working class" because they had very little industrial development. Soviet scholars attempted to alleviate this problem to a degree by focusing on the formation of a "peasant proletariat." This peasant proletariat was said to be in the process of formation due to the increasing commercialization and mechanization of agriculture, a process ironically accelerated by agrarian reform in certain countries, which had been conducted in the interests of the bourgeoisie rather than the mass of peasants and consequently had only exacerbated class differentiation in the countryside by creating a new "kulak" class.[39] Meanwhile, Soviet scholars insisted that the working class, despite its small size, still played an important part in the struggle for national independence and that its rapid growth allowed it to assume a central position in the "state of national democracy," though apparently more so in Asia than in Africa.[40] However, the idea of "national democracy" really hinged on the concept of the "national bourgeoisie," which was distinguished from the "comprador" bourgeoisie and the "monopolist" bourgeoisie by having nationalist and anti-imperialist sympathies due to its competition with international capitalist interests.[41] Since, ultimately, the interests of the national bourgeoisie would not include the total elimination of private property, the success of the "state of national democracy" in instituting the path of "non-capitalist development" depended upon the class coalition that formed the government moving constantly to the left until the national bourgeoisie had been subsumed under a peasant-worker union.[42] True to form though, Soviet policy explicitly discouraged achieving this by violent means; "The working class and peasantry are deeply interested in building the independent state of national democracy through a peaceful path, without armed struggle."[43] This still left the problem of the state, however, since the state was supposedly the instrument of the ruling class, and the ruling class in a state of "national democracy," at least initially, would be the "national bourgeoisie." Consequently, Soviet scholars needed to argue that state structures in the developing world had become so complicated that, while they still fundamentally reflected bourgeois interests, they were no longer just naked tools of class oppression.[44]

The "state of national democracy" had been charged by the Moscow Declaration with the rather vague imperatives of defending national independence, realizing deep democratic transformation, and enabling social progress.[45] Soviet theoreticians transformed these into three more concrete tasks. The first of these involved the completion of the "antifeudal" struggle by implementing radical agrarian reform, including, when possible, the development of cooperative methods of agriculture. The second of these was industrialization through the government sector. Finally, the state was supposed to achieve "democratization," by which was meant the inclusion of the masses in national politics.[46] Boris Ponomarev, the head of the International Department of the Central Committee of the CPSU, even argued that a "state of national democracy" should include "freedom of speech, of the press, of assembly, the right to create political parties and social organizations, and to participate in the determination of state policy," though this was primarily meant as a critique of those Western-leaning states that had curtailed the freedoms of local communists.[47] Of these three tasks, however, it was state-led industrialization that came to be seen as the most crucial to the process of political and socioeconomic development. Ponomarev wrote that any country seeking to strengthen its national independence must develop its national industry and that "one cannot achieve authentic independence without the liquidation of foreign monopolies in the economy, without the creation of a material basis for further independent development—a strong, independent national economy, especially in branches of heavy industry."[48] The implication that the anti-imperialist struggle depended upon industrialization, in light of the emphasis of the Chinese and many African countries on agriculture, was not accidental.

The key international factor in the advent of the "state of national democracy" and the possibility of the "noncapitalist path" was the existence of the socialist camp. Each discussion of the national liberation movement in the developing world began with the assertion that it was "second in historical significance" to the creation of the world socialist system, a point directed against the Chinese claim that the developing world had become the primary arena of the world revolutionary struggle.[49] Only the existence of the socialist camp made skipping the capitalist stage possible and, consequently, the internal development of "national democracies" was said to be dependent upon international factors, namely ties to the socialist bloc. "It is understood, that the state sector will be able to operate on a democratic basis and develop independent of foreign monopolies only in the case in which progressive patriotic forces will be able to offer certain pressure on the state of the country, and the state sector itself will cooperate with socialist countries."[50] This, of course, attached foreign policy criteria to the "state of national democracy." Nevertheless, Soviet scholars insisted that the choice to follow the "noncapitalist path" was left up to the countries themselves, and they vigorously protested against accusations of "exporting revolution."[51]

The "ideal type" of the "state of national democracy" set forth by Soviet theoreticians demanded an extensive attempt to evaluate the realities of each individual country's political and economic reality in light of the model in order to determine its current situation and likely direction. This produced endless classifications of countries by various Soviet authors, and it often seems that political rather than economic considerations determined the classification of a particular country at any given time. Nevertheless, Soviet scholars maintained that "without a differentiated approach to the characteristics of the class structure of society in the sovereign states of Asia, Africa, and Latin America it is impossible to give the correct evaluation of the relations of class and political forces in these countries in the contemporary stage of the development of the national liberation revolution."[52] While considerations of foreign policy may have intruded upon these evaluations at times, it should not be taken for granted that they therefore had no effect on the direction of Soviet policy.

Discussion about the "state of national democracy" and the "noncapitalist path of development" was not merely an attempt to justify Soviet penetration into the newly emerging nations. The priorities of foreign aid programs and political analyses were based on these theoretical structures, and the attempt to interpret events in this light occupied diplomats and policymakers as well as academicians. The case of Indonesia, one of the Soviet Union's earliest and largest aid recipients in the developing world, is illustrative. Soviet aid to Indonesia was based upon careful political, social, and economic analysis, and it was geared toward the transformation of society from below through expansion of heavy industry and state control of the economy. As early as March 1955, Khrushchev told the Indonesian ambassador in Moscow and future foreign minister Subandrio that the USSR was interested in helping Indonesia develop its industry in order to make a decisive stand against the colonialists.[53] Later that year, the Soviet ambassador in Jakarta, D. Zhukov, wrote to his superiors in the Foreign Ministry that Indonesia was in desperate need of industrial equipment and trained cadres if it was going to build and maintain an independent national economy.[54] In early 1956, in anticipation of Sukarno's upcoming visit to the USSR, Zhukov analyzed Indonesia's first five-year plan, and he suggested focusing aid on hydroelectric power and black and colored metallurgy.[55] Sukarno's visit subsequently resulted in an aid agreement in which the USSR pledged a $100 million credit to help Indonesia industrialize.[56] However, at this stage, the priority of Soviet aid seemed to be directed at altering Indonesia's international orientation. As the economic attaché of the Soviet embassy in Jakarta wrote in July 1956, "The foreign policy course of the Indonesian government will depend greatly on the results of the economic cooperation between our country and the Republic of Indonesia."[57] Hopes for deep domestic transformation were still limited.

By 1960, Sukarno's establishment of a regime of "directed democracy" focused on building "Indonesian socialism" via an eight-year plan would raise some Soviet hopes of domestic transformation. During his visit to Indonesia that year, Khrushchev gave Indonesia a further $250 million credit to aid in the fulfillment of the plan. The aid was meant primarily for the development of black and colored metallurgy, and the chemical and textile industries, specifically "in the main for the development of the key branches of the economy without which it would be impossible to secure the economic independence of the country."[58] The Soviet embassy believed that Sukarno might finally turn his attention to the economy. Reporting on the eight-year plan, it asserted that "the Indonesian government is devoting and will devote great efforts toward its completion, because it is relying on putting this plan into practice to improve the difficult economic situation in the country."[59] The significance of the plan was not only domestic, since "the expansion and strengthening of the state sector in the Indonesian economy . . . will exert a positive influence on other countries of Asia and Africa in choosing their paths of developing their economies."[60] However, the rhetoric of "Indonesian socialism" gave the Soviet government pause. The Southeast Asia Division of the Soviet Foreign Ministry claimed that "in presenting their conception of socialism, Sukarno and his group are working from the assumption of the possibility of building a socialist society without a revolutionary breaking of bourgeois relations of production, in conditions of the hegemony of the small and middle bourgeoisie and the preservation of subordinate position for the working classes and their avant-garde—the Marxist-Leninist Communist Party."[61] Analyzing the content of "Indonesian socialism," the Soviet embassy concluded that its claims to unify all classes of society and incorporate religion marked it as a petit-bourgeois concept, but, given the suppression of political freedoms for all political parties in Indonesia, little could or should be done to openly combat it. However, measures could be taken to encourage the obvious appetite of Indonesians for "true" socialism. In addition to putting greater emphasis on "true socialism" in published materials in Indonesia, the embassy stipulated that "in unofficial conversations with Sukarno during his trip to the USSR, support the acceptable parts of his teaching on Indonesian socialism, especially those touching on economic construction, and express doubt about those propositions which could lead to the growth of capitalism in Indonesia."[62] Combined with concrete shifts in the economy accomplished with Soviet aid and advice, perhaps Indonesia could be put on the path toward "scientific" socialism.

In the event, Soviet enthusiasm turned out to be unjustified. The economic situation of Indonesia continued to deteriorate, budget deficits ballooned, and the construction projects stipulated as part of the eight-year plan, including those to be built with Soviet aid, were delayed due to bureaucratic neglect and lack of resources. The Soviets were in no in doubt as to the culprit. In a report to the Southeast Asia Division of the GKES, Yuri Ganovskii, a researcher at the Institute of the Peoples of Asia, pointed out that military expenditure took up nearly 80 percent of the budget in 1962, and that "the steady and rapid growth of military expenditures appears to be the most serious obstacle to the allocation of means for budget outlays in the interests of the spheres of material production and more rapid social-cultural progress."[63] The story of Soviet frustration with the priorities of the Indonesian government will be continued in the next chapter. What this episode demonstrates is the concern registered throughout the Soviet foreign policy apparatus with the promotion of its economic model. Soviet diplomats in Indonesia, as well as GKES officials involved in crafting and implementing aid programs, paid close attention to the economic, social, and political structures of Indonesia as well as to the ideological pronouncements of its leading figures in order to figure out how best to promote the eventual construction of scientific socialism through Soviet aid and diplomacy. Indonesia, because of its powerful interest groups, particularly the military, and its existing economic relationships with the capitalist world, turned out to be too difficult a target. The USSR, though, would look for easier ones.

Even before the Kennedy administration would begin to apply its developmental model in the developing world, the first Soviet attempt to demonstrate the applicability of the Soviet model of socialism in the developing world was under way in Guinea, to be followed soon after by efforts in Mali and Ghana. Unlike Indonesia, these countries seemed to provide more of a blank canvas on which to work. Soviet scholars R. Avakov and G. Mirskii argued at the time that Africa did not yet have a fully formed national bourgeoisie because whatever businesses of any scale that had existed had been owned by Europeans. At the same time, certain African countries did have small, though active, working classes.[64] This fact meant that, in practical terms, there would be much less political resistance to Soviet involvement in economic planning in certain African countries than in India, where economic experts objected to "hard plans" with an "obligatory character,"[65] or in Indonesia, where ratification of a Soviet-Indonesian aid agreement was held up for two years in parliament.[66] Ideology and political opportunism were certainly not strangers in this case. Furthermore, Avakov and Mirskii categorized Guinea, Ghana, and Mali as a unique group, distinguished by the supposed fact that "the relationship of class and political forces in them is arrayed in such a way that increasing weight is being acquired by forces pushing for the noncapitalist path of development."[67] Whatever the reason for their selection, however, their importance for Soviet policy in the developing world was unmistakable. The ruling parties in Guinea, Ghana, and Mali sent delegations to the Twenty-Second CPSU Congress in October 1961, the first noncommunist parties ever invited to do so. President Sekou Touré of Guinea was awarded the Lenin Peace Prize in 1961, followed by President Kwame Nkrumah of Ghana in 1962 and President Modibo Keita of Mali in 1963. Consequently, the initial practical application of the concepts of the "state of national democracy" and the "noncapitalist path" would largely be focused on these three states.

Guinea was the earliest site of Soviet involvement where efforts were most intense. After Guinea voted to leave the French Union in September 1958 and subsequently declared its independence, France immediately abandoned Guinea, taking everything that was not bolted down and destroying most things that were. The USSR stepped into the breach. The two countries signed a trade agreement in February 1959, temporarily making the USSR Guinea's main trading partner, and then in August the Soviets agreed to a $35 million agreement for financial and technical aid.[68] It was not, however, until Guinea decided to embark upon economic planning in the spring of 1960 that the Soviet approach changed from merely an attempt to win friends and influence people to making Guinea a showcase for the Soviet development model in Africa.

The formation of the first plan was actually conducted largely under the leadership of Charles Bettelheim, an Austrian Jew who became a member of the French Communist Party (PCF) and who only a year earlier had written an essay titled "China's Economic Growth" based on his visit to China in 1958.[69] In that essay, Bettelheim remarked upon the "extraordinary impression created by the disappearance of all the social stigmas of 'underdevelopment' . . . in a country that goes ahead at an unbelievable speed and which, in this respect, outdoes all the performances that could have been achieved elsewhere."[70] Guinea's three-year plan was introduced by Minister of Planning Keita N'Famara at the Economic Conference of the Guinean Democratic Party in April 1960 in a speech that was subsequently republished in an abridged form first in *Pravda* and then in *Narody Azii i Afriki*.[71] N'Famara declared that the plan would liquidate "social differentiation" and that "the development of our country will not go along the path of the creation of a bourgeoisie, a class of exploiters, on the capitalist path that has outlived its time; it will go along the path to which belongs the future."[72] However, N'Famara acknowledged that the plan did not foresee the immediate development of heavy industry due to the lack of capital and of qualified technical cadres and workers. Instead, the three-year plan "will above all be a plan of the development of agricultural production."[73]

Despite the declared emphasis on agriculture, the Soviet reaction was enthusiastic. At a meeting of socialist ambassadors in Guinea on July 25, 1960, Soviet ambassador Solod excitedly said that the Guinean leaders wanted to follow the socialist path, including economic planning, nationalization, and agricultural collectivization, following a "mass line" in domestic politics, and a foreign policy of stated neutrality while, in fact, leaning toward the socialist camp. The only reason Guinea was not yet willing to call itself a "People's Democracy," the term applied by Moscow in Eastern Europe, was fear of prejudicing the outcome of African decolonization before it was completed.[74] When the Bulgarian ambassador proposed turning the African Independence Party, a pan-African underground party headquartered in Senegal, into a full-fledged Communist Party, Solod responded that "for now it is not appropriate to found a Communist Party in Guinea, the reason being that the present direction of the Guinean Democratic Party is socialist; there is still no need to found a Communist Party."[75] This same Bulgarian ambassador, immediately following the announcement of the plan in April, had breathlessly told the Chinese ambassador that Guinea would enter socialism by 1968, after the completion of this three-year plan and a following five-year one.[76]

Accordingly, Soviet aid and experts began to flood into Guinea. Soviet aid accounted for 33 percent of the investment forecast by the three-year plan, or 42 percent of Guinea's total foreign aid, and, at the beginning of 1962, there were some 448 Soviet specialists in Guinea.[77] Soviet aid went toward many projects, including a radio station, a hotel, a rice farm, a stadium, and even, according to one eyewitness report, the supply of tropical Guinea with snow-removal equipment.[78] Industry represented a significant part of the Soviet aid program, including geological prospecting, factory installations, and a polytechnical institute.[79] Guinea's main industrial resource, however, was already spoken for. Guinea contains approximately one-third of the world's high-grade bauxite deposits, but in the early 1960s the only mining operation for bauxite in Guinea, which had started under French control in 1957 in the town of Fria, was under the control of an international consortium known as the Fria Company. Soviet involvement in Guinean bauxite production would not come until 1969, when a new agreement would lead to the opening of a Soviet-constructed mine and railroad in Débélé.[80] From the Soviet perspective though, industrial development, regardless of under whose auspices it was conducted, was more important than the construction of an autarchic, nonindustrial economy.

The reason for this was that industrialization would lead to the advent of a working class, which would in turn manufacture new political realities. While the Guinean planning minister had explicitly defined one of the goals of the three-year plan to be the liquidation of social differentiation, Moscow's intentions were opposed to those of its small West African client. As early as July 1960, Y. Bochkaryov wrote in regard to Guinea that "the situation is such that it will be impossible to avoid a certain amount of differentiation. Although the bourgeoisie is weak and has not yet set itself up as a force in opposition to the people, it is growing. On the other hand, the economic plans and the resultant industrialization will lead to the growth of the working class. In these circumstances new social trends and even organizations may quite possibly arise."[81] Boris Ponomarev stated in May 1961 that "national democracy" will inevitably entail certain processes, and "it is understood that such processes in countries which have been liberated from imperialist oppression, arise not by the will or desire of one or another party or personality, but rather due to the strength of contradictory basic interests of different classes."[82] The differences between the nonclass conceptions of "African socialism" and the Soviet agenda of a "noncapitalist path" leading to "scientific" socialism were clearly evident between those who had written Guinea's three-year plan and those who were largely in charge of fulfilling it.

These differences would not remain on the pages of academic journals. In 1961 the Soviet embassy in Conakry began to criticize high-ranking officials in the Guinean government, including Ismail Touré, the president's half-brother, claiming that the regime was "turning right," the Guinean people were dissatisfied, and that the situation of political power in Guinea was unstable.[83] The North Vietnamese ambassador reported that, unlike a year earlier, the Soviet ambassador said that "now we can consider the question of founding a new opposition party," and the Soviet embassy was supposedly supporting the activities of the African Independence Party against Touré's regime.[84] The activities of the Soviet embassy did not escape the notice of the regime. When the Guinean Foreign Ministry gave the Soviet ambassador a notice prohibiting the distribution of their press materials, the latter promptly tore the paper apart.[85] Meanwhile, the Guinean side became increasingly dissatisfied with the quality and quantity of Soviet aid.[86] Soon enough, the situation exploded. The details of exactly what occurred are still unclear, but in late November a teacher's strike led to student demonstrations on the night of November 23–24.[87] On December 11, Touré gave a speech blasting the demonstrators as "counterrevolutionaries" and ordering their arrest. The Soviet news correspondent in Conakry described those who were arrested as "communists" and "leftists," hardly the terms normally employed to describe the opponents of a friendly regime.[88] Claiming that the Soviet embassy had been responsible for this subversion, Touré expelled the Soviet ambassador two days later. In a meeting with the socialist ambassadors on December 14, Touré accused them of engaging in illegal activities, subversion, and espionage, except for the Chinese and North Vietnamese. Other Guinean government officials then went on to attack the conduct and activities of the experts, as well as the projects they were working on, once again excepting the Chinese and Vietnamese.[89]

Not willing to let Guinea go without a fight, First Deputy Chairman of the Soviet Council of Ministers Anastas Mikoyan immediately flew to Conakry, ostensibly for the opening of a Soviet trade exhibition at the

Conakry fairgrounds.[90] He signed a new trade deal for 1962, increasing trade by 70 to 80 percent over 1961, which also included a new loan of two billion Guinean francs. There was one demand that Mikoyan would not concede. Guinea had 500 students studying in the USSR at the time and claimed that the Soviets had been propagandizing them against the regime. In particular, they demanded the return of forty students who were said to have supported the conspiracy. Mikoyan refused, explaining that the Soviet Union could revoke their scholarships, but it could not force them to return to Guinea against their will.[91] For the rest of 1962, the Soviets would continue to include Guinea whenever Moscow listed progressive states in Africa. By the beginning of 1963, however, the continued refusal of Sekou Touré to submit to Soviet tutelage had led to a change of policy. Now Moscow not only refused to allow Guinea to draw upon the 1962 loan, but it also insisted that trade now had to be balanced, and Guinea had to start repaying old loans.[92]

Moscow, however, had already begun planning for a break with Guinea as soon as its ambassador was expelled. After concluding his negotiations in Guinea in January 1962, Mikoyan immediately flew to Mali, where he signed an agreement on economic and technical cooperation that would provide aid for the fulfillment of Mali's current five-year plan (1961–65), and he described Soviet-Malian relations as "comradely." From then on, the Soviets began officially calling Mali "socialist." President Modibo Keita visited Moscow in May 1962, and Khrushchev addressed him as "comrade president," pronouncing his happiness at Mali's choice of the "socialist path of development."[93] Continuing his tour, Mikoyan then visited Ghana, praising Nkrumah's "socialism" and announcing at a banquet that "your desire to build socialism unites us." This was not merely a diplomatic show. At the end of the year, the Soviet ambassador averred in a meeting of socialist ambassadors that he "does not doubt that Nkrumah has an honest desire to go down the socialist path."[94]

Relations with Mali soon began following the same pattern as they had with Guinea, however. The Soviets gave Mali a 56 million ruble credit in January 1963, and soon 200 to 300 Soviet experts were working in Mali. Despite the fact that Mali had learned from Guinea's experience and was more vigilant regarding Soviet activities, on February 14, 1963, President Keita felt the need to call a meeting with the ambassadors of the socialist countries, criticizing their aid, saying the prices charged for equipment were too high, and claiming that, except for China, all other socialist countries conducted trade relations more or less in the same manner as capitalist countries. Finally, echoing the accusations of Sekou Touré one year earlier, Keita claimed that Malian students in the Soviet Union and Czechoslovakia did not even feel as if they were in socialist countries, and the deputy head of the Malian youth organization said that he knew that Moscow and Prague were trying to turn the students against the Bamako government.[95] The Soviet government seems to have learned its lesson though, and it managed to avoid the expulsion of another ambassador.

Despite the fact that Ghana was usually grouped with Guinea and Mali in Soviet statements, relations with Accra were qualitatively different. Nkrumah's socialist rhetoric belied the fact that Ghana's state planning, in fact, relied much more on private enterprise, a fact attributable both to the higher level of development of the Ghanaian economy at the time of independence and the greater involvement of the United States and the United Kingdom in Ghanaian politics and economics, particularly the former's massive aid in building a hydroelectric project on the Volta River. Ghana served the important purpose, though, of serving as the mouthpiece for Soviet foreign policy positions in West Africa, as Nkrumah could be counted on, unlike Touré and Keita, to support peaceful coexistence, holding a conference supporting a "world without missiles" in Accra in 1962. According to the Chinese, after the Soviet ambassador was kicked out of Guinea, "Ghana became the most important target and most convenient venue for current Soviet cultural and propaganda activities, as well as the dissemination of the revisionist point of view, in West Africa."[96]

By the middle of 1962, however, the difficulties encountered by the Soviets in trying to build socialism in Africa, and in Guinea in particular, had led to a certain level of disenchantment with African leaders and a consequent hardening of policy. Whereas the theory of the "state of national democracy" had depended upon the inclination of the "national bourgeoisie" toward the completion of "anti-imperialist" tasks, the Soviets now began to push a more militant working-class line, arguing that the period of the utility of the national bourgeoisie in the revolutionary process would soon be exhausted if it had not been already. While it still had some use in foreign policy, Soviet writers argued that "the national bourgeoisie is afraid to conduct general democratic transformations, for this will develop the revolutionary initiative and enable the development of the class self-consciousness of the laborers, that is, strengthen those sociopolitical factors that in the final count can turn against the very same bourgeoisie."[97] In a speech in Sofia in May 1962, Khrushchev affirmed that many leaders of the newly independent states were talking about socialism, and that this was good, but the question was:

> What kind of socialism do they have in mind? . . . We are convinced of one thing—time and the trend of historical development will face the former colonial countries with the choice of taking either the capitalist path or the non-capitalist path of development. Which path to choose will be decided by the peoples themselves. And those leaders who really have the best interests of the people, the working masses, at heart will sooner or later have to realize that only by leaning on the working class as the most consistent, most revolutionary class of society, in alliance with the peasantry and with the support of all progressive forces, can they bring about victory and the correct solution of fundamental social problems. They will either grasp this fact or they will be followed by others with a better understanding of life's demands.[98]

Soviet frustration with the ostensibly progressive African political leadership was now leading to thinly veiled threats against that leadership. When Malian president Keita visited Moscow later that month, Khrushchev educated him publicly, saying, "It would be wrong to think that it is enough to proclaim the slogan 'We are for socialism' and then lie in the shade of a tree waiting for everything to arrange itself. . . . We would like our Malian friends to see and understand the complexity of the tasks which arise in the building of a new society."[99] As Sergey Mazov argues, in the wake of the disaster in Guinea, Khrushchev demanded a greater level of "ideological purity" from his would-be acolytes in West Africa.[100] This Soviet willingness to risk damage to its relations with African states and its standing on the African continent for the sake of influencing the domestic policies of African states speaks deeply to the priorities of the Soviet leadership, priorities that were not shared in Beijing.

All along, the Chinese had taken a dim view of the Soviet attempt to build socialism in the developing world. Despite having signed on to the Moscow Declaration, which introduced the concepts of "national democracy" and the "noncapitalist path," Chinese propaganda rarely employed them, and they seemed to play no role at all in the formation of Chinese policy. Instead of states of "national democracy" (民族民主) the Chinese talked about states of "national independence" (民族独立), reflecting the Chinese prioritization of independence from Western influence over socialistic domestic politics. Beijing saw Moscow's ventures as an attempt "to create in African countries an example of not going through capitalism, reaching socialism through peaceful development," thereby validating its theory of "peaceful transition."[101] Guinea represented the first attempt to showcase this theory because, along with Mali, its leaders had had ties to the French Communist Party in the colonial era. The CCP Central Committee wrote to the Liaison Committee regarding Guinea and Mali that, after independence, "both countries enacted and advanced a bourgeois reformist line, [and] the Soviet Union produced illusions about them, attempting in economics and politics to increase its attraction and control."[102] This was followed by an "unprincipled" promotion of Ghana as the next demonstration of peaceful transition and the noncapitalist path.[103] To do this, the Soviets even encouraged Ghana to accept an offer of American aid, directly contradicting the chief slogan of development promoted by Beijing, "raising oneself on one's own forces" (自力更生).[104] The Chinese called the entire Soviet theory of the noncapitalist path and the peaceful transition to socialism "preposterous" (荒谬).[105]

At this stage, however, China did not yet offer a comprehensive alternative to the model of development promoted by the Soviet Union. Visitors to China were lectured on the Chinese "revolutionary experience and experience of socialist construction," and they were often taken to view factories and people's communes.[106] Chinese diplomats abroad and those receiving foreign guests at home eagerly solicited comments upon the supposed great successes of Chinese construction, the particular applicability of Chinese experiences to the developing world, and the increasing popularity of the thought of Mao Zedong.[107] However, Beijing's prescription for development seemed to be limited to the exhortation to develop using one's own forces, a slogan which had become popular within China in the aftermath of the withdrawal of Soviet advisers. The application of this particular slogan to the developing world, however, revealed the Chinese preoccupation with foreign policy and the "anti-imperialist" stances of the newly independent states. The Chinese thought that any talk of socialism or industrialization was premature, and consequently what mattered most was the total elimination of Western influence from Asia, Africa, and Latin America. A copy of the PLA's *Bulletin of Activities*, captured by French soldiers in the Congo in 1961, revealed that the Chinese saw Africa as far from the stage of socialist revolution. "At present some parts of Africa are going through experiences similar to what we experienced in China 60 years ago in the Boxer uprising. Some of the events are like those which occurred during the Xinhai revolution, while others resemble what happened around May 4th [1919]. We have not yet begun the period of the Northern Expedition and that of the War of Resistance against Japan, and we are still far from the events of 1949 in China."[108] Though at the time it was obtained some expressed skepticism about whether this document was an accurate representation of Chinese thought at the highest level, Foreign Ministry documents seem to confirm that the Chinese still saw true socialist revolution in Africa at this time as a remote prospect.[109]

As a result, Chinese coverage of the newly independent states focused on their anti-imperialist measures, such as nationalizing foreign businesses, eliminating foreign military bases, and "Africanizing" the bureaucracy, rather than on socialist-type measures, such as planning and cooperativization.[110] China had an aid program as well, though on a smaller scale than the Soviet Union, but that program was focused more on building bilateral relationships through anti-imperialist solidarity rather than any attempt to reshape the socioeconomic structures of the states involved. Chinese aid agreements with Guinea and Nepal famously specified that the living standards of Chinese experts should not exceed those of their local counterparts, a condition that was given a significant amount of coverage in the local press.[111] By contrast, the supposed "great power chauvinism" with which Soviet and Eastern European experts related to Africans and their excessive material demands led to significant complaints in Guinea and Mali, among others.[112] The comparatively beneficial terms of the Chinese aid offers began to concern certain Soviet officials. A report from the Institute of the Peoples of Asia to deputy foreign minister V. V. Kuznetsov in July 1961 titled "Development of Economic Ties of the PRC with the Countries of Asia, Africa, and Latin America," despite expressing the hope that increasing Chinese engagement would be a net benefit to the socialist camp, discussed the dangers of Chinese aid, which was often offered as either grants or interest-free loans in contrast to Soviet loans, which were offered at a rate of 2.5 percent. "Such forms of economic relations could create the impression of a naked political, propagandistic maneuver, which could be used by anticommunist propaganda . . . together with this, such 'generosity' from the PRC could put in a slanderous position the Soviet Union and other socialist countries who offer aid to underdeveloped countries on conditions in great measure tied to the principle of mutual benefit."[113] Though such concerns were not yet widely shared at the top, events would soon lead the Soviet leadership to take note of the growing Chinese challenge.

The different approaches of the Soviet Union and the PRC to the novel scenario posed by the newly emerging states in the early 1960s and the intensifying battle for influence with the West in general, and the United States in particular, reveal much about the nature and focus of Soviet and Chinese policy. For the USSR, the overriding concern was the creation and demonstration of a viable model for the implementation of socialism in the developing world, even if this meant risking relations with African leaders who were otherwise inclined to be supportive of the broader aims of Soviet foreign policy. The Chinese, by contrast, were satisfied with a militantly anti-imperialist policy, expressed externally as opposition to the United States, the United Nations, and a host of other issues, and internally in terms of expelling all Western influence at any cost. On issues such as whether or not to accept Western economic aid, the two agendas came into direct conflict. As an extreme illustration of the different philosophies of the two countries, Sekou Touré reported that during his first visit to Moscow in 1959, Khrushchev actually asked him directly why he had voted for independence, implying that the USSR did not approve of the choice.[114] Touré, and the Chinese, were incredulous. Nevertheless, this entire episode points to a different understanding of the relationship between the Soviet and Chinese revolutionary projects than the common idea that the Chinese Revolution was simply a younger, more radical version of the Soviet one. Rather, the two revolutionary projects were fundamentally different, and each was the more radical in its own way. The Soviet project prioritized anticapitalism, and the Soviets certainly made a much greater concrete effort to promote socialism than the Chinese did. Meanwhile, the Chinese saw anti-imperialism as the chief goal of their revolutionary program, and they prioritized that goal over any attempt to build socialism in the developing world. Even while the Sino-Soviet Split was still relatively quiet at the level of bilateral relations throughout most of 1961, the differences between the Soviet and Chinese Revolutions expressed themselves quite clearly in their respective policies in the developing world.

The Twenty-Second Congress and Its Aftermath

The tentative truce in bilateral Sino-Soviet relations that had existed since the 1960 Moscow meeting was shattered decisively by the Twenty-

Second CPSU Congress, which began on October 17, 1961. The congress was intended as the crowning moment for Khrushchev's reforms, introducing a new party program to replace the one adopted in 1919, one which boldly proclaimed that the Soviet Union would surpass the United States economically by 1970 and that it would achieve communism by 1980. The program announced that the Soviet Union had achieved a classless society, and consequently the party would be open to all. In many ways, the ambitious new program seemed to be a response to the Kennedy administration's agenda, especially in the developing world. In a break with Soviet policy of only a few months earlier, the program blasted American "imperialism" and "neocolonialism," criticized the new American aid programs, and even specifically mentioned Kennedy's speech to the U.S. Congress about loans to developing countries.[115] The Chinese, however, saw the program as a direct attack upon themselves and the Albanians.[116] Mao said that the program "is like an old woman's foot-binding bandage, not only long but also stinking."[117] Nevertheless, the Chinese leadership did not react to the program publicly in advance of the congress, deciding that its policy should be to maintain both principle and solidarity, not engaging in polemics unless directly provoked.[118] In Khrushchev's opening address to the congress, however, he launched into vehement unanticipated attacks on Stalin and Albania, forcing the other CPSU speakers to rewrite their speeches and precipitating the removal of Stalin's embalmed corpse from the mausoleum on Red Square.[119] On instructions from Mao and Liu Shaoqi, two days later, Zhou Enlai, representing the PRC at the congress, fired back, criticizing the public attack upon a fellow party. On October 21, the Chinese delegation went to lay a wreath in honor of Stalin, who had not yet been interred, and, following talks with the Soviet party leadership on October 22, Zhou returned to Beijing while the congress was in mid-session.[120]

Beijing immediately began a diplomatic offensive against the Twenty-Second Congress, explicitly soliciting opinions upon the CPSU's policies and searching for like-minded people. The Chinese Foreign Ministry instructed all of its personnel abroad to study the Soviet program and Zhou's speech, holding meetings within the embassies to discuss documents related to the conference in preparation for the propaganda offensive.[121] On November 16, the Chinese embassy in Bamako invited the Malian propaganda minister to talk about the congress, and the Malian promptly launched into a defense of Stalin. On the 30th they invited a representative of the African Independence Party stationed in Mali for the same purpose.

He supported the Chinese positions on Stalin and Albania as well.[122] The same scene played out in numerous Chinese embassies around the world. Ho Chi Minh said in a meeting with officials from the Chinese embassy in Hanoi that the conference had proven that there were now two groups within the international communist movement; one consisting of the Soviet, East European, French, Italian, and certain other European and African parties, and the other including the Chinese, Koreans, Vietnamese, Indonesians, and other East Asians.[123] Ho nevertheless thought that Albania had also acted incautiously in its response and hoped for reconciliation. Che Guevara, meeting with the PRC ambassador in Cuba, remarked that he agreed "100 percent" with China, but he said that Soviet support was crucial for Cuba and so he could not express this publicly.[124] The Chinese embassy in Cuba, however, reported that while the top leaders, such as Fidel, Raul, and Che, seemed to have "correct" positions on international issues, there was another group in the party leadership, including Anibal Escalante, Carlos Rojas, and Rafael Rodriguez, with decidedly pro-Soviet views.[125] Meanwhile, Chinese embassies reported that the attitude of the Eastern European governments had become noticeably colder toward them since the conference.[126]

In the aftermath of the Twenty-Second Congress, Beijing also placed increased attention on Soviet activity in Asia and Africa. On January 30, 1962, the Chinese Foreign Ministry forwarded a report from the embassy in Burma indicating that since the Twenty-Second Congress the USSR had increased its activities in the country, promoting the revisionist line while pressuring the "true leftists." The Chinese embassy claimed that the Soviets were promoting the idea that the "national democratic revolution" must be led by the bourgeoisie in order to prevent any armed uprising and forestall the establishment of a pro-Chinese party.[127] The Chinese Foreign Ministry then asked the embassies in India, Indonesia, Pakistan, Ceylon, Nepal, Afghanistan, UAR, Iraq, Ghana, and Mali for similar reports on Soviet activity. On February 12, the PRC embassy in Moscow produced a report on the supposed increase of Soviet efforts abroad since the congress. After listing the growing number of trips abroad of high-level Soviet officials, such as Brezhnev and Mikoyan, along with foreign visits to the USSR, the report talked about Moscow's attempts to build up certain leaders, such as Nehru and Nkrumah, in order to use them for their own purposes. Meanwhile, the Soviets were increasing trade, as well as technical and particularly military, aid to gain greater loyalty. In addition to a long list of recently signed economic agreements, the Chinese report mentioned new massive arms deals with the UAR, India, and Indonesia.[128] All of this was seen as a Soviet attempt to promote the revisionist line of the Twenty-Second Congress, bolster its flagging status in the developing world, and, most importantly, weaken China's "ever-increasing" influence in the region, even to the extent of encouraging right-wing groups to conduct anti-China activities, in India especially.[129]

The renewed tension in the wake of the congress soon expressed itself in a series of international meetings. The Chinese showed up at an executive committee meeting of the AAPSO in Gaza in December 1961 with the largest delegation there, and the Soviet delegation quickly found out what that meant. They were confronted by an angry Algerian delegation and concluded that "somebody is confusing them about our position on the struggle of the Algerian people."[130] The main issue at the meeting centered on the idea of convening a tricontinental conference, including representatives from Latin America as well. The Soviets wanted to hold the conference under the auspices of the World Peace Council (WPC), but the Chinese and their allies argued that the WPC was "not an anticolonial, anti-imperialist organization."[131] The Chinese saw an attempt by the Soviets to subsume the more militant Afro-Asian solidarity movement under the Moscow-controlled WPC, while the Soviets saw the Chinese as attempting to sever the two organizations completely, thereby cutting Moscow off from any influence in Africa and Asia. The battle continued at a WPC meeting in Stockholm following the Gaza meeting, where the Chinese, along with a number of East Asian and African delegations, loudly accused the USSR and WPC of betraying the cause of national liberation in Asia and Africa. SCSCAA acknowledged the success of the Chinese arguments, pointing out that even African students studying in the USSR itself seemed to believe that Soviet calls for disarmament included disarming liberation movements in Algeria, Angola, and elsewhere.[132] By the time of the Afro-Asian writers' conference in February 1962 in Cairo, it was clear that there were now two set lines, and all future Afro-Asian conferences would see battles between them. While the Chinese argued that Afro-Asian countries could liberate themselves without any outside help, "operating on their own forces," the Soviets felt they had no choice but to openly discuss their disagreements with the Chinese.[133] Nevertheless, the Soviets felt themselves overwhelmed by the extent of Chinese preparation, and it was all they could do to moderate a conference resolution in effect written by the Chinese.[134] Despite winning modest victories, including perfunctory mentions of peaceful coexistence and disarmament, in the resolution, SCSCAA grimly predicted that "the struggle will continue in the same atmosphere of contradiction as before."[135] Given the Chinese successes, some SCSCAA members now suggested shifting their focus to Latin America, which was at a "different stage of historical development" than Africa and would consequently be more receptive to the Soviet position.[136]

The Chinese propaganda offensive that accompanied this change in relations began to concern Soviet officials, especially due to the perceived inadequacies of Soviet propaganda efforts. A correspondent of the newly created international Soviet news agency Novosti complained that Chinese propaganda vastly overwhelmed Soviet propaganda in Mali, while a member of the SCSCAA Presidium noted that Chinese propaganda was flooding into Africa, and the works of Mao Zedong could be found even in Conakry.[137] Meanwhile, another high Novosti official, reporting on an extensive trip through Africa in November 1961, wrote that the Soviets were failing to set the agenda even on the issue of the Twenty-Second Congress itself, since most African news sources were getting their information from Western press agencies that focused largely on the issues of Stalin and Albania.[138] Submitting a proposal to the Central Committee for the expansion of Soviet propaganda in Africa based on this report, the head of Novosti warned that "in general forces of the PRC are deployed toward putting out bulletins wherever there is a Chinese representation, as well as the distribution of popular ideological literature (cheap editions of the articles and speeches of Mao Zedong, magazines, photo materials)."[139] A particular point of concern was the emphasis of the Chinese on what the Soviets interpreted to be issues of nationalism, particularly regarding the notion that countries should develop independently of foreign aid. This "nationalism" of the Chinese seemed to be directed toward galvanizing suspicion among Asians and Africans toward Europeans, in general, and the Soviets and their Eastern European allies, in particular.[140] The Soviets were especially concerned that the Chinese were attempting to use arguments of racial solidarity to weaken the influence of the "white" Soviets. In Chinese propaganda, the Soviet Union became essentially another white, imperialist power, whose past experience of building socialism in an industrialized former Great Power was irrelevant to the experience of newly independent colonies, and which would always prioritize its relations with the West over the welfare of the developing world.

At this stage, however, few at the top of the Soviet leadership were listening to these warnings from below. The head of the radio administration under the Ministry of Communications in a March 1961 report on the state of Soviet radio propaganda wrote that Radio Beijing was more easily heard than Radio Moscow in almost all of Latin America, but he still had to ask that someone in the Soviet embassy in Havana actually be given the job of listening to its broadcasts.[141] More ominously, the KGB reported that on February 26, 1962, Radio Beijing first began beaming programs in Russian to the Soviet Union, though as of yet its content was not considered prejudicial.[142] However, when the KGB itself a year earlier had proposed the creation of a radio center in Tashkent for broadcasting to Africa, Southeast Asia, and the Near East, the International and Agitprop departments of the Central Committee had weighed in, saying the project was unnecessary and too expensive. In the end, the center was not built.[143] Similarly, when in the wake of the Twenty-Second Congress, the editor in chief of *Problemy Mira i Sotsializma,* the global journal of the international communist movement published in Prague, wrote to CPSU secretary Frol Kozlov about the deficiencies of Soviet propaganda in Asia, Africa, and Latin America in the wake of the Chinese propaganda offensive, proposing among other things the creation of a division of the Central Committee in charge of foreign agitprop, the International Department quickly dismissed the idea as unnecessary.[144] Repeated calls by SCSCAA to publish the journal *Aziia i Afrika Segodnia* in English and French were going unheeded,[145] and when the vice chairman of SCSCAA, Anatoly Safronov, asked in the wake of the Twenty-Second congress what was being published in Asian languages, the answer came back—almost nothing.[146] As the summer of 1962 wore on, the weight of the Soviet propaganda machine remained focused on peaceful coexistence and disarmament, especially in advance of the "World Disarmament Conference" held in Moscow in July 1962. Tellingly, the WPC and Soviet Peace Committee, which were organizing the conference, needed to rely on SCSCAA to invite Africans since they themselves had few contacts in Africa.[147]

Nevertheless, the Chinese embassy in Moscow did notice a certain hardening of the Soviet line over the course of 1962, though it considered this stiffening to be merely a tactical and not a fundamental shift. A report filed by the embassy on August 31 presents an interesting contrast to the one mentioned above from February. The author writes that the

Soviet leadership was taking certain measures now to elide its growing contradictions with the national liberation movement.[148] While still emphasizing peaceful coexistence and disarmament, the Soviets were now acknowledging that sometimes armed struggle was necessary, claiming that the Soviet Union had never shrunk from supporting the struggle of peoples for freedom and independence. Furthermore, disarmament was for nuclear powers first; as for people struggling for independence, the USSR would continue to provide them with arms. The Chinese reaction to this shift demonstrates clearly the changes in Chinese policy toward the USSR that had taken place since the Twenty-Second Congress. Beijing was no longer interested in reforming Soviet policy; it was now interested only in competing with it. The PRC embassy wrote: "The above corrections in the Soviet Union's policy toward the countries of the intermediate zone are due to the current situation, and it also received some training in its struggle with us. These corrections not only do not change the original position at all, but they [the Soviets] continue to adopt any type of attractive measures toward bourgeois ruling groups which serve its pacifist foreign policy, divide the revolutionary forces, and at the same time they also use all efforts to diminish our country's influence, even encouraging right-wing forces to oppose China."[149]

In the summer of 1962, domestic political events in China were setting the stage for what would soon be an explosion of Sino-Soviet confrontation. Chen Jian, Niu Jun, and Lorenz Luthi have shown that, in the course of 1962, Chinese foreign policy would increasingly become a function of the efforts of Mao to reestablish his dominance within the CCP leadership.[150] The so-called 7,000-Cadres Conference from late December 1961 to early February 1962 ended up as a significant political defeat for Mao, who withdrew to Wuhan in the wake of the conference to watch the political developments in Beijing from afar.[151] Meanwhile, during the conference, the head of the Liaison Department, Wang Jiaxiang, gathered his leading colleagues, including Liu Ningyi, head of the Chinese Afro-Asian Solidarity Committee, and Wu Xiuquan, to work out a proposal for a more moderate Chinese foreign policy. They came up with a policy that Mao later derisively labeled *sanhe yishao* (三和一少), or "three reconciliations and one reduction," advocating some level of reconciliation with the USSR, USA, and India along with the reduction of ideologically based foreign aid.[152] While it is unclear to what degree some or all of Wang's recommendations ever found expression in the concrete formation of Chinese policy,[153] the appearance of such a clearly articulated, ostensibly "revisionist" foreign policy position among the leadership would prove a useful tool for Mao in his return to power. At the Beidaihe work conference from July 25 to August 24, Mao returned from Wuhan to make a threatening speech, arguing that the economic reforms pursued by Liu Shaoqi and Deng Xiaoping in the wake of the Great Leap Forward were infected with revisionism. At the Tenth Party Plenum in September, he tackled the issue of foreign policy and, in particular, Wang's proposals. He asserted that Wang's foreign policy was friendly both toward imperialism and revisionism, that China no longer needed to rely on any big power including the USSR, and that the focus of Chinese foreign policy should definitively shift toward Asia, Africa, and Latin America.[154] In the wake of the plenum, Mao introduced the slogan *fanxiu fangxiu* (反修防修) (oppose revisionism [abroad], prevent revisionism [at home]), clearly linking Chinese foreign policy with domestic political battles.[155] Events would soon allow Mao to implement this more militant policy with a ferocity that would ultimately cause Moscow to reevaluate its own foreign policy.

The Cuban Missile Crisis and the Road to Open Confrontation

In the wake of deteriorating Sino-Soviet relations following the Twenty-Second Congress and the beginnings of what Niu Jun has called China's "turn to the left" in the summer of 1962, the Cuban Missile Crisis played a decisive role in turning the Sino-Soviet relationship in the developing world into an outright battle for influence. Thus far, competition with the United States had remained the dominant consideration in Soviet policy vis-à-vis the newly independent states as evidenced by the continued emphasis on peace and disarmament, a policy oriented toward public opinion in the West and the more centrist countries of Asia, Africa, and Latin America at the expense of a certain amount of influence among the more radically minded people in the developing world. Similarly, the Soviet obsession with aid and development models thus far found its primary competitor in the Kennedy administration rather than in Beijing. While the Soviets were aware of growing Chinese influence, especially in Africa and among the Communist Parties of East Asia, competition with China in the developing world was still unquestionably a lower priority for Moscow. For the Chinese, the competition with the USSR had become more central to its agenda, especially since late 1961, but the need to devote resources and attention to domestic issues in the wake of the failure of the Great Leap Forward took precedence, such that even the rather modest Chinese aid agreements signed with Mali and Ghana in 1961 specified that the credits not be drawn upon until mid-1962.[156] In the aftermath of the Cuban Missile Crisis, however, a resurgent Mao and the deteriorating Sino-Soviet relationship would lead China to devote far more resources to its competition with the USSR.

Despite the fact that the Cuban Revolution had occurred through armed struggle in the countryside, similar in some ways to the CCP's own experience, Sino-Cuban relations initially got off to a slow start. The Chinese were unsure what to make of the various groups in the initial coalition of power in Havana, and the lack of Communist Party participation in the revolution made them wary. Even Che Guevara was described as having only "advanced bourgeois democratic revolutionary thought" with some Marxist-Leninist influence.[157] The situation was confusing enough for the CCP that Zhou Enlai submitted an entire analysis of the Cuban Revolution in late 1959 to other top CCP leaders simply in order to explain the decision to establish a Xinhua post there, on Cuban invitation. In the end, Zhou justified this primarily by saying that "in reality, it will be our political observation post in Cuba for all of Latin America."[158] When Cuban delegations visited Yugoslavia, Egypt, and others in January 1960, signing a joint communiqué with Tito, the Chinese embassy in Cairo worried that Cuba's "bourgeois nationalists" were trying to unite with other bourgeois nationalists in Asia, Africa, and Latin America, including Nasser and Nehru, to create a neutralist bloc.[159] A major obstacle in the way of developing relations was Cuba's continuing diplomatic ties with Taiwan, which became a significant consideration in Chinese deliberations regarding aid and trade.[160]

The Soviet Union, meanwhile, was far more enthusiastic about the possibilities of the Cuban Revolution, and consequently much more active in developing a relationship. After Mikoyan's trip to Cuba in early 1960, he pushed for aid to Cuba in Moscow, telling the Chinese that Fidel Castro was someone the socialist world could rely on politically.[161] Now the Chinese began to worry that Soviet influence was growing rapidly in Cuba and in particular that the Cubans found the Soviets militarily reliable.[162] Che himself said that "Soviet support for Cuba is a true indication of the Soviet policy of peaceful coexistence."[163] After a Cuban delegation led by Che visited China in November 1960, the Chinese became somewhat more convinced of Cuba's sympathy for its own more militant line, especially after a discussion on guerrilla warfare tactics between Che and

Mao,[164] but despite increasing aid and trade relations, Soviet aid still reigned supreme, preventing the Cubans from breaking their public façade of neutrality to reveal any underlying sympathy with Chinese positions.[165] The significant Soviet military and economic aid to Cuba, combined with a major propaganda offensive, seemed to be diminishing even the underlying sympathy between two revolutionary regimes recently forged in long years of guerrilla warfare.[166] By the end of 1961, the chairman of SCSCAA, reporting on his recent trip through Latin America, summarized the situation by saying, "In the course of this year, which has been difficult for the Cubans, they have become convinced that from the Chinese they can get only revolutionary slogans and loud yelling, but real aid from the Chinese is not visible and they couldn't see it, because the Chinese don't have the means and the possibilities to offer any kind of significant real aid. But our real aid there is very visible, it hits everyone in the face."[167]

On the day before the discovery by the United States of the Soviet missiles in Cuba, Che Guevara expressed confidence to the Chinese ambassador that, even though the Soviets had not explicitly said what they would do in case of attack, he was sure that world war would be the result. At the same time, Che expressed a rather cavalier attitude toward the struggle with revisionism, which disturbed the Chinese. He told them that "I don't understand why Yugoslavia is still at the center of the question, Yugoslavia has already become history."[168] After the Soviets agreed to remove the missiles under threat of an American attack, the Cuban tone changed considerably. When Mikoyan came to Havana to meet with Cuban leaders at the beginning of November, Che would not come to the airport, even apologizing to the Chinese ambassador for his remarks during their conversation of October 13.[169] Mikoyan still would not put into concrete terms what the Soviet response would be in case of an American attack, and now the Cuban leadership discussed the possibility of fighting on alone.[170] The Chinese embassy reported frequently on the mood in Cuba, eagerly cataloguing every negative change in the attitude of both the leadership and the people toward the USSR.[171] The feeling on the Soviet side was mutual. After Mikoyan gave his report to the Presidium on his visit to Cuba, his colleagues called the Cubans "unreliable allies."[172]

Immediately before, during, and after the missile crisis, Soviet policy had been rather congenial toward the Chinese in the hope of gaining Chinese support. While the crisis was going on, border clashes had once again erupted between China and India due to China's attempt to reverse the results of India's "forward policy" of 1961. This time, the Soviet leadership took a more clearly pro-Chinese stance with the intention of improving relations. On October 13, three days before Kennedy discovered the missiles, Khrushchev told departing Chinese ambassador Liu Xiao: "It would be most appropriate to open a new, blank page [in our relations] . . . to squeeze out the cold and replace it with warmth."[173] The next day at a Presidium meeting Khrushchev decided to hold back on providing the MiG-21s to India as had been agreed upon. He called the Chinese policy "rational," described India's demands as "humiliating" for the PRC, and instructed the Soviet ambassador to India to tell Nehru that Moscow was "disappointed."[174] Khrushchev even ordered Chervonenko, the Soviet ambassador in Beijing, to offer the MiGs to the Chinese, an offer which was refused.[175] Even after the Cuban Missile Crisis and the hostile Chinese reaction, the Soviet Presidium decided that, as far as the leadership of the CCP was concerned, "do not burn bridges."[176] Unfortunately for them, it was no longer their choice to make.

With Mao now openly pushing for an open split, the Chinese exploited the Cuban Missile Crisis for its full propaganda value. The image of the small, heroic island of Cuba facing the full might of the American imperial colossus, willing to risk annihilation in the cause of socialism, only to be betrayed by the cowards in the Kremlin, had captured the world's attention and seemed to distill into its purest form everything the Chinese had been saying about the Soviet policy of peaceful coexistence and its consequences for world revolution. Khrushchev rued the "cheap" propaganda victory with which he had provided the Chinese.[177] Publishing Soviet materials in Cuba suddenly became much more difficult.[178] Meanwhile, the Chinese began publishing a series of polemics against the USSR composed under the supervision of Mao himself.[179] These polemics, among other Chinese materials, were distributed in multiple languages around the world at rapid speed. One report claimed that an item published in Beijing was available in bookstores in Algiers five days later.[180] Increasingly alarming reports were arriving about the greater quantity, quality, and availability of Chinese propaganda in the developing world and Africa in particular, in some places where Soviet materials were practically unknown, and, even worse, the receptive audience that these Chinese publications found.[181] The director of the press division of the Foreign Ministry, in a report to Central Committee secretary L. F. Il'ichev of March 7, 1963, based on reports from Soviet embassies in Africa, emphasized the recent growth in the propaganda activity on the continent, especially radio broadcasts, and outlined a plan for getting out the Soviet point of view. The report noted: "In view of the activization of Chinese propaganda in Africa," Soviet propaganda needed to "in a calm tone, gainfully and convincingly explain to African society our point of view on questions of peaceful coexistence, the possibility of the peaceful path to socialism, the possibility of preventing war, the national liberation movement."[182]

The extent of the damage to Soviet standing in the developing world was manifested at the third AAPSO Conference in Moshi, Tanganyika, in February 1963. The Chinese saw this as their chance to decisively wrest leadership of Africa and Asia from the Soviets and they prepared for battle. In December 1962, after the conference had already been delayed once, the Chinese Peace Committee wrote to all Chinese embassies in Asia and Africa that this conference "is an important arena of struggle in the current battle between us and the contemporary revisionists for leadership of the mass movement in the Afro-Asian region" and that, unlike previous conferences where the Chinese delegation was instructed to preserve solidarity, this time they would "maintain the struggle until the end" (坚持斗争到底).[183] In particular, the Chinese delegation was instructed to talk about Cuba as much as possible.[184] SCSCAA meanwhile still hoped to make peace and disarmament the central issues of the conference.[185] The Chinese were so confident before the conference that they had Africa "in their pocket" that, when they met the Soviet delegation, they asked them simply, "Why did you come? There is nothing for you to do here."[186] After extensive preconference wrangling over the text of the general secretary's speech, the proposed resolutions, and whether or not to invite representatives of international organizations, such as the WPC, and Eastern European states, the two fiercest points of contention at the conference itself ended up being the Sino-Indian border conflict and the proposed tricontinental conference. On the first issue, despite strong Indian pressure for the AAPSO to take a position, the Chinese continually refused to agree to any resolution whatsoever, leading India to leave the conference. In the end, under pressure from the Tanganyikans who wanted to assure the success of the conference, the Chinese agreed to a very mild "recommendation" after India had been formally reprimanded by the chairman for its behavior. The issue of the Tricontinental Conference was the most hotly contested point of Sino-Soviet conflict. A resolution to hold the conference had been passed at the executive committee meeting in Gaza in 1961. Fidel Castro sent his ambassador to Mali to the conference with an invitation to hold the Tricontinental in Havana, which the Chinese strongly supported, planning to coordinate their activities with the Cubans at the conference.[187] The Soviets, wary about the militant views of the Cubans, flew in uninvited representatives of Latin American Communist Parties with an alternative plan to hold the conference in Brazil under the auspices of the WPC. After hearing the speech of José Carrillo, the Cuban representative, the Soviets sent the Brazilian delegate to threaten him, saying, "Your speech cannot represent the Cuban government, if you speak like this, you will be condemned when you return home."[188] In the event, the conference overwhelmingly supported the Chinese, preventing the Latin Americans from even attending the small committee meetings, and the conference was to be held in Havana. Liu Ningyi and the Chinese delegation wrote back elatedly to Beijing, detailing their victory and declaring that Africa and Asia were awash in militant anti-imperialism. "The Soviet Union and its partners were completely on the defensive and isolated, in the end they slipped away in the middle of the night, heads bowed and discouraged" (最后垂头丧气地于深夜溜走).[189] SCSCAA's evaluation was more terse; the conference, it noted, was "very difficult."[190]

Despite their success at the conference, the Chinese could see difficulties in the road ahead. Decolonization was proceeding apace, and with the independence of Algeria and Kenya now won, two of the most intense struggles had been completed. Even though the Chinese had managed to gain the upper hand rhetorically and ideologically in a period of anti-imperialist militarism, Chinese diplomats began to warn as early as late 1962 that "from now on we need to increase our material forces [aid], in order to coordinate political struggle."[191] The Soviet Union was increasingly using aid to gain political influence, taking advantage of China's "temporary economic difficulties."[192] Only a month after the conference in Moshi, the Chinese embassy in Dar es Salaam reported increased Soviet activity in the region, particularly in terms of attempts of the USSR to expand its economic penetration and "buy" certain nationalist leaders.[193] It did not take long for the effects of the Soviet strategy to become apparent. When Fidel Castro visited the USSR in April–May 1963, signing a joint communiqué in which he supported many Soviet foreign policy positions, the Chinese embassy in Moscow wrote that Castro had traded his principles for economic and military aid and that the visit had been a success for Khrushchev.[194] The Chinese would need more than slogans if they were to win an open competition for influence with the USSR.

The Moshi Conference would turn out to be an important step in this direction. Now that the liberation struggle had shifted almost completely to southern Africa, Dar es Salaam would become the focal point, due to the many liberation movements that were headquartered there. While China had earlier considered Nyerere to be insufficiently anti-imperialist due to his "illusions" about the West, nonviolence, and "nonracism,"[195] and it had even supported an opposition party in Tanganyika,[196] the Chinese delegation to the third AAPSO conference brought representatives from numerous organizations in order to prolong their stay after the conference, establish close, friendly relations, and possibly work out a deal on economic and technological cooperation.[197] At the same time, in North Africa, Algerian independence provided the Chinese with another potential ally. China, unlike the USSR, had recognized the Provisional Government of Algeria almost immediately after its founding, provided it with aid and weapons, and even exchanged government delegations in order to sign economic agreements in advance of independence. Now the victorious Algerian FLN represented an African regime that had come to power through armed struggle and which was determined to promote armed struggle in the rest of the continent. Consequently, Tanganyika (soon to become part of Tanzania) and Algeria would become central to China's effort to compete with the Soviets for influence through a newly expanded aid program in Africa, as the next chapter will discuss.

In the early 1960s, the Soviet Union found itself increasingly caught in a political trap. Soviet ideology saw the defeat of capitalism and its replacement with socialism as the chief objective of its foreign policy, and this necessitated two things. The first was the growth of the revolutionary struggle of the working class in advanced industrial countries, and this required a positive attitude of the populations of those countries toward the USSR, not least in order to improve the political environment for their respective domestic Communist Parties. The second, and it was always referred to as "second in historical significance" by Moscow in this period, was the national liberation movement in the developing world, increasingly conceived as including Latin America in the wake of the Cuban Revolution. Now the two had become connected as the new administration in Washington had made development in what the West was now calling the "Third World" its priority and was hard at work developing the theory and practice of what could be called a "nonsocialist path of development." To fulfill its objectives then, the USSR adopted a policy of promotion of peace and disarmament, which was quite popular with its intended European audience, and it created and promoted its own development model for the newly independent states, calling it the "noncapitalist path of development."

The problem was that in promoting this policy, which was created with the intention of competing with the capitalist world, the Soviets were increasingly antagonizing the Chinese and many others in Asia, Africa, and Latin America who shared the Chinese view, whether with or without prodding from Beijing. As long as relations with China were reasonably amicable, the Soviets could afford to concentrate on the capitalist world as the primary competitor. However, the combination of Khrushchev's outburst at the Twenty-Second Congress and Mao's return to political dominance in Beijing rendered this no longer possible. Now the Soviets would be forced to choose. They could keep pursuing peaceful coexistence and hope to win the battle with capitalism by demonstrating the viability of socialism as an economic system within the Soviet Union and through the example of its protegés in the developing world. Alternatively, they could abandon peaceful coexistence in order to reinforce their rear against the Chinese challenge, risking relations with the West in order to promote a more militant brand of revolution.

Meanwhile, the Chinese were to discover the difficulties of the path they had chosen. When they had simply been attempting to mobilize anti-imperialist sentiment in the hopes of preventing a Soviet-American rapprochement, the particularities of a potential Chinese alternative did not require the kinds of resources that China did not possess at this juncture. As the Chinese were more concerned with the anti-imperialist struggle than the anticapitalist one, believing that any talk of "socialism" in most of the developing world was grossly premature, this foreign policy situation was suitable. However, now that the Chinese leadership led by Mao had chosen a course of open competition with the Soviet Union for leadership of an Afro-Asian and possibly Latin American bloc, the Chinese would have no choice but to offer something to compete with what was available from Moscow or Washington. The naked battle for power between Moscow and Beijing that would take place between 1963 and 1965 would require both sides to reevaluate their positions and policies in order to emerge victorious.

CHAPTER THREE

Battle for Supremacy

Competition and Adaptation, 1963–1965

In the spring and summer of 1963, the divide between the Soviet Union and China exploded in public recrimination. In the wake of the Cuban Missile Crisis and second Sino-Indian border conflict, Soviet and Chinese delegations had clashed with increasing intensity at a series of Eastern European party congresses between November 1962 and January 1963, during which the Chinese were faced with the solidarity of the Eastern Europeans with a Soviet leadership that now, properly incensed at Chinese accusations of Soviet weakness and betrayal of Cuba, would brook no more hints of neutrality.[1] If it had not already been the case, the missile crisis and its aftermath personalized the dispute with China for Khrushchev, who felt the need to assert in his memoirs that "the Caribbean crisis was a triumph of Soviet foreign policy and a personal triumph in my own career as a statesman and as a member of the collective leadership."[2] The escalating war of words during the party congresses sparked an attempt to find a way to resolve the dispute by a number of concerned Communist Parties, led by the Vietnamese, who called for "the unity of the international communist movement" on February 10.[3] The Soviets, however, would not agree to the proposal of a new meeting of Communist Parties similar to the Moscow meetings of 1957 and 1960, which had been proposed by the Chinese in November in the hopes of humiliating the Soviets. Instead, the CPSU Presidium decided on January 2 to write a letter to the Communist Party of China (CCP) proposing bilateral talks and an end to the polemics, though the letter was not delivered until February 21.[4] Both sides treated the talks as nothing more than a forum to jockey for position. The Chinese responded to the Soviet proposal on March 9, agreeing to meet and suspend published attacks, the day after publishing the third in a series of scheduled polemics. Meanwhile, the "central antirevisionist drafting group," convoked by Mao under the leadership of Kang Sheng and Chen Boda, worked "day and night" for the next three weeks to "prepare the documents for the Sino-Soviet Split."[5] The Soviet reply of April 1 restated Moscow's ideological positions, leading Mao to direct the drafting of an article that would lay out the Chinese program for the international communist movement. The result was the publication on June 14 of the "Proposal Concerning the General Line of the International Communist Movement," which distilled the Chinese position into twenty-five points.[6] Four days later, the CPSU Central Committee released a resolution attacking the Chinese letter, and the subsequent CPSU Plenum was filled with accusations that the Chinese were responsible for the state of affairs, ultimately producing a resolution empowering Khrushchev to defend the line of the Twentieth, Twenty-First, and Twenty-Second Congresses against the "slanderous attacks" of the Chinese in the upcoming party talks.[7] The actual party talks, held from July 6 to 20 in Moscow, were little more than an angry exchange of lengthy diatribes that resulted only in a public Soviet reply to the Chinese "General Line" on July 14, and the resumption of Chinese polemics.

With the world now aware of the nature and severity of the Sino-Soviet split, Moscow and Beijing were left with no alternatives to a naked competition for influence. The advent of this era of open competition, however, found the Soviets starting from a position of disadvantage vis-à-vis their antagonists in Beijing. The Cuban Missile Crisis had been a serious blow, and Khrushchev desperately tried to invite Fidel Castro to Moscow to change his mind and stop the bleeding. When Khrushchev subsequently reported on his successful finessing of Castro, who now saw the merits of the Soviet perspective, at a Presidium meeting in early 1963, Boris Ponomarev, head of the CPSU Central Committee's International Department, immediately responded that "this must be widely distributed in all countries, especially where there are inclinations toward the Chinese."[8] Meanwhile, Soviet relations with the Democratic Republic of Vietnam (DRV) had been deteriorating since 1960, reaching a nadir in the joint Sino-Vietnamese communiqué of May 16, 1963, in which the Vietnamese Workers' Party (VWP) openly supported Chinese positions on a range of issues, began a campaign of popularization of Chinese positions in the lower ranks of the party, and essentially prohibited the distribution of Soviet propaganda.[9] Cuba and Vietnam had a symbolic importance disproportionate to their size since they were seen as the countries on the front lines of the struggle with imperialism. In Africa, May 1963 saw the founding conference of the Organization of African Unity (OAU) in Addis Ababa, which placed a militant emphasis on decolonization, involving the creation of a Liberation Committee headquartered in Dar es Salaam to coordinate the provision of material aid, including arms, to liberation movements struggling against the remaining white-ruling regimes, primarily in southern Africa. Of particular concern to the Soviet leadership was the fact that the avalanche of Chinese propaganda was making an impression even within the Soviet Union itself, as reports of meetings of party organizations recorded Soviet citizens asking questions such as "Are we not in fact compromising with imperialism over West Berlin?" and "Why did the USSR stop giving aid to China when we still give aid to bourgeois countries such as India, Syria, Iraq, and the UAR?"[10] The fact that the Chinese had already been directing their attacks largely against the USSR while the Soviets were still focused on the Americans had taken its toll.

A successful policy response to the Chinese challenge on the part of the Soviet Union would require something of a reverse of the policies that had been pursued by the Khrushchev-led regime since the late 1950s. "Peaceful coexistence," misunderstood or not, was clearly an Achilles' heel in some circles, one that the Chinese had exploited to paint the USSR as nonrevolutionary and willing to sacrifice the interests of people in Asia, Africa, and Latin America for the sake of peace, and maybe even collusion, with the white, Western, capitalist powers. The Soviet project of building socialism in the developing world as the way to advance the anticapitalist revolution had also produced mixed results at best, with the Soviets expelled from Guinea and nearly expelled from Mali, confirming the fears of communist influence present in many developing countries that had been exacerbated by Western influence and propaganda. What remained to be seen was how willing Khrushchev would be to change the policy approach he himself had largely developed. The signing of the Partial Test Ban Treaty on August 5, 1963, between the USSR, United Kingdom, and United States, at the very moment of the public eruption of the Sino-Soviet Split, solidified the impression of Soviet commitment to peace with the West at the expense of the South, and it became a centerpiece of Chinese propaganda for months and years to come.

Meanwhile, Beijing no longer had the luxury of merely mobilizing discontent in the developing world against the Soviet Union. Now that it had publicly staked its claim to the mantle of leadership of the world revolution with the publication of its proposal for the "General Line," the People's Republic of China (PRC) had to present itself as a full-service alternative to the Soviet Union, with an aid program and development model in addition to its rhetoric of militant anti-imperialism. With the effects of the Great Leap Forward still being felt, the continuing diplomatic isolation of China—a large majority of countries in Africa and Latin America still recognized the Nationalist regime on Taiwan—and the suspicion of China sown by numerous forces, including Western propaganda and local anti-Chinese sentiment, particularly in Southeast Asia, the Chinese regime certainly faced a difficult task as well.

The years from the summer of 1963 to the end of 1965 would see the most intense period of direct competition between the USSR and the PRC for influence and allegiance in the developing world. China made a bold attempt to cut the Soviets out of the political structure of the Afro-Asian bloc while the Soviets, in turn, tried to discredit the Chinese as irresponsible and unreliable, and consequently not an adequate potential replacement for Soviet revolutionary leadership. The Soviet Union would expand its activities, particularly in terms of diplomacy and propaganda, and direct its efforts more specifically against the Chinese during Khrushchev's last year in power. However, the failure of Khrushchev to transform Soviet policy would lead to the continuing deterioration of the Soviet position vis-à-vis China and the developing world, a fact that would play a role in his ouster in October 1964. The subsequent leadership under Leonid Brezhnev and Alexei Kosygin, after a brief attempt at reconciliation with Beijing, would abandon that tactic in favor of intensified competition, but this time without the restraint of established policy precedent that had hampered Khrushchev. Soviet policy in the immediate aftermath of the leadership change would become noticeably more militant, both in practice and in rhetoric, a circumstance that alarmed the Chinese greatly by 1965. In turn, China unleashed a diplomatic and aid offensive in these years, which, while not neglecting the more militant aspects of the anti-imperialist struggle, nevertheless focused far more than in the past on aid, development, and building relationships with established governments. By 1965, the battle largely became concentrated on the struggle for influence over certain key states, particularly the DRV, United Arab Republic (UAR), Indonesia, and Algeria, as well as the related issue of China's attempt to convene a second Bandung Conference without the Soviet Union. By the end of the year, Chinese foreign policy was in a shambles due to the collapse of Indonesia, its most important ally, and the failure to hold a second Afro-Asian conference. However, it would prove to be something of a Pyrrhic victory for the Soviet Union, which had been forced to come to terms with a political agenda in the developing world different from the one it had imagined in the halcyon days of decolonization back in 1960.

Moscow Responds to the Chinese Challenge

By the beginning of September 1963, relations with the Chinese had become critical enough for Khrushchev to declare at a Presidium meeting regarding efforts to combat Chinese attacks: "This, comrades, is now for us task number one, this is the chief of our foreign policy tasks."[11] Explaining that now, "we should not only defend ourselves, we should attack," Khrushchev called for a vast propaganda offensive, beginning with writing three letters, one to members of the CPSU, one to the Chinese leadership, and one to people in Asia, Africa, and Latin America.[12] Ever since the Cuban Missile Crisis, the Soviets had begun adopting the tactic of questioning China's own anti-imperialist bona fides, with Khrushchev remarking sarcastically about China's actions in support of Cuba, saying at a Communist Party plenum in November 1962 that "the Chinese demonstrated for three days in Beijing. If this is their way of fighting imperialism, the imperialists could not give a damn."[13] In the series of preparatory meetings in advance of the AAPSO conference in Moshi, Tanzania, each time the Chinese brought up the issue of Cuba the Soviets would respond by pointing out China's continuing failure to liberate Taiwan, leading the Chinese to angrily assert that the two had nothing to do with each other.[14] Consequently, the Soviet propaganda offensive would focus on exposing what Moscow saw as China's own hypocrisy to discredit its message and undercut its revolutionary image, as well as seeking to trumpet and clarify the Soviet line.

One of the primary methods of conducting this propaganda war was the use of the international Soviet press agency Novosti to distribute Soviet documents in vast quantities in numerous languages worldwide. The CPSU Central Committee passed a resolution on August 3 directing Novosti to distribute copies of the July 14 "Open Letter of the CPSU to the CCP," and by September it had done so, distributing 3.2 million copies in thirty-five languages to eighty-five countries.[15] In a report to the Central Committee in September 1963 on its anti-Chinese activity, Novosti detailed its efforts to publish materials abroad in the foreign press, in its own magazines, and in separate brochures. It also systematically commissioned articles from Soviet scholars and reprinted articles from journals such as *Kommunist* and *Aziia i Afrika Segodnia,* with a particular focus on attacking individuals who "Chinese authorities present as authoritative representatives of the national liberation movements of Asia, Africa, and Latin America."[16] Following a Central Committee decision of October 1963, Novosti began publishing a new organ, "Questions of the World Communist Movement," specifically devoted to the conflict with China, in English, French, Spanish, and Russian.[17]

Individual Soviet embassies also began devoting considerable resources to anti-Chinese propaganda. The embassy in India, a country where the local Communist Party was threatened with a split due to the strength of pro-Chinese forces, submitted a report in November 1963 titled: "On the strengthening in the local country of the external and internal policy of the Soviet Union, on explication and examination of the most important documents and materials of the CC CPSU and Soviet government attacking the anti-Soviet, schismatic activity of the Chinese leaders."[18] The report not only detailed efforts to publish and distribute copies of government documents and journal articles in local languages, but also called for soliciting local Indian writers to write anti-Chinese articles, creating a thematic database of material to be used in local "progressive" and "bourgeois" papers alike, meeting with leading editors and journalists of Indian papers no less than two or three times per month as well as conducting lectures, press conferences, and film viewings. Similar reports were submitted by many other embassies in Asia and Africa.[19] The Soviet embassy in Ghana held a meeting of the staff to discuss ways to combat Chinese propaganda.[20] In addition, Soviet embassies made special efforts to get materials in the hands of top political figures, while tailoring their propaganda output to the particular situation of the country in question, especially focusing on Chinese involvement with local opposition parties and figures.[21]

Mikhail Suslov's lengthy diatribe against the PRC at a Communist Party plenum in February 1964 would become the seminal Soviet ideological text in this propaganda offensive. As the CPSU's chief theoretician, it was left to Suslov to delineate the fundamental sources of disagreement between the CPSU and CCP and place them in a proper Marxist-Leninist context. In his speech, Suslov called the Chinese "contemporary Trotskyites" and compared them to both the old Socialist

Revolutionaries and the "Workers' Opposition" of 1921, three familiar ghosts from the Soviet/Bolshevik past.[22] He asserted that the Chinese sought to de-center the working class within the revolutionary movement, which was impermissible within Marxist-Leninist ideology, and that the Chinese advocated armed struggle as the path of revolutionary development to the exclusion of all others.[23] Furthermore, argued Suslov, the Chinese saw the national liberation movements of Asia, Africa, and Latin America, rather than the socialist world or workers' movement, as "that area, where supposedly the fate of humanity is being decided."[24] On the contrary, railed Suslov, the success of the national liberation movements was possible only due to the existence of the world socialist system and to assert otherwise would be to abandon class positions. More insidiously, the CCP leaders "count on playing on the mistrust of Europeans which took hold in many Afro-Asian countries during the period of colonial oppression, igniting nationalist and even *racial* prejudices"[25] [italics mine]. This played into the hands of the enemy, as there are states "where national independence (*samostoiatel'nost'*) serves only as a cover for the domination of the most extreme, reactionary, tyrannical regimes, which operate with the support of imperialism."[26] This last point was crucial, as it provided a starting point for explaining not only the sources and nature of the Chinese heresy, but also the reasons for its enthusiastic reception in many corners.

Suslov's speech was only the beginning, however. The Soviet propaganda effort to counteract Chinese claims required a serious reexamination of the ideological issues involved. As A. Rumyantsev, a member of the Central Committee as well as editor of *Problemy Mira i Sotsializma*, the journal of the international communist movement based in Prague, wrote to Khrushchev in early 1964, "It is impossible to completely expose the mistaken concepts in the realm of practical politics [of the Chinese] without uncovering their theoretical bases."[27] Rumyantsev noted both the particular attention paid by the PRC to developing countries and the attraction of Maoist ideology among those escaping colonialism and seeking to avoid the long, hard slog of "scientific socialism." The core issue, according to Rumyantsev, was that a certain excessively tolerant attitude had pervaded Soviet thought and policy toward the developing world concerning the problem of nationalism. Similar to Suslov, he argued that it was excessive, malignant nationalism that stood at the core of the Maoist heresy, and that nationalism was the common point between Maoist dogmatism and Titoist revisionism. *Aziia i Afrika Segodnia* concurred, writing in the wake of a Communist Party plenum calling on Soviet orientalists to renew their efforts in the area of ideology in July 1963, that Chinese ideology was "characterized by a rejection of Marxist-Leninist historical science and the replacement of it with chauvinist nationalist and even racist conceptions."[28] *Narody Azii i Afriki* went further, arguing: "Dogmatism inevitably . . . leads to the replacement of proletarian internationalism with the ideology of bourgeois nationalism."[29] Soviet scholars, who had developed the theory of the "national democratic" state that was to pursue the "noncapitalist path of development" as an expression of popular will through a wide national front, now had to adapt that theory to account for the dangers of excessive nationalism.

The centerpiece of the theory of the "national democratic" state had been the role of the "national bourgeoisie," whose nationalism had caused them to take the leading role in the independence struggle and whose predominance in national politics led them to be the crucial element in the wide national coalition. However, given that "nationalism" now presented the primary danger in the Soviet view of the revolutionary process in the developing world, the "national bourgeoisie," as the repository of nationalism, came under suspicion from Soviet theorists. This danger of "nationalism" had to be diagnosed in class terms in order to make it useful for identifying allies and enemies. G. Kim, writing in October 1964, argued that while initially the "lower" and "middle" strata of the "national bourgeoisie" had been dominant, now the "great" strata was dominant, and its interests were increasingly oriented toward rapprochement with imperialism.[30] Consequently, the previous concepts of "People's Democracy" and "National Democracy" were replaced in the imagination of Soviet theorists with a new concept: "revolutionary democracy." "Revolutionary democracy" was still merely a transitional form of the national liberation movement moving toward the noncapitalist path of development, not yet an actual form of socialist revolution, and it was still to be headed by a class coalition, but this time the coalition consisted primarily of the peasantry and what was alternatively referred to as the "petite bourgeoisie" or the "middle urban strata."[31] Given the demotion of the "national bourgeoisie," the state of "revolutionary democracy" was meant to be less susceptible to nationalist deviation. Furthermore, Kim acknowledged the still undeveloped nature of the working class in developing countries, asserting that this placed a greater importance on the leadership of the global working class, making the connections between the struggle of world socialism and the global working class to the national liberation struggle even more essential. This shift in the Soviet ideological paradigm for the developing world even produced some divisions between those who had been the more enthusiastic promoters of the theory of the state of "national democracy" and those who now argued that that theory had diverged too much from strict class analysis and assigned insufficient importance to the role of the working class.[32]

While Soviet scholars expounded upon the dangers of nationalism, they nevertheless changed their rhetoric on the issue of armed struggle. Soviet promotion of peaceful coexistence, through the efforts of the Chinese, had hurt them significantly in the eyes of the developing world and while the Soviet state, Communist Party, and propaganda institutions continued to promote the slogan of peaceful coexistence along with specific examples, such as the Partial Test-Ban Treaty, they began increasingly to emphasize that peaceful coexistence did not exclude armed struggle in the developing world. E. Alekseev wrote in December 1963 that while most former colonies achieved independence peacefully, this did not mean that the nature of imperialism had changed and "it does not follow from anywhere that there is only one path to the conquering of national independence—the peaceful one."[33]

In addition to a propaganda offensive directed at the Chinese and ideological adjustments to the model of "national democracy," the Kremlin's response entailed a repackaging of the Soviet Union itself. Chinese propaganda had portrayed it as a white, imperialist power whose experiences of revolution and economic construction were not relevant to those countries that had recently gained independence. The geographic and racial image of the USSR was not a new problem. As early as 1959, in the wake of the questions raised about the presence of the USSR at the Afro-Asian economic conference in Cairo, the chairman of the presidium of the All-Union Chamber of Commerce, in a letter to Mikoyan, suggested creating a separate Central Asian Chamber of Commerce to be located in Tashkent, which would handle Soviet representation at future Afro-Asian conferences.[34] However, as the attempt to exclude the USSR from Afro-Asian forums due to Chinese intervention began to gain steam, Soviet organizations came to revisit the notion of using the Central Asian republics to present the USSR as an authentic Asian power. Because it was on the front lines of the struggle, SCSCAA was unsurprisingly one of the first organizations to adopt this tactic. At a Presidium session in January 1962, SCSCAA discussed raising the profile of the solidarity committees in each of the Central Asian and Trans-Caucasian republics, increasing their work, as well as having the republican committees invite foreign delegations to visit Central Asia.[35] In subsequent sessions, SCSCAA members would call for ever more activity on the part of the republican committees to combat Chinese attempts to kick the USSR out of the AAPSO and to combat racial prejudices against the USSR.[36] In June 1964, the State Committee on Cultural Ties (GKKS) sent a plan to the Ideology Department of the Central Committee on the use of international organizations such as the UN for the purposes of Soviet propaganda. The committee emphasized the need both to attract more Central Asians to work as Soviet representatives in those organizations and to hold more Afro-Asian events in Soviet Central Asia and Transcaucasia.[37] As the struggle to attend the planned second Afro-Asian heads of state conference heated up, Soviet leaders began to insist on calling their country "Eurasian" in joint communiqués, emphasizing that the vast majority of Soviet territory was in Asia and even distributing pamphlets on the "Asianness" of the USSR.[38]

Repackaging the Soviet Union was not only a matter of geography or ethnicity, however. Soviet organizations also attempted to combat Chinese claims that the PRC's experiences and economic model were more relevant to the conditions of the recently liberated developing countries than those of the USSR. Soviet representatives argued that the USSR in the immediate aftermath of the October Revolution was also a feudal, agrarian state, whose initial development tasks were very similar to those being faced by many countries in Asia and Africa. One Soviet orientalist suggested focusing on the trajectory of Soviet development since "the Soviet people have in practice shown how, in the lifetime of one generation, having taken a course for socialism, for communism, it is possible to take a backward and poor country to the very peak of progress."[39] In addition to heavy industry, Soviet organizations involved in policy toward the developing world began to emphasize tasks such as fighting illiteracy and feudalism and establishing basic health care, relying especially on the experience of the Central Asian republics.[40]

Central Asia also provided the key, Moscow hoped, to navigating a particular issue in its relations with the developing world that had proven to be very dangerous: religion. Particularly in Islamic countries, antisocialist and anti-Soviet forces tended to mobilize around religion, and this forced even the more radical nationalist leaders, such as Ben Bella in Algeria and Sukarno in Indonesia, to incorporate it into their programs. The Algerian minister of religious affairs insisted that "Islam is a socialist religion,"[41] while Sukarno's political program reflected the fact that much of Indonesian nationalist thought had been constructed by students returning from the Middle East imbued with reformist Islam.[42] Soviet scholars sought to blunt criticism and avoid ideological problems by arguing not only that Marxism does not advocate a war on religion, but also that Islam in many cases serves an important unifying function in national liberation movements. They asserted that the declaration of Islam as the national religion in the UAR, for example, not only does not hurt the revolution, but also it would be "adventurism" to fight it.[43] The Soviet leadership tried to use Central Asian representatives to employ Islam to its advantage, for example, bringing an Indonesian delegation to visit Soviet Muslim communities in Central Asia under the auspices of SCSCAA and its member Babakhanov, who was also a mufti.[44] It sent a Central Asian delegation to the Afro-Asian Islamic conference in Indonesia in early 1965 as well, hoping to use this as a backdoor to achieving recognition as an Afro-Asian state and therefore attendance at the planned heads of state conference later in the year.[45] Despite this effort, in many cases Soviet policy was never able to overcome the obvious discrepancy between the antireligious campaign at home and its supposed promotion of freedom of conscience abroad.[46]

The greater Soviet attention both to combating the Chinese and to increasing Moscow's influence in the developing world did produce some fruit in terms of improving Soviet standing in Asia and Africa. In the AAPSO, having learned their lesson at the Chinese-dominated Moshi conference earlier in the year, the Soviets managed to dominate the council meeting in Nicosia, Cyprus, in September 1963. Despite the Chinese delegation's best efforts, they failed to prevent the passage of a resolution in favor of the Partial Test Ban Treaty, and, in a move that the Chinese had opposed consistently for years, the council decided to establish permanent ties with the solidarity committees of the Eastern European countries. According to SCSCAA, this result could partially be attributed to the fact that the Africans "somehow grew up."[47] Soviet success continued at the Executive Committee meeting in Algiers in March 1964, where unrelenting Chinese belligerence was met with at least half-hearted Soviet attempts to present a façade of calm and reasonableness, leading the newspaper *Alger Républicain* to write: "Only the Chinese delegate did not understand the importance of calm debate."[48]

The culmination of Khrushchev's policy in the developing world came in May 1964 when he made his first trip to Africa to preside at the ceremony marking the completion of the first stage of the Aswan High Dam, the largest Soviet aid project to date. Khrushchev's visit was announced immediately following Zhou Enlai's tour through ten African countries, which will be discussed below, as well as the meeting of the Jakarta preparatory conference for the second Afro-Asian heads of state conference, which had decided not to invite the USSR. Khrushchev therefore needed Nasser to help reestablish Soviet prestige in the developing world and Nasser needed Khrushchev too, to raise his standing in Africa and the Arab world as well as to rescue his deteriorating economy. In addition to a Soviet promise to provide Nasser with a new loan of 252 million rubles (about $300 million), the visit resulted in a grand tour of the country, including visits to numerous public meetings, as well as talks with Ben Bella, who had traveled from Algeria for the event. During the course of the visit, Nasser announced his desire to build "socialism" in the UAR, and Khrushchev legitimized this goal, labeling the UAR a "democratic socialist country," addressing Nasser as "comrade," and even awarding him the designation "Hero of the Soviet Union." The Soviet press trumpeted the success of the visit, with *Izvestiia* gleefully writing about how the reception of Khrushchev made the Chinese leaders look "pathetic" and their hearts empty of all but "hypocritical revolutionary phrases." The Chinese, however, were not so sure. The Chinese embassy in Cairo remarked that Nasser did not totally cave to Khrushchev. Despite Khrushchev's constant raising of Sino-Soviet issues, Nasser refused to take sides, nor did he endorse Soviet attendance at the planned Afro-Asian conference. They concluded that "whether from the visit-concluding Soviet-UAR joint communiqué, Afro-Asian countries' reactions, or the judgments of the Western press, the results and influence of Khrushchev's visit cannot be compared to those of the Prime Minister's [Zhou's] visit to Africa."[49]

In the end, despite his best efforts, Khrushchev could not fundamentally alter the dynamics of the Sino-Soviet battle for influence in the developing world, at least not without a much greater renunciation of his previous policies than he was willing to countenance. Without a more public rejection of peaceful coexistence and an enthusiastic embrace of armed struggle, the image endured of the Soviet Union as a satisfied, European power unwilling to engage in the revolutionary struggles of the developing world. The extent of the damage was evident in a series of KGB reports on international delegations to the World Forum for Solidarity of Youth and Students in the Struggle for National Independence

and Peace held in Moscow in September 1964. While the KGB reported
on the efforts of the Chinese to turn the delegates against their Soviet
hosts, it became clear that the supposed lack of Soviet support for armed
struggle in the developing world was the key to Chinese success and that
many delegates, in fact, believed the essence of the Chinese claims. For
example, the delegations of Congo-Léopoldville, South Africa, Mozambique, Angola, and Guinea-Bissau expressed anger at the lack of attention
paid to their struggles at the conference, and they began to wonder why
they had even come, according to the KGB.[50] It was not until a reception
at the Kremlin at which Khrushchev himself addressed the delegations,
explicitly affirming Moscow's willingness to supply arms, that many delegations changed their minds. The Iraqi delegation said that they were in
a great mood because before coming to the Kremlin reception they truly
did not believe that Moscow was willing to supply weapons. Similarly, the
delegation from Dahomey said that the speech made an enormous impression, and that they would go back and tell their people that the Soviet
Union was on the side of the fighters.[51] It would take a much greater shift
in rhetoric and policy, however, to convince the rest of the world.

Events were already underway that would enable this shift to take
place. The month before the Youth Forum, Washington alleged that its
ships had been fired upon in the Gulf of Tonkin, and the situation in
Vietnam threatened to escalate precipitously. In short order, Vietnam
would take center stage in the view of the world as the chief battleground
of both the anticapitalist and anti-imperialist struggles. This meant that
Vietnam would see not only a desperate struggle between the capitalist
and communist worlds, but also an intense struggle between Moscow
and Beijing to be seen as the chief patron of the DRV and the National
Liberation Front (NLF), and consequently the true leader of world revolution. Unfortunately for the Soviets, their relations with the North
Vietnamese had reached a low ebb by this point. On the eve of the Gulf
of Tonkin incidents, the Soviet embassy reported that "now, nothing remains of the earlier 'middle line' taken by the Vietnamese between the
CPSU and CCP except for small differences between the lines of the
CCP and Vietnamese Workers' Party (VWP) on internal problems of
socialist construction in each country and certain tactical questions."[52]
On international issues, the VWP supported CCP positions on imperialism, nuclear warfare and the Partial Test Ban Treaty, the role of the
CPSU and USSR, the cult of personality, Albania, Yugoslavia, South Vietnam, and the Sino-Indian border conflict.[53] The VWP even continued to

support Chinese claims about Soviet "cowardice" during the Cuban Missile Crisis after Fidel Castro had publicly supported Soviet actions. The VWP simply claimed that Castro was being "sentimental."[54] Consequently, the DRV was instrumental in supporting Chinese positions in the AAPSO, the WPC, and other international organizations. By June 1964, Soviet–North Vietnamese relations had deteriorated to the point where even Soviet military attachés were no longer being briefed, an action justified by the claim that "Soviet military doctrine does not suit the conditions of the DRV."[55] The DRV was increasingly adopting Chinese military strategy and the Military Affairs Bureau of the Central Committee of the VWP reportedly decided to gradually shift the DRV army from Soviet weaponry to Chinese.[56] At the time of the Gulf of Tonkin incident, USSR-DRV relations seemed to be dangerously perched on the precipice of total collapse. Improving relations would quickly become one of the top priorities of Khrushchev's successors.

Ultimately then, despite undertaking a massive diplomatic and propaganda effort since the outbreak of the open split, the Khrushchev-led Soviet leadership had largely failed to win back the ground it had lost from the Chinese over the previous three years. In part this was because of Chinese foreign policy successes during this time, particularly in Africa, as China undertook an unprecedented diplomatic and aid offensive in 1963–64, while continuing to support armed struggle in rhetoric and, increasingly, in practice as well, as will be discussed in the next section. However, despite its best efforts, Beijing would never have been able to match Soviet capabilities in either quantity or quality of aid, either military or economic, and so the continuing failure of the Kremlin to turn the tide during this period must rest with its own policies. The increasing détente with the West and with the United States, in particular, especially in the wake of the Partial Test Ban Treaty, undercut any attempts the Soviets made to present themselves as true militant revolutionaries, a problem compounded by Moscow's failure to embrace supposed "left-wing" positions on issues such as Congo, Palestine, and South Vietnam in favor of compromise with the West and preservation of the status quo. Furthermore, Soviet aid was tarnished by the implicit political conditions that accompanied it, the condescending behavior of Soviet experts, and the conditions of repayment that made many countries inclined to equate it with Western aid. Chinese aid had not yet acquired this sort of reputation, and it might have been perversely aided by the anti-Chinese propaganda of both the West and the USSR, in comparison with which the behavior of the actual Chinese with which Asians and Africans came into contact must have seemed surprisingly benign.

The Chinese Alternative

In contrast to the USSR, China had reason to feel confident about the diplomatic fallout from the public split in the summer of 1963. Chinese embassies around the world reported back on conversations with local political figures, journalists, activists, and others in finding a significant amount of sympathy for their side in the dispute. Besides the standard claims that the Soviets were revisionists who did not actually support national liberation movements in the developing world, considerable pique seemed to be manifested at the way the Soviets behaved toward Afro-Asian countries and the way they presented themselves in the public exchange of letters with the CCP. The Guinean foreign minister said that "we are not willing to see one country consider itself above others," a thought echoed by Algerian minister of defense Houari Boumedienne.[57] The Ghanaian ambassador in Algeria described the Partial Test Ban Treaty as "three big businessmen doing business in a café."[58] Sekou Touré objected to the idea that because the USSR was the first country to build socialism, it must necessarily be the only source of Marxist-Leninist thought.[59] The deputy head of the Eastern European Division of the Indonesian Foreign Ministry made his fears explicit, saying that he thought the USSR would ally with imperialism and that "white people will turn around and together oppress Eastern and colored peoples."[60] Meanwhile, a number of countries were irritated at the way that the Soviets took credit for what they saw as their own accomplishments. An official in the Algerian Defense Ministry remarked, "The open letter said that the Soviet Union gave Algeria aid—I am clear about how much moral and material aid China gave us, but I can't think of any from the Soviet Union."[61] The antirevisionist offensive ordered by Beijing thus seemed to have a receptive audience.

Not all Chinese diplomats, however, saw making antirevisionism (i.e., anti-Sovietism) the top priority as the best strategy. A report from the Chinese embassy in Guinea in November dissented from the central directive to emphasize antirevisionism as the best means of opposing imperialism, saying that "if you want to oppose revisionism, you must hold the banner of anti-imperialism even higher."[62] The report asserted that not only was imperialism the cause of revisionism, but also any likely future scenario would involve revisionism collapsing of its own accord before imperialism. Presciently, the report argued that the difference between Chinese antirevisionism and the nationalist antirevisionism of the "intermediate zone" was class analysis, saying, "We cannot demand of the intermediate zone nationalists that they be exactly like us on the class ideology of antirevisionism."[63] While China should continue to pursue both unity (with the revolutionary forces) and struggle (against revisionism), the emphasis should definitely be tilted toward unity, as struggle might have the effect of alienating too many political actors. If this policy were to be pursued correctly, the report affirmed, "the intermediate zone will not only be our allies against imperialism, but might also become our allies against revisionism."[64] In the end, however, Beijing continued its increasingly militant policy of forcing leaders to take sides between it and Moscow, thereby creating the impression that it was driving the split in the world revolution, while asserting that questions of Marxist ideology that seemed obscure and parochial to many should be the top items on the global agenda, positions that contributed to its eventual diplomatic disaster.

In the meantime, the PRC's diplomatic fortunes were rising rapidly. The month of July 1962 witnessed the independence of Algeria, and this removed one of the main obstacles preventing China from establishing relations with a number of African countries. Edgar Faure, the envoy of French president Charles De Gaulle, was secretly sent to China in October 1963, leading to a French agreement to cut off ties with Taiwan in December in preparation for the dramatic announcement of the establishment of Sino-French relations on January 27, 1964.[65] Consequently, France no longer opposed its former African colonies establishing relations with the PRC as well. In addition, the independence of Kenya, Zambia, and Zanzibar, as well as a coup in Brazzaville overthrowing the right-wing government of Abbé Youlou in February 1964, meant that the number of African states recognizing the PRC had gone from ten in 1962 to nineteen by 1965. This was reflected in the nearly annual vote on whether to seat Beijing in the UN. In 1963, thirteen African states had voted in favor with sixteen against and five abstentions, while in 1965 the totals were eighteen for, ten against, and eight abstentions.[66] As China established diplomatic relations with more African countries, the number of African delegations visiting China rose from thirty-seven in 1962 to 113 in 1963, while Chinese delegations to Africa jumped a year later, from fifty in 1963 to eighty-seven in 1964.[67]

The most famous Chinese delegation to tour Africa in this period, one that garnered a considerable amount of attention from the global press, was that led by Prime Minister Zhou Enlai and Foreign Minister Chen Yi to the UAR, Algeria, Morocco, Tunisia, Ghana, Mali, Guinea, Sudan, Ethiopia, and Somalia in late 1963 and early 1964. Originally the Chinese leaders had hoped to visit Kenya, Tanganyika, and Zanzibar as well, but that was prevented by political disturbances, including a military mutiny in Tanganyika and a revolution in Zanzibar. The trip had several purposes. The first was to explain China's side of the dispute with the Soviets, as illustrated by the fact that Zhou decided to include a stop in Burma on his way back from Africa to meet with Ne Win. He did this after receiving a report from the Chinese ambassador in Rangoon that Ne Win sought to take a neutral position in the Sino-Soviet split, which might be due to a lack of understanding, "but it is also possible that he received a certain amount of Soviet influence, so I advise that you consider at an opportune time discussing with Ne Win the true nature of the Sino-Soviet split, such as after the current trip of Prime Minister Zhou to Africa."[68] The second objective was to promote the plan to hold a second Bandung Conference, from which China hoped to exclude the Soviet Union, which had not been present at the first one, and thereby solidify its position as the leader of an Afro-Asian bloc. On these two fronts, the results of the trip were mixed, as few countries were willing to publicly side definitively with the Chinese, even if they secretly sympathized with them (or told Zhou or other Chinese officials that they did). For many countries, the upcoming second Non-Aligned Movement conference, which would ultimately be held in Cairo in October, was a higher priority. In a broader sense, however, the trip was a tremendous success. The trip was Zhou's first to Africa, and it established China in the minds of many on the continent as a stable, responsible partner, a view that testified to Zhou's diplomatic skills. One of the most revealing episodes on the trip occurred during the delegation's visit to Tunisia, where President Habib Bourguiba criticized Chinese policy on a number of international issues at a state banquet with Zhou present, without any serious reaction on the part of the Chinese.[69]

Beyond the improvement in its public profile and diplomatic impact, Zhou's trip marked a more important change in China's foreign policy. At a farewell banquet in Accra on January 15, 1964, Zhou laid out China's eight principles of foreign aid, emphasizing aid based on mutuality and equality, respect for sovereignty, interest-free credits, provision of top-quality equipment, training of local technical cadres, and living standards for Chinese experts not to exceed their local counterparts.[70] When matched against the litany of complaints voiced by Guinea in 1961 and Mali in 1963 regarding the aid provided by the USSR and the Eastern bloc, the origin of many of these points is quite evident.[71] By this means did China announce its full-scale entry into the aid competition. The Chinese aid program, however, did not come in the absence of its own development model, despite the attempt made to distinguish Chinese aid from the oppressive, paternalistic aid programs of the USSR and the Western powers. The fourth principle declared: "The goal of the Chinese government in providing aid is to help countries gradually go down the road of *raising themselves on their own forces* (自力更生) and independent economic development (italics mine)," affirming China's own development philosophy and attempting to cut out the USSR. The importance of this goal for Chinese policy was brought home by the author of an article in *Shijie Zhishi* who was covering Zhou's trip, which declared in terms eerily reminiscent of Khrushchev's pronouncement at the Twenty-Second CPSU Congress that "if you want to achieve complete, true independence, political independence alone is not sufficient, you must toil to develop the national economy, achieve economic independence."[72] While "raising oneself on one's own forces" was still the primary means to achieve this, the article conceded that some external aid was not necessarily problematic as long as it did not include any special treatment or conditions and was given between equals rather than between greater and smaller powers. In a clear attempt to disqualify China's competition, the article also strongly implied that Afro-Asian countries should accept aid only from each other.

The following year *Shijie Zhishi* provided a blueprint for developing an "autonomous independent economy" in listing seven steps modeled on China's own experience.[73] First, immediately after the revolution one should eliminate all foreign privileges, following which one should take the central components of the economy under national control. Then one should promote "social democratic" (社会民主) reforms in order to increase people's productivity and expand the domestic market. In developing the economy, "first one should appropriately resolve the problems of the greater part of the people with regard to their 'eating,' 'wearing,' and 'using' needs" (首先适当地解决广大人民的"吃""穿""用"的需要问题) and only then should one turn one's attention to the development of heavy industry. In directing investment, one should focus on areas in which productivity can be raised rapidly and where results can be produced quickly, as the products of the domestic economy must be used to procure foreign exchange. Finally, it is essential to train national cadres and develop domestic science and industry so as not to be reliant on foreign powers. The article ended with the affirmation that "reality has shown that each people's revolutionary construction, whether a country is large or small, whether its population is large or small, they are all able to rely first on their own forces, and only secondarily on foreign aid."[74]

The model of development presented here is substantively different from the Soviet model of the "noncapitalist path of development." First, the Chinese model is not focused, at least not explicitly, on the eventual road to socialism; rather, it is focused on achieving economic autonomy. Perhaps for that reason, the Chinese model shows less concern with the issue of ownership of the means of production than with the growth of production in general, even to the degree that it might allow for the introduction of small-scale market mechanisms to increase productivity, possibly not unlike the New Economic Policy that the Soviet Union itself used to escape its dire economic circumstances after seven years of international and civil war. Finally, the Chinese model emphasizes agriculture and light industry rather than heavy industry in early economic development, which would be reflected in the nature of actual Chinese aid agreements, though it should be noted that China itself, during the Great Leap Forward, sought to develop heavy industry first. These distinctions illustrate quite clearly the different priorities of an anti-imperialist development model as opposed to an anticapitalist one.

In the event, Chinese aid pledges in 1963–64 totaled $266.3 million to nine African countries, as opposed to only $72.2 million to six countries in the years prior to 1963, not including military aid.[75] Following the principles outlined above, Chinese aid projects went primarily to agriculture, light industry, and infrastructure projects rather than the metallurgical and mining projects predominant in Soviet aid agreements. Chinese projects included a 5,000-acre state farm in Tanzania as well as a fully integrated textile mill and two high-powered transmitters. In Somalia, China pledged to complete the construction of a highway, set up a textile mill, and establish a state farm to grow rice.[76] Textile factories were also constructed in Ghana and Congo-Brazzaville. In addition to aid, Chinese trade with Africa increased by roughly 170 percent between 1962 and 1965.[77] Most of these aid projects were on a small scale, however, and they did not demonstrate that China had either the economic or the technological capacity to replace the Soviet Union, let alone the West, as potential aid partners in the developing world.

But the project that would eventually become China's signature aid contribution in the developing world, a calling card similar to the Aswan High Dam for the USSR, was broached by Beijing at this time, although a number of issues, including the outbreak of the Cultural Revolution, would delay the signing of a final agreement until 1970. This was what would ultimately become the Tan-Zam railway. After years of discussion by the London and Rhodesian Mining and Land Company (Lonrho) about the possibility of linking the copper mines of Northern Rhodesia with the Indian Ocean by way of the Tanganyikan Central Line, Tanganyikan president Julius Nyerere seized upon the idea and attempted to attain financing, either from the United States, the United Kingdom, or an international consortium. A pessimistic World Bank report submitted in May 1964, however, doomed those efforts.[78] The following month, Abdul Babu, an old Chinese ally who had been the minister of external affairs of revolutionary Zanzibar, accompanied Tanzanian vice president Rashidi Kawawa to Beijing. While no official announcement about any offer regarding the railway was made, it appears that the topic was brought up, as George Ivan Smith, the UN representative in East Africa who happened to be on the same plane as Kawawa returning via Nairobi, subsequently wrote a confidential letter to UN Secretary-General U Thant indicating that China might step in to help build the railway if other sources of aid were not forthcoming.[79] It was no coincidence that the Chinese had broached such a possibility less than a month after the conclusion of Khrushchev's triumphant opening of the Aswan Dam. On the eve of Nyerere's first visit to the PRC in February 1965, Zambia's only daily newspaper, the *Northern News,* announced for the first time that the Chinese were ready to finance the construction of the railway.[80] Nyerere's visit greatly impressed him and, following Rhodesia's Unilateral Declaration of Independence (UDI) in November, Zambian president Kenneth Kaunda was on board with the Chinese plan as well. Though completion of the project would take a long time, and much of the world would remain skeptical of the ability of the Chinese to complete it, the desire to undertake such a project at this time signals the lengths to which Beijing was willing to go to prove itself as an alternative aid source to the Soviet Union.

In addition to economic aid, China continued to provide arms and military training to many on the African continent. However, even

Chinese military aid policy at this time demonstrates its concern with maintaining the good will of the governments of the continent. In the aftermath of the mutiny of troops in Tanzania, China offered to replace the arms that had been lost, following which Nyerere invited Chinese military instructors to train his troops.[81] In September 1964, Ghanaian president Nkrumah invited the Chinese to provide instructors to train guerrilla fighters for combat in African countries still fighting for their independence. Huang Hua, the Chinese ambassador to Ghana at the time, describes how his embassy's analysis of the unstable political situation in Ghana led him to recall the advisers to the embassy in Accra in November 1965; thus, by the time the military government, which overthrew Nkrumah in February, was looking for them, they had escaped to Algiers.[82] The deepest area of military involvement of China in Africa at this time was with the rebellion in the eastern Congo. However, when the prime minister of Congo-Brazzaville approached the Chinese embassy with a request to be very cautious and quiet in its dealings with the various rebel groups for fear of bringing down international retribution on his country, the Chinese Foreign Ministry ordered its embassy in Brazzaville to avoid contact with those claiming to be nationalists as much as possible.[83] Contrary to the image of China at this time as a reckless promoter of armed struggle, Chinese policy, in fact, reflected the desire to maintain its anti-imperialist policies while raising its conventional diplomatic profile.

Chinese aid policy also reflected both its pragmatism and its emphasis on anti-imperialist struggle, which gave it a certain degree of flexibility with regard to the capitalist/communist divide. In Angola, the MPLA, due to its roots in various Communist organizations in Portugal and Angola and the ideological pronouncements of its leaders, had been the early favorite for Communist support in that country's liberation struggle. By the middle of 1963, however, ideological splits within the MPLA had divided the movement right at the moment that the newly founded Organization of African Unity (OAU) Liberation Committee was holding its first meeting in Dar es Salaam. This led the latter to recommend that all aid be funneled instead to Holden Roberto's National Front for the Liberation of Angola (FNLA), as well as that all OAU member states recognize Roberto's Revolutionary Government of Angola in Exile (GRAE). Roberto, whose organization had been labeled as pro-American and was even rumored to be funded by the CIA,[84] took this opportunity to appeal to Moscow for aid but was summarily rebuffed.[85]

Beijing was much more open to the FNLA. Given that the FNLA seemed to have the largest organization on the ground in Angola, it had played the main role in the beginning of the armed uprising in February 1961, and now it was endorsed by the OAU, the Chinese Foreign Ministry argued that, despite its ties to the United States, "according to our policy of great support for national liberation movements, we should give Roberto appropriate support and aid."[86] Chen Yi told Holden Roberto in January 1964 that the PRC would welcome a delegation from the GRAE and might even be willing to provide aid and arms.[87] Preparations for a visit were soon underway, and the background reports produced by Chinese embassies in Africa were surprisingly balanced and nuanced, with the embassy in Brazzaville even drawing a distinction between aid from American groups and aid from the U.S. government.[88] The visit was delayed by various logistical questions, however, giving leftist activists in Africa time to raise enough of a din to inspire hesitation in the Chinese Foreign Ministry, which ultimately put off the visit indefinitely.[89] Despite this, Beijing decided to maintain ties with the GRAE,[90] and the Portuguese suspected it of arming the FNLA.[91] The "visit that never was" nevertheless reveals much about Beijing's approach to foreign policy at this time. The Chinese leadership was willing to overlook the socialist inclinations of the MPLA and the Western ties of the FNLA in the name of effective anti-imperialist solidarity. Though the visit was ultimately cancelled, it seems to have been because Beijing was afraid of the impact on its anti-imperialist image in Africa. This episode therefore illustrates as clearly as any the practical differences between the PRC's anti-imperialist priorities and the USSR's anticapitalist ones.

Whether the PRC could sustain its challenge to the USSR over the long term was a different matter. Eying the Chinese economy, some in Moscow saw great difficulties ahead in Beijing's effort to maintain its new foreign aid program. A report from the Institute of the Economy of the World Socialist System to Secretary of the Central Committee P. N. Demichev in May 1965 forecasted that, when the final totals were in, Chinese agricultural production in 1964 might reach the levels of 1957, before the Great Leap Forward, but that industrial production was still far below the level of 1957.[92] The primary bottleneck in the Chinese economy, according to the report, was the lack of machines for agriculture, tractors in particular, and at the current rate China would be able to produce the 1 million tractors needed only in 140 years.[93] China's economy, despite recovering from the disaster of the Great Leap Forward, was still growing at a slower rate than all other socialist economies. This meant, according to the report, that China was in desperate need of foreign aid, in particular in heavy industry for agricultural machines, and that it would increasingly turn toward the capitalist world for trade and possibly even aid, which would lead toward more tension with the USSR. Interestingly, the report maintained, however, that China could potentially sustain its own foreign aid at a level no higher than that of 1964, i.e., roughly $125 million per year.[94] By contrast, according to the Chinese Foreign Ministry, from 1954 through 1964, the USSR had given a total of $3.861 billion of economic aid and $2.285 billion of military aid to some twenty-two Afro-Asian countries.[95] Consequently, at the rate forecast by the report, it would be very difficult for China to compete directly with the USSR on the basis of aid over the long term.

For a time, though, due to the widespread dissatisfaction produced by Soviet attitudes and policies, China was able to present enough of a specter of competition to significantly threaten the Soviet position in the world. In the course of 1963–64, Chinese policy took anti-imperialism from a mobilizing slogan to a comprehensive development model, one that could not only compete with the Soviet anticapitalist model, but also seemed to be more appealing to many. This was coupled with a diplomatic offensive that decreased China's isolation significantly and removed its "rogue" status in the eyes of many around the world who had been wary of it before, particularly in Africa. As a consequence, China began to take greater account of its relations at the state level, prioritizing peaceful relations with influential governments over revolutionary adventures, such as in its endorsement of Tanganyika's merger with erstwhile revolutionary Zanzibar in early 1964. At the same time, China managed to retain its revolutionary image through rhetoric and well-placed military aid, particularly in the Congo. Soon after Khrushchev's removal, China would take one more important step in presenting itself as a viable alternative to the USSR; on October 16, 1964, it exploded its first nuclear weapon. As a nuclear power, China could more convincingly pose as an international heavyweight and champion of Africa and Asia. To defeat the Chinese challenge then, the Soviet leadership that succeeded Khrushchev would need to adopt policies from the Chinese, taking a more militant stance in both theory and practice to reassert its self-appointed position as the leader of the world revolution.

Changes in Moscow

When Khrushchev's ouster was announced, two days before China's nuclear test, a thought briefly fluttered across the minds of leaders in Beijing: They had won.[96] The KGB reported that Chinese students studying in Moscow were similarly triumphant, quoting one student's letter home saying "many are congratulating us, they say that China has won, that Mao Zedong has become the leader of the world."[97] The Chinese decided to take the opportunity to send a delegation to Moscow for the forty-seventh anniversary of the October Revolution, and the Soviet leadership took this as a promising opportunity to achieve reconciliation. While the Soviet leadership made it clear to the Chinese that they did not intend to change the fundamental elements of Khrushchev's policies, they hoped that a new leadership and a change in tone would perhaps be enough to find a *modus vivendi.* The attempt was an abject failure, and the visit of the Chinese delegation to Moscow and the subsequent Communist Party talks only aggravated the situation. Though it was certainly not a decisive factor in Soviet policy on this question, reconciliation with China at this point would have also had some adverse consequences for the Soviet position in the international communist movement, as many parties had gone too far in their support of the Soviets and commitment to a peaceful transition to socialism to turn back now. Luis Corvalan, general secretary of the Chilean Communist Party, told a visiting Soviet delegation five days after the leadership change that "if now the CPSU comes to an agreement with the Chinese on the disputed issues, we will find ourselves in an even more difficult situation," complaining that "our Soviet comrades do not take into account the effect that these actions have on the situation of Communist Parties in capitalist countries."[98] Even with Khrushchev gone then, reconciliation was not in the cards.

The new Brezhnev-Kosygin leadership's primary foreign policy objective was to resurrect the Soviet Union's international status as the unquestioned leader of the world revolution, with Chinese acquiescence if possible but more likely, as they soon discovered, without it. This meant that the Soviet Union had to reestablish order within the international communist movement and restore the revolutionary reputation of that movement within the developing world where the Chinese had done so much damage to its standing. While Khrushchev had become somewhat more militant in his rhetoric in 1963–64, and the Soviet Union had continued providing arms covertly to countries such as the UAR, in support of its war in Yemen, as well as to India and Indonesia, he ultimately chose not to risk his policy of peaceful coexistence with the capitalist world for the sake of competition with the PRC. His successors would see things differently, embracing a more openly militant and confrontational policy that would cause a deterioration of Soviet-American relations. The Brezhnev-Kosygin leadership also took power at a time of economic difficulty in the Soviet Union and, partially for that reason, the Soviet Union would spend less on economic aid in the aftermath of the leadership change, eschewing projects on the scale of the Aswan Dam or the Bhilai metallurgical factory. Rather, aid would be dispersed not only more strategically, but also more publicly. Within several months of the leadership change, Beijing noticed the changes in Soviet policy and acknowledged the results they had produced.

In 1964, both Moscow and Beijing reacted to their battle for leadership of the world revolution in a similar way. They each decided that the best thing to do would be to hold a prominent conference of their constituency, real or imagined, in order to affirm their own leadership position and ostracize and condemn the other. For Beijing, this meant an all-out effort to hold a second Bandung Conference—a meeting of the leaders of Afro-Asian states—without Soviet participation. For Moscow, this meant an attempt to hold a new meeting of the international communist movement, similar to the ones that had been held in Moscow in 1957 and 1960. In his speech on the anniversary of the October Revolution in 1964, with Zhou Enlai in the audience, Brezhnev called for a "new international meeting of the fraternal parties."[99] At a Communist Party plenum nine days later, Brezhnev announced that, so far, sixty-one Communist Parties had agreed to the international meeting (there had been eighty-one at the 1960 Moscow meeting) and nineteen of the twenty-six members of the earlier meeting's editorial committee had agreed to serve again.[100] Meanwhile, the Soviet leaders tried to rebuild relationships with China's allies, if they could not do so with the CCP itself, in order to isolate the Chinese. Soon after Khrushchev's removal, they tried to contact the leaders of the Communist Parties of the DPRK, DRV, Japan, and Indonesia to discuss their differences.[101] They invited D. N. Aidit, the leader of the Indonesian Communist Party (PKI), to Moscow and tried to improve relations with the Cubans as well, in what the Chinese saw as a switch from Khrushchev's policy of attacking wayward parties to more of a carrot-and-stick approach.[102] In advance of the planned international communist meeting, the Kremlin decided to organize regional meetings of Communist Parties to use its predominance among the leadership of most parties to pull dissenters back into line. In November 1964, a conference of twenty-two Latin American Communist Parties was held during which the attendees attacked "factionalism," meaning groups within their own parties that did not follow Moscow's line, and that resulted in a nine-party delegation sent to Moscow and Beijing with a resolution calling for the end of polemics.[103] On December 7, the group was received warmly in Moscow by Brezhnev, Podgorny, Suslov, Ponomarev, and Andropov, and the CPSU Central Committee signed the resolution. The Chinese leaders perceived the resolution as a conspiracy to pressure them, and when the delegation came to Beijing, they defended the importance of polemics and rejected the need to make peace with those who were not even Marxists.[104] In December and January, an "Arab Communist Conference" was held in Moscow and Prague under the leadership of strongly pro-Moscow Syrian Communist leader Bagdash, including representatives of the parties of Iraq, Syria, Jordan, Egypt, Lebanon, Iran, and, according to a rumor reported by the Chinese Foreign Ministry, Israel.[105] The conference affirmed the correctness of the CPSU line of the last three congresses, promoted the "socialism" of Nasser and Ben Bella, both of whom had suppressed their local Communist Parties, and called for the creation of a united Arab Communist Party. Despite the lack of African Communist Parties, the USSR even tried to organize an "African Marxist Conference" under the leadership of Nkrumah in Accra.[106]

In the end, however, the Soviet effort to hold a full-scale international communist meeting in 1965 failed. The best they could do was to transform what was supposed to have been a meeting of the editorial commission into a "consultative meeting" in March 1965 with nineteen Communist Parties present. Many parties were hesitant about joining what was essentially an attempt by the CPSU to isolate the CCP, especially the Romanian, British, and Italian Communist Parties. Both the Vietnamese and Koreans refused to attend, saying that to do so would endanger their relations with the PRC. However, the conference did produce a statement that was decidedly more militant than previous documents of the international communist movement, calling for "active support of liberation movements and defense of peoples opposing imperialist aggression."[107] Despite this setback, the Soviet leadership would not give up on its goal of holding a new Moscow meeting to restore the unity of the international communist movement.

In addition to their attempt to restore order to the communist movement, the new Soviet leaders sought to improve their diplomatic standing throughout the developing world. Their first priority was to reassure their closest allies that their policy of support would continue. Three days after Khrushchev's ouster, the Soviet ambassador in Cairo gave Nasser a letter from Kosygin saying Soviet-UAR relations would not be affected.[108] In December, Aleksandr Shelepin, a member of the Politburo, visited the UAR and confirmed that all of Khrushchev's aid pledges would be honored.[109] Overall, the change in leadership was followed by an unprecedented diplomatic offensive. In the first five months after the switch, Moscow sent eighty-two delegations to thirty-eight countries, with forty-eight of those being official party, government, military, or legislative delegations. During the same period, they received twenty-eight delegations from twenty-one countries and invited many prominent foreign leaders to visit, including Ben Bella, Modibo Keita, and Sekou Touré, among others.[110] One of the primary objectives of these visits was the proposed second Bandung Conference. While Khrushchev had chosen not to campaign openly for Soviet attendance, the new leadership made sure that nothing would be spared to prevent the conference from being held without the USSR. On November 21, the Soviet ambassador in Beijing told the Chinese that the USSR had the "right" to attend, while Shelepin asked the UAR to push for an invitation for the USSR during his visit to Cairo the following month.[111]

While the new Soviet leadership did not sign new aid projects on the scale of those Khrushchev had offered, aid did play a role in Moscow's diplomatic strategy. Officials signed new aid agreements with India, Afghanistan, Uganda, Senegal, and Congo-Brazzaville totaling 236 million rubles in the first five months after coming to power. The Kremlin also made use of smaller grants to gain good will, giving free military, economic, medical, and cultural gifts to twelve Afro-Asian countries, in particular Algeria and the DRV. In addition to giving new aid, the Soviet leadership cancelled the interest on a loan to the DRV, agreed to delay Guinea's repayment schedule by five years, and forgave half of the UAR's debt, totaling some half a billion dollars.[112] In a move that had more symbolic than practical importance, given that imports from the developing world were generally part of repayment for Soviet loans, the Kremlin announced that it was removing all import tariffs on goods from Asia, Africa, and Latin America beginning on January 1, 1965.[113] However, a combination of domestic economic considerations and the popularity of the Chinese rhetoric on aid and development led the Soviets to begin to emphasize self-reliance as well. The head of the Institute of Africa, Vladimir Solodovnikov, wrote in the aftermath of the first UN Conference on Trade and Development (UNCTAD) that "the scale and tempo of economic development, undoubtedly, depends first of all on the mobilization of internal sources of accumulation, on the depth and character of internal socioeconomic transformation. External economic aid can serve only as supplementary means in overcoming economic backwardness and the rebuilding of the economies of developing countries."[114] As far as external aid, the Soviets argued that the socialist countries would not be able to meet all of the needs of the developing world, and they encouraged developing countries to seek aid from the capitalist countries, arguing that with socialist support they would be able to conclude such agreements on the basis of equality.[115] Despite this stance, Moscow continued to provide plentiful aid to certain key states that it saw as crucial to the battle with China for leadership.

The most important policy shift of the new leadership was a willingness to promote a far more militant policy than Khrushchev had advanced. Soviet organizations on the front lines of the struggle had long realized the importance of this change, as illustrated by the comment of a member of the SCSCAA Presidium on the agenda of the Soviet delegation to a session of the World Peace Council that put the "struggle of peoples" at the top, that "this is very important because arriving in Asia and Africa the first question is certainly not that of disarmament or peace."[116] The new leadership went beyond merely the rhetorical promotion of struggle, and it changed Soviet policy on a number of crucial issues. While under Khrushchev the Kremlin had promoted peace negotiations and UN intervention in the Congo, the new leadership made a public statement on November 25 announcing the provision of aid to the rebels, and it followed through the following month by providing certain weapons by way of Algeria and the UAR, as well as sending IL-12 planes to Algeria for transport.[117] Khrushchev had similarly been reluctant to support Sukarno's policy of *Konfrontasi* against Malaysia. In contrast, the new leadership expressed significant support, manifested in a statement of the Soviet ambassador on January 20 and Kosygin's condemnation of "American imperialism's use of Malaysia as an anti-Indonesian containment conspiracy" at a public meeting in Hanoi. In a reversal of Khrushchev's refusal to provide arms to Indonesia for the struggle, Foreign Minister Subandrio reported that the Soviet ambassador had told him they were prepared "to provide any aid that Indonesia needs, especially aid needed within the scope of Indonesia's 'smash Malaysia' struggle."[118] While the USSR had earlier been reluctant to condemn Israel to the satisfaction of its Arab interlocutors, on his visit to Cairo in December 1964 Shelepin denounced Israel as a "tool of neocolonialism" and, according to Chinese reports, offered to provide small arms to Palestinian fighters through the UAR and Iraq.[119] The new Brezhnev-Kosygin leadership certainly seemed to see burnishing its anti-imperialist credentials as worth the price of a certain level of deterioration in relations with the West.

The key shift would occur regarding policy in Vietnam. On November 9, only weeks after the leadership change, Kosygin received a delegation led by DRV prime minister Pham Van Dong, who complained about the weak Soviet support for the DRV in the wake of the Gulf of Tonkin incident.[120] This time, though, the meeting produced an understanding on military aid to the DRV.[121] By the end of the month, the DRV ambassador in Moscow was already telling the Chinese ambassador that the new Soviet leadership was more committed to supporting national liberation movements and anti-imperialism.[122] In December, the Kremlin invited the National Liberation Front of South Vietnam (NLF) to open a permanent representation in Moscow.[123] Meanwhile, at a Politburo session of the VWP in Hanoi discussing the change in Moscow, the DRV leadership adopted a tactful line of approach to relations with the USSR, hopeful for improvement while prepared to return to "struggle" if their hopes were disappointed.[124] In the following months, the signals coming out of Moscow were increasingly positive from Hanoi's point of view, as the Soviet leaders publicly condemned U.S. "aggression" in South Vietnam and offered all necessary support for the struggle of the "Vietnamese people."[125] In early February, Kosygin visited Hanoi, a visit that would become more eventful than he had planned. Soon after his arrival, the NLF killed eight U.S. Marines in a raid on a base in Pleiku. The Johnson administration responded immediately with air attacks on the DRV, which Kosygin and the USSR took as a personal insult.[126] Kosygin's visit included talks on a new defense agreement, which had suddenly been given new impetus, and the agreement was completed back in Moscow. After his return, he began organizing military support for the DRV from the rest of the Warsaw Pact as well.[127] The Kremlin clearly understood that as the war heated up, it could not allow itself to continue to follow

Khrushchev's policy of trying to restrain the DRV and resurrect the Geneva agreements without risking major damage to its revolutionary image.

Nevertheless, Moscow also did not want the escalation in Vietnam to lead to a complete breakdown of relations with Washington. Soviet policy reflected a delicate balancing act between providing the DRV with all the necessary military aid and attempting to save détente by seeking a negotiated outcome to the war.[128] Consequently, Moscow employed diplomatic back channels to prevent the Americans from acting on the basis of public Soviet declarations.[129] The Chinese tried to expose Moscow's game, arguing that the West, in fact, wanted the USSR to aid the DRV to counteract Chinese influence and perhaps provide a useful lever for pressuring the North Vietnamese when the time came.[130] Meanwhile, to cover their left flank, the Soviets tried to come to an agreement with Beijing on a plan of coordinated aid to the DRV. Kosygin stopped by Beijing for talks on his way back from Hanoi. However, the Soviets and the Chinese had completely different objectives in Vietnam, and Kosygin returned empty-handed.[131] Unbeknownst to Kosygin, Mao did not want peace in Vietnam, nor did he even want a complete Communist victory; what he wanted more than anything was continued war.[132] As the year 1965 progressed and the Soviets looked for ways to organize peace negotiations, the Chinese firmly opposed every one of their attempts, leading the Soviet embassy in Moscow to write that the Chinese had made clear their desire "to fight against the Americans to the last Vietnamese soldier."[133] As the war progressed, accusations back and forth between Moscow and Beijing over aid to the DRV and support for the struggle would take center stage in the battle for leadership of the world revolution.

During the initial period of the Brezhnev-Kosygin leadership, the Chinese Foreign Ministry was closely monitoring any changes, or lack thereof, in Soviet policy. The ministry produced secret reports throughout the first half of 1965 for the Central Committee on the overall foreign policy of the new Soviet leadership as well as separate reports on Moscow's new policies in Africa, Latin America, the Arab world, and Southeast Asia. The Chinese analysis of the Kremlin's new policy affirmed that its ultimate goals were the same as before, namely winning the competition with China for leadership and the destruction of Afro-Asian militant solidarity in the service of détente with the West.[134] However, the Soviets were increasing their "fake" anti-imperialism in the form of belligerent statements, open criticism of the United States, and even provision of arms to fighters in places such as Congo-Léopoldville, Vietnam, and Palestine.[135] Another element of the new Soviet policy that the Chinese saw as mere "opportunism" was the increasing promotion of their key allies in the developing world, particularly Nasser and Ben Bella, as "socialists," using the theory of "revolutionary democracy" to almost completely neglect the role of actual Communist Parties in the transition to socialism.[136] To the Chinese, this theory reflected the complete elision of class contradictions, supporting the notion of class merger that Khrushchev had fought against in his criticisms of "Arab" and "African" socialism. The Soviets increasingly built party-to-party relations with the ruling parties of these countries, including Algeria's FLN, the UAR's Arab Socialist Union, and Mali's Sudanese Union. The Chinese Foreign Ministry admitted that the new Soviet policy had produced results in terms of creating "illusions" about Soviet anti-imperialism through its "tricky" rhetoric, as well as through exploitation of the fact of economic need in many countries.[137] Nevertheless, as the revolutionary situation improved in Africa and Asia, the "fake" anti-imperialism of the USSR would inevitably be exposed, and economically, just as before, the "great power chauvinism" of the USSR would lead to contradictions between it and its aid recipients.[138] Just to be sure, the Africa Division of the Foreign Ministry still said that China could help this process along by doing whatever it could to strengthen African economies in order to decrease the pressure from the "revisionists" as well as by sending an ever-increasing number of delegations abroad to promote Chinese policies.[139]

Key Battlefields: UAR, Algeria, Indonesia

As the battle for political influence between Moscow and Beijing heated up in 1964 and 1965, the competition began to focus on certain states, which, for reasons of geography, size, political influence, or revolutionary prestige, held an outsized symbolic value for the developing world as a whole. Within the communist world, as has been discussed above, Cuba and the DRV held this sort of symbolic importance. In the rest of the developing world, such status was less clear and more ephemeral, often tied to the rise and fall in global prestige of leaders such as Kwame Nkrumah or Gamal Abdel Nasser. However, by the mid-1960s, Soviet aid statistics told a large part of the story. Of the total of $2.4057 billion in economic aid given by the USSR to Asian countries from 1954 to 1964, some 39.4 percent of that went to India.[140] Meanwhile, 70.8 percent of Soviet military aid to Asia over the same period, or nearly 1 billion dollars, went to Indonesia. In Africa, 53 percent of all economic aid, over $800 million, went to the UAR while another 14 percent, roughly $225 million, went to Algeria.[141] These four countries were seen as key potential allies of the Soviet Union in its battle with the PRC, and the more intense the competition grew, the more intense became the diplomatic efforts to woo their respective governments. Having fought two wars over the course of the previous five years, the chances of Beijing winning the favor of New Delhi were quite slim, and China acted accordingly. However, the PRC hotly contested the loyalties of the other three governments, with great symbolic value attached to whether or not they would agree to invite the USSR to the planned second Bandung Conference.

While Cairo's position at the center of the Afro-Asian world, with its pretensions to dominate both Arab and African spheres, had made it perhaps the key state in the emerging Afro-Asian movement in the late 1950s and early 1960s, China's position there had never been very strong. Nasser's attempt to maintain the favor of both Washington and Moscow, in order to keep aid flowing from both, meant that, on the one hand, the Chinese saw him as a pseudo-revolutionary at best yet, on the other hand, one whose unwillingness to commit fully to one superpower might mean that they could nevertheless deny Moscow his full allegiance. While Nasser's relations with Moscow had hit a high point after the 1956 Suez crisis, the period of unification between Egypt and Syria from 1958 to 1961 saw him shift slightly toward the West, repressing Communists in both Egypt and Syria, leading to Soviet disillusionment with their erstwhile ally.[142] In May 1961, the head of the International Department had listed the UAR as an example of a country where reactionary, imperialist forces were increasingly employing dictatorial means, alongside Pakistan,[143] while the head of the State Committee on Cultural Ties complained to the Central Committee about the restrictions on Soviet propaganda there.[144] In the aftermath of Syrian secession from the UAR in September 1961, Nasser turned his attention toward deepening the revolution at home, enacting a new wave of nationalizations, rapidly regaining Moscow's favor.[145] Soon, in addition to Moscow's massive aid project to dam the Nile, the Soviets and Egyptians were cooperating secretly hand in glove (or glove in glove) in Nasser's ever-expanding war in Yemen.

As detailed above, the Chinese closely observed Khrushchev's visit to the UAR in May 1964, noting that both sides had benefited but that Nasser had still managed to hold back, remaining aloof from the Sino-

Soviet dispute and refusing to endorse Soviet attendance at a second Bandung Conference. Hoping to maintain the status quo, the PRC in December 1964 gave the UAR an interest-free credit of $80 million for industrial equipment and machinery for its second Five-Year Plan.[146] It was a drop in the bucket, though, compared to Soviet aid. Shelepin's visit in December 1964 had raised the stakes, as the Soviets were now directly pressuring Nasser to support their attendance, with the implicit connection this held for continuing Soviet aid. Nasser's position had become far more precarious in the meantime. By 1962, roughly 50 percent of the UAR's wheat was being provided by the United States under the "Food for Peace" program. In the course of 1964, however, U.S.-UAR relations deteriorated rapidly for a number of reasons, including Egypt's actions in Yemen and its arms supplies to rebels in the Congo. In November 1964 the United States suspended all non-food aid to the UAR and then, on January 5, a week after Shelepin left Cairo, the Johnson administration suspended indefinitely sales of wheat to Cairo.[147] The UAR's food situation was now a ticking time bomb, and salvation lay in Moscow.

The Soviets stepped in and promised 300,000 tons of wheat to the UAR. Nasser continued to attempt to walk a fine line diplomatically, but he could no longer avoid tilting toward Moscow. Worried about where this was heading, Beijing dispatched Zhou Enlai to Cairo in June. Nasser explained the situation to Zhou, claiming that his country only had forty days' food supply, and while the Soviets had promised to supply them, just twelve days earlier Moscow had written him a note demanding public support for Soviet attendance at the conference.[148] Nasser hedged, saying that they had to support Soviet attendance, but they would not do so "actively." Zhou was uncompromising; he told Nasser that on such questions one must "maintain principled struggle until the end" (到底), and he asked him to encourage Moscow to abandon its desire to attend. Nasser did make some concessions to the Chinese in terms of his public stance on Soviet attendance, and the Soviet reaction was not long in coming. The Soviets reduced the promised aid to 200,000 tons, to be paid back in wheat or rice within two years at 2 percent interest.[149] The Radio Moscow correspondent in Cairo angrily told his Egyptian colleagues that "you should know, food was stolen out of the mouths of Soviet people to rescue yours."[150] The Soviet offer was indeed a great sacrifice, as the USSR itself had become a grain importer in recent years (a shipment of wheat bound for Odessa was diverted to Alexandria in June 1965) and it could not provide a permanent solution.[151] As Nasser went to Moscow on August 27, 1965, Soviet patience with his diplomatic games had run out. The naked pressure and horse-trading that ensued inspired the Chinese embassy in Moscow to call it a "filthy transaction" (肮脏的交易). Moscow forgave half of Cairo's debt, rescuing it momentarily from economic apocalypse, and in return Nasser caved to the Soviet position, calling for Soviet attendance in the joint communiqué. In the aftermath of the visit, China's view of Nasser had completely soured. The Chinese Foreign Ministry now pointed to a pattern of Nasser's continuous shift toward the right throughout 1965, particularly in the wake of the Algerian coup in June, saying that Nasser's position in the communiqué clearly showed that he did not care about Sino-Egyptian relations.[152] Nasser's class nature was invoked to explain his continuing turn toward the right and this was expected to continue, although eventually his utilitarian streak would require him at times to make concessions to the anti-imperialist interests of the Arab people. Hopefully and perhaps vengefully, the Chinese Foreign Ministry declared that the day will yet arrive "when he will come begging to us" (有时间还会求于我).[153]

While the Chinese had hoped to be able to prevent Nasser's complete capitulation to Soviet demands, the UAR never represented for them a true potential comrade-in-arms in the world revolution due to the perceived class nature of the regime and its neutralist stance going back to the late 1950s. Instead, the Chinese invoked Nasser as a cautionary tale about dependence on foreign aid. Algeria and Indonesia, however, were a different matter. In the early 1960s, both regimes had a certain revolutionary cachet for Moscow and Beijing, due to Algeria's successful war against the French and militant support for African independence and Indonesia's large, powerful Communist Party. These two countries would be the most hotly contested battlefields in the Sino-Soviet dispute in 1964–65, outside of Vietnam, and there is a strange parallel between the two in this fateful period. Both countries played crucial roles in the drama of the second Bandung Conference, with Jakarta holding the preparatory conference in April 1964 that decided to hold the conference in Algiers in March 1965, and before the end of 1965, the larger-than-life revolutionary heroes-cum-presidents of both countries would be displaced by military coups.

On the surface, Algeria should have been very promising terrain for the Chinese. While Moscow failed to recognize the Provisional Government of Algeria during the war for fear of upsetting France, and its support was meager if not nonexistent, Beijing had recognized the new government soon after its announcement and supplied arms and training, with several National Liberation Front (FLN) delegations visiting Beijing.[154] Shortly before independence, the FLN, under the control of its left wing led by Ben Bella and Houari Boumedienne, published the Tripoli Program, which called for building a new Algeria following "socialist perspectives," including the nationalization of French-owned enterprises and the formation of agricultural cooperatives.[155] As French *colons* abandoned their property and headed back to France by the hundreds of thousands after independence, Algerians began seizing the land and factories, setting up *ad hoc* "self-management committees" that were temporarily approved by the government in October 1962. Following French nuclear tests in the Sahara, in March 1963 the government decided to distribute the lands and enterprises of French colonists who had decided to stay as well. After the adoption of a constitution by referendum in September, followed by a more radical agrarian reform program that called for the nationalization of all large landholdings—both French and Algerian—Ben Bella declared in November that the Algerian government "is a dictatorship of the poor, the peasantry, and the workers, and it will exist here for a long time."[156] In April 1964, the FLN held its first congress and adopted a new program called the "Algerian charter," declaring that power belonged to the workers and peasants, following which the FLN began widening its social base and integrating other socialists from outside the party.

In foreign policy, Algeria promised to serve as an incubus of revolution the likes of which Africa had never seen. A French journalist, describing the scene of Ben Bella speaking at the founding conference of the OAU in 1963, wrote: "I do not think that I have ever had such a profound sense of African unity as when I listened to Ben Bella, tears in his eyes, visibly moved, urge his listeners to rush to the assistance of the men dying south of the equator."[157] The Algerian leader was as good as his word. In one of the first acts passed after the adoption of the constitution, Algeria created a "Committee for Aid to the Peoples of Africa," and soon guerrilla fighters from all over Africa—South Africa, Angola, Portuguese Guinea, Congo, and elsewhere—were being trained in camps in Algeria.[158] A particularly close relationship developed between Algeria and Cuba. Cuba sent hundreds of troops along with tanks and artillery to

Algeria during a border war with Morocco in late 1963, following which Algeria became a transit point for Latin American guerrillas trained in Cuba to be sent back to Latin America, along with arms.[159]

All of the above made Algeria an irresistible example for the Chinese version of the anti-imperialist revolutionary model. From Beijing's perspective, "The great victory of the Algerian people's armed struggle has once again proven to all the world's people that an oppressed people faced with the armed oppression of American imperialism need only to employ revolutionary arms to oppose counterrevolutionary arms, and only then can they defeat the enemy, achieve national independence and liberation."[160] In addition, Algeria's aid to others fighting for liberation epitomized the Chinese view of anti-imperialist solidarity. Meanwhile, in the aftermath of the open split in 1963, Algerian officials told Chinese diplomats that they wanted to follow China's path of "raising oneself on one's own forces."[161] Algeria had taken over the imperialists' property, began educating its own technical cadres, and had even formed production cooperatives that echoed of China's own communes.[162] For the first time, the Chinese began promoting the economic reforms of a noncommunist country, calling Algeria a "national democratic" state undergoing "social reforms" and "revolutionary construction" with the most important aspect being that "it relies on its own efforts" (主要依靠自己的努力).[163] China wasted no time in building its ties with Algeria. A delegation from the Chinese Ministry of Defense arrived in October 1962 with a $1.8 million grant to balance the budget.[164] A year later the two countries signed agreements on cultural exchange and economic cooperation, including an interest-free $50 million credit, followed by a visit of Zhou and Chen Yi in December 1963, and finally a delegation led by the Algerian economic minister to China in early 1964 to sign a trade agreement.[165] At the height of relations, the Chinese staged an economic exhibition in Algiers in September 1963, with over 150,000 Algerians visiting.[166]

While the Soviet Union began from a disadvantageous position and consequently got off to a slower start, the Kremlin understood that Algeria was too important to be conceded to the Chinese. Khrushchev himself told the Algerian ambassador that Algeria was the key to the ideological competition with Beijing in Africa.[167] The question was, how did the USSR see developments in Algeria ideologically and what did it have to offer Algeria in terms of a development model? In late 1963 in the first substantial Soviet article on the Algerian economic program, I. Genin wrote that Algeria was "searching" for the noncapitalist path of development and that while the Tripoli program differed in some ways from the program of the Communists, "it serves the interests of the Algerian people and will enable the creation of objective conditions for the building of socialism."[168] The invocation of socialism makes this sound more impressive than it is from a Soviet perspective since the "objective conditions" for socialism can mean little more than economic growth, in almost any form. A year later, after the first FLN Congress and the subsequent visit of Ben Bella to the USSR, the Soviet evaluation had changed dramatically. Y. Potemkin now labeled the Algerian leadership an example of "revolutionary democracy" which had chosen the noncapitalist path, seeing "self-management," which seemed more Chinese or Yugoslav than Soviet, as being acceptable because it arose out of necessity due to the abandoned property of the *colons* rather than ideological predisposition.[169] In fact, he argued that "self-management is the objective result of **socialist revolution, which has already begun**" (bold in original).[170] Algeria showed that "in countries with underdeveloped, predominantly agricultural economies, the peasantry is not only a mass base for the struggle of national liberation. Under certain conditions, the more 'proletarianized' part of the peasantry, agricultural workers, enable also the crossing to social transformations." Adequate leadership could be provided by intellectuals and petite bourgeoisie who as "revolutionary democrats, by the very logic of class struggle, are led to stand on the ideological position of the proletariat, on the position of scientific socialism."[171] The most important thing at this stage was the formation of a "vanguard" political party to unite all socialists, and the FLN had taken the first step toward this at the congress, adopting what Potemkin called "democratic centralism" and "collective leadership," while giving the party sole control of the state. In short, the FLN was becoming a mini-CPSU. All that was left, said Potemkin, was the official adoption of the ideological program of scientific socialism, which was "inevitable."[172]

Soviet relations with Algeria got off to a rocky start. Defense Minister Boumedienne told the DPRK ambassador that when he visited in 1963 the Soviets put three conditions on the provision of military aid: open opposition to China, acceptance of peaceful coexistence, and legalization of the Algerian Communist Party.[173] At the end of the year, an FLN party delegation got a warmer reception, receiving a $100 million credit, though they still refused to cave in to Moscow's demands.[174] A few months later, on the heels of the first FLN Congress, Ben Bella arrived in Moscow to a hero's reception similar to that received by Fidel Castro a year earlier. Praising Algerian "socialism" built on "Marxist analysis," the Soviets gave them a new loan of about $126.5 million, which included several large-scale projects that ranged from mines to technical schools. Ben Bella extolled the Soviet Union as Algeria's "loyal friend," even thanking it for its support during the war, while praising Khrushchev and the USSR's accomplishments. However, in foreign policy, other than support for the Partial Test Ban Treaty, which made sense given Algeria's opposition to French nuclear tests in the Sahara, Ben Bella did not concede much to Khrushchev. He repeated the Chinese line that "as long as there exists oppressed and oppressing nations in the world, there cannot be real peace" and the foreign press discerned "Chinese notes" in Ben Bella's tone.[175] Given that he also refused to enter into Sino-Soviet issues or legalize the Communist Party, the Chinese were satisfied that he had made the absolute minimum number of concessions, despite his "illusions" about the USSR and the impression that the Aswan Dam had made upon his economic imagination.[176] Just to be safe, the PRC embassy in Algiers suggested inviting him to Beijing as soon as possible.

Instead, Chen Yi visited Algeria in October, followed by Zhou Enlai in March. Both were concerned to make sure that Algeria, as the host nation, would not allow the Soviets to attend the upcoming second Bandung Conference. Zhou tried to convince Ben Bella to drop his call for peace talks in Vietnam and instead support the DRV and NLF, with some success.[177] The Chinese were concerned that Algeria was, as Ben Bella put it, at the "crossroads of contemporary international political trends," and, as such, they thought it natural that he would vacillate, and the closer the conference got and the fiercer the struggle became, the more intense those vacillations would become.[178] It was certainly a creative way of maintaining the illusion that Algeria could still be in their camp despite the fact that Soviet pressure and aid were beginning to show results. All of a sudden, Ben Bella's anti-imperialism was just "tough talk, weak action" (咀硬手软), and the embassy in Algeria questioned whether he had the courage to use "revolutionary means" to overcome Algeria's economic difficulties.[179] Ben Bella was still redeemable because his "active side is leading" (他的积极面还是主导的) but, as Zhou's visit had shown, it would take patient convincing and a lot of flattery since "the Algerian ruling group is very arrogant and conceited, but its tiger's ass can still be petted" (他的老虎屁股还是可以摸的). Meanwhile, Boumedienne was visiting Moscow, and the Chinese speculated that he might be negotiating a new arms deal. That seems to have been the case and, in what might have been a cryptic reference to what was to come, Boumedienne assured Brezhnev "that Soviet weapons in Algerian arms will always serve the goals of the liberation struggle."[180]

On June 19, 1965, Houari Boumedienne led a military coup that overthrew Ben Bella, taking the world, and apparently Moscow and Beijing, by surprise. By now, the Chinese were happy to see him go, and they recognized the new government almost immediately, hoping that the second Bandung Conference could still be salvaged. The Soviet ambassador in Algeria even suspected that the Chinese might have been involved.[181] Moscow began openly promoting the return of Ben Bella, claiming that 70 percent of Algerians supported him, while Beijing said that Moscow only wanted him back because they had spent so much money on him and he had been turning to the right consistently in the last year.[182] While the new Algerian government was understandably more congenial to the Chinese position on the conference, the Soviets won the day by arguing for postponement, as the coup, and Chinese support for it, had unsettled established regimes in the rest of Africa. Beijing could already see the writing on the wall, however, as Moscow was using its allies in Eastern Europe for the fiercest condemnations, preparing for the day when it would need to woo Boumedienne to restore its position in North Africa. While Moscow at first flirted with the idea of supporting a guerrilla struggle against the new government, on July 15 Kosygin called Boumedienne to congratulate him on being named prime minister.[183] By December, Boumedienne was on his way back to Moscow, and Beijing found cold comfort in the thought that Soviet influence in Algeria would never match that of the French.[184]

In the end, Soviet success in Algeria stemmed from a combination of a superior aid package and the policy changes of the new Soviet leadership. The USSR had provided more than $225 million in credits, including funds for building and staffing schools for the training of technological cadres as well as some 150 tanks, twenty airplanes, sixty pieces of artillery, and six naval ships, in addition to sending military experts and accepting Algerian officers for training.[185] However, Soviet aid to Algeria already far exceeded Chinese aid before Khrushchev's removal, when all of the credits had already been granted. It was the fact that Moscow had moved closer to him that allowed Ben Bella to move closer to Moscow. Of Khrushchev's original three conditions as presented to Boumedienne in 1963, the Soviets no longer demanded open opposition to China, except on the issue of the conference, nor did they demand that he endorse peaceful coexistence. The increasingly militant Soviet policy, including helping Algeria supply arms to the Congo, condemning Israel, and militarily supporting the North Vietnamese, allowed Ben Bella to accept Soviet influence without abandoning anti-imperialism. On the final demand, namely that the Algerian Communist Party be legalized, the concept of "revolutionary democracy" made the whole issue irrelevant. The FLN itself was becoming an adequate substitute. It is certainly the case then that aid played a role in the outcome of this second "Battle of Algiers," but it is far from certain that aid would have been decisive had Khrushchev remained in power.

Indonesia presented a much more advantageous situation for Moscow relative to Beijing. While the armed uprising by the Indonesian Communist Party (PKI) in 1948 resulted in the death of most of the party leadership who had spent World War II in Moscow and was followed by a series of strongly anticommunist governments, in January 1953 the new leadership, led by Aidit, met with Stalin in Moscow and claimed all disagreements had been resolved.[186] This move paved the way for a golden age of Soviet-Indonesian relations in the late 1950s and early 1960s. Indonesian president Sukarno paid his first visit to the USSR in 1956 to a hero's reception, while Indonesia received a $100 million credit that same year. It helped as well that Subandrio, the future foreign minister, was currently serving as ambassador to Moscow and considered decidedly pro-Soviet. Khrushchev and Sukarno exchanged visits again in 1960–61, in the wake of the CIA-supported separatist rebellion in 1958, which led to the proclamation of "directed democracy" and the banning of the Muslim Masyumi Party, associated with the Sumatran aristocracy, that had been complicit in the rebellion as well as the Socialist Party (PSI), which was tied to social democrats back in the Netherlands, the former colonial power. This meant that Sukarno and a rejuvenated PKI were now coming to dominate what had been a very complicated Indonesian political landscape. New aid agreements were signed in 1959 and 1960, the latter for more than $250 million, as well as a military aid agreement worth roughly $400 million in January 1961 in support of Indonesia's intensifying conflict with the Netherlands over West Irian.[187] That same year, Sukarno introduced an eight-year plan meant to lead Indonesia to "socialism," and a delegation of the Indonesian National Planning Council was soon dispatched to Moscow for consultations in the "Homeland of the Planned Economy."[188] Though "Indonesian socialism" did not meet Soviet standards for "scientific socialism" as discussed earlier, it was at least seen as an opening toward social transformation, especially in light of the rising fortunes of the PKI.

Meanwhile, Sino-Indonesian relations were careening between periods of crisis and relative calm, primarily due to the large numbers of ethnic Chinese in the country. Many Chinese had arrived during the period of Dutch colonialism and took advantage of preferential treatment and expansive trading networks to dominate commerce in much of the archipelago, causing a considerable amount of local dissatisfaction. Beijing began large-scale efforts to convince the local Chinese to support it instead of the Nationalists in Taiwan, and the specter of a hated foreign economic elite becoming loyal to a large, hostile Communist neighbor set off alarms in the Indonesian body politic. A 1955 treaty to eliminate dual citizenship resolved the problem for a while, but in May 1959 Indonesia revoked the trading licenses of aliens in rural areas and the military ordered the removal of all aliens from the countryside for "security reasons."[189] Removal efforts soon led to violence and riots, which prompted the PRC embassy to send its own people out into the countryside. When that failed, Beijing called the overseas Chinese back home, devastating the Indonesian economy. The dispute heated up until a widely publicized murder of two Chinese women by Indonesian soldiers, following which both sides chose to step back from the precipice, leading to the restoration of diplomatic concord when Chen Yi visited in April 1961.[190] Nevertheless, the powerful Indonesian military remained hostile to, and suspicious of, Beijing, at the same time that it was being armed, to the tune of over 1 billion dollars in 1961–62, with weapons, including warships and aircraft, as well as trained by Moscow.[191]

The situation began to change rapidly in early 1963. The West Irian issue had been resolved peacefully in Jakarta's favor and the Soviets now thought that it was time for Sukarno to get serious about economic reforms.[192] Soviet dissatisfaction with the pace of socialist development, in particular due to heavy spending on the military, had led them to avoid including Indonesia in their list of "revolutionary democracies."[193] Sukarno had other priorities, however. As early as the first NAM conference in 1961, Sukarno had spoken in favor of a radical altering of the global political structure, emphasizing the confrontation between North and South over that between East and West. This concept began to crystallize into an idea known as the "Conference of New Emerging Forces" (CONEFO), which would replace the UN and stand in opposition to the established world powers and that even led to the holding of the Games of New Emerging Forces (GANEFO) in 1963 as an alternative to the Olympics.[194] Sukarno's version of militant anti-imperialism thus suited Beijing, which was calling for Afro-Asian solidarity. The PRC was not represented in the UN anyway, which was not the case for Moscow, one of the pillars of the existing global power structure. The idea for a second Bandung Conference was pushed equally hard by both Jakarta and Beijing, even though India, with Soviet support, successfully lobbied to hold the conference in Africa rather than in Bandung again. The differences over how to confront anti-imperialism crystallized when Sukarno announced his policy of *Konfrontasi* vis-à-vis the newly proposed Malaysian Federation, which he saw as an imperialist plot to contain Indonesia, in February 1963.[195] The Soviets feared that promotion of the doctrine would lead to military clashes between Indonesia and the United Kingdom, and they refused to support Sukarno, in contrast to the Chinese, who were arguably even more enthusiastic than Sukarno himself.

In the meantime, as the Sino-Soviet dispute heated up within the communist movement, the PKI, the largest nonruling Communist Party in the world, became a firm ally of the CCP in international conferences, especially on the issue of individual party autonomy from the CPSU.[196] In 1963, the PKI officially adopted the rhetoric of "antirevisionism," exchanging hostile letters and polemics with the CPSU. Aidit complained about Soviet efforts to split the party, telling the editor of *Pravda* that he was trying to control the PKI to prevent it from becoming even more pro-Chinese.[197] In mid-1964 the Soviet ambassador in Jakarta wrote Moscow that "in the recent period the positions of the PKI and CCP on a number of contemporary issues have merged and become identical."[198] Mikoyan visited in June 1964 in order to improve the situation from Moscow's perspective, but his continued refusal to openly support the *Konfrontasi* policy against Malaysia made the visit unsuccessful.[199] The other purpose of his visit was to bring the PKI into line, harshly if necessary. In a meeting with Aidit, Mikoyan actually threatened to mobilize the Indonesian bourgeoisie against the PKI, telling him that the 7,000 Indonesian officers trained in the USSR and 1,500 Soviet military experts in Indonesia opposed the PKI, and that if Moscow decided to act, "the Indonesian bourgeoisie will have a change in attitude toward the PKI, and it will not be good for the PKI."[200] Mikoyan at the same time tried to woo Sukarno and Subandrio with promises of military aid, which continued during Subandrio's subsequent trip to Moscow, but Aidit was confident that they were only humoring Moscow to try to get arms.[201]

The Soviet ambassador in Jakarta agreed with his assessment, writing that *"we are confronted with what is in effect a united, even if temporary, position of the leadership of the republic and the PKI leadership on questions of international development"* (underlined in original).[202]

After Khrushchev's ouster, the new leadership tried to mend ties with the PKI, but the latter saw Brezhnev and Kosygin as no better than Khrushchev, viewing their efforts as a renewed attempt to bully the PKI into submission.[203] Moscow tried to improve ties with Sukarno and the military instead by supporting the *Konfrontasi* policy, even offering new military aid as mentioned above, but this time they were one step behind. When Malaysia was voted onto the UN Security Council, Sukarno announced on January 7, 1965, that Indonesia was leaving the UN altogether. This Moscow could not countenance, as it reflected a real step toward creating a new world order of the type that Beijing wanted, pitting the developing world, the "world village," against the "world city" that encompassed all of Europe and North America, and Kosygin wrote Sukarno a letter criticizing the move while the Soviet press spoke out in favor of the UN.[204] As the Soviet ambassador in Jakarta wrote, Indonesia's policy reflected a belief that "the newly emerging forces carry the main weight of the struggle against imperialism," and this approach could not but lead to the marginalization of Moscow.[205] The new Soviet leadership was willing to embrace anti-imperialism only insofar as it was anti-imperialism under the Soviet umbrella. Even when it came to military aid, there were certain lines Moscow would not cross. Sukarno began expressing a desire to acquire nuclear weapons and asked for Moscow's help on this, but the Soviets tried to dissuade him. Meanwhile, it seems that Chen Yi in August 1965 indicated that the PRC would be willing at least to consider the transfer of nuclear technology to Indonesia, and Mao asked a visiting Indonesian delegation on September 30, "Do you want to build an atomic bomb?"[206] It was no surprise then when, in a speech on August 17, 1965, Sukarno proclaimed the advent of a "Jakarta-Phnom Penh-Hanoi-Beijing-Pyongyang axis."[207]

As Sukarno moved ever closer to the PKI in 1964–65, the PKI moved closer to the CCP. While the PKI had always been a predominantly urban party and followed the strategy of an electoral road to power, now the PKI sought to broaden its base in rural areas to prepare for a potential "guerrilla struggle in the countryside."[208] In mid-1964 the PKI began taking the matter of the stalled enactment of the Agrarian Law of 1960 into its own hands, initiating seizures of land, clashing with local Muslim landholder groups, and provoking suspicion in the military leadership.[209] Making matters worse, the PKI began advocating for the creation of a "Fifth Force" consisting of armed workers and peasants, which gained Sukarno's endorsement, in a clear demonstration of the fact that Sukarno's primary power base was now the PKI, and he was relying on it against the military.[210] It was not a small base either, as by August 1965, the PKI estimated that more than 26 million people, out of a total population of roughly 100 million, were members of the party or affiliated organizations.[211]

The whole picture changed on the night of September 30–October 1, 1965. Though the sequence of events remains unclear to this day, the result of the turmoil that night was the installation of an anticommunist military government led by General Suharto, the physical destruction of the PKI, the resignation of Sukarno, and the breaking of relations with the PRC. The correspondent of *Pravda* in Jakarta initially wrote to Suslov that he was unsure of the role of the PKI in the coup, but it was clear in any case that they were dreadfully unprepared.[212] In a subsequent top secret analysis sent by the Soviet ambassador in Jakarta to the Central Committee, the former claimed that the PKI decided at a meeting in May to "force the struggle for power," though he felt it had "overestimated the 'revolutionary situation.'"[213] Ultimately, Moscow was not as troubled by the coup as Beijing was, and it saw the demise of the PKI as a cautionary tale against following Beijing's line of excessive "adventurism,"[214] while maintaining ties with Suharto and even completing certain aid projects.[215] For Beijing, the coup was devastating. It had lost its closest ally, the fifth most populous country in the world with the largest nonruling Communist Party, one that had openly declared an alliance with Beijing and one on which the PRC had hoped to underpin the building of an Afro-Asian-Latin American power structure. The consequences for the PRC's foreign policy would be enormous as it descended into the self-isolation of the Cultural Revolution.

Despite the ultimate outcome, however, the course of events in Indonesia revealed the limitations of the shift in policy of the new Soviet leadership. The Kremlin was willing to support a more militant version of anti-imperialism but not if it risked actual war with a major Western power and not if it threatened to upset the global power structure that the USSR had helped construct and of which it was a major beneficiary. It showed the limits of Soviet toleration of dissent within the international communist movement, as Moscow not only threatened to support bourgeois forces against the PKI, but also even dabbled in extending support to the Murba Party, a Marxist rival to the PKI, which was exactly the type of "splittist" activity of which Moscow accused Beijing.[216] Finally it showed the limits of aid, as the vast quantitative and qualitative superiority of Soviet aid offers, both military and economic, as compared with the Chinese, could not overcome the ideological confluence among Beijing, Sukarno, and the PKI.

The Demise of the Second Bandung Conference

Throughout 1965, thanks to the concerted efforts of the Kremlin,[217] the decision that the PRC had successfully fought for in Jakarta in April 1964 to hold a second Afro-Asian heads of state conference without the USSR disintegrated. Under the twin pressures of diplomacy and aid, one country after another—India, UAR, Ghana, Cyprus, Iraq, Laos, Senegal, Nigeria, and the list goes on—came out in favor of Soviet participation in the conference. Gromyko and Suslov maintained a constant correspondence on the issue in the summer of 1965, ticking new countries off their shopping list while Beijing watched countries slip through its fingers.[218] When Ben Bella sent out the official invitations for the conference in late May to begin on June 29, the question of Soviet attendance was very much up in the air, and Gromyko told Suslov that the question might be decided only days before the opening.[219] By June 29, of course, Ben Bella was no longer in power and, on June 27, in the conference hall in Algiers, the Soviet-backed proposal to postpone the conference carried the day against the wishes of Beijing and Boumedienne. While Beijing pushed for a new preparatory meeting to be held in November, it became clear that the USSR now had majority support for its attendance, and suddenly it was the USSR and India pushing to hold the conference. The PRC promptly declared that it would not attend and tried to scuttle the meeting. On October 28, 1965, Gromyko sent a lengthy proposed directive for the Soviet delegation at the conference to Suslov, Andropov, Ponomarev, Semichastnyi, and Shevliagin for consultation. The proposal outlined a Soviet approach and agenda to the conference in the event that the PRC chose to attend as well as if it did not.[220] This time, though, Beijing succeeded, and the conference was never held.

By the end of 1965, the PRC's foreign policy, such as it was, had collapsed. The Indonesian coup had eliminated its most important ally and the failure to hold a second Bandung Conference ended its hopes of creating an Afro-Asian bloc to bolster its self-professed status as the leader of the world revolution. This meant the failure, at least for the time being, of the attempt to compete head to head with the Soviet Union. Nevertheless, China had succeeded in changing the nature of the debate within the "socialist camp" and possibly the world at large regarding the issues of imperialism, colonialism, and neocolonialism as well as aid and development, forcing the USSR to adapt its own policies in these areas in order to maintain its global status.

The question is: what accounts for this relative Soviet success? Many commentators have argued that the preponderance of Soviet resources relative to those of the PRC that could be distributed in the form of aid, especially the higher technological development of the USSR, led countries, when forced to choose between Moscow and Beijing, to choose Moscow. Certainly the USSR's aid totals in these years far surpass those of the PRC, and the PRC could not have completed a project of the technical difficulty of the Aswan Dam. Aid is therefore part of the story, but it is not the whole story. Much more Soviet aid was granted during the Khrushchev period than in the aftermath of his ouster, and yet Chinese political fortunes were probably at their highest in October 1964. Soviet aid did not win over Sukarno, nor did it win over Ben Bella without an accompanying shift in Soviet policy toward the support of so-called national liberation movements. It was this shift toward a more militant anti-imperialist policy that changed the terms of the debate and meant that countries no longer had to give up their anti-imperialist policies for "peaceful coexistence" and a "state of national democracy" under Soviet tutelage to receive Soviet aid. Instead, they could have both communist guns and butter, in a manner of speaking.

However, Soviet anti-imperialism was a very particular kind of anti-imperialism. Soviet anti-imperialism was built on the notion of class, not race or ethnicity, and it insisted that the leadership of the world revolution still remained in the hands of the proletariat of the socialist countries along with the workers' movements in the capitalist countries. Soviet anti-imperialism allowed for the possibility—and occasionally even the desirability—of armed struggle, as long as it did not threaten to lead to a full-scale war with the West. Soviet anti-imperialism did not allow for any major alteration of the global power structure, and Moscow did not want to encourage the diffusion of power, such as in the form of new nuclear powers. Nationalism was acceptable within Soviet anti-imperialism, but only up to a certain point, one to be determined by Moscow. As the experience of Indonesia showed, not all were satisfied with this version of anti-imperialism. The Afro-Asian conference that China and Indonesia had fought for might not have been held, but the Tricontinental Conference, which China and Cuba had worked to convene since 1963, would be held in Havana in January 1966, and it would demonstrate the continuing appetite for radical anti-imperialism beyond the comfort zone of Moscow.

CHAPTER FOUR

The Cultural Revolution and Its Discontents, 1966–1969

"The principle of peaceful coexistence is not applicable to the relations between oppressors and oppressed, between colonizers and the victims of the colonial yoke."[1] In the early 1960s, such statements were common in conferences, joint communiqués, and editorials by Beijing and its Afro-Asian allies attacking the Soviet policy of peaceful coexistence. In 1966, however, those words were spoken by Leonid Brezhnev himself at the Twenty-Third CPSU Congress. Much had changed in the last few years. To combat the Chinese challenge for the mantle of leader of the world revolution, the Kremlin had embraced the anti-imperialist cause in both rhetoric and policy, particularly since the leadership change of October 1964. However, the foreign policy imperatives that had originally led the Soviet leadership to adopt the policy of peaceful coexistence had not disappeared. The Kremlin continued to seek a de-escalation of tension with the West in order to avoid a devastating conflict, and peace still seemed to be a popular slogan for many communists seeking political influence through electoral channels in Western Europe and Latin America. At the same time, the Soviet embrace of militant anti-imperialism had not led to the reconstitution of Moscow's influence as the center of world revolution. As China descended into the chaos of the Cultural Revolution, Havana and Hanoi increasingly began to put themselves forth as the true centers of world revolution. At the Tricontinental Conference in Havana in January 1966, the Cuban regime carried the day, producing resolutions explicitly calling for the support of armed struggles around the world. The secretary general of the newly created Organization of Solidarity of the Peoples of Asia, Africa and Latin America (OSPAAAL) Osmany Cienfuegos sought to replace the old AAPSO headquartered in Cairo, arguing that the Sino-Soviet split was causing more harm than good and that the world revolutionary movement would do better without Moscow and Beijing, under the leadership of Havana.[2] Meanwhile, increased Soviet aid to Hanoi did not seem to produce greater opportunities for Moscow to influence Hanoi's policies, and the North Vietnamese continued to resist Soviet peace initiatives, preferring to seek a military solution instead.[3] Hanoi's militarism was supported by the Cuban leadership, as well as Che Guevara, who called for "two, three, many Vietnams."[4]

Even more problematic from Moscow's perspective was the unexpected direction that events in the developing world were taking in the mid-1960s. Beginning with the overthrow of Brazilian president João Goulart in March 1964, a series of military coups overthrew some of the leading lights of the so-called national liberation movement. Ben Bella of Algeria was overthrown in June 1965, followed by Sukarno in October and then Kwame Nkrumah of Ghana in February 1966, the latter while in Beijing on his way to Hanoi to propose peace negotiations. The strongly left-leaning regime of President Massamba-Débat in Congo-Brazzaville was saved from a similar fate in June 1966 only through the determined efforts of roughly 200 Cuban soldiers.[5] Finally, in November 1968, Modibo Keita of Mali was overthrown as well. By the late 1960s, the number of developing world regimes friendly to Moscow and Beijing had decreased significantly in this way. Furthermore, progress on decolonization seemed to have stalled. After the independence of Zambia in 1964, the decolonization process had hit a brick wall in the southern part of Africa due to the determination of the Portuguese as well as the white South Africans and Rhodesians to hold on to power. As liberation wars dragged on in these countries, supplied by both the USSR and the PRC, very little progress was being made and the frustration of Africans with the impotence of their Communist patrons grew. The promise that decolonization had held in the early 1960s to redress the balance of power in the world against the West and the idea that the political and economic circumstances of people in the developing world made them naturally inclined toward socialism and potential allies of the socialist world seemed to be dissipating.

Consequently, from the Soviet point of view, the diplomatic triumph over China in 1965 was not as triumphant as had been anticipated. Furthermore, while the nature of the Chinese challenge had changed, it had not disappeared completely. Chinese foreign policy during the Cultural Revolution was in a state of disarray, but the voice of Maoism emanating from Beijing had become even louder and more forceful than before, and it had begun to attract a new audience, particularly in the West. The battle for influence with the Chinese would therefore increasingly become a matter of ideas and propaganda directed toward masses of protesters rather than aid projects and diplomacy aimed at political leaders. Within this context, the symbolism of the Vietnam War would become ever more crucial due to its high global profile and mobilizing effect among youth in the West.

The late 1960s therefore presented the Kremlin with new challenges resulting from its success in meeting an older one. The Soviet leadership had succeeded to a significant degree in co-opting the anti-imperialist rhetoric and policy of the Chinese, but the logic of that policy conflicted with certain underlying Soviet interests, leading to tragic results in Latin America, Vietnam, and, most shockingly, the Middle East. The Soviet solution to this would be control. If the USSR was going to try to promote both anti-imperialism and détente at the same time, it would need greater control over its allies and this would be achieved the only way the Soviet leadership knew how: through the twin mechanisms of party and ideology, that is the same means the Communist Party of the Soviet Union (CPSU) used to maintain control within the USSR. The greater emphasis on ideology dovetailed with the Soviet response to the Cultural Revolution, as the battle against Maoism replaced the battle against Beijing, at least in the international sphere. The students in the West, however, presented a more difficult problem, since Moscow's traditional methods of control were not available. Instead, Communist Parties in Western Europe would begin to slip away from Moscow's grasp in order not to lose their constituency at home. The Soviet invasion of Czechoslovakia in 1968 contributed to this growing divide between the standing of the Soviet Union in the developing world and in the developed world as, in a sort of preview of global reaction to the events of Tiananmen Square in 1989, the West was far more troubled by the use of force than was much of the rest of the world. By the end of the 1960s, then, the USSR was also increasingly turning its revolutionary ambitions away from the West and toward the South.

The Cultural Revolution and Chinese Foreign Policy

As the Chinese Cultural Revolution began to take shape between November 1965 and August 1966, few outside observers had a clear understanding of the causes and nature of the seemingly bizarre series of events in the PRC, or where they might be heading. The Soviet leaders were no exception. In the beginning they saw it as a battle for control of the PRC between those elements of the CCP that remained faithful to Marxism-Leninism and the "Mao clique" that was seeking to wipe them out.[6] What was unmistakable, however, was the effect of the Cultural Revolution on Chinese foreign policy. By the middle of 1967, Chinese standing around the world had deteriorated as Beijing's diplomats abroad had created diplomatic incidents through the distribution of propaganda, foreign representatives in Beijing had been harassed and attacked, ethnic Chinese in Southeast Asia had started their own mini–Cultural Revolutions, and all Chinese ambassadors but one, Huang Hua in Cairo, had been recalled to Beijing. The imperatives of domestic politics, not only on the institutional level, but even on the individual level, were overriding those of foreign policy, and the consequences were disastrous. In less than two years, China's effort to build itself up country by country from an ostracized, dangerous pariah state to a powerful player on the international stage, painstakingly forged by Zhou Enlai and Chen Yi since the Geneva conference of 1954, seemed to be in tatters.

In terms of its effect on the conduct of Chinese foreign policy, the Cultural Revolution was somewhat delayed by the efforts of Chen Yi and Zhou Enlai. Through the summer of 1966, Chen Yi headed the Communist Party work committee that was in charge of the Cultural Revolution in the Foreign Ministry. Three high-profile targets were found in order to demonstrate adherence to the policy while forty-four young translators who called for a more radical attack on the ministry hierarchy found themselves the subject of investigation.[7] Meanwhile, Zhou and Chen had decided that Chinese embassies abroad should not get involved.[8] However, things began to change with the arrival of two letters in August. These two letters, supposedly written by Chinese sympathizers abroad, criticized the "bourgeois" behaviors and consumption patterns of Chinese diplomats abroad and contrasted them with the egalitarian ideals of the Cultural Revolution. On September 9, Mao instructed Chen Yi to spread the Cultural Revolution to the embassies abroad and begin bringing staff members back to Beijing.[9] Subsequently, in early 1967, Zhou Enlai ordered the return of all Chinese ambassadors from abroad, except for Huang Hua, who had only recently been moved to Cairo from his previous post in Accra, where a military coup had led to the severing of relations with China.[10] Upon their return to Beijing, the staff of each embassy, along with its ambassador, was housed in a large room in an old condemned building belonging to the Foreign Ministry, where it was supposed to conduct its struggle against the "bourgeois elements" of its embassy.[11] The staff of each embassy quickly divided into conservative and radical factions, mirroring divisions among Red Guards more broadly, with the more numerous faction of each embassy leading the Cultural Revolution in its own room, often devolving into the physical torture of ambassadors.[12]

As the Cultural Revolution became increasingly radical, the Beijing staff of the Foreign Ministry fared little better. With the seizure of Shanghai's municipal party committee and government by rebels in January 1967, subsequently condoned by Mao, Zhou Enlai could see the writing on the wall for the Foreign Ministry. Within days, he encouraged the so-called Lianluozhan, or liaison station, which had been formed within the ministry at a meeting on December 20 with approximately 100 to 200 of the roughly 2,000 members of the ministerial staff, to seize power, in order to forestall a seizure of power by Red Guards who were not affiliated with the ministry.[13] Zhou thereby hoped to place the Foreign Ministry in the hands of those who would be amenable to his plan for limiting the Cultural Revolution to struggle within the ministry itself, while leaving the conduct of foreign policy outside the purview of the rebels since, as he told the Red Guards, "Specific foreign affairs cannot be discussed in big-character posters, nor can replies be made. What effect will they have? Only a negative effect."[14] However, while Chen Yi initially went along with Zhou's plan, submitting to the takeover of the ministry by the Lianluozhan, in a meeting of the Politburo and the Central Cultural Revolution Group (CCRG) at Huairentang in February 1967 he joined a number of other Politburo members in speaking out against the excesses of the Red Guards and Cultural Revolution policies. Informed of the events at the meeting, Jiang Qing appealed to Mao, who connected this outburst with supposed manifestations of opposition to the Cultural Revolution. Mao then instigated a series of enlarged Politburo meetings under Zhou's chairmanship to condemn what he labeled the "February Adverse Current." Despite Zhou's best efforts to control the process and save Chen Yi, events soon spun out of even his control, and on April 17 the *Lianluozhan* officially put forward the slogan "Down with Chen Yi."[15] By August, Zhou Enlai was forced to accede to the demands of the Red Guards for a meeting in order to criticize Chen Yi, and although Chen Yi managed to survive physically, his duties were largely taken over by Ji Pengfei, and he was essentially marginalized until his death in 1972.[16]

The nadir of the Cultural Revolution in the Foreign Ministry would be reached in August 1967. On August 7, Wang Li, a member of the CCRG, gave a talk to members of the *Lianluozhan* expressing dissatisfaction with how the Cultural Revolution was being carried out in the ministry. He encouraged the Red Guards to seize power, arguing that, in comparison with the affairs of Red Guards, there was nothing complicated about foreign affairs.[17] This was seen as a direct challenge to Zhou Enlai, who was the new target of the ire of the CCRG. Radical elements of the *Lianluozhan,* mobilized by Wang's talk, seized control of the Political Department of the Foreign Ministry on August 16, the department in charge of ideology and personnel in the ministry.[18] For a while it was not clear who was in charge of the Foreign Ministry, and Mao would later remark that he had lost control of the Foreign Ministry for a month and a half.[19] However, the burning of the office of the British chargé d'affaires in Beijing on August 22, resulting from a dispute over the treatment of workers in Hong Kong, signaled that things had gone too far. Along with a strange series of events in Wuhan in July 1967 in which Mao himself was perceived to have been in physical danger, the tide began to turn against the most radical elements of the CCRG and Wang Li was soon arrested after a personal appeal by Zhou to Mao.[20] Wang Li and others became identified with the so-called May 16th elements, a radical conspiracy that was supposed to have taken its name from the circular adopted by the Central Committee on May 16, 1966, criticizing the "moderation" of the Cultural Revolution to that point. Zhou used the campaign against "May 16th elements" to combat the *Lianluozhan* as well, and the latter was disbanded on October 18, 1967.[21] The worst of the Cultural Revolution was over in the Foreign Ministry, but the damage to Chinese foreign policy had been significant.

During the Cultural Revolution, it was difficult to speak of a "Chinese foreign policy" with the implication it contains of a policy directed by central organs, carried out at home and abroad, to achieve particular objectives in relation to other countries. Instead, order within the ministry at home and embassies abroad collapsed as the struggles of the Cultural Revolution and the imperatives of individual survival overrode the conduct of any sort of foreign policy. Individuals understandably feared the personal consequences of being perceived as insufficiently revolutionary to be worse than those of offending other countries with excessive revolutionary actions that broke with diplomatic protocol. Consequently, workers in embassies abroad and ministry staff at home devoted themselves to distribution of propaganda, Mao badges and pins, and the overt display of revolutionary enthusiasm. According to one estimate, over 5 billion copies of *Quotations from Chairman Mao*, otherwise known as the "little red book," were distributed at a time when the world population was only roughly 3 billion.[22] As one country after another severed relations with China, the director of the Information Department of *Renmin Ribao* asserted that "severance of relations can do us no harm. . . . Severance of relations will only make a mess of things politically and economically for a given country, since we can then support the people of that country to make revolution."[23] The number of African delegations visiting China dropped from 116 in 1966, due to invitations proffered earlier, to twelve in 1968, while Chinese delegations going to Africa went from forty-eight in 1966 to fourteen in 1968.[24]

The Soviets were thrilled that the Chinese were doing their work for them better than they could ever hope to do it themselves. Many Africans approached Soviet diplomats to condemn the Cultural Revolution, leading the Soviet embassy in Uganda to write that "if earlier the 'revolutionary' phraseology of the Chinese was taken by certain official leftist circles and especially youth as true currency and found among them known support, now they are 'disillusioned' with the ability of the leaders of the PRC to lead Africa (*povesti za soboi Afriku*)."[25] The situation was not helped by the fact that the Chinese ambassador to Uganda had been recalled and the embassy staff had been cut from twelve to two—only the second secretary and a translator remained.[26] Even the Cubans were shocked. The vice president of the Cuban Academy of Sciences, returning from a trip to China in October 1966, told a Soviet diplomat that "it is hard to imagine, to what type of idiocy the ranks of the "Red Guards" and the people led by them reach. The Hitlerites could have learned something from them."[27] With the exception of Albania, no country was exempt from the fury of the Cultural Revolution. Even North Korea and North Vietnam came under criticism, as well as Cuba. Yao Wenyuan, a member of the CCRG, even labeled Fidel Castro a "revisionist."[28]

Despite these developments, the Chinese press published a flood of supposed global acclamations in support of the Cultural Revolution. Between January and May 1967, more than 110 articles praising the Cultural Revolution were published by representatives of forty-two Afro-Asian countries.[29] Few of the pieces were the products of influential overseas supporters; many, in fact, were by foreigners living in Beijing under the patronage of the Chinese regime, such as Angola's Viriato da Cruz. They invariably spoke of the Cultural Revolution as a great global phenomenon and praised Mao Zedong as the leader of all revolutionary people around the world. The culmination of this manufactured praise was the "International Seminar on the 25th anniversary of Mao's speech in Yan'an on Literature and Art," held in Beijing in late May and early June 1967 with representatives from thirty-four countries.[30] Nevertheless, actual support for the Cultural Revolution in Africa and Asia was scant indeed. Despite the best efforts of his Chinese hosts, Zambian president Kenneth Kaunda, visiting China in June 1967, refused to endorse the Cultural Revolution even while negotiating for Chinese aid for the Tanzam railway. The foreign country that came closest to adopting Cultural Revolution–type policies of its own was Tanzania, where President Nyerere issued the Arusha Declaration on February 7, 1967, laying out a project of Tanzanian socialism on the basis of self-reliance.[31] Soon young Tanzanians wearing green shirts were christened the "Green Guards," and they were issued with "little green books" containing quotations from President Nyerere.[32]

Overall, however, the Cultural Revolution was an unmitigated disaster for Chinese foreign policy. Most Afro-Asian observers were horrified by the course of events in China as well as offended by crude Chinese attempts to spread the Cultural Revolution abroad, and little in terms of an economic, political, or ideological model seemed attractive to Afro-Asian elites trying to build up their own countries. By late 1967, then, China's standing in the developing world was lower than it had been in a decade.

The Curse of Victory

For the Soviet Union, the temporary demise of Chinese foreign policy did not solve all of its international problems. Whether or not they would have wanted to, there was no way for the Soviet leaders to go back to the halcyon days of the postcolonial era in the early 1960s, with its dreams of peaceful coexistence and building socialism in the "state of national democracy." The newly militant Soviet anti-imperialist policy had created certain expectations among friends and foes alike and backtracking would be difficult, if not impossible. Indeed, Moscow was now caught between the logic of its rhetoric, the belligerence of its allies, and its desire to avoid confrontation with the West. The result would be unrest among Communist Parties in Latin America devoted to the electoral path, an inability to restrain Hanoi, and a disastrous war in the Middle East.

Meanwhile, what had seemed like solid socialist gains in the developing world were reversed in one military coup after another and the Cultural Revolution was affecting not only Chinese prestige, but also the image of socialism throughout the world. The Soviet solution that would eventually emerge in response to these difficulties would be a switch in emphasis from economics to politics and ideological indoctrination. The introduction of the concept of "revolutionary democracy" in 1964 had already begun this shift, but the events of the late 1960s would provide it with a great impetus. If the USSR was going to be able to promote anti-imperialism without unwanted explosions of conflict, it would need greater control over its allies. This would mean not only greater Soviet involvement, but a more reliable military and political structure to facilitate that involvement. The ideologically nebulous unstable class coalitions of the "state of national democracy," which had proven to be so fragile and unpredictable, would need to be replaced by more ideologically orthodox Leninist-style party structures. The Cultural Revolution, which Soviet analysts began to see as a potential danger facing all postcolonial agrarian societies, only confirmed the danger of ideological heterodoxy and political instability. In turn, however, the Soviet economic model would become somewhat more flexible. While the focus of the "state of national democracy" was on having a broad national coalition implement policies of agrarian reform, industrialization, and expansion of the state sector, "revolutionary democracy" would focus on the development of the party-state structure, while allowing for a more pragmatic economic policy. Though the clearest applications of these new Soviet policies would not be seen until the 1970s, the overall direction had become clear by the end of the 1960s.

The Soviet policy of peaceful coexistence had not been without its partisans in the developing world. Chief among them had been the Communist Parties of Latin America, which, with the exception of the Venezuelan Communist Party and certain elements of the Brazilian Communist Party in the wake of the 1964 coup, were even more committed to the notion of the "peaceful road to power" than the CPSU. As mentioned earlier, the Chilean Communist Party general secretary Luis Corvalan warned the Soviets in the wake of Khrushchev's ouster that they could not approve of reconciliation with the Chinese.[33] Beijing had been very active in creating Maoist splinter parties in Latin America, and the Moscow-oriented parties had spent much of the last five years fending off Chinese-inspired attacks.[34] More threatening, however, was the specter of Cuba. Havana not only promoted armed struggle, but also was actively involved in exporting it to the mainland with or without the consent of the local Communist Parties, since, after all, Fidel Castro's band of rebels had taken power through armed struggle while the established Cuban left dawdled. Soviet participation in the Tricontinental Conference in Havana, with its militant declarations, unsettled many in Latin America. The Chilean ambassador in Moscow immediately went to see Vice Foreign Minister Yakov Malik, asking him whether or not this meant that "the USSR will support morally and materially the struggle in Peru, Venezuela, Colombia, Guatemala and other countries of Latin America in accord with the results of the mentioned conference."[35] Malik nervously assured him that the USSR remained committed to peaceful coexistence and noninterference, rather incredibly explaining that the Havana conference was attended by representatives of the people, not the state, and so the position taken did not reflect that of the Soviet government. Just to be sure, the head of the Foreign Ministry's Latin American division summoned the Chilean ambassador to present him with an official Soviet statement to that effect, though he asked that the statement be kept out of the public sphere.[36]

In reality, the CPSU leadership was not any happier with Havana than their Latin American comrades. While the Kremlin encouraged the Cubans to moderate their policies and seek recognition from their neighbors for their own economic benefit,[37] Havana took the opposite tack, criticizing the USSR in turn for its insufficient support for the Arab states in the wake of their 1967 defeat while bemoaning the "lonely" struggle of the Vietnamese people.[38] In his June 1967 plenum speech, Brezhnev went so far as to group the Cubans with the Chinese as examples of countries that promoted their own national interests without regard for the rest of the socialist world, remarking ominously that the Politburo was taking "certain measures" to combat these tendencies in the Cuban leadership.[39] Perhaps one of the measures he was referring to was the apparent Soviet directive to Manuel Monje, the head of the Bolivian Communist Party, not to aid Che Guevara and his small band of rebels who had arrived in Bolivia in late 1966. Though the series of events leading to Che's death in October 1967 remain shrouded in mystery, undoubtedly Moscow did not miss him as he had become a focal point of disagreement between Moscow and Havana, and the Soviet leadership was determined to see him fail.[40] Despite Che's death, however, relations between Moscow and Havana continued to deteriorate while the other Latin American Communist

Parties, which had broken with the Cubans by now, appealed to Moscow for support.[41]

The dilemma of Soviet anti-imperialism would produce even more tragic consequences in the Middle East. In the early 1960s, the Soviets had refused to join in the general Arab chorus for the elimination of the state of Israel. After all, the USSR had voted in favor of the UN partition plan in 1947, and, consequently, it had recognized Israel as a legitimate state rather than merely an outpost of colonialism. However, as seen earlier, the Soviet turn toward a more anti-imperialist policy included, for the first time, rhetorical support for the Palestinian cause along with armaments, though the latter were given only to Arab states while the Palestine Liberation Organization (PLO) itself was left to seek support from Beijing.[42] Increasing Soviet support emboldened Nasser and, as the situation in the Middle East deteriorated, the Soviets found it difficult to de-escalate given the steady drumbeat of accusations coming from Beijing that Moscow was selling out the Arabs.[43] On May 19, Nasser took what Brezhnev would subsequently call a "not-well-thought-out step" by ordering UN troops to leave the Sinai without prior consultation with Moscow.[44] Nevertheless, the public support from Moscow was unequivocal. The CPSU Central Committee released a public statement supporting the "Arab countries in their just struggle for national liberation," including the guarantee that any "aggression" in the Middle East "would be met not only with the united strength of the Arab countries but also with strong opposition . . . from the Soviet Union."[45] Despite a series of secret attempts to head off war at the last minute by gaining assurances from Nasser that he would not attack, the continued public support for the Arabs by the Soviets in the UN undoubtedly led Nasser to feel confident enough to take provocative steps that he would not have taken without full-fledged Soviet backing.

Given the results of the war, it is not surprising that the Soviet leadership denied any part in encouraging it. However, what is striking about Brezhnev's lengthy speech on the war at a Communist Party plenum on June 20, 1967, is the degree of implied blame directed at the Soviets' Arab allies, given that the official Soviet position was that the war was the sole product of Israeli aggression. After affirming Nasser's assent to Soviet demands for peace, Brezhnev remarked that "at the same time, for full orientation on the situation on the eve of Israeli aggression, it will be useful for members of the CC to know the following: According to the data from our embassy, the positive development of events, in the opinion of the UAR leaders, strengthened the mood among the generals of the UAR armed forces in favor of a preventative strike on Israel; it was characteristic that even the head of the operational General Staff of the UAR in a conversation with a senior group of Soviet military specialists in the UAR on June 3 announced that not all Egyptian military leaders approve of the line of Nasser 'for restraint.'"[46] He went on to assert that the Syrians were even more optimistic about their military chances and that Syrian prime minister Yusuf Zayen told the ambassador several times that "now is the best time for a decisive blow against imperialist forces in the Near East, and this moment must be used."[47] Despite the public Soviet position, behind closed doors the Soviet leadership viewed the war as at least partially the product of excessive confidence and militarism on the part of its Arab allies.

In the aftermath of the war, the Soviet push to get the Arabs to agree to some form of armistice was again undermined by the demands of its anti-imperialist policy. Despite prompt Soviet resupply of the Egyptian and Syrian militaries, the Chinese, and to a much lesser degree the Cubans, were loudly blaming the USSR for the defeat and urging the Arabs to keep fighting. Zhou Enlai called on the Arab states "to continue the war at any cost" and "not to enter into any peaceful regulation of the conflict."[48] Anti-Soviet riots broke out across the Arab world and Algerian president Houari Boumedienne, in Moscow for talks on June 12 and 13, called for "more decisive" Soviet action and asked Moscow to end its policy of "peaceful coexistence."[49] Obviously, despite the impractical offers of Chinese aid, the burden of supporting any renewed conflict would fall on Moscow, not Beijing.

The dilemma of Soviet anti-imperialism was never clearer. Moscow had inadvertently encouraged a war it had never wanted by emboldening its allies to move to the precipice of war, and the logic of the Soviet position made it very difficult for the Soviets either before or after the war to exercise significant restraint upon the actions of their allies for fear of being labeled a fake anti-imperialist. The Kremlin would find a way to square this circle through the greater exercise of control over its allies. Already in diagnosing the causes of defeat, in addition to Israeli arms and Arab disorganization, Brezhnev cited the fact that Arab leaders, including Nasser, did not feel the need to discuss matters with their socialist "friends."[50] He argued that the Arab leaders were not yet Marxist and therefore they were still susceptible to petite bourgeois nationalism. This failure could be solved by deepening Soviet ties.[51] In the past, the Soviets had sent arms and military advisers to many countries, but their responsibilities were limited to helping the locals operate the equipment. When they offered to help the Arabs in the past with planning and strategy, they had been turned down. Now the Arabs were willing to accept hands-on help, and the Soviets would play a more active role in training and planning wherever they supplied arms, and not only for military personnel but diplomatic personnel as well.[52] Returning to the issue in April 1968, Brezhnev reported that about 600 Soviet military advisers had been sent to the UAR and they were working on strategy and tactics, while pushing the line that any increase in military aid must be matched by an increase in political ties and influence over policy.[53]

Consequently, the difficulties resulting from increased Soviet support for anti-imperialism led Moscow to seek to impose a greater level of political control and ideological orthodoxy on its allies. The dilemma of anti-imperialism, however, was not the only thing pushing Moscow in this direction. The series of military coups that struck leftist regimes in the developing world in the mid-1960s awakened Soviet scholars and policymakers to the dangers of dependence upon unstable, ideologically heterodox regimes of dubious class origin. In particular, Soviet scholars began paying a great deal of attention to the class composition and political organization of armies. Looking through Soviet journal articles on the developing world in the early 1960s, one would be hard pressed to find any devoted to the question of armies. In September 1966, though, in response to what it claimed was a flood of letters from readers asking for information on Afro-Asian militaries, *Aziia i Afrika Segodnia* published an article titled "The Army and the Liberation Movement." The article discussed the historical and social composition of armies, arguing that in some countries young officers with revolutionary ideas could contribute to the work of liberation, citing as examples the coups that had brought Nasser and Ne Win to power in Egypt and Burma, respectively. Recently, though, imperialist penetration of militaries had increased the possibility of armies being used against left-leaning regimes.[54] *Narody Azii i Afriki* then published a series of articles on the issue in 1967–69. The articles revealed an open disagreement between Soviet scholars on the degree to which armies were independent actors or were simply products of political and class forces operative in various countries. What they did agree on, however, was that the rise of the influence of the military in politics was a product of political stalemate and indecision.[55] The solution, as advanced by G. Mirskii, was the creation of cohesive political parties with socialist agendas that could unite the people and advance the revolution.[56]

The danger of military coups was not the only factor threatening the political trajectories of left-leaning states in the developing world. The Biafran war in Nigeria had strikingly demonstrated the threat of tribalism, and Soviet scholars saw more centralized political organization on a class, rather than an ethnic, basis as the solution to that as well.[57] Despairing of constructing proper socialist allies on the basis of economic transformation alone, some writers pointed to the crucial importance of what they termed the "subjective" factors of leadership in the process of building socialism in the developing world.[58] Consequently, the more "far-seeing" leaders of developing nations were tying themselves ever more closely to the socialist world.[59] No less an authority than Karen Brutents, one of the key officials in the CPSU's International Department working on the developing world, asserted that the important questions determining the direction of developing countries were the organizational and ideological development of national democratic parties.[60] Tellingly, Brutents said very little about economic questions in his article.

In accordance with the idea that the main criteria in evaluating the revolutionary potential of developing countries were now political and ideological rather than economic, Soviet journals began examining party structures and ideologies more closely.[61] *Narody Azii i Afriki* praised Algeria, where Boumedienne's regime was retreating from the earlier policy of self-management of enterprises, and Tanzania, which had recently adopted the Arusha Declaration, as examples of countries that placed greater emphasis on political organization and class struggle than on nationalization and the state sector and therefore represented a higher stage of revolutionary development than countries where "socialism" merely meant state control of the economy.[62] Soviet promotion of industrialization policies was now qualified by the need to take into account the size of the domestic market and the international division of labor.[63] Meanwhile, the Soviets held a series of ideological seminars on "Problems of the Development of Revolution and the Struggle for Socialism in Liberated Countries" in Cairo, Algiers, and Baku in 1966–67.[64] Confronting instability in the developing world, Soviet scholars had come full circle in acceding to the Leninist position that political and ideological control, in the form of a centralized party structure, could compensate for economic concessions while economics alone was not enough to assure the success of revolution.

Soviet analysis of the Cultural Revolution would go a long way toward confirming this position. By late 1967, the earlier confusion in which the Kremlin saw events in China as reflecting an internal battle for leadership that they hoped the "true Marxists-Leninists" would win had disappeared in favor of deeper attempts to understand the social, political, and economic processes underlying the Cultural Revolution. The main theoretical organ of the CPSU, *Kommunist*, ran an almost monthly series of articles on China throughout 1968 in response to a barrage of requests by readers, and then it ran a similar series in 1969 after the military clash between the PRC and USSR on the Ussuri River in March of that year. Now Soviet analysts saw events in China not merely as the idiosyncratic distortions of one particular country with a megalomaniacal leader, but rather as a potentially troubling vision of the dangers that faced all developing countries if their revolutionary trajectories were thrown off-track. Fedor Burlatskii, in an early work on the subject titled "Maoism or Marxism," delineated four criteria that identified countries vulnerable to Maoism: a backward economy, an overwhelmingly peasant population, a heavy threat of imperialist and nationalist prejudice, and the lack of a hardened proletarian party and leadership.[65] Rostislav Ul'ianovskii, an official of the International Department, wrote that nationalism led countries to "absolutize" their experience, as seen in the "Sinicization" of Marxism, which led them to heretical versions of socialism. These deviations could be prevented by circumscribing nationalism, not trying to achieve economic transformation too quickly, and, most importantly, tying local movements to the world workers' movement led by Moscow.[66] The connection between Maoism and nationalism, seen as a particular danger for countries that had only just recently liberated themselves on the back of nationalist movements, was emphasized by the director of the Institute of Marxism-Leninism P. N. Fedoseev at a Communist Party plenum in June 1969.[67]

Clearly, an ideological heresy that was characteristic of underdeveloped, predominantly agrarian countries with strong nationalist sentiments was a significant danger to Soviet ambitions to spread its ideology in the developing world. Furthermore, the excesses of the Cultural Revolution did not merely discredit the PRC but, as evidence gleaned from the world press demonstrated, the idea of socialism as a whole. Brezhnev called the Cultural Revolution the greatest propaganda victory the imperialists had ever had.[68] Given the fact that Chinese foreign policy was nearly paralyzed by the chaos of the Cultural Revolution, this meant that the

Soviet struggle on an international scale had largely ceased to be against Beijing so much as against Maoism. As a result, rather than diplomacy and aid, ideological propaganda would have to take center stage. To this end, Moscow invited representatives of the International Departments of all members of the Warsaw Pact, with Romania replaced by Mongolia, to meet in Moscow in December 1967 to coordinate their respective anti-China propaganda efforts in the founding meeting of what came to be known as *Interkit,* or the "International on China."[69] The meetings would continue on a nearly annual basis at least through the 1970s.

The increased emphasis on ideology and construction of proper socialist parties did not, however, mean the complete neglect of economics. Given both the content and the form of Marxist thought, the complete isolation of ideology from economics would have been a contradiction in terms. In fact, the Soviets held a series of seminars for underdeveloped countries on economic development between 1967 and 1972 in Baku, Alma-Ata, Frunze, and Tashkent. Rather, it was the focus of economic policy that changed. The reasons for the change were perhaps best explained by the deputy director of the Institute of Africa, Starushenko, at a meeting of the entire SCSCAA *aktiv* in February 1969: "Our work lacks ideological ignition, ideological potential. . . . And now, when the struggle on the international stage has intensified, and especially it has intensified in developing countries, it is necessary to give answers to the most pressing questions that move society. We are often forced to ascertain that in these or those Asian or African countries our ideological opponents are operating successfully—the representatives of imperialist propaganda and the representatives of the left-dogmatic worldview."[70] In addition to its ineffectiveness, Starushenko argued that previous Soviet aid policy was too costly: "We put forth the idea of the noncapitalist path of development. It is completely obvious that this idea in its old version when the socialist states and the Soviet Union took upon themselves the burden of the construction of socialism—now we cannot take upon ourselves such a burden." Instead, he argued that the solution lay in moderating recommendations for "sudden, total nationalization" in favor of encouraging "private initiative" and "foreign aid." The new Soviet aid policy then would be more pragmatic in seeking cheaper ways to encourage economic growth, no longer offering to shoulder the burden of large-scale state-led industrialization.

Thus, the late 1960s saw the USSR, for reasons that included the dangers of uncontrolled anti-imperialism, weak, unstable allies, the ideological threat of Maoism, and domestic economic considerations, shift even farther away from its earlier model of the "state of national democracy." The new Soviet policy put ideology and politics first, seeking to build strong Marxist-Leninist parties that would be less vulnerable to the political danger of military coups and the ideological temptations of Maoism. The danger of nationalism, which lay at the bottom of Soviet concerns, would be combated with internationalism, which meant loyalty to Moscow's line. Economic policy, however, would be characterized by greater flexibility, something that Moscow could afford given stronger Soviet influence over political and military policy and which would also reduce the aid burden on the Soviet Union.

Hanoi between Moscow and Beijing

The exception to the Chinese disengagement from foreign affairs during the Cultural Revolution was the war in Indochina. Needless to say, it was not a trivial exception. During the second half of the 1960s, the Vietnam War brought the struggles between communism and capitalism in the developing world, as well as the "national liberation movement," into the immediate consciousness of people around the world in a way that Congo, Palestine, or Angola did not. Consequently, the competition between Moscow and Beijing for influence in Hanoi itself as well as on the world stage to be seen as Hanoi's primary patron heated up during this period. The two objectives were not distinct; influencing the policy of Hanoi, because of its visibility and symbolic importance, was seen as a key way to promote each side's model of struggle. The situation for both the Soviets and the Chinese was further complicated by the direct involvement of the United States. As Sino-Soviet bilateral relations deteriorated to the point where each side began to perceive a potential security threat from the other, both leaderships also began to view developments in Vietnam through the prism of their own relationships with the United States, as well as that of their opponent. Despite the massive increase in Soviet aid in 1964–65 under the new Kremlin leadership, the Soviets found Chinese influence in Hanoi very difficult to dislodge. Nevertheless, during the late 1960s a number of factors, including shifting aid balances, strategic transformations, leadership changes, and the negative effect of the Cultural Revolution on the Vietnamese perception of China, led Hanoi to move slowly but surely closer to Moscow.

The ties that had been forged between Beijing and Hanoi were not easily severed by the Soviets. Ho Chi Minh and other Vietnamese leaders had spent their formative years in contact with many Chinese leaders, both as students in Paris and during the early years of the CCP struggle in the 1920s. China had been Hanoi's sole provider of aid, as well as its strategic adviser, during the war against the French, and Chinese influence had been predominant during the early years of constructing socialism after the first Geneva conference. The Soviets were latecomers to the game, and they knew it. A December 1965 report by the Soviet embassy in Hanoi complained about the significant Chinese influence over domestic and foreign DRV policy, as well as nearly uniform DRV support for Chinese positions. Given the categorical Chinese opposition to the peace negotiations that the Soviets were trying to promote, the embassy ruefully wrote that "the danger of such presentations by the Chinese side is that it constrains the actions of the Vietnamese, reinforces their inflexible positions in relation to the use of political means of struggle in the international arena and in practice means the tying of the Vietnamese side to the Chinese line."[71] As the quote indicates, the Soviet embassy was aware of the fact that the predominant view in the DRV leadership itself was against negotiations at this time; it was not solely the doing of the Chinese. In any case, the lack of traction provided by Soviet aid frustrated Moscow. A Vietnamese journalist, talking to *Izvestiia* correspondent Mikhail Il'inskii, said, "What is the Soviet Union's share in total assistance, received by Vietnam, and what is the share of Soviet political influence there (if the latter can be measured in percent)? The respective figures are: 75–80 percent and 4–5 percent."[72] Il'inskii remarked in his report to the Central Committee that while these figures might be exaggerated, they were basically correct.

Moscow was also well aware of just how crucial Vietnam was to the Chinese, especially given their current circumstances. In January 1966, the Soviet embassy in Beijing reported that "the great misfortunes of Chinese foreign policy in Asia and Africa necessitate that the Chinese leaders now concentrate their efforts ever more first of all on Vietnam and the other countries of Indochina, which in this way, take on for the Chinese a special significance since the defeat of Chinese policy in the region after the failure in Indonesia would mean the most complete bankruptcy of the special Chinese course and the ideas of Mao Zedongism."[73] The Chinese, therefore sought to present the war in Vietnam as the focus of the entire global struggle against imperialism. At a banquet in honor of a visiting delegation from Mauritania in February 1967, Chen Yi declared: "Now in the entire world, a great bitter battle rages between the forces of revolution and counterrevolution, and the focus of this battle is the war of the Vietnamese people against American imperialism for the salvation of their homeland."[74] More problematic for Moscow was the fact that this was also a point of convergence between Beijing and Hanoi. North Vietnamese diplomats and the North Vietnamese press essentially told a global audience that "your position on Vietnam is your position on imperialism."[75]

Given the convergence between Hanoi and Beijing on a view of the conflict and a strategy inimical to Moscow's desires as well as the difficulty the Soviets had in edging their way into the discussion, one might reasonably ask why they chose the path of direct competition with the Chinese to be Hanoi's revolutionary patron. There was an alternative. The hard-line North Vietnamese position was not nearly as popular in the developing world as Hanoi or Beijing would have had people believe. Many saw the DRV's position as dangerously provocative, foolish in its confrontation with an American army that many doubted could be defeated, and one that contained the possibility of igniting a global conflagration. A report by the Soviet embassy in Hanoi on DRV relations with Africa detailed the ambivalent reactions to Hanoi's policies.[76] According to the report, even left-leaning African governments refused to express support for the DRV's four points or the NLF's five points. In June 1965, a DRV delegation with the task of gaining support in Africa was able to visit only the UAR, Guinea, and Mali because no other invitations were proffered. The African leaders, according to the report, "were frightened off by the sharp political and anti-American direction of the position of the DRV."[77] Nasser, Nkrumah, and Ben Bella were only three of the Afro-Asian heavyweights who tried to offer themselves as mediators in peace negotiations. The Soviets themselves were certainly very interested in a peaceful solution to the conflict in order to prevent the deterioration of their relations with the United States.[78] Furthermore, they understood that the Chinese wanted to exacerbate the conflict specifically in order to cause a U.S.-Soviet confrontation that conjured images of the ultimate Soviet nightmare during this period, namely a Sino-American rapprochement.[79] They knew as well that not all DRV officials agreed with the confrontational policies adopted by the leadership with Chinese support. An October 1965 report from the Soviet military attaché in Hanoi to the Central Committee detailed the dissatisfaction on the part of some DRV military officers with the leadership "which, to please the Chinese, conducts a policy which does not reflect the national interests of the Vietnamese people."[80] On top of everything, Moscow was simply not as sanguine as other socialist countries regarding Hanoi's chances of defeating the United States.[81] Given the tremendous risks and meager rewards, along with the existence of a practical alternative, Moscow's policy choice to support the DRV's war cannot be taken for granted.

Nevertheless, support the war it did, with increasing rhetorical belligerence and massive aid. The Soviet leadership even began to adopt public positions very close to those of the DRV and PRC. Brezhnev declared that "relations to the unity of action in the face of the imperialist assault on Vietnam serve today as the decisive criterion of international responsibility and devotion to the ideals of progress and revolution."[82] The phrase "unity of action" was meant as an attack on the Chinese, who continually rejected Soviet proposals to develop a united plan of action in support of Vietnam. In other words, the Soviet leadership, rather than taking the position of peacemaker and mediator for the reasons outlined above, chose publicly to attempt instead to outflank the Chinese from the left by accusing them of being insufficiently supportive. The logic of Soviet anti-imperialism dictated that it was much more dangerous for the position of the USSR in the world to be seen to be insufficiently revolutionary than excessively revolutionary, since its political and ideological appeal rested on being seen as the center of world revolution. Therefore, once again, the Soviets found themselves supporting a war that threatened their interests. Even worse, the need of the Soviets to be seen as anti-imperialist reduced their leverage over Hanoi, since the North Vietnamese could always threaten to publicly praise Chinese aid more than Soviet aid, with the attendant problems that doing so would entail for the desired Soviet image. Consequently, even when Moscow thought it could possibly exert enough pressure on Hanoi to get it to agree to negotiations, it demurred, for fear of losing influence to Beijing.[83]

As a result, Soviet aid poured into the DRV in ever-increasing amounts. Though starting from a position far below the Chinese, Soviet aid to the DRV reportedly exceeded that of the Chinese by 1968, accounting for half of all socialist aid.[84] Chinese aid remained very significant, however, and its impact was magnified by the fact that between 1965 and 1968 more than 320,000 Chinese troops served in the DRV, primarily in air defense, engineering, construction, minesweeping, and logistical units.[85]

Soviet personnel did not arrive on a similar scale, and the presence of so many Chinese could not but affect the impressions of Vietnamese on the ground. Since Soviet aid had to be transported by rail through China, it required the cooperation of the Chinese, which, given the state of Sino-Soviet relations and the chaos in the country during the Cultural Revolution, was bound to be a source of trouble. The Soviets continually accused the Chinese of delaying or stealing shipments of weapons, while the Chinese in turn argued that they were transporting everything, for free no less, and that the Soviets were merely using transport issues as an excuse for the insufficiency of their aid. Hanoi tried to find a middle position by praising Soviet aid but refusing to publicly mention transportation issues. Instead, the DRV press criticized "rumors" in the Western press about the Chinese delaying shipments and stealing arms, which led the frustrated Soviets to ask the North Vietnamese where they thought such rumors might originate.[86] Behind closed doors, however, the North Vietnamese were becoming ever more frustrated with Chinese transport issues, and Pham Van Dong expressed this sentiment on a visit to Beijing in April 1967.[87] When Beijing suggested that if the Soviets were dissatisfied they could try shipping aid instead, the Soviets took this as an attempt by the Chinese to ignite a Soviet-American conflict on the high seas.[88]

As time went on, however, rifts began to emerge between Hanoi and Beijing, and the position of Moscow grew ever stronger. One of the early fruits borne by Soviet aid was the attendance of a DRV delegation at the Twenty-Third CPSU Congress in 1966. Liu Shaoqi and Deng Xiaoping, in meetings with the North Vietnamese on their way to and from Moscow, told them that "if you are consistent revolutionaries and firm Marxist-Leninists, then you must politically and organizationally detach yourselves from the CPSU, view it as an enemy, a renegade from Marxism-Leninism, and conduct struggle against it."[89] Deng even threatened to withdraw Chinese troops from the DRV.[90] The Vietnamese in turn explained that they depended on the Soviets for aid, and, consequently, they could not afford not to attend. In the words of Le Duan, "You are saying that the Soviets are selling out Vietnam, but we don't say so."[91] The Cultural Revolution would have the effect of significantly accelerating the process of Hanoi's shift from Beijing to Moscow, partly because of the further radicalization of the Chinese position and partly because of the reaction in the DRV to the Cultural Revolution. As early as June 1966, some Vietnamese intellectuals were worried about the possibility of a Cultural Revolution in the DRV and they asked the VWP for clarification on its policy. The VWP answered that "the Cultural Revolution is an internal matter of the Chinese comrades. The situation in the DRV is different from the situation in China, the class struggle in Vietnam has other forms which differ from the Chinese. The struggle with American aggression for the salvation and unification of the motherland demands the maximal unity of all, including intellectual, forces of the Vietnamese people."[92] As the Cultural Revolution progressed, Hanoi's reaction became ever more negative. The DRV ordered the return of its 4,000 students from the PRC to avoid their participation in the Cultural Revolution.[93] In September, the VWP distributed a document among party cadres saying "one should not support the ideas of the Cultural Revolution; however, it is not necessary to loudly proclaim our disagreement with these ideas."[94] As that directive indicated, pressure from the Chinese for the Vietnamese to support the Cultural Revolution was intense. The PRC's chargé in Hanoi told the DRV foreign minister that the Cultural Revolution had the same significance for the PRC as the armed struggle for the DRV, and consequently Vietnamese support was required.[95] Publicly, Chinese pressure produced results, and the seventeenth anniversary celebration of the PRC led to the first public DRV mention of the Cultural Revolution; however, privately, Chinese pressure for support only frightened and angered Hanoi.[96] The Soviet embassy took notice, reporting in March 1967 that "currently the process of improvement of relations between the CPSU and VWP continues, as well as the weakening of the influence of the CCP, which is enabled to no small degree by the so-called Cultural Revolution in China."[97]

Ultimately, the shift of influence from Beijing to Moscow made itself felt in the North Vietnamese conduct of the war. Beginning in August 1966, Chinese pressure on Hanoi to avoid negotiations became ever stronger, while the North Vietnamese, in turn, became ever more doubtful of the wisdom of the Chinese approach, especially because of their doubts of whose interests it was meant to serve.[98] In mid- to late 1967, this attitude resulted in a North Vietnamese decision to launch a massive offensive in early 1968 contrary to Chinese demands to avoid large-scale warfare.[99] At the same time, the VWP conducted a purge known as the "Revisionist Anti-Party Affair" that included well-known generals on the staff of Vo Nguyen Giap, who was thought to be pro-Moscow himself, in part to allay Chinese fears that the offensive would signal a tilt toward Moscow.[100] The following spring, however, the direction of Hanoi's policy became clearer. The DRV agreed to Johnson's offer of peace negotiation on April 3, 1968, without consulting the Chinese, who furiously and absurdly accused the Vietnamese of thereby contributing somehow to the death of Martin Luther King Jr. the following day.[101] A shift in the leadership seems also to have played a part in the Vietnamese decision. Ho Chi Minh was in Beijing at the time receiving medical treatment, and when Zhou Enlai asked him about the decision to negotiate, it became apparent that Ho had not been consulted.[102] In 1968, as negotiations began, Chinese troops began leaving the DRV, and they had all left by the end of 1970.[103] While Soviet influence began to predominate over Chinese, Hanoi still tried to keep Beijing in the picture in order to maintain its strategic independence from Moscow.

By 1968 then, the Soviets had largely achieved their objective of gaining influence over Hanoi and diminishing Chinese influence. This was due, partly, to their own increased aid and, partly, to the Cultural Revolution and Hanoi's discomfort with Chinese pressure. It is not clear, however, to what degree Moscow achieved its larger goals. The growth of Soviet influence in Hanoi did not necessarily reestablish Moscow as the leader of the world revolution. Publicly Hanoi made sure that China remained very much in the picture. In addition, Moscow seemed to be a reluctant follower of Hanoi's policy, an example of the tail wagging the dog, rather than the vanguard of the world revolution. Soviet anti-imperialism was making burdensome claims on Soviet policy and resources without necessarily producing benefits for Moscow.

Cue the Students

In the late 1960s, the Sino-Soviet split, and particularly the struggle for influence in Vietnam, found a new audience: the student movement in the West. Though there had been student protests earlier in the decade, it was not until late 1967 and early 1968 that Moscow and Beijing really began to take notice.[104] Once they finally did so, however, they were confronted with an unexpected puzzle. Marxist theory had always predicted a revolution in the industrialized countries and now, suddenly, millions were marching in the streets. However, for the most part they were not workers and neither were they led by their local Communist Parties. Nor were the slogans of "free love" or "turn on, tune in, drop out" reflective of the kind of revolution that leaders in either Moscow or Beijing had in mind. Compounding the problem were the difficulties both the Soviets and the Chinese were having with their own youth at the time.[105]

The Kremlin worried that Soviet youth were becoming increasingly dis-
affected and disenchanted with Communist ideology while Mao and
others were desperately trying to stuff the youth genie back in the bottle
by putting the People's Liberation Army (PLA) in charge of the Cultural
Revolution. Nevertheless, both leaderships decided to try to appeal to
the students in the West, viewing them selectively as authentic revolutionary forces. This attempt to appeal to the students in the West added
further motivation to their efforts to be seen as Hanoi's patron since the
Vietnam War seemed to be the primary galvanizing issue. This was especially true for the Soviets, who were worried that, despite the damage
the Cultural Revolution had done to China's influence in the developing
world, the appeal of Beijing in the developed world was proving far
stronger than that of Moscow.

The Kremlin had actually tried to encourage opposition to the American effort in Vietnam well before the peak of the student protests. As early
as May 1965, a draft resolution had been submitted to the CPSU Central
Committee with the goal of igniting a worldwide campaign against American involvement in Vietnam, charging the KGB to "take measures for the
organization through its channels of presentations by visible political and
social activists of foreign countries, including in the press, which will enable the mobilization of wide social circles for active demonstrations
against the aggressive policy of Johnson."[106] However, little mention was
made of anti–Vietnam War protests in the West in either the Soviet press
or speeches at Party plenums for the next two and a half years. By the beginning of 1968, the Kremlin had begun to take notice. In March, Brezhnev
gave a speech at a Moscow Communist Party conference in which he discussed the source of youth rebellion in the West, attributing it to the accelerating crisis of capitalism.[107] The following month the Institute of the
United States and Canada submitted a report to the Politburo on relations
with Washington discussing widespread domestic opposition to American foreign policy.[108] In a speech at a Communist Party plenum the very
same month, Brezhnev spoke about the unrest in the United States, asserting that now American society was nearly split on the question of
the war with the Soviets supporting the "democratic forces" against the
war. He declared that Soviet propaganda should make sure that the
whole world could hear the voice of that Soviet support.[109]

Embracing the students in the West as comrades-in-arms, however,
was problematic given their class identities, cultural behaviors, and ideological predilections. The Soviet press solved this dilemma by presenting

a sanitized version of the students that could fit within the Marxist-Leninist schema. Contrary to the picture often presented in the American media of privileged youth on college campuses protesting a war being fought by their lower-class contemporaries who, by and large, supported it, the Soviet press presented the students as a group made up predominantly of the children of the petite bourgeoisie as well as one characterized as intrinsically oppressed due to the economic difficulties of being a student and the tightening job market that they faced.[110] Politically, while the students might be somewhat naive, the great mass of them were "essentially progressive, democratic, and just."[111] Furthermore, while student dissatisfaction with the capitalist system could be taken at face value, critiques of communism were dismissed as the products of ignorance and exposure to years of capitalist propaganda.[112] Third World liberation struggles, and the Vietnam War in particular, held a special appeal for these students because of the "connection between the unquenchable thirst for freedom for their own social group, their own country, and the understanding of the universal significance of the liberation struggle of other social groups, other peoples, even in the farthest ends of the earth."[113] Vietnam was therefore the easiest way for Moscow to connect with the youth in revolt in the capitalist world.

In addition to the desire to improve its global image, the Kremlin's attempt to connect with Western youth through the Vietnam War might have had another objective: appeal to Soviet youth. A KGB report of November 1968 described the pervasive political apathy and cynicism of Soviet students, who were disillusioned with the Communist Party and had even lost faith in the ability of Marxism to "predict the future course of events."[114] What did excite Soviet youth according to the report, however, was copying their Western counterparts. Long hair, rock and roll, and even whatever they could manage in terms of narcotic and sexual experimentation filled minds that should have been occupied with thoughts of Lenin. By late 1968, the situation had become particularly serious, as the Soviet leadership had seen up close what could happen with youth in a socialist country in the Prague Spring. Most ominously, the KGB report quoted one student in saying, regarding events in Czechoslovakia, "I wonder, could something similar happen here? I would personally participate."[115] Perhaps the Soviet leadership hoped that changing the prevailing view of the USSR among youth in the West would help change the views of their Soviet counterparts who tried to imitate them.

A significant problem for the Soviet leadership, however, was what seemed to be the much greater appeal of Mao and China in the West, particularly the high visibility of Maoist student groups in the Paris uprising of May 1968. While Beijing had paid little attention to the protests and demonstrations before Paris, Chinese reports claimed that on May 21, more than half a million "workers, Red Guards, revolutionary teachers, students, and cadres" demonstrated in Beijing in support of the "progressive student movement in Europe and North America."[116] The demonstrations continued, encompassing a reported 20 million people from May 21 through May 26.[117] The Chinese press attributed the revolutionary upheavals to the dissemination of the thought of Mao Zedong around the world.[118] Though these claims were certainly exaggerated, the chairman of the Committee on Press under the Council of Ministers wrote to the Central Committee in early 1969 calling for the urgent need to produce more anti-Chinese propaganda for export, given the success of Chinese propaganda in Europe and the United States.[119] The second Interkit meeting, held in East Berlin in January 1969, paid particular attention to the appeal of China in the West. According to the report presented at the meeting, "The facts of the recent period have shown that the student movement, in which anarchist, Trotskyite, and other ultra-left voices (*Stimmungen*) have found a significant audience, can be used by Beijing as a favorable means for the expansion of its influence."[120] China had already called for a conference of pro-Chinese youth to be held in Albania later in the year, and the concern was that the Chinese were preparing a major offensive to undermine the established pro-Soviet Communist Parties in Europe.[121] Given the way in which the French Communist Party, one of the largest and most loyal on the European continent, had found itself marginalized in May 1968 by the radical left, such a threat must have seemed all too real indeed.

In 1968–69 then, the youth movements in the West served as another focus of Sino-Soviet conflict. The 1969 Moscow meeting of the international communist movement officially recognized the youth of bourgeois societies as the major new variable in the revolutionary equation, and the assembled Communist Parties agreed to set the objective of "winning it over (*zavoevat'*) for the side of Marxist-Leninist ideology."[122] Their major opponents were the various leftist alternatives running the gamut from Mao to Marcuse.[123] The centrality of the Vietnam War to the various youth movements therefore made it a key vehicle for the conduct of this battle for the allegiance of Western youth. The student unrest in the West unquestionably raised the stakes for the battle between Moscow and Beijing to be seen as the liberator of the world's oppressed peoples, and no people was perceived to be under greater assault from imperialism at this time than the Vietnamese. More broadly, the youth movements had destabilized the political calculus that underlay the Soviet policy of peaceful coexistence. With the weakening of the political fortunes of the major Western Communist Parties in favor of radical student groups, promoting the popularity of the Soviet Union and socialist revolution required more, not less, militancy.

Moscow Declares Victory, but the Game Changes Again

While China's stock was on the rise in the West, however, the red sun of Mao was in eclipse almost everywhere else. China's diplomatic isolation was underlined in late 1968 when Havana and Hanoi, despite heavy pressure from Beijing, publicly supported the Warsaw Pact invasion of Czechoslovakia, thereby officially signaling their return to the Soviet orbit. The Soviet leadership, therefore, saw this as an excellent opportunity to consolidate its victory. In 1969, the CPSU finally managed to hold the meeting of the international communist movement that it had been trying to organize since 1964. Before that, however, the Soviets would take the lead in organizing two conferences in Africa. These conferences would end up demonstrating that dissatisfaction with Moscow remained, even without a strong Chinese alternative. Consequently, as the Chinese leadership, frightened domestically by a Cultural Revolution that threatened to spin out of control and internationally by a perception of direct military threat from the Soviet Union, began to reenter the international arena, it would find a surprisingly welcome reception.

In January 1969, under the auspices of the WPC in which China had ceased to participate by this time, two conferences were organized, one in Cairo for Arab issues and one in Khartoum for the African liberation movements. The Cairo conference brought together representatives from seventy-five countries and fifteen international organizations, but the Soviets were disappointed to find that the conference agenda was dominated by militant calls for armed struggle on behalf of the Palestinians.[124] The SCSCAA Presidium suggested that it was time to get serious about building ties to Palestinian organizations not just among the so-called nongovernmental organizations but through the Foreign Ministry as well.

The KGB would soon become heavily involved, recruiting the head of foreign operations of the Popular Front for the Liberation of Palestine (PFLP) Dr. Wadi Haddad as an agent in 1970.[125] Yasser Arafat would make his first official visit to Moscow in 1972, though he had visited earlier as part of Nasser's entourage in 1968.[126] The Khartoum conference was focused primarily on the liberation struggle in southern Africa. Each country in the region that was still under foreign or minority rule, Angola, Mozambique, Rhodesia, Southwest Africa, and South Africa, had at least two liberation movements of which one was more closely identified with Moscow and the other with Beijing, though the lines of actual contact and influence were not always so clearly defined. The Chinese-leaning movements were not invited to Khartoum and the goal was to designate each of the Soviet-supported movements as the sole legitimate representative of its nation. This Soviet agenda did not meet with the approval of several key African governments. The logical place to hold the conference would have been Dar es Salaam, the headquarters of the OAU Liberation Committee, but the Tanzanian government, which had close relations with Beijing, would not participate. The same was true for Zambia and Guinea, which, like Tanzania, were tied closely to the Chinese as well as with several of the liberation movements not invited to the conference.[127] A number of African states, including Tanzania, disapproved of the conference as opening the door to outside interference in African affairs. Consequently, the conference was something less than a complete victory for Moscow.

The 1969 Moscow meeting of the international communist movement, held in June, was very difficult to organize. Brezhnev's report on the meeting to a Communist Party plenum later in the month began with a litany of all the ideological problems that had dogged the communist movement throughout the decade: right and left "opportunism," questioning of the role of the working class and the dictatorship of the proletariat, and nationalist and isolationist tendencies.[128] The preparation of the meeting had taken years, and over one thousand amendments had been offered to the proposed documents.[129] The meeting had originally been called for November 1968, but many Communist Parties refused to participate in the wake of the invasion of Czechoslovakia. Nevertheless, in June 1969 representatives of seventy-five parties came to Moscow, which was fewer than the eighty-one that had attended the last meeting in 1960. Fourteen parties did not attend, including, most significantly, the Vietnamese and Koreans, although the Cubans did attend.

While no delegation tried to openly defend the Chinese, the meeting demonstrated just how much control the Kremlin had lost. At least seven parties openly criticized the invasion of Czechoslovakia.[130] A number of parties, primarily in Western Europe, approved only parts of the final document or added their own opinions. It was clear that the Western European parties had come to decide that their chances of political success did not lie along the road laid out by Moscow. They had been repulsed by Prague and frightened by Paris, and they knew that the unpopularity of the USSR meant that they themselves could soon be marginalized by the New Left. Led by the Italians, they called for opening the communist movement to all sorts of moderate leftist forces as well as putting forth a socialist model that would allow for the preservation of multiparty democracy. Brezhnev criticized the Italian Communist Party's "retreat from Marxist-Leninist principles to adapt to the positions and opinions of petit bourgeois strata among the Italian population in the hopes of increasing its influence in that strata."[131] The CPSU had come face to face with what would come to be called Eurocommunism, which would be a bane of Moscow's existence throughout the 1970s. Nevertheless, Brezhnev admitted that there was little the Soviet Union could do since the Chinese were attempting to attract anyone "we push away from ourselves," and with the Chinese "a serious front of struggle has been opened—it has been opened, judging by everything, for a long time."[132] The Moscow meeting had demonstrated that all the Kremlin's horses and all the Kremlin's men could not put the international communist movement together again, and even though the CPSU worked feverishly to convene a new international communist meeting until finally giving up in 1985, this would turn out to be the last one.[133] On one issue, however, the meeting showed that the world's Communist Parties could still reach agreement: the anti-imperialist struggle and particularly solidarity with Vietnam.[134]

In Beijing, the Chinese leadership began slowly to reemerge from its international isolation. On March 17, 1968, Mao issued an instruction for a "resolute and systematic reform in external propaganda." As the year progressed, he warned against attempts to impose Chinese ideology on foreigners, forbade the distribution of Mao badges abroad, and ordered that "from now on, such self-praising terms as 'Mao Zedong Thought' should be omitted from all documents and articles related to foreign affairs."[135] By June, the Institute of the Far East sent a report to the Soviet Foreign Ministry on the reactivization of Chinese policy in Africa, including a renewed diplomatic and aid offensive.[136] More than 3,000 Chinese specialists were already in Tanzania and Zambia to begin work on the railroad there, and Chinese relations with both countries became increasingly close, including other economic and military aid as well as increased arms to national liberation movements headquartered in Tanzania. President Nyerere visited Beijing shortly after the report was written. Chinese engagement was not limited to Tanzania and Zambia. In May 1968, China signed an agreement with Guinea and Mali to build a railroad to give Mali an outlet to the sea that would not pass through hostile Senegal. With the overthrow of Modibo Keita in November, however, that project never materialized.[137]

The invasion of Czechoslovakia, combined with the military clashes between the PRC and USSR over Damanskii/Zhenbao Island in the Ussuri River in March 1969, shifted Beijing's return to the international arena into high gear due to the increasing fear of Soviet attack. On April 1, the Ninth CCP Congress began with the goal of bringing order to the Cultural Revolution and possibly winding it down. Though the conference ultimately resulted in a prolongation of the Cultural Revolution, it was now to be conducted under the control of the People's Liberation Army (PLA), which was given the task of "purifying class ranks," and it began to look more like a traditional purge than the chaotic clashes of 1966–68. In June, a special group of four marshals, including Chen Yi, who had been tasked with evaluating the international situation and China's foreign policy, submitted a report on the possibility of war.[138] The conclusion that a Soviet attack was unlikely did little to dampen the growing war paranoia. By October it had reached fever pitch, and most of the leadership was evacuated from Beijing while the entire PLA was put on alert.[139] Fear of invasion made it imperative that China begin reestablishing contacts with other countries. In June, Zhou Enlai ordered the Foreign Ministry to begin the process of once again dispatching ambassadors abroad, beginning with France, Vietnam, and Albania.[140] Fifteen ambassadors were sent out before the end of the year, followed by another fourteen in 1970.[141] The most dramatic step taken by Beijing was, of course, the first tentative approaches to its sworn enemy in Washington, where Richard Nixon, who had made his desire to reengage with the PRC known, was now in power. The Sino-American rapprochement would have tremendous implications for China's relations with the developing world and its anti-imperialist position, which will be discussed in the next chapter.

The course of events in the late 1960s demonstrated just how little the Soviet Union had gained from its diplomatic triumph over the PRC in the wake of the latter's descent into domestic chaos and international isolation. Moscow's adoption of anti-imperialism as a policy had proven to be very troublesome and created problems for Moscow in Latin America, the Middle East, and Indochina. To a significant degree the results of the anti-imperialist policy confirmed in retrospect the wisdom of the policy of peaceful coexistence from the Soviet perspective, but it was difficult to go back now without completely abandoning Moscow's revolutionary pretensions. Meanwhile the eruption of revolutionary unrest in the industrialized West, the dream of Soviet leaders since Lenin, Trotsky, and the Bolsheviks had taken power in 1917, turned into a cruel joke as Western youth preferred Mao Zedong, Ho Chi Minh, Che Guevara— almost anyone—to what the Kremlin had on offer. Instead, the youth revolt led only to the abandonment of the Soviet line by the Western European Communist Parties, confirming that the shattering of communist unity was now permanent.

The Soviet response to these developments was to seek greater political and ideological control over its allies in the developing world. This way Moscow could hopefully be rhetorically belligerent without having to worry about thereby finding itself involved in undesired wars. Soviet involvement in the developing world did not decrease as a result of the disappointing results of its policy in the late 1960s. On the contrary, the 1970s would see even more resources devoted to Asia, Africa, and Latin America than had been proffered in the 1960s. After all, Soviet prospects in the West were in some ways bleaker than ever. However, large numbers of Soviet military and political advisers would now accompany the economic experts and, in some cases, they would come instead. These advisers would pay much more attention to political organization and ideological orthodoxy, and they would focus on building parties and armies rather than dams and factories. In other words: more guns, less butter.

The Chinese, however, would emerge from the Cultural Revolution surprisingly unscathed internationally, especially given that their most recent isolation had occurred largely through a seemingly concerted effort to offend as many governments as possible in the shortest amount of time. In part, this development reflected dissatisfaction in the developing world with both of the superpowers, which would lead to a new "Third World"-ist movement in the 1970s that China would once again try to turn into its own constituency. Meanwhile, the Sino-Soviet split increasingly took on the trappings of a more conventional bilateral security issue. The Soviets, however, redoubled their efforts to fight Maoism around the world. While the Chinese had labeled the Kremlin's policies after October 1964 "Khrushchevism without Khrushchev," the Soviets would increasingly be fighting "Maoism without Mao" due to the remaining influence of Chinese ideology around the world despite the new course of the Chinese leadership and even though Mao was still alive and very much in power (though they would not use the term themselves until Mao died in 1976). Soviet diplomats, experts, journalists, and scholars would chase the ghost of Maoism around the globe in the 1970s.

CHAPTER FIVE

"Three Worlds" versus the Three "D"s
Détente, Development, and Disarmament, 1970–1976

As the 1970s dawned, the Soviet position in the world, though perhaps not ideal from the perspective of the Kremlin, had at least reached a comfortable and seemingly stable plateau. The 1969 Moscow conference of the world's Communist Parties had certainly not brought back the glory days of the Comintern, and new fissures with the Western Europeans had become evident, but, nevertheless, the event demonstrated that very little support for the Chinese remained within the international communist movement. The new equilibrium in the international communist movement was clear during the preparatory meetings, during which a number of Communist Parties objected to the very notion of trying to work out a united ideological platform. As the Italian Communist leader Enrico Berlinguer declared, "We have decided that its [the conference's] task is not the discussion and approval of a common ideological platform, but rather unification in the struggle against imperialism." Karen Brutents observed that at the two previous international communist meetings in 1957 and 1960, the notion that a common ideological platform would be adopted was never even brought into question.[1] Essentially the Communist Parties had now decided to agree to disagree, and the struggle against imperialism, in Vietnam and elsewhere, had now replaced any clear-cut notion of the struggle against capitalism in their own countries as their core, shared precept.

In this struggle against imperialism, the Soviets had by 1970 managed to allay many of the doubts of the 1960s about their willingness to confront the West and support armed struggle. Ever-increasing Soviet aid to Hanoi contrasted with diminishing Chinese aid. Chinese aid to the DRV in 1970 was lower than at any point since American marines had arrived in Da Nang in 1965, and all Chinese troops had left the country by the end of the year.[2] In the Middle East, Moscow's support for the Arab struggle against Israel had never looked more solid. In early 1970, the Soviets sharply increased their aid to Egypt during the War of Attrition and Soviet missile units landed in broad daylight and paraded down the main streets, while Soviet pilots flew missions over the Suez Canal talking in Russian over their radios. Israel was consequently deterred from bombing Egypt, and some frantic superpower diplomacy soon produced a ceasefire reluctantly accepted by both Nasser and the Israeli leadership.[3] Moscow had, at least temporarily, achieved both of its objectives: it had flexed its military muscles in support of anti-imperialism and, by doing so, it had avoided open conflict with the United States and achieved a more peaceful situation, albeit one that would prove difficult to maintain.

Contributing to Moscow's sense of stability at the start of the decade was the new man in charge in Washington. Though the Soviets were somewhat nervous about the election of Richard Nixon because of his anticommunist reputation, and they had even taken the step of offering Hubert Humphrey "any conceivable help," including financial aid, during the campaign, they soon discovered that they could work with the Nixon administration.[4] By the end of 1969, SALT negotiations had been restarted, new channels of communication between the White House and the Kremlin had been opened, and Brezhnev declared at a Communist Party plenum in December that Nixon was very amenable to negotiations and compromise.[5] Now that Moscow had seemingly repulsed the Chinese challenge and reaffirmed its anti-imperialist credentials, it could return to its policy of peaceful coexistence, in the form of détente.

However, while the view from Moscow was promising, if not actually rosy, at the start of the 1970s, it was decidedly less so from the developing world. Whereas the 1960s had been the decade of hope, the 1970s were to be the decade of discontent. According to UN statistics, 44.6 billion dollars in aid had been provided by Western countries from 1959 through 1967, with nearly another 10 billion dollars from the socialist world.[6] This aid had come in the context of all sorts of development schemes from the "noncapitalist path" to the Union for Progress during the first United Nations Development decade, but it had yielded little actual development. Average annual per capita GDP growth in Sub-Saharan Africa was 1.3 percent over the decade, starting from a very low base. Meanwhile, the agricultural situation was even worse. Food production in Africa grew 2 percent annually in the 1960s, while population grew by 2.5 percent.[7] This reality was compounded by a prolonged drought in the

Sahel region from 1968 to 1973. In retrospect, the 1960s would turn out to be independent Africa's best decade in the twentieth century. At the time, though, the rate of growth was far from matching the millennial hopes that had accompanied the continent's emergence from colonialism. Compounding the problem was the fact that growth in the industrialized West had accelerated in the 1960s and so the gap between developing and developed countries was growing ever larger. As the so-called scientific-technological revolution took off in the West, average annual growth in labor productivity grew 3.8 percent annually from 1953 to 1967 in contrast to only 2.65 percent in developing countries, leading one Soviet author to admit that, perhaps, the colonial system was not as important to the economies of the capitalist countries as had previously been thought.[8]

As the extent of the developing world's economic problems became evident, a political shift began to occur as well, with the focus of the anti-imperialist struggle moving from issues of independence and armed conflict to the realm of international economic relations. The beginnings of the shift were evident at the Third Summit of the Non-Aligned Countries in Lusaka, Zambia, in 1970, where Julius Nyerere announced that "the real and urgent threat to the independence of almost all nonaligned states thus comes not from the military, but from the economic power of the big states." The summit went on to produce a set of economic resolutions known as the "Lusaka Declaration" based on the idea that "the poverty of developing nations and their economic dependence on those in affluent circumstances constitutes a structural weakness in the present economic order."[9] Increasingly, therefore, developing countries began to view development not as a matter of domestic reforms but rather as one of international injustice. As Raúl Prebisch, an Argentine economist and one of the originators of "dependency theory," remarked while resigning from his position as the first secretary-general of the United Nations Conference on Trade and Development (UNCTAD) in March 1969, "If we do not succeed in effective and vigorous economic development the alternatives are clear. The deteriorating situation in the have-not countries will demonstrate that the extremists are right. Black power, now merely a U.S. phenomenon, will become brown, yellow, and black power on a world scale."[10]

Enter the Chinese. Beijing had spent much of the 1960s painting the Soviet Union as a white, industrialized power that would inevitably betray the interests of the forces of revolution in the developing world for collusion with its fellow rich, white states. Now, the Soviets were pursuing détente with the Americans just as anger over economic injustice was bubbling over in the Third World. Though Moscow had successfully demonstrated its willingness to support armed struggle, the main battlefield of anti-imperialism was now shifting to the economic realm and from that perspective the Soviet Union looked more like part of the "Rich North" than the "Red East." China needed to rebuild its global standing in the wake of the most chaotic stage of the Cultural Revolution at a time when the Soviet threat to its security was viewed as more dangerous than ever, and it sought help in the Third World. The mantle of "Third World unity" in the struggle for economic justice against the "two superpowers" provided just the platform it needed, especially as rapprochement with the United States reduced its credibility somewhat in the most radical revolutionary circles. All that China still required to play this role was a diplomatic opening, one which arrived in October 1971 with the entry of the People's Republic of China (PRC) into the UN, following a vote in the General Assembly in which the rest of the world refused to maintain the diplomatic isolation of the PRC that the United States itself had now repudiated.

Once again, the Soviet Union found itself playing catch-up while trying to reestablish its revolutionary credentials in the eyes of the majority of the world's population. In the 1960s it had rebuffed the Chinese challenge only by adopting much of Chinese rhetoric and tactics. In the process the very terms of the revolutionary conversation had shifted from being about workers in industrialized capitalist societies controlling the mean of production to being about nationalism, racism, and anti-imperialism. Now the pattern would repeat itself to some degree as Moscow would reestablish its revolutionary superiority over Beijing, but not before it had shifted its own discussion about economic development from internal revolutionary transformation to global struggle against neocolonialism. The key for Moscow in this new battle was not to concede the division of the world into three parts, pitting a developing Third World against the two superpowers. Instead, Soviet efforts would focus on creating a "natural alliance" between the developing world and the socialist camp against the West. In the end the Soviets would win, thanks in large part to a series of self-serving Chinese foreign policy decisions, culminating in its association with the apartheid regime in South Africa on the Angolan issue in 1975–76 that significantly reduced China's standing in the Third World (which had been reluctant to adopt a new "leader" in any case). However, by this point, China seemed not to regret the loss, as domestic political changes had led Beijing to begin prioritizing economic growth over geopolitical standing

in 1976. The Soviets, having won the competition and reestablished themselves as the preeminent leaders of the world revolution, were once again
left with the responsibility for supporting that revolution around the
world and with the task of confronting the West face-to-face.

Peaceful Coexistence Redux: Soviet Policy in the Early 1970s

As discussed above, at the beginning of the 1970s, Moscow was in a more
stable position internationally than it had been since the Sino-Soviet
split in the early 1960s. Since certain Soviet interests, first and foremost
the desire to avoid a military conflict with the West and shift resources
from the arms race to the economy, persisted from that time, the Soviet
leadership saw the opportunity to resurrect certain elements of its policy
of a decade earlier. At the top of this list were the twin issues of peaceful
coexistence and disarmament. At the same time, a comparison with Soviet policies of the early 1960s also demonstrates how the geopolitical
terrain had shifted irrevocably in certain ways. Now the Soviets were
openly supplying large amounts of arms to their allies and clients in the
developing world, loudly supporting their various struggles. There was
no more talk of preventing local wars for fear that they would lead to
world war, as in the days of Khrushchev. The experience of Vietnam had
put an end to that. This time around, Moscow was meticulous about making sure to express support for armed anti-imperialist struggle whenever
it talked about peace, and it would prove to be especially sensitive to any
charges that its commitment to détente in any way compromised its military commitment to its allies and to the goal of revolution in the developing world more broadly.

On the economic front, Moscow had been too burned by the reverses
of the 1960s to return to a policy of large-scale economic aid, which had
been provided to a great number of states with little regard for their existing political and economic structures in the hopes that the aid itself
would serve as the catalyst for transformation. Instead, the Soviet leadership would focus its aid largely on what were now labeled countries of
"socialist orientation." This aid would also be heavily directed toward
constructing political and military institutions, in particular the creation of "vanguard parties." Soviet experts poured in to the countries of
"socialist orientation" in an attempt to inculcate and enforce ideological
orthodoxy. The emphasis on domestic policies and institutions in the
quest for development and especially the strong distinction drawn by

Soviet policy between countries of socialist orientation and the rest, who were presumably following some version of a capitalist path, contrasted sharply, however, with the promoters of dependency theory. The latter argued that the source of continuing underdevelopment was to be found in the unequal international economic system, and that all developing countries were fundamentally in the same boat.[11]

The Twenty-Fourth CPSU Congress, held in the spring of 1971, showcased a party that thought it had been victorious on the international stage and could now return to focus its efforts on building the economy at home. Immediately before the congress, while outlining the content of his foreign policy address to a Communist Party plenum, Brezhnev explained that the section on the "anti-imperialist struggle" would be short because of the considerable attention that had been devoted to the topic in recent years.[12] The domestic emphasis of the congress was evident even in Soviet journals devoted to foreign policy, where the primary international significance of the congress was declared to be the economic example set by the USSR.[13] When the issues facing the developing world were addressed at the conference, they were characterized as increasingly issues of internal political and socioeconomic transformation rather than international struggle against imperialism, with the obvious exceptions being Indochina, the Middle East, and southern Africa.[14] The congress outlined two key factors that distinguished countries of socialist orientation: close cooperation with the world socialist system and the unification of all "patriotic, anti-imperialist forces," in particular in the form of cooperation between communists and so-called national democrats.[15] According to Boris Ponomarev, it was this political cooperation between Communists and other progressives on a national scale, and between the world socialist system and states of socialist orientation on a global scale, that was the new element introduced into Soviet foreign policy by the conference. "Ties of this kind, established these days by many fraternal parties, actually represent a fundamentally new form of solidarity between the world communist movement and the forces of national liberation."[16] Soviet policy would now focus on more intense ties with a smaller number of key states that possessed a deeper institutional and ideological connection with the Kremlin.

There was one other major item on the international platform of the Twenty-Fourth Congress: peace. Brezhnev's keynote address introduced a six-point "peace program" which was immediately trumpeted in the Soviet press and became the basis for Soviet initiatives in the international sphere.[17] The program called for the rejection of the use of force as a means of settling international disputes, the signing of bilateral and regional peace pacts, the limitation by agreement and ultimately prohibition of all "weapons of mass destruction," the calling of a global disarmament conference, liquidation of foreign military bases, reduction of military budgets, and the development of peaceful international cooperation. Despite the utopian tone of the program, other points demonstrated what Moscow had learned about the anti-imperialist struggle during the 1960s, and what it had not yet learned: the program expressed unqualified support for the ongoing armed struggles in Indochina and the Middle East and condemnation of the imperialist aggressors as well as calling for the liquidation of apartheid and all remaining colonial and racist regimes. The program said nothing, however, about reforming the international economic order. Nevertheless, Moscow wasted little time in acting upon this program, calling for a disarmament conference of the five nuclear powers and delivering an invitation to the PRC on June 15, which was turned down.[18] The global propaganda side of the Soviet peace effort would culminate in October 1973 with the World Conference of Peace-Loving Forces in Moscow, which would coincide with what was, along with the Cuban Missile Crisis, perhaps the closest brush the world has had to date with nuclear war.

Such gestures as the peace program and the appeal for a world disarmament conference, however, were recognized by most international observers in the early 1970s as rather transparent propaganda efforts. Détente, though, was a different matter. From the Kremlin's perspective, détente represented a serious enough revision of the global Cold War order that, as the Watergate scandal progressed, it presented a much more persuasive explanation for events than some third-rate burglary. Addressing a Communist Party plenum in December 1973, Brezhnev remarked, "It is clear that the situation which has come about as a result of the so-called Watergate affair . . . those who are attempting in any way to use it are those who are dissatisfied with the foreign policy course, which Nixon has been conducting, especially in relations with the USSR."[19] Interestingly, this seemed to be one of the few topics on which Moscow and Beijing agreed at the time, as evidenced by remarks made by a Chinese delegation to Nicolae Ceauşescu in the aftermath of Nixon's resignation.[20] Therefore, it was no surprise that as one agreement followed another between the United States and the Soviet Union and as Nixon and Brezhnev began to make summits an annual event, Soviet allies in the developing world had reason to be concerned about what consequences détente might hold for them.

Moscow attempted to allay these fears at an early stage of détente by signing an unprecedented series of "friendship treaties" with its key allies in the developing world in 1971–72. The most important of these treaties were the ones signed with Egypt and India, the two main bulwarks of Soviet support throughout the 1960s. The death of Nasser in September 1970, with whom the Soviet leadership had long cultivated a close personal relationship, significantly destabilized the bilateral relationship as the new president, Anwar Al-Sadat, made noises about reducing Soviet influence and subsequently removed the pro-Soviet head of the Arab Socialist Union, Ali Sabri, on May 2, 1971. The subsequent friendship treaty, which Brezhnev labeled a document "of a new type" between socialist and "young nationalist" states, was signed on May 27 after a high-level Soviet delegation, including Podgornyi, Ponomarev, and Gromyko, flew to Cairo to rescue the relationship.[21] Nevertheless, Sadat's international ambitions, as well as his fear of being sold out in the name of détente, remained, and he warned the Soviets before Nixon's first trip to Moscow in May 1972 not to accept any agreements relating to arms limitations or the Arab-Israeli conflict.[22] Soviet-Egyptian relations remained uneven at best until the October 1973 war, and although some recent scholarship has thrown doubt upon the standard narrative that Sadat expelled Soviet advisers in July 1972, Craig Daigle has argued in a recent, authoritative work that "Sadat's decision must be viewed as a direct consequence of detente."[23]

The friendship treaty with India proved to be far more successful. Relations between India and China had been hostile since the border clashes of 1959–62 and, as China began to build a closer relationship with Pakistan in the late 1960s, India sought support elsewhere to prevent encirclement. When the Nixon administration implemented a policy of "tilting" toward Pakistan as well, India was faced with the prospect of a hostile Washington-Beijing-Islamabad axis. The situation reached a boiling point as tensions in East Pakistan in 1970–71 led millions to take refuge in India. When the Congress Party faction led by Indira Gandhi, who had been assiduously cultivated by the Soviets since 1953, won a decisive victory at the polls, the stage was set for a Soviet-Indian agreement.[24] The Treaty of Peace, Friendship and Cooperation with Moscow was signed in August 1971 and Brezhnev clearly explained the Soviet motivation for doing so at a Communist Party plenum three months later: "We understand well the significance of India, the Politburo considers its important task to do everything necessary to maintain this most powerful Asian country on positions of struggle against imperialism so that it will be our friend."[25] When war broke out only weeks later between India and Pakistan, the USSR stood unequivocally on the side of India, and the subsequent Indian triumph was seen as a victory by Moscow as well over a nascent Beijing-Washington entente, leading one Soviet diplomat to proclaim that "this is the first time in history that the United States and China have been defeated together."[26] Soviet-Indian relations grew closer in the wake of the war, aided by the fact that, as one KGB official remarked, India became "a model of KGB infiltration of a Third World government."[27]

The effect of détente on Soviet policy in Vietnam differed from the cases of Egypt and India for two reasons. The first was that extricating itself from Vietnam was the primary concern of the Nixon administration at the time and so the Soviet leadership knew that without significant efforts to force concessions out of the North Vietnamese, Washington was unlikely to see détente as worthwhile. The second was that Hanoi had long been able to use the threat of moving closer to China to keep Moscow in check, but now, given Beijing's rapprochement with Washington, Hanoi's leverage had suddenly decreased dramatically. Despite the increase in Chinese aid in 1971–72 (from a low point in 1970), Beijing would have had difficulty credibly accusing Moscow of abandoning anti-imperialism in the context of its own shocking diplomatic about-face. In fact, Hanoi seemed to view the prospect of Nixon's visit to Moscow less harshly than his visit to Beijing, though it was certainly not happy about either event.[28] Le Duan, the leader of the Vietnam Workers' Party (VWP), told the visiting Soviet delegation, which had come in October 1971 to discuss Nixon's visit, that Soviet foreign policy was "directed mainly toward providing for the tasks of the defense of the entire socialist camp, including Vietnam, for the defense of world peace."[29] Meanwhile, Zhou Enlai, when asked by Alexander Haig about the improvement in Soviet-DRV relations due to the Sino-American rapprochement, grimly asserted that China was willing to "bear the consequences of the Sino-American accommodation."[30] Lien-Hang Nguyen affirms that, based on Vietnamese archives, it was the feeling of being boxed in by both of its patrons that led Hanoi to plan the Easter offensive of 1972.[31] The offensive was launched after Nixon had gone to Beijing but before he went to Moscow, endangering the latter summit. Hanoi put pressure on the Kremlin to cancel Nixon's visit, but the Soviet Politburo ultimately decided to go ahead with it, not least out of anger at the behavior of the North Vietnamese, whom they suspected of launching the offensive with the deliberate intent of sabotaging détente.[32] In the wake of the offensive, the political realities facing Hanoi became quite clear. Both the Soviets and the Chinese sent delegations to Hanoi advising the North Vietnamese to settle, and soon both Moscow and Beijing were decreasing their military aid to Hanoi, putting the latter on the defensive and forcing it to shift to a "strategy of peace," which, as Nguyen writes, was "an admission of failure, not a declaration of victory."[33] Victory, however, was exactly how the Soviets saw the subsequent peace treaty, ending a battle now labeled a "test of strength of two social systems," and Brezhnev, at a subsequent Communist Party plenum, took full credit for supposedly winning a war that his predecessor had wanted no part of a decade earlier.[34]

Overall then, détente did relatively little damage to the Soviet image in the developing world regarding its standing in the anti-imperialist struggle, especially in comparison with the disastrous results, for Moscow, of the policy of peaceful coexistence in the early 1960s. Despite the images of Nixon and Brezhnev meeting cordially that graced the world's newspapers and television screens in the early 1970s on a regular basis, few in the developing world now questioned the Soviet willingness to support anti-imperialist struggle with military means. In part, this was because of the changes in Chinese policy, which were not limited to the rapprochement with Washington but rather entailed a much broader shift away from the open encouragement of guerrilla warfare, as will be discussed below. However, it was also largely due to the fact that the Soviets were now much more aware of the political dangers of the promotion of "peace," and they made sure both to openly and to loudly proclaim its limits as well as to reassure their allies with formal commitments and large amounts of armaments. In Vietnam, this meant that Moscow managed to aid in ending the war while maintaining détente and strengthening its influence in Hanoi at the same time. It was also due to the closer political relations and more intense ideological influence that characterized Soviet relations with many of the countries now labeled countries of socialist orientation.

The term "countries of socialist orientation," which came into use in Soviet discourse in the early 1970s, did not explicitly replace earlier terms such as "state of national democracy" and "revolutionary democracy," but, nevertheless, the phrase seemed to carry different implications from those earlier iterations of the Soviet postcolonial development model, judging by the way it was used. In particular, it implied a significantly higher level of political and ideological development than the earlier terms, which had basically referred to states in which the broad national anti-imperialist coalitions that had won independence would now turn their attentions to socioeconomic transformation in the form of agrarian reform, industrialization, and expansion of the state sector. Soviet authors still spoke of a "united front" but now, rather than referring to the unity of various classes or social strata, they were referring specifically to the unity of action between local Communists and "revolutionary democrats," i.e., those leftist leaders who had been thrust into power in the wake of independence and pushed a progressive agenda but were (not yet) true Marxists.[35] It was precisely the effects of the earlier stages of socioeconomic reform that were supposed to have opened new class fissures in society, exacerbating class struggle and radicalizing the process of reform and thereby opening the way for an ideological leap to the left by the "revolutionary democrats." Rostislav Ul'ianovskii and Karen Brutents, two high officials in the International Department, argued over exactly how far along the road toward socialism countries of "socialist orientation" were said to be. According to Brutents, "social progress in these countries is now nearing the point where the implementation of new fundamental changes in social relations and political structure can make the noncapitalist choice irrevocable."[36] Clearly, the talk about "preparing the way to cross over to the noncapitalist path" was now passé for Brutents. Ul'ianovskii put it in even more stark terms. He argued that such countries were now at the stage where "the crossing of the more progressive parts of the radical democratic parties of these countries to the positions of the proletariat and scientific socialism is not only desirable, but theoretically and practically possible."[37] Even for Brutents, "the widening of paths and legal possibilities for the dissemination of Marxist ideas is a not insignificant particularity of the development of the spiritual (*dukhovnoi*) life of many countries of socialist orientation at the current stage."[38] In short, the socioeconomic transformations that had been accomplished in the early stages of independence had now radicalized the class struggle, necessitating the creation of more decisive, powerful political forces in the form of new political parties in which Communists would unite with the ruling progressives and gradually win them over to Marxism. This was the new model that the USSR would follow in its relations with countries of socialist orientation in the 1970s as evidenced by its relations with Syria, Iraq, Congo, South Yemen, and, later on, with others such as Ethiopia, Benin, and Angola, where a high-level East German delegation held a six-week seminar to teach Marxist ideology and economic planning to leaders of the Popular Movement for the Liberation of Angola (MPLA).[39]

Once Marxists had taken control, however, Moscow advocated a careful, gradual transition to a socialist economy as opposed to the violent, revolutionary methods used under Stalin in Eastern Europe and in Mao's Great Leap Forward. The election of Salvador Allende as president of Chile in September 1970, the first Marxist freely elected to head a government, provided the Soviets with an excellent test case for this theory of "peaceful transition." Leonid Brezhnev underlined the significance of the Chilean experiment in Moscow's eyes at a Communist Party plenum in March 1971. While outlining the foreign policy section of his address at the upcoming party congress, he remarked: "In connection with the situation in Latin America, space is allotted to the recent victory of the forces of National Unity (*Unidad Popular*—UP) in Chile. For obvious reasons at the congress this will be talked about rather guardedly, but here in our auditorium it is possible to add that the coming to power of Communists and Socialists through the constitutional path—if, of course, they manage to hold on to power and realize their declared program (in substance a program for building socialism)—will have immense principal significance and could seriously influence the further development of many Latin American countries."[40] As a consequence of this, the Soviets advised a very cautious path of reform directed toward winning over the middle classes in order to solidify the government's electoral future. The Chilean Communist Party, led by Luis Corvalan, and President Allende himself, despite being a member of the more radical Socialist Party, generally agreed with Moscow's strategy and preferred to focus on building public support for continued Marxist control rather than attempt an immediate revolutionary overhaul of the economy. The Soviets were especially cognizant of the example that Chile would set around the world. As a middle-income Latin American country with a long democratic tradition, a moderate, constitutional revolution could make socialism palatable in much of the developed world, where welfare policies had made violent working class revolution passé. A turn toward violence and repression, on the other hand, would give credence to the arguments of anticommunists the world over.

The Socialist Party, however, led by its new general secretary, Carlos Altamirano, with close ties to Cuba, and by Foreign Minister Clodomiro

Almeyda, a long-time supporter of Mao, constantly pushed for a more radical approach, leading to destabilizing tension within the ruling coalition. In just one example on the all-important question of land reform, the Communists, backed by advisers from Moscow and East Berlin, called for nationalizing only landholdings larger than eighty irrigated hectares, therefore pitting the majority of the country against the large latifundists and assuring small and middle farmers of their property holdings. The Socialists, though, committed themselves at a party plenum in August 1971 to nationalizing all landholdings above forty hectares, which was explicitly designed to produce *enfrentamiento,* or violent class confrontation.[41] As that confrontation became increasingly imminent, the Soviets were willing to supply arms to defend the regime in an anticipated civil war. The question was simply to whom those arms should be provided. Since the armed forces themselves were politically suspect, the choice came down to the Communists, who wanted to avoid a violent confrontation and therefore did not want the arms, and the Socialists, who were all too eager to fight but politically too radical for the Kremlin's tastes. In the end, Moscow asked Corvalan whether they should arm the Socialists, and he counseled refusal since the Socialist Party was composed of "heterogeneous elements" that had very recently followed "anti-Soviet" and "anticommunist" positions.[42] It appears that no arms ended up reaching Chile from the USSR, though it is possible that one ship was sent with that intention.[43]

Nevertheless, in the aftermath of the coup, Moscow's primary concern seemed to be, as a member of the Soviet International Department told his East German comrades, to "work out and publicize a correct analysis of the events in Chile, that the theory of the peaceful path to socialism in view of the existence of the socialist camp is correct."[44] What mattered most was that the overthrow of Allende would not have the consequence of bolstering the radical arguments of those, often devotees of Mao or Che Guevara, who believed that violent revolution was the only path. Chile, therefore, provides an excellent window into viewing Soviet priorities in the developing world at this time. Moscow wanted politically popular, ideologically reliable Marxist coalitions which would, nevertheless, pursue socialization of the economy at a careful and measured pace.

The increasing Soviet emphasis on internal political dynamics and ideological orthodoxy, however, did not match well with the new economic theory that was gaining traction abroad as the gap between the developed and developing countries continued to widen: dependency theory. Dependency theory essentially evolved in the 1960s as a response to "modernization theory," which argued that all societies follow similar trajectories of socioeconomic development and that the newly emerging states were merely at an earlier level and therefore required aid, reform, and integration into the world economy to grow. In contrast, proponents of the various versions of dependency theory asserted that the position of the newly emerging states had unique aspects, most importantly the fact that they had suffered under colonization and were, as a result, pushed into a weaker and peripheral role in the world economy. One of the most prominent dependency theorists argued that global capitalism created uneven development and that, in fact, the wealth of the industrialized countries was predicated upon the continued, active process of advancing the underdevelopment of other regions, a process he called the "development of underdevelopment."[45] Some, such as Raúl Prebisch, advocated high tariffs and import substitution as a path out of underdevelopment, but many on the Latin American Left in particular found this solution unsatisfactory. Even if it succeeded, it would place a heavy burden on Latin American consumers and enrich a small, politically connected bourgeoisie.[46] They argued instead that the solution had to be found in a restructuring of the global trade regime because the current international economic order was dominated by the wealthy industrialized countries, one that, rather than accelerating growth in the developing world, actually served to suppress it.

For the Soviets, dependency theory presented two major problems. First, it diminished the role of domestic political and economic transformations in favor of an analysis based on global economic mechanisms. Second, it divided the world not between East and West, socialism and capitalism, but between the "poor South" and the "rich North," which once again separated the socialist and developing worlds and grouped the Soviets with the capitalist powers. By 1970, Soviet scholars were already writing about the dangers of the new ideological pressures being created by the growing development gap. As one author argued, poor urban masses, the so-called *lumpenproletariat*, of developing countries contained great revolutionary potential but were extremely fickle and, as they compared their own material situation with that of Europe, they grew increasingly dissatisfied, even with "progressive" governments.[47] He asserted that economic progress would not be achieved until productivity had been raised and this would require major social and ideological changes since "the striving for progress, whether in the realm of productive relations or in the realm of social relations, is not a typical aspect of the social-psychological storehouse of traditional 'eastern' societies."[48] Brutents admitted that governments of socialist orientation had, by and large, achieved more in the social realm than in the economic one so far.[49] The solutions offered by Soviet scholars, however, focused almost exclusively on domestic political measures. One article offered eight potential solutions ranging from eliminating corruption to encouraging tourism, even advising caution in enacting nationalizations of potentially unprofitable areas of the economy, but it said nothing about reforming the relations between developed and developing countries on a global scale.[50] Ironically, Soviet economists were just rediscovering the benefits of trade, particularly in terms of development, at the time.[51] The Soviets were therefore dismayed when UNCTAD III, meeting in Santiago, Chile, in the spring of 1972, turned into a pitched battle between the Third World, in the form of the Group of 77, and the developed countries, with calls for a radical reformation of the global economic system that ultimately found concrete expression in the "Charter of the Economic Rights and Obligations of States," an early form of what would become the New International Economic Order (NIEO) by 1974. The main Soviet foreign policy journal, in its coverage of the conference, criticized some developing countries for seeing UNCTAD as a vehicle solely for advancing the interests of the Third World without taking into account the nature of imperialism and the role of socialist countries, "mechanically putting in one dock both imperialist and developed socialist countries, without considering the fundamental opposition of their social systems and relations to the Third World."[52] The article included the hopeful note, from the Soviet perspective, that "the further the process of economic, social, and political differentiation in the Third World goes, the stronger can become the centrifugal forces shaking unity."[53] Given the overwhelming popularity at the time of calls for Third World solidarity, nothing demonstrated more starkly the divide in interest perception between Moscow and the developing world than the open Soviet desire for disunity. Of course, the cause of Third World unity had now gained a new proponent, which the article identified as the "new pretender" for leadership of the Third World: China.

Consequently the battle for leadership of the world revolution, which in the 1960s had taken place primarily within the international communist movement and the left-leaning movements, parties, and regimes that together constituted the "national liberation movement," would now shift largely to the realm of interstate relations on a global scale. The ground on which the battle would be fought had shifted as well from the sphere of armed struggle and revolution to one of global economic confrontation and reform. Both battles ultimately boiled down to a clash between the agendas of anti-imperialism, arising from decolonization, and anti-capitalism. In some ways, the NIEO paralleled the call of China and Indonesia in the mid-1960s for a Conference of New Emerging Forces (CONEFO) to replace the imperialist-dominated international political order. Just as Moscow had answered that call by adopting anti-imperialism within acceptable limits that did not challenge its place in the world, so too the Soviet challenge would now become to assimilate enough of the agenda of the new Third World movement without conceding a radical political restructuring of the international order.

The Aspiring New Leader of the Third World

During the initial stages of China's emergence from its international isolation during the Cultural Revolution, it was not clear whether Chinese activity on the world stage would now be any different. In 1969 and 1970, so far as most of the outside world could see, no sea changes had taken place, as China's return to the international arena consisted primarily of sending ambassadors back to countries with which it already had relations and giving large amounts of aid to countries with which it already had established close ties, particularly Tanzania, Zambia, and Pakistan. In 1970, the Soviet press was still employing the old charges of "'ultra-left' phraseology" and support for "adventurist actions" against the Chinese.[54] The clear signals of rapprochement with the United States in 1971, however, would change the picture. China established relations with fifteen new countries in 1971 and eighteen in 1972 in contrast to only five in 1970.[55] China's aid pledges would balloon at the same time. China's rapprochement with the United States, and its subsequent emergence onto the world stage as a recognized world power with a permanent veto in the UN Security Council, did not come without a major restructuring of Chinese global strategy. The failure of China's pre–Cultural Revolution foreign policy seems to have led to a reevaluation of policy away from the open promotion of armed revolution toward increased emphasis on interstate relations and the principle of noninterference in internal affairs. The new opportunities and limitations provided by the rapprochement with the U.S. and the seat in the UN, along with the pressing imperative to hedge against the Soviet threat, further pushed China to seek to build an independent power base in the world separate from both superpowers among the states of the so-called Third World. As calls for Third World unity and militancy grew, China sought to ride the wave to a position of influence that would enable it to escape the embrace of either Moscow or Washington.

To the close observer, two important changes in Chinese rhetoric in 1970 already signaled the potential shifts in Chinese policy. Throughout the 1960s, Beijing had continually proclaimed the inevitability of world war, but in a conversation on May 11, 1970, with Le Duan, Mao acknowledged that both superpowers were reluctant to start a nuclear war.[56] On May 20, Mao announced a change in the standard formula that the two main tendencies in the world were war and revolution, declaring that "now, however, the main tendency in the world is revolution."[57] The new formula was codified at a subsequent Communist Party plenum in September. With world war no longer imminent and inevitable, Beijing could now conduct a foreign policy based on the premise that the current world order would be fairly stable in the short and medium term. The other major shift in Chinese rhetoric had actually occurred in the wake of the invasion of Czechoslovakia, when Beijing labeled the USSR "social imperialist," thereby preparing a basis, not least domestically, for shifting the focus of the "anti-imperialist struggle" against Moscow and consequently leading to an opening to the United States.[58] With these two changes in its ideological and rhetorical position, Beijing had opened the door to a new foreign policy of seeking support and legitimacy within the existing international framework, one that would be directed primarily toward confrontation with the USSR, which it now saw as its primary adversary.

As with so much else on Soviet policy in the developing world, SCSCAA served as the canary in the coal mine regarding China's impending return to international organizations, as well the receptiveness in evidence in Africa and Asia for just such a move. The fourth AAPSO conference in Winneba, Ghana, in 1965 had called for holding the next conference in Beijing in 1967, but, as the date approached, many countries, led by the USSR, called for moving the conference for fear of the disaster that would have ensued had an international conference been held in Beijing at the height of the Cultural Revolution. The Chinese objected and pledged that they would hold their own conference, but, in the end, no conference was held and the Chinese left the AAPSO. Now, in 1971, movement was afoot once again to hold the long-awaited fifth

AAPSO conference and the big issue was whether China should be invited to rejoin the organization. At a session of the executive council in preparation for the upcoming conference in June, i.e., even before the announcement of Nixon's visit on July 15, several SCSCAA members noted rising Chinese influence in a number of regions of the world, particularly sub-Saharan Africa.[59] When asked why they supported the Chinese, a number of Africans told the Soviets that "you are still white, but they are yellow, closer to us."[60] SCSCAA was divided on how to react, with some calling for a delay of the conference, while others sounded a new note in terms of responding to the Chinese. Several SCSCAA members argued that, given the evident sympathy for the Chinese, attacking them directly would only be counterproductive.[61]

It was not long before the new Chinese problem had exploded far beyond the AAPSO. On July 15, the Sino-American rapprochement went public and the process of diplomatic recognition of the PRC soon accelerated. On October 25, the UN General Assembly voted to admit the PRC and expel Taiwan. The PRC was unprepared for the vote and a meeting of the CCP Leading Team of the Foreign Ministry the next day initially decided not to send a delegation to the UN as China was not yet ready, a position which Zhou Enlai shared. Mao, however, sent Wang Hairong to summon Zhou and several others to him where he overruled the decision and decided instead to send a delegation.[62] On November 15, the head of the PRC's new UN delegation, Qiao Guanhua, delivered a speech that would set the tone for China's diplomatic and ideological stance for the next several years. Qiao declared: "An increasing number of medium and small countries are uniting to oppose the hegemony and power politics practiced by the one or two superpowers and to fight for the right to settle their own affairs as independent and sovereign states and for equal status in international relations. Countries want independence, nations want liberation and the people want revolution, this has become an irresistible trend of history."[63] The self-proclaimed guiding principle of Chinese activity in the UN over the next few years would be the uniting of the Third World in opposition to the two superpowers.[64] Accordingly, China supported almost any international proposal originating in the Third World, especially if the USSR did not support it, such as proposals for declaring the Indian Ocean a zone of peace, which China voted for every year from 1971 to 1976 while the USSR abstained, as well as the Latin American proposal to extend the limits of territorial waters to 200 miles offshore, again opposed by Moscow.[65] As in 1964, when China declared that its nuclear bomb would be the "Afro-Asian bomb," so now it proclaimed its Security Council veto the "Third World veto," and the Kenyan UN representative, for one, echoed the sentiment.[66] Many in the developing world accordingly looked to China to help redress the balance of power in the UN in opposition to the developed countries.

The Soviets were immediately alarmed both by the nature of the Chinese position and the enthusiastic reception that it had received. One week after Qiao's speech, the director of the Institute of World Economy and International Affairs informed a Communist Party plenum that China was trying to build a hostile coalition of Asian, African, and Latin American countries to oppose the USSR in the UN "on the basis of the false Peking-ese (sic) thesis of the hostility between the rich north and the poor south."[67] In SCSCAA, one member ominously reported first hand the standing ovation China received when its representatives first entered the UN, followed by its embarking on an anti-Soviet course in pushing the "poisonous" theory of the "two superpowers."[68] Now a number of African delegations were insisting that there could be no fifth AAPSO conference without China and some SCSCAA members began to fear that the Afro-Asian sympathy for China was ineradicable.[69] In the event, the conference was held in January 1972 without an actual Chinese presence but with heavy Chinese influence as calls to liquidate the movement or throw the Soviets out of the leadership proliferated.[70] At UNCTAD III, while the Soviets found themselves in the dock with the West facing a unified Group of 77, the Chinese role was lauded in the mainstream African press. One paper praised China as the most active participant in the conference, pronounced its presence "historic," and declared that the poor countries were elated to have China lead their struggle.[71] Another described how Chinese speeches denouncing the superpowers for exploiting and destroying the Third World precipitated massive student demonstrations during the conference on the streets of Santiago.[72] While rising Third World unity and militancy were seen as a threat by the USSR, that threat was magnified many times by the specter of Beijing leading the charge.

China's dramatic entry onto the scene at the UN was soon followed by a massive aid and diplomatic offensive. Despite the fact that Qiao, in his speech at the UN, had described the Chinese economy as "backward" by way of explaining why China's ability to provide material aid was "very limited," the Chinese aid offensive of the early 1970s dwarfed that of the 1960s.[73] Chinese economic aid to Africa from 1970 through

1977 totaled some $1.882 billion in comparison to $428 million between 1954 and 1966. Chinese aid to Africa over this period significantly exceeded the Soviet total of $1.04 billion.[74] While a sizeable portion of that aid went toward the construction of the Tanzam railway, the number and political variety of Chinese aid recipients increased as well. China pledged new aid to fifteen African countries between 1971 and 1973, among them such traditionally Western-aligned states as Ethiopia, Zaire, and Senegal.[75] Needless to say, Soviet observers were alarmed. The Soviet mission to the UN sent a report to the Foreign Ministry on the Chinese aid offensive in early 1972, concluding that "the outstanding fact in the policy of Chinese provision of aid to developing countries is that its development proceeded and proceeds in parallel with the active efforts of Chinese diplomacy directed toward the establishment of diplomatic and trade relations with the maximum possible number of countries, especially in the Third World."[76] The following year, the Soviet representative at the UN in Geneva sent a similar comprehensive report on Chinese aid, describing the goal as "limiting the activity of the Soviet Union and undermining its ties with these [developing] countries and at the same time becoming the leader of the Third World."[77] The burden of this new aid offensive, especially coming in the wake of the most chaotic period of the Cultural Revolution, was enormous, however. Zhou Enlai claimed in an interview in 1972 that foreign aid consumed 5 percent of the Chinese budget, and he might have been underestimating.[78] According to Ma Jisen, the proportion of the Chinese budget going to foreign aid in 1972, 1973, and 1975 was 6.7 percent, 7.2 percent, and 6.3 percent, respectively.[79] How long China could sustain such expenditures on foreign aid would become a serious question for the leadership in Beijing.

China's aid offensive was accompanied by an equally impressive diplomatic offensive as a parade of foreign leaders came to Beijing in the early 1970s from countries all across the political spectrum. Haile Selassie, Joseph Mobutu, Isabella Peron, and the Shah of Iran were just some of the high-profile and politically eclectic cast of characters from among the twenty-five Third World leaders between June 1973 and April 1975 who made the pilgrimage to Beijing. During each visit, as with all of the formal interactions between Chinese and officials from the developing world at this time, China sought recognition of its status as a developing country and member in good standing of the Third World.[80] Chinese leaders sought to find common ground with each visiting foreign head of state, often agreeing to their requests in order to get the Third World line included in the joint communiqué, which seems to have been the case with the visit of the president of Mexico in April 1973, leading China to sign the Treaty of Tlateloco calling for a non-nuclear Latin America (which the Soviets refused to sign).[81] Similarly, China found common ground with the Shah on the issue of opposing foreign naval bases in the Indian Ocean and with the Peronist regime in Argentina on the issue of opposition to the superpowers, even though Argentina was more concerned about the United States than the USSR.[82] Argentina would become an important supporter of the idea of a Third World opposing the two "imperialisms," especially in the Non-Aligned Movement, where it was a strong proponent of the policy of "equidistance" supported by China.[83] The visit of Senegalese president Léopold Senghor, the chief exponent of the ideology of "Negritude," highlighted the importance of skin color in world politics, as the Senegalese press, covering the visit, remarked that the experiences of China and Senegal showed that colonialism was not only about the hegemony of developed over developing countries, but also that "skin color played if not the chief (*glavnuiu*) role then at least the primary (*preimushchestvennuiu*) role."[84] While China displayed much greater flexibility in its diplomatic interactions with foreign states, its propaganda efforts abroad became decidedly more tame and courteous. The Soviet embassy in Rwanda, reporting on a Chinese film showing at the embassy in Kigali, found that now there were no Mao portraits on the walls, no propaganda literature on offer, and the film itself had no obvious political content.[85] Chinese policy was now clearly focused on building the broadest possible base of support, and the widest front of Third World unity, to oppose Soviet hegemony.

This shift in Chinese policy, however, was not well received in all corners. China had spent a lot of time and effort building Maoist parties and splinter groups all around the world, pushing some to conduct guerrilla warfare, and the new policy encountered dissatisfaction and resistance both from those who had bought into the radical Maoist line of the 1960s and from those governments, particularly in South and Southeast Asia, that had been its targets. The Communist Parties of Thailand, Malaysia, and Burma had been headquartered on Chinese territory where they were trained and armed, and Maoist splinter groups conducted guerrilla operations in other countries in the region.[86] As China began to try to normalize relations with its southern neighbors, the ongoing guerrilla struggles presented a significant obstacle, as became evident in the course of negotiations with Malaysia and Burma.[87] Consequently, China began to decrease its support for guerrilla struggles in the region, leading to great difficulties for Maoist parties.[88] In public, Chinese leaders maintained that they had not stopped supporting the guerrilla struggles and that they would never sacrifice others for their own diplomatic gain. Zhou Enlai told Le Duan and Pham Van Dong in early 1971: "We hold that support to the people's revolutionary struggles cannot be sacrificed for the sake of relations between governments. Only traitors do that."[89] Chinese officials were still using very similar language in 1975 as evidenced in a conversation with the Romanians, and Zhou asserted that China was still supporting the Burmese Communist Party's struggle even after establishing relations with Rangoon.[90] Nevertheless, the evidence was clear that China had in fact significantly reduced, if not totally eliminated, its support for many Maoist groups. Two former leaders of the Maoist splinter group in Sri Lanka, in an interview with a TASS correspondent, provided a detailed narrative from the advent of the split within the Sri Lankan Communist Party in the early 1960s to their virtual abandonment by Beijing in 1971 and the subsequent chaos that led to the disintegration of the party. The Soviet ambassador in Sri Lanka forwarded the transcript directly to the International Department with the remark that "in our view, the conversations contain interesting material on the history of Maoism in Sri Lanka, of its pernicious influence on the development of the whole democratic movement in the country, which, to a significant degree, is typical for a whole slew of states in the Third World."[91] The Chinese shift toward normalization of relations with states was causing similar problems with Maoist groups in Latin America.[92] One journalist writing in *Le Monde*, catching the eye of the Soviet Foreign Ministry, derided the new Chinese foreign policy with the slogan, "Power holders of the world, unite!"[93]

Though China's new foreign policy strategy did allow the Soviets to gain some traction with more militant elements on the issue of China's "betrayal" of revolution, overall Moscow was very concerned with the success of the new Chinese approach. The result was in part a typical series of condemnatory analyses of Chinese policy in Communist Party plenums, Interkit meetings, and Soviet scholarly journals, which declared that China had thrown off its pseudorevolutionary cover and was now openly siding with imperialism in order to achieve its great power aims by making the Third World its political domain.[94] In April 1973, Mikhail Suslov announced that "now almost nothing remains of the leftist verbal shell of the international policy of the Maoists."[95] However, there was also a realization that China's new approach had found a real audience and simply attacking China in response would not be sufficient. Soviet diplomats abroad reported that the perception was real that China had interests in common with the developing world that the USSR did not, and so the theory of the two superpowers was in fact gaining traction.[96] Writing about the success of Chinese propaganda during Brezhnev's visit to the United States in August 1973, the Soviet embassy in Nairobi remarked that "the biggest danger is that Chinese slogans of struggle against the 'hegemony and monopoly of the superpowers' in international relations, [and] demagogic statements of support by the Chinese for any demands of the developing countries are evaluated by many African countries as answering to their interests."[97] More specifically, the Institute of Latin America wrote to the Central Committee recommending that it review its policy on the 200-mile marine territorial boundary issue and the denuclearization of Latin America because of the success of Chinese advocacy of those positions in the region.[98] There was a realization then that answering the Chinese challenge once again would require a shift in approach to Soviet policy in the Third World.

Nevertheless, the question may still be legitimately asked: were Mikhail Suslov, a journalist for *Le Monde*, and countless others at the time and since then correct? Had China in fact betrayed its revolutionary ideology for security and stability in the international arena? Had the rapprochement with the United States irrevocably compromised the Maoist call for revolution? For many who thought that Beijing had, in fact, done so, the label of "social imperialism" attached to the USSR seemed like the ultimate ideological façade, a classic Orwellian "black is white" rhetorical move. However, as the political trials and tribulations of the Cultural Revolution, which, though they had passed through their most chaotic phase, were still continuing in the early 1970s, attest, "revisionism" was not a matter to be taken lightly in Chinese politics at the time. As Roderick MacFarquhar, perhaps the foremost historian of the Cultural Revolution, has argued, if it had only been a power struggle, it would have been over by 1967.[99] There certainly was a reorientation of Chinese policy, as countless Maoist guerrillas in the jungles of Southeast Asia found out. However, a country that was spending 7 percent of its budget on foreign aid at a time of extreme economic difficulty was not merely paying lip service to the idea of Third World solidarity. It will be recalled also that Chinese foreign policy in the 1960s was never as reckless in its promotion of the armed overthrow of existing governments as its extreme rhetoric suggested.[100] It seems therefore that the shift in Chinese policy in the early 1970s does not demonstrate a complete about-face and betrayal of its revolutionary ideology. Rather, it demonstrates that the ideology had, in fact, never been what it had seemed to some. If the Chinese priority had been the promotion of socialism and the defeat of capitalism, then its policies of the early 1970s do indeed seem like a betrayal. However, if Beijing's ideological priority was taken all along to be anti-imperialism, then the story makes much more sense. The Soviet Union appeared to be equally as powerful, and more aggressive, than the United States at this time, and it was increasingly extending its global reach into the developing world. Those Asian Communist Parties were useful at a time when the goal was weakening the pro-Western governments on China's southern rim, but when the priority shifted to keeping Soviet influence out of the region, stable relations with the existing governments seemed a safer bet. Even North Vietnam, after the Paris agreement, had now become an outpost of Soviet "imperialism," which was presently threatening the PRC with encirclement.[101] It would be hard to untangle rhetoric from reality in terms of how much China saw the threat of Soviet expansionism as a true threat to the entire Third World beyond its borders. In time, the relative evaluations of the Soviet threat by Beijing and other governments in the Third World would lead China to make political decisions that would ultimately significantly reduce its standing among the latter. However, the changes in Chinese foreign policy in the early 1970s make more sense in the context of a shift in the evaluation of relative imperialist threats rather than as a complete betrayal of the "Revolution" by septuagenarian life-long revolutionaries in the midst of the Cultural Revolution.

Moscow Fights for the Third World

The challenge with which the Kremlin was presented in the wake of the PRC's entry into the UN and subsequent diplomatic offensive had both new and familiar aspects. The Soviet leadership had already been faced with the specter of a Chinese attempt to build a political base in Asia, Africa, and Latin America by appealing to national and racial categories. Then, as now, the Soviet Union was grouped with the Western powers as a white, industrialized, imperialist power whose purported revolutionary intentions could not be trusted. However, the Chinese challenge was now taking place in the context of the United Nations and other international organizations with the United States as a de facto Chinese ally. The terrain was no longer the international communist movement and the left-leaning solidarity movement where Soviet rhetorical and practical demonstrations of revolutionary fidelity could carry the day. Now the battleground included states where appeals to Marxist revolutionary ideals held no attraction. Moscow would have to prove that it shared and promoted the expressed interests of the Third World even, to some degree, if they did not match its own revolutionary agenda. At the same time, what the Soviets could not allow was a firm division between the Second and Third Worlds. Consequently, Moscow needed to do what it could to convince states in the Third World that the division of the world between the "rich North" and the "poor South" was neither accurate nor conducive to achieving their goals.

The intensified Soviet effort to influence the Third World was prominent at the Fourth Non-Aligned Summit in Algiers in September 1973. Soviet interest and involvement in previous meetings of the group had been fairly minimal, but, in the current political context, the Kremlin realized the importance of the forum for furthering its objectives. At an April 1973 plenum, Brezhnev outlined the importance that the Non-Aligned Movement had now taken on and declared that "we intend to conduct work so that, with the help of Cuba, Chile, Yugoslavia, India and several other countries, we can try to give the decisions of this conference a more militant, directed anti-imperialist character."[102] He went on to explain that the sudden increase in the political weight of the developing states, especially in Latin America, made them crucial potential Soviet allies. Moscow accordingly conducted an intense propaganda campaign on the eve of the summit.[103] Since the Soviets themselves could not attend the summit, however, the most prominent exponent of the Soviet view in Algiers was Fidel Castro, attending a meeting for the first time. Castro loudly attacked the Chinese theory of the "two imperialisms" whose most enthusiastic proponent at the summit was the Peronist regime in Argentina.[104] The summit marked the beginning of a concerted effort by certain socialist states, chiefly Cuba but later Vietnam, North Korea, and others that joined in the next few years, to make alliance with the socialist world an essential part of Non-Alignment. The debate between proponents of that so-called natural alliance and their opponents, led by the Yugoslavs, arguing for "equidistance" between the two blocs, would divide the movement well into the 1980s, though it peaked in intensity at the Havana summit in 1979, with Moscow consistently supporting the former position.[105] The suddenly increased Soviet attention to the Non-Aligned Movement in 1973 was noted by the Chinese. Zhou Enlai told a Romanian delegation even as the summit was still going on that the Soviets were heavily influencing its proceedings, having had a hand in making India the president of the political commission, which marked a major departure from the relative indifference with which the Kremlin had treated the Non-Aligned Movement until that point.[106] Despite this effort, the West German press still considered the summit a Chinese victory. The Soviet embassy in Bonn summarized the local verdict in saying that "the overwhelming majority of states participating in the conference unambiguously came out for the point of view of the Chinese on the division of the world into a 'world village' and 'world city,' a 'poor South' and 'rich North' and indirectly spoke against 'Russian imperialism.'"[107] Nevertheless, when Brezhnev visited Cuba in February 1974, the resulting joint communiqué emphasized that "the Non-Aligned countries have achieved an important role in international politics in recent years."[108]

As the battle for the Third World intensified, Cuba increasingly came to serve as the chief Soviet advocate in forums where Moscow's own representatives could not enter. Though Havana and Moscow had had a very tense relationship throughout most of the 1960s, by 1970 the Soviet embassy in Havana reported that the Cuban regime had shifted many of its international positions, specifically on issues of armed struggle and peaceful coexistence. (It did not mention that, in some ways, the Soviets had moved closer to the Cuban position as well.) Cuban relations with the Eastern bloc as well as with the Moscow-oriented Communist Parties of Latin America had improved noticeably. At the same time, "significant attention is devoted by the Cuban government to the development of relations with certain countries of the Third World (Algeria, Syria) whose positions on the national-liberation movement are either close to or coincide with the Cuban position."[109] The return of Cuba to the fold was noted in several of Brezhnev's foreign policy reports to the party in the next few years, calling Cuba more "mature" and underlining that the Cuban attitude toward Maoism was "practically identical with ours."[110] Cuba was thus the perfect spokesman for Moscow in the ensuing battle with China for the Third World. Cuba's increasing integration into Latin American politics, facilitated in large part by the Allende regime in Chile, allowed it a greater voice in Third World politics. The Chilean government, as the host of UNCTAD III in 1971, worked hard to get Cuba into the conference as well as the Group of 77, and the Cuban foreign minister met with Allende and Chilean foreign minister Clodomiro Almeyda to work out a united platform for both meetings.[111] At the Group of 77 meetings in preparation for UNCTAD III, as the Cuban Foreign Ministry reported to the Soviet embassy, Cuba firmly opposed any attempts to put the developed capitalist and socialist countries on the same level.[112] By the end of 1972, the Soviet embassy in Havana noted that Cuba was supporting the Soviet position in a number of international forums, including the Non-Aligned Movement, UNCTAD, UNESCO, the Group of 77, and the UN General Assembly.[113] Cuban support, however, would not come cheap for Moscow. Between 1970 and 1975, the Cuban military was equipped with $3 billion worth of the most sophisticated Soviet weaponry free of charge, twice the amount it had received during the 1960s, and Moscow began subsidizing the Cuban economy to the tune of $4–5 billion a year.[114] The increasingly close Soviet-Cuban alliance would be of tremendous importance for Moscow in repulsing Chinese efforts to move the Third World in opposition to the Second in the mid-1970s and, as Cuba came to follow the Soviet economic and political model ever more closely, it would serve as a practicing demonstration of the Soviet model in the developing world.[115]

Having Cuba advocate on Moscow's behalf, however, by itself would not have been sufficient to turn the tide. The Soviets made some tactical changes such as, belatedly, agreeing to the Latin American demand for a 200-mile maritime exclusive economic zone.[116] One SCSCAA member suggested another tactic in December 1973: "There is one theme, very advantageous (*vygodnaia*), which would allow us to unite all opponents of imperialism, on which we will not meet any resistance. But we need to be more active in using this problem to arm ourselves (*vziat' na vooruzhenie*)—this is the struggle against racism and racial discrimination. Here everyone agrees: leftists, democratic movements, everyone agrees, there are no opponents." He went on to point out that the UN was already passing many resolutions on the issue, some on Soviet initiative, and that the opportunity existed to "acquire great political capital."[117] Moscow also attempted to make détente and disarmament popular in the developing world by tying their advancement to proposals to dedicate a certain percentage of the savings in military expenditures to economic aid, promoting a sort of "disarmament dividend." Each of these tactics helped in improving the Soviet image in the developing world.

However, the main issue at the time was the Third World attempt to overturn the existing international economic order. In April 1974, the

UN held its Sixth Special Session on the initiative of the current president of the Non-Aligned Movement, the Algerian president Houari Boumedienne. The meeting convened in the wake of the OPEC oil boycott, which had demonstrated as never before the potential economic power of the Third World, and many developing countries were consequently in a heightened state of militancy and eager to press their advantage. The Third World came to the conference with the explicit aim of adopting a "New International Economic Order" (NIEO) based on the framework outlined at the Non-Aligned summit in Algiers the previous year. Seventeen developing states met again in Algiers in March 1974 and produced a declaration calling for a guarantee "of preferential and nonreciprocal treatment to developing countries in all fields of international economic cooperation."[118] They demanded an agreement on higher and stable prices for commodities, better terms of trade, reduced tariff barriers, increased foreign aid, and the right to control their own natural resources. Some countries spoke of forming cartels for all sorts of other commodities on the OPEC model. The USSR, like the United States, did not respond positively to the Algerian call for the session, but it passed by majority vote anyway. In the end, the session adopted both the declaration and the program of action of the NIEO based on the voting strength of the Third World bloc, and Soviet and American proposed amendments were rejected.

China played a prominent role at the session. It was in this forum that Deng Xiaoping made his famous speech outlining China's "Three Worlds" theory, which divided the world into three parts: the two superpowers, the developing world, and the other developed countries caught in the middle. Deng went on to endorse each item on the NIEO agenda, attacking the USSR even more than the West for plundering the Third World and preaching economic self-reliance, which he defined as each nation's control over its own economy and natural resources rather than refusal to accept foreign aid. He put China firmly in the camp of the Third World and declared: "If one day China should change her color and turn into a superpower, if she too should play the tyrant in the world, and everywhere subject others to her bullying, aggression, and exploitation, the people of the world should identify her as social-imperialist, expose it, oppose it and work together with the Chinese people to overthrow it."[119]

The USSR, though, had clearly been on the defensive at the special session. In the wake of UNCTAD III the Soviets had held a conference on economic development in the developing world in Tashkent, where the delegates had once again propounded the Soviet view of the non-capitalist path that largely ignored the growing focus on international economic relations.[120] The special session had shown that that approach was clearly not in tune with the political tide in the Third World and that the USSR faced marginalization if it did not change its approach. The initial Soviet coverage did not diverge from the line promoted by Soviet foreign minister Andrei Gromyko at the session, asserting that while the NIEO documents constituted an indictment of the inability of the capitalist system to raise the development level of poor countries, they were not yet truly "anti-imperialist" documents because they did not attack the very bases of the capitalist system itself, nor did they speak at all about internal transformation.[121]

The Soviet position, however, had already begun to change by the time of the Seventh UN Special Session in 1975, the second meeting held on economic development, while China overreached diplomatically by trying to insert explicitly anti-Soviet language into UN documents.[122] By the time of UNCTAD IV in Nairobi in 1976, the shift in the Soviet position was obvious. Brezhnev announced at a meeting of European Communist Parties that year that "the struggle for equality of political and economic relations of former colonial and dependent states is an important part of the general international duty of our parties," and he made equality in trade relations between developed and developing countries an explicit goal of Soviet foreign policy at the Twenty-Fifth CPSU Congress.[123] At the conference itself, the Soviet representative, Minister of Foreign Trade N. S. Patolichev, declared: "We now have the right to say that in the world there exists not only two opposing socioeconomic systems, but two principally opposed approaches to relations with developing countries."[124] The socialist countries came to the conference prepared this time with a joint statement containing a "scientific" analysis of world trade and the place of developing countries as well as endorsing the Manila Declaration, which had been adopted by the Group of 77 as its basis for negotiation.[125] Soviet coverage attempted to ideologically justify this shift by arguing that the tendency of developing countries to attack imperialism on the basis of trade relations stemmed only from declining terms of trade, but also "has under it a distinctly expressed social basis."[126] Finally, the Soviets now even heartily endorsed Third World unity, congratulating the Group of 77 on "overcoming centrifugal tendencies" in Nairobi—the very same tendencies they hoped would tear the movement apart after Santiago.[127] By 1977, Moscow was unabashedly proclaiming itself the defender of the international rights of developing countries in the "new phase" of decolonization that had begun with the special session of 1974.[128]

At the same time as the Soviet Union was trying to turn itself into the champion of the developing countries, though of course not the Third World, since that was an imperialist invention, a series of foreign policy issues damaged China's own candidacy for the post. China's veto on the entry of Bangladesh into the UN in the fall of 1972, after the latter declared its independence from the government in Islamabad, a long-time Chinese ally, following a very bloody conflict, went against overwhelming global sentiment and was seen as distinctly hypocritical, coming from a country that itself had been kept out of the UN for so long.[129] China's maintenance of relations with Chile after the overthrow of Allende hurt its image in Latin America and the refusal of the PRC to vote for the UN resolution condemning Israel in the wake of the October 1973 war further isolated it from the vast majority of the Third World.[130] The Soviet press agency Novosti decided to capitalize on the anger at China in Latin America in the wake of the Chilean coup by publishing a series of brochures titled "Why Maoism Is Dangerous for You."[131] The PRC justified these moves as defending the Third World from Soviet hegemony and, in the case of Pinochet, respecting the principles of national sovereignty and noninterference, but, as time went on, fewer and fewer developing countries were buying the Chinese line. By mid-1975, Soviet officials were already reporting that Chinese efforts were increasingly meeting with failure. In January 1975 when China sought admittance to the Group of 77 at a meeting of the United Nations Industrial Development Organization (UNIDO), it was refused, and China instead ended up associated with the Group of 77 though not actually a member.[132] In May, the Soviet representative at the international organizations in Vienna reported: "It is still premature to give a final evaluation of the existing situation on the given question, but the existing facts allow one to say that the attempts of the PRC to achieve recognition as a developing country belonging to the Third World have been unsuccessful. The overwhelming majority of the countries of the Third World relates cautiously to the actions of the PRC leaders in the international arena and do not accept its foreign policy conceptions."[133] Soviet officials reported similar decreases in Chinese prestige at the conference on sea rights and the Seventh Special Session later that year.[134]

The coup de grace for China's standing in the developing world would come in Angola. Both China and the USSR had been involved in the

Angolan liberation struggle from Portuguese rule since before the outbreak of armed struggle in February 1961, and, by the outbreak of all-out civil war between the rival liberation movements in the wake of official independence on November 11, 1975, China and the USSR were supporting opposing sides. In the eyes of African public opinion initially neither side had an automatic claim to legitimacy; however, African opinion turned decisively in favor of the Soviet- and Cuban-backed MPLA once it became public knowledge that South African troops had entered the war on the same side as China and against the former. The image of the PRC siding with the apartheid regime in Pretoria was unforgivable, and the last straw in the eyes of many. When Agostinho Neto, the leader of the MPLA, called for an international solidarity conference in Luanda in early 1976, the Soviets attended with the expressed intent of capitalizing on the Chinese error and passing an explicitly anti-Chinese resolution.[135] For the first time in the history of the Afro-Asian solidarity movement, they succeeded.[136] A report from the Soviet embassy in Guinea-Bissau later that year reported that, despite the long history of Chinese support for the struggle of the ruling PAIGC in that country, the events in Angola had fatally undermined the attitude of the government toward Beijing. The chairman of the State Council, Luis Cabral, said at a closed meeting of government leaders that "objectively China presents itself together with the Republic of South Africa, a country where people with black skin, the same as you and me, are not considered people." Cabral was actually one of those the Soviet embassy considered more favorably disposed to China.[137] As late as May 1977, a Soviet Foreign Ministry delegation told the East Germans that "in relations with the countries of the Third World Beijing has still not redeemed itself from the shock of Angola."[138] By that time, however, China had moved on to other priorities and had essentially conceded the Third World to Moscow.

1976: Year of Divergence

For a decade and a half, China had been fighting a prolonged geopolitical battle with an opponent far richer and stronger than itself while undergoing tremendous turmoil at home. Resources that were desperately needed to rebuild the economy were going to build railroads in Africa and factories in Albania. By 1975, the CCP, as of the beginning of that year under the day-to-day control of the rehabilitated Deng Xiaoping, was ready to prioritize development at home. The long-delayed Fourth

National People's Congress was held in January 1975 and Zhou Enlai, in what was in effect his political swan song, called for concentrating state efforts on the "Four Modernizations": agriculture, industry, defense, and science and technology.[139] Though the difficult political situation would hamper the attempts to act on this platform for the next two years, one impact was felt immediately. On April 23, 1975, the CCP Central Committee decided to cut China's foreign aid, citing the fact that "the living standards in some recipient countries being higher than that in China, as well as more and more countries of the Third World asking for aid from China."[140] Even before the death of Mao in September 1976, the Chinese leadership had already begun its disengagement from the Third World. Zhou Enlai died on January 8, 1976, and the battle for control of the party between Deng and his followers and the Gang of Four heated up. After Mao's death, the struggle for succession reached a climax and on October 6, 1976, the Gang of Four was arrested. The path forward was unclear and would proceed in a series of fits and starts, but the clear priority from now on was to be domestic economic growth. Leadership of the world revolution was no longer the goal.[141]

The Soviets, in 1976, proceeded in the opposite direction. At the Twenty-Fifth CPSU Congress that year, Leonid Brezhnev laid out the agenda for the developing world: "The complete liquidation of all remnants of the system of colonial oppression, limitations on equality and independence of peoples, all hotbeds of colonialism and racism; development and strengthening of all-around cooperation of the USSR with the liberated countries; the deepening of ties of the CPSU with revolutionary-democratic parties and movements; the elimination of discrimination and any artificial obstacles in international trade, all manifestations of inequality, *diktat*, and exploitation in international economic relations; the liquidation of remaining military bases, and above all the realization of a just and solid settlement in the Near East; and the provision of collective security in Asia."[142] It will be recalled that at the Twenty-Fourth Congress in 1971, little was said about the developing world besides statements of support for armed struggle in Indochina, the Middle East, and southern Africa. Now, Moscow had adopted the Third World agenda and declared itself the protector and promoter of the interests of developing countries. The Twenty-Fifth Congress had an air of triumph regarding the international situation, coming as it did in the wake of communist victories in Vietnam and Angola. The movement in support of the NIEO was now considered to represent a new, higher stage in the international struggle against imperialism and capitalism. Meanwhile, ties between the USSR and the countries of "socialist orientation" were getting ever closer and it seemed that they might be finally becoming true Marxist-Leninist states that could then serve as examples for the rest of the developing world. The supposedly growing interest in Marxist-Leninist theory meant that now was the time to promote real "scientific socialism."[143] One Soviet author captured the optimism of the moment: "The experience of the development of the countries of socialist orientation, in our opinion, demonstrates that in the current epoch, when world socialism has become the decisive social force in the development of humanity, even with weak economic development and a numerically small working class, on the first steps even small parties of national revolutionaries, sharing the basic propositions of Marxism-Leninism, striving to plant this teaching and recognizing the leading political role of the working class, are able to lead the struggle for national progress and the socialist goal."[144] The Soviet Union believed that it had successfully recaptured the mantle of leadership of the world revolution, spearheading the struggle of the entire developing world against imperialism and inequality while disseminating the ideology of Marxism-Leninism through an inner circle of countries of socialist orientation. The future was bright—this was to be Moscow's moment.

And so the Soviets had defeated the Chinese for the mantle of leadership of the world revolution. But what revolution were they leading? In 1976, the Soviets managed to organize a meeting of twenty-nine European Communist Parties in East Berlin. Despite the modest size of the gathering, it was the closest they would come to having a full meeting of the international communist movement ever again. Even so, the document adopted was a compromise version, "rather revisionist" from the Soviet perspective.[145] In 1980, they organized an anti-imperialist forum, held in East Berlin as well. It was attended by seventy-seven Communist Parties and eighty-nine "revolutionary democratic parties and national liberation movements." It turned out that the revolution the USSR was now leading was a revolution whose main direction was anti-imperialism. In effect, the international communist movement had ceased to exist. Eurocommunism had been enshrined at a meeting of the Western European Communist Parties in January 1974 in Brussels and, in any case, the revolutionary tensions of the late 1960s in the West had subsided by the mid-1970s. In Asia, the Chinese and the Koreans were going their own way while many other parties had been severely damaged by the Sino-Soviet split. What remained was a devastated Indochina, which would burden the Soviets for the rest of the Cold War. African communism, to the degree that it existed, was being created by the barrels of Soviet and Cuban guns. In Latin America, Communist Parties were battling military juntas and fighting guerrilla wars. These groups had little left in common, let alone enough to bring them to a table to reestablish a united movement. What had begun in the late 1950s as a fight within the communist movement over revolutionary tactics in the international arena had ended up as a struggle over the relevance of an ideology, developed in the industrialized world, to the circumstances of a world in which the sharpest grievances came from preindustrial societies emerging from colonialism. In the end Moscow had reasserted its revolutionary leadership by adopting large parts of the Third World agenda. It had sacrificed peaceful coexistence in the name of anti-imperialism, supporting armed struggle morally and materially around the world. It had made the struggle for a restructuring of the international economic order its own and limited the promotion of its revolutionary model to a small circle of states for which it bore heavy financial and political responsibility. It made the battles against racism, Zionism, and apartheid its central slogans in the international arena. Instead of an international working class that "knows no national boundaries," Soviet policy in effect now supported a view of the world in which workers in the First World and workers in the Third World were enemies. Such was what remained of the revolution the Soviet Union had fought to lead.

For the Chinese, their defeat had freed them from the burden of competing for world revolutionary leadership. They were able to do what the Soviet Union would not be able to do a decade later—they realized that they were losing the competition and that, in any case, the downsides of competing outweighed the benefits—so they gave up and went home, attending to their own needs. The road ahead for the Chinese would be smoothed by the fact that, as Boris Kulik, one of the Soviet Union's top China experts, wrote in looking back in 2000, "the leadership of the CCP from the beginning had never considered the construction of socialism any sort of self-justifying goal, but saw the possibilities of socialist construction as the most effective for the resurrection of a great and mighty China."[146] As long as that belief remained, Beijing would embrace socialist economic principles domestically. Nevertheless, the Chinese Revolution was not merely self-serving. On the contrary, there were real ideals behind the global projection of Chinese revolutionary influence. Those ideals, however, were about independence, anti-imperialism, economic development, and resurrecting the dignity of people who had suffered through the depredations of European colonialism. The Chinese Revolution was the revolution of decolonization, and combating capitalism only played into that insofar as it served as an obstacle to the defeat of imperialism and neocolonialism. The Marxist-Leninist conviction that one world revolutionary process would lead to the demise of both capitalism and imperialism, however, led the leaders in Moscow and Beijing to think that they were fighting over ownership of the same revolution. As a result, the Chinese challenge, which consolidated the political impact of decolonization, changed the terms of the revolutionary conversation with the result that Moscow ultimately fought, and won, on China's terms.

So where did all of this leave the Third World? The developing world would never again attain the heights of political power and influence that it had reached during the heyday of the New International Economic Order in 1974–75. Now the Soviet Union sought to make itself the protector of the developing world and the states closely allied with Moscow—Cuba, Vietnam, Laos, Cambodia, Angola, Afghanistan, Ethiopia, South Yemen, etc.—increasingly joined and participated in organizations such as the Non-Aligned Movement and the Group of 77. Rather than strengthening solidarity and broadening it to encompass a joint "Third World–Second World" front, this had the effect of dividing the developing world. Such organizations would be rent by divisions over the issue of ties to the socialist world and the promotion of socialist policies, and united action would become impossible. The beginnings of a willingness to compromise evidenced by the developed world at the Seventh UN Special Session in 1975 would evaporate as the West recovered economically from the shocks of the 1970s, and the indebtedness of the developing countries grew. Instead, the new political calculus of Soviet support and influence in the Third World, combined with a reinvigorated Cold War, would taint the entire program of Third World solidarity, the NIEO, and nonalignment with the stench of communism.

CONCLUSION

The Revolution is Dead—Long Live the Revolution

The Sino-Soviet split was very difficult for contemporaries to decipher. No less an authority than Nikita Khrushchev admitted to being baffled. During Fidel Castro's visit to Moscow in early 1963, in response to Castro's request for an explanation of the differences between the Soviets and the Chinese, Khrushchev replied, "I am also asking, what differences? We are for peace and they are for peace. We are for coexistence, and so are they. What's the problem?"[1] Of course, rare is the political leader who is openly against peace or justice, in whatever way he or she understands these concepts. But the reasons for Khrushchev's confusion run even deeper in this case. In the Marxist-Leninist view, imperialism is merely a stage of capitalism—the highest stage—and so the struggles against capitalism and imperialism are one and the same. Furthermore, it is capitalism and its by-product imperialism that are the sources of violence, oppression, and inequality in the world. Consequently, the two can only be defeated together, and only by defeating them can one bring peace and justice. One cannot simultaneously be for peace and justice and against ending the capitalist/imperialist system. Because of their explicit adherence to Marxist-Leninist ideology, then, both the Soviet and Chinese Communists necessarily took this as a fundamental premise of their worldviews and the ultimate goal that shaped their policies. What differences, indeed?

The differences came from the fact that two very different revolutionary programs underlay this Leninist synthesis. An important connection exists between imperialism and capitalism, just as nationalism, religion, science, technology, and many other concepts are connected to imperialism. Imperialism, however, did not begin with capitalism, nor is its demise tied to the demise of capitalism, as even the Chinese acknowledged when they began to label the USSR a "social imperialist" power. The Soviet Communist Party, descending as it did from a long heritage of Russian populism and European socialism, took the replacement of the capitalist economic system with something superior as its raison d'être to the very end. Socialism and communism were meant to succeed capitalism on the stage of history, most importantly in the centers of industrial capitalism. This seemed to be a reasonable strategy as capitalism floundered during the Great Depression, but it turned out to be a failure in the post-1945 era. "Peaceful coexistence" was essentially a continuation of this strategy—an attempt to prevent the capitalists from uniting to destroy "really existing socialism" before it could demonstrate its superiority in the economic sphere. On its own, this strategy would likely not have succeeded anyway, but the USSR was forced to abandon it in any case in order to try to take the reins of the anti-imperialist struggle as well. In its earliest days, the nascent Russian Socialist Federated Republic had sought to hitch the anti-imperialist revolution to the anticapitalist one, but its resources were meager and the anticolonial movement was still at an early stage, with independence decades away. Even at that time, however, tensions had already arisen between the interests of the revolution in Europe and those of revolutionaries in Asia, Africa, and Latin America. The various Comintern shifts of policy between radical isolation and the "Popular Front" were products more of circumstances in Europe than in the colonies, and Comintern adherents in the latter often suffered the consequences. In the wake of the rapid wave of decolonization that crested in the decades after World War II, the Soviets would find that sacrificing the interests of the anti-imperialist revolution to the Europe-centered anticapitalist struggle would mean abdicating leadership of a global Marxist-Leninist revolution.

The Chinese Communist Party was a product of that anti-imperialist revolution. China had a long, proud imperial tradition of its own, and the humiliation it suffered at the hands of the West and Japan over the course of a century had sparked a radical movement to rebuild a strong, united, independent, modern, and prosperous China. Early on, Chinese intellectuals had come to see their own oppression at the hands of imperialism as part of a global system that needed to be destroyed, and, due to its size and success in military struggle as well as its charismatic leader, the new People's Republic of China provided a compelling champion for a global anti-imperialist struggle. For a while, the PRC and the USSR remained allies, though it was an alliance often fraught with tension. The alliance rapidly deteriorated once the Chinese leadership saw enough evidence in Algeria, Vietnam, and Congo as well as its own border conflict with India, among other places for it to conclude that the USSR meant to betray the anti-imperialist cause in the name of peaceful coexistence. Though this was not the only cause of the split, it was the split's primary international significance, and the one that transformed an ideological dispute between the CPSU and the CCP into a rift that tore through the heart of the global communist movement.

While the issue of war or peace, militant anti-imperialist struggle or peaceful coexistence and economic competition, was the most obvious and most divisive issue arising from the clash of priorities between the anti-imperialist and anticapitalist revolutions, it was not the only one. The different models of development proposed by the Soviets and Chinese for the newly emerging states in the 1960s reflect some of these other divisions. The Soviet model reflected a concern with demonstrating the superiority of an economic system based on state-led industrialization and social control of the means of production. This meant a focus on building heavy industry, even in the least-developed regions, an openness to foreign investment, and a disregard for raising living standards connected to a neglect of light industry, suppression of private trade, and promotion of collectivized agriculture. The Chinese model arose from China's own experience and stressed the elimination of foreign influence and the construction of a strong, cohesive society. This meant focusing on efforts to raise living standards immediately to allow people to enjoy the fruits of independence by promoting light industry and small-scale private trade while eliminating any foreign economic presence. The economic expression of the divide between the two revolutions was matched in the sociopolitical realm by a fundamental question of how the dynamics of oppression were to be conceived and, consequently, combated. Was the revolution about class or about something else, whether that meant race, nation, or ethnicity? This last question was perhaps the most dangerous one for the Soviet claim to leadership because the USSR was always perceived as a "white" power by people throughout the developing world. The Chinese leadership understood the power of this issue from their own experience and they managed to credibly argue for affinities between themselves and other recently colonized peoples, even when the representatives of those peoples espoused views far from Maoism ideologically. Whether the source of oppression was ultimately economic or racial-ethnic-national in origin would become a defining issue for the Left everywhere, one that would destroy old coalitions and ideologies and create new ones.

The outcome of the Sino-Soviet clash would therefore have fateful consequences for the Left around the world. Though the Soviets emerged victorious from their struggle with the Chinese by the late 1970s, it was a Pyrrhic victory. To defeat the Chinese challenge to their leadership of the "world revolution," the Soviets would have to adopt much of the Chinese agenda because that agenda derived, in large part, from the agenda of the anti-imperialist revolution, and the Soviets had to adapt their own agenda to the anti-imperialist one in order to lead it. As the revolutionary battleground shifted to the Global South, and the working classes in the West became less revolutionary, sticking with the anticapitalist agenda was a losing prospect for the aspiring leader of the world revolution. This meant that Moscow had to embrace militant anti-imperialism, and issues of race and nation, including the anti-Zionist and anti-apartheid struggles, gained higher profiles on the Soviet agenda. The Soviets similarly adapted their political and economic model for developing states, taking a more pragmatic approach to the development of industry by focusing on profitability and consumption, while allowing more room for private trade and cautioning against too-hasty collectivization of agriculture. This shift away from the project of "building socialism" in the early 1960s, which focused on social control of the means of production, was balanced by two other imperatives: the creation of Marxist-Leninist vanguard parties and the embrace of proposals for a new international economic order, one which would shift the terms of trade to favor developing states. The Soviets therefore replaced peaceful competition and evolution with militant struggle, global class solidarity with racial and national identity, and domestic economic reform with promotion of international redistribution. They were now leading a very different revolution, a fact that some leading Soviet policymakers would realize in hindsight.[2]

Even this adulterated victory would soon turn sour for Moscow. The Soviet support for militant revolutionary struggle in the late 1970s would lead to a breakdown of détente and the return of the Cold War in the early 1980s to a level of intensity not seen in decades. Furthermore, the burden of supporting the USSR's various client states around the Third World would prove to be quite heavy. When East German State Planning chairman Gerhard Schürer appealed to his Soviet counterpart Nikolai Baibakov for more fuel in 1981, Baibakov responded, "Should I cut back on oil to Poland? Vietnam is starving . . . should we just give away Southeast Asia? Angola, Mozambique, Ethiopia, Yemen . . . we carry them all. And our standard of living is extraordinarily low."[3] In 1990, the USSR for the first time published a list of the foreign debts that it was owed, and the total came to 85 billion rubles, of which two-thirds was owed by Moscow's "friends." Cuba ranked first among the USSR's debtors with Vietnam third, India fourth, Syria fifth, Ethiopia eighth, and Angola eleventh.[4] As the burden on Soviet foreign policy and the Soviet economy grew while the latter headed toward zero growth, the voices calling for a reassessment of Soviet policy in the developing world grew ever louder. Back in December 1974, Nikolai Leonov, then head of the Information-Analytic Bureau of the KGB, wrote in his diary: "Another wonder of wonders has occurred. In distant, poor Dahomey, in Cotonou, local president Kereku has pronounced himself a Marxist-Leninist from December 6 of this year, and his country—going down the path of constructing socialism. He wants our help in organizing the army, special services, not to mention the economy. Our ambassador, to whom he entrusted all of this, sweated from fear and could not answer yes or no. . . . The action of the Dahomeians seems absurd. Eighty percent of the three-million strong population is illiterate, power is in the hands of a group of military people. There is no industry, no party, no classes. I wish very much that it were permitted to say the truth, even if it is forbidden!"[5] At the time, he did not speak the truth as he saw it, and, sure enough, Moscow was soon embroiled in an intense effort to build the revolution and combat Maoism in tiny Benin, as revolutionary Dahomey was renamed.[6]

By November 1982, however, with Brezhnev dead and Yuri Andropov about to assume the office of General Secretary, skeptics of the utility of Soviet developing world policy were soon to have greater influence on the course of events. On the eve of taking office, Andropov echoed their skepticism, saying, "It is one thing to proclaim socialism . . . and quite another to build it."[7] Andropov's protégé Mikhail Gorbachev, upon assuming control in March 1985, did not necessarily disavow the USSR's role in the developing world. He still affirmed the need to support the "anti-imperialist path" of Angola, Ethiopia, and Mozambique, as he told Fidel Castro,[8] and he considered the setbacks the USSR had suffered in Asia, Africa, and Latin America to be "temporary."[9] Anatoly Chernyaev, his new foreign policy aide who had replaced the longtime incumbent A. M. Aleksandrov-Agentov, was frustrated because he believed that Gorbachev's thinking was still "contaminated by ideological and class mythology" and was marked by "contradictions and inconsistencies."[10] At the end of 1985, the USSR even sent 1,000 instructors and 1 billion dollars' worth of military equipment to Angola to prepare for a massive offensive with the objective of destroying UNITA in the southeastern part of the country.[11] However, Gorbachev also believed that the USSR had overemphasized "subjective" factors, such as "socialist consciousness" and "dedication to ideals," that led Moscow to ignore the fact that societies such as Angola and Ethiopia were a very long way away from being ready to build socialism.[12] At the same time, given the state of the Soviet economy, Gorbachev declared that it was time for foreign policy to serve the interests of domestic policy rather than the other way around, as had been the case for so long.[13] Along with the new foreign policy came a change of personnel, involving the replacement of such longtime hardliners as Foreign Minister Andrei Gromyko and Boris Ponomarev, head of the International Department, with younger figures who were regarded as "liberals," namely Eduard Shevardnadze and Anatoly Dobrynin. While Gorbachev himself remained committed to a Marxist view of the world in which countries would defect from capitalism to socialism over time, the policy of *glasnost* allowed voices to be heard that rejected Soviet policy in the developing world on a much more fundamental level. Dmitrii Volskii, an influential foreign affairs commentator, wrote in December 1988:

> It happened more than once that some African or Asian state turned out to be completely different from the way many of our press organs depicted it. True, this could only be established after the regime had fallen. Only then did it become known that "national-patriotic forces," on coming to power, had behaved like feudal or even prefeudal princes, that "important industrial projects," created at the wave of a hand using the people's money, were needed to indulge their vanity, that the country, after embarking on the path of "progressive transformations" and "strengthening national independence," had arrived at an economic catastrophe, and that its tired and indignant people had finally lost patience and overthrown their rulers.[14]

The disillusionment with the effort to build socialism in the developing world led some to question the binaries that had governed the Soviet worldview since at least the days of Andrei Zhdanov, Stalin's ideological architect of the "two-camp" model, if not earlier. Andrei Kolosovskii, a Soviet assistant deputy foreign minister, wrote that "[experiences] demonstrate clearly that by no means does every regime that has quarreled with the Americans follow a course of social progress, justice and democracy."[15] When Nelson Mandela was released from prison in 1990 and the apartheid regime in South Africa crumbled in what was perhaps Moscow's last major victory in the Third World, some voices in the USSR rejected the outcome and sided instead with the pro-apartheid forces.[16] Given the prevailing mood, the Soviet aid budget was cut to only 400 million rubles by 1991.[17] In that all-too-brief moment in the early 1990s when Russia embraced the West, leadership of the anti-imperialist struggle, which Moscow had fought so hard for, became not only unnecessary, but also a liability and a rueful memory.

The PRC, which had lost the competition for leadership of the world revolution, followed a very different path. In the wake of Mao's death and the arrest of the Gang of Four in the fall of 1976, the new CCP leadership under Deng Xiaoping disengaged from the competition with the USSR and began to chart an unprecedented path of economic reform. Though many would ask whether the USSR could have followed the path of Chinese reform, the fundamental differences between the CPSU and the CCP, and the Russian and Chinese Revolutions, dictate otherwise. The legitimacy of CPSU rule in the USSR was based upon its ability to construct an economic system superior to capitalism. If it could not do that, it had no reason to rule, even in the eyes of its General Secretary. The CCP, however, had taken power with the mandate to build a strong, united, independent, prosperous, and modern China. Many of its leaders were convinced that socialism provided the best way to do this, but once that proved to be misguided, new means had to be found to achieve the same goals. When the Communist regimes in Eastern Europe began to fall in 1989, the Chinese regime stayed firm because its anti-imperialist basis for legitimacy, and consequently the belief of the CCP leaders in their own cause, remained intact. On June 9, 1989, Deng Xiaoping told a group of officers in Beijing that "They [the demonstrators] had two key goals: one was to overthrow the Communist Party, the other was to topple the socialist system. Their aim was to establish a bourgeois republic totally dependent on the West."[18] Yao Yilin, a member of the Politburo speaking four days later at a conference of the Central Committee, was even more explicit: "The bourgeois republic they [our students and intellectuals] planned to establish would eventually become a vassal state attached to a certain imperialist or capitalist nation. *Without the leadership of the Chinese Communist Party and socialist system, it is impossible for China to exist in the world as a genuine independent state!*"[19] (italics mine). In the words of the CCP leaders attempting to justify their own positions, the alternative to a China under Communist Party rule was not a capitalist China, but a dependent, perhaps even a colonial, China.

The CCP conducted an extensive analysis of the reasons for the Soviet collapse, and its conclusions reflect its concern with independence and anti-imperialism over egalitarianism and social control of the means of production. On the one hand, Gao Di, editor in chief of *Renmin Ribao* (People's Daily), writing on August 30, 1991, vilified Gorbachev and Yeltsin as "traitors and agents of the West . . . [who] acted . . . in accordance with orders from America."[20] On the other hand, the chief defects of the Soviet system were identified as its allegiance to the planned economy and its refusal to introduce any market mechanisms. David Shambaugh notes: "Virtually all assessments were in agreement that the totalism of the command economy and the absence of market mechanisms were fundamental failings of the Soviet economic system. They also agreed that this failure was the result of economic determinism and excessive ideological dogmatism that dismissed certain reforms as 'capitalist' and thus inappropriate."[21] The Soviet collapse consequently had the effect of not only affirming China's market-oriented path, but also accelerating it, thereby revivifying the pace of reform that had slowed in the wake of the June 1989 repression.[22] In its analysis of the success of the Cuban Communist Party in maintaining its rule, the *Zhonglianbu* praised the Cubans for "combining indigenous ideology (Marti Thought) with Marxism-Leninism" and for "refusing to adopt a Western multiparty system," but not for any particular achievements in the economic sphere.[23] Looking at the CCP today, Shambaugh asserts: "Aside from these propagandistic clichés, what the party has consistently advocated is really little different from the core themes that all Chinese rulers since the Self-Strengtheners of the 1870s have advocated: attaining wealth and power, enhancing nationalism and international dignity; and preserving unity and preventing chaos."[24] This approach, Shambaugh argues, has been effective: "Though not original, these core visions do resonate deeply in China and do lend the current party leadership legitimacy and continuity with the past."[25] While China has changed dramatically since the 1980s, at its core the mission guiding its rulers has actually changed very little over more than a century, and thus far the CCP has proven itself to be most successful at fulfilling that mission.

This story, then, of the Sino-Soviet competition for influence in the developing world and the clash between the anticapitalist and anti-imperialist revolutionary agendas should also be seen as grounds for humility both for American policymakers and for some historians of American foreign policy. Not only China and Russia but also smaller countries such as Egypt, Algeria, Chile, and Guinea have their own national narratives and priorities that sometimes involve the United States and sometimes do not. The tendency to see the Cold War as a bilateral struggle between the United States and the Soviet Union, between capitalism and communism, often involved, and continues to involve, interpreting every move by one side as a response to the other. Robert F. Kennedy, for example, when running for president in 1968, argued that Guinea's decision not to allow Soviet flights to Cuba at the height of the Cuban Missile Crisis was evidence of its sympathy for the United States.[26] Given the extremely tense relations between Guinea and the Soviet Union in 1962, as illustrated in chapter 2, this conclusion appears presumptuous. Perhaps the most consequential instances of this perception surrounded Soviet and Chinese support for North Vietnam. Many in Washington during the war agreed with the notion that Soviet policy constituted a "combination of continued aid to the North with diplomatic and propaganda strong-arm tactics designed to inhibit us," as one high-level analysis from 1966 concluded.[27] However, it seems that rather than focusing on pressuring or humiliating the United States, Soviet policy in Vietnam might actually have been a product of a situation in which other priorities, namely the struggle for revolutionary leadership with the PRC, took precedence over concerns with Soviet-American relations. American policymakers then would be well advised to consider the perspectives from other capitals and the forces operating on their policies, keeping in mind that the role of the United States might itself be secondary.

From the American perspective, this could have a significant ameliorative impact. A tendency has been prevalent in certain corners to see the world in terms of "the West and the Rest," in Kyshore Mahbubani's phrase. The notion of non-Western countries as having fundamental interests in common and likely to present some sort of united front was both one of the great hopes and one of the great fears of the Cold War era, and it has been resurrected at times in the post–Cold War era, such as in Samuel Huntington's conception of a "Confucian-Islamic connection."[28] However, the story of the failure of both the Soviets and the Chinese to build this sort of coalition due not only to differences of interests but also to ideology should dampen thoughts about the inherent likelihood of such an arrangement. Even the common ground of anti-American rhetoric has often proved to be an insufficient basis for unity. Assimilating this lesson might help American policymakers to decide which battles are worth fighting and which should best be avoided as well as what correlation of interests can be productively exploited.

In the introduction to his book *The Global Cold War*, Odd Arne Westad writes that he has little doubt that historians of the future will regard the Cold War "as one of the final stages of European global control."[29] From a political and economic perspective this seems quite likely to be true; after all, European (and American) economic hegemony certainly seem to be diminishing and it appears that Europe will regress to somewhere closer to its historical norm as a percentage of the world economy. Where economic influence goes, political and military influence will soon follow. But to see the Cold War in the Third World as simply an attempt by Europeans, broadly speaking, to control the rest of the world seems to be to miss something important about what was really going on in the second half of the twentieth century. The Cold War was first and foremost a battle over the future of humanity, over the structure of economies, states, and societies. For a number of reasons, this battle overlapped with the emergence of the majority of humanity from colonial rule, leading a vast number of new states to seek to build themselves up from almost nothing to achieve a dignified and prosperous existence in the international arena. The confluence of states looking to sell a political and economic model while many others were looking to buy one created a massive global marketplace in which new models were created or modified and others failed and disappeared. It would be incorrect to see either the sellers or the buyers as simply disinterested agents on behalf of their peoples and even more incorrect to ignore the power discrepancies between the superpowers and developing states and the terrible, tragic consequences that power discrepancies and cynical pursuit of interests caused around the globe during the Cold War. But something important is also lost if we do not see the second half of the twentieth century for what it was: an attempt by many around the world to catch up to the most developed countries and achieve a more just and egalitarian division of wealth on both a domestic and an international scale. The Cold War may be over, and the particular models that it represented may be largely discredited, but the fundamental problem of inequality still remains and the search for a solution will continue.

Notes

Abbreviations

AHM	*Arquivo Histórico de Moçambique* (Historical Archive of Mozambique)
AJ	*Arhiv Jugoslavije* (Archive of Yugoslavia)
AMAE	*Arhive Diplomatice ale Ministerul Afacerilor Externe* (Diplomatic Archive of the Ministry of Foreign Affairs, Romania)
AMREC	*Archivo Histórico del Ministerio de Relaciones Exteriores* (Historical Archive of the Ministry of Foreign Relations, Chile)
ANIC	*Arhivele Naționale Istorice Centrale din România* (National Historical Archive of Romania)
AVPRF	*Arkhiv Vneshneĭ Politikoĭ Rossisskoĭ Federatsii* (Archive of the Foreign Policy of the Russian Federation)
CFMA	中国外交部开放档案 (*Zhongguo Waijiaobu kaifang dang'an—*[Declassified] Chinese Foreign Ministry Archive)
GARF	*Gosudarstvennyĭ Arkhiv Rossisskoĭ Federatsii* (State Archive of the Russian Federation)
IAN/TT	*Instituto dos Arquivos Nacionais da Torre do Tombo* (Institute of National Archives of the Torre do Tombo, Portugal)
RGAE	*Rossisskiĭ Gosudarstvennyĭ Arkhiv Ekonomiki* (Russian State Archive of the Economy)
RGANI	*Rossisskiĭ Gosudarstvennyĭ Arkhiv Noveisheĭ Istorii* (Russian State Archive of Contemporary History)
RGASPI	*Rossisskiĭ Gosudarstvennyĭ Arkhiv Sotsial'no-Politicheskoĭ Istorii* (Russian State Archive of Socio-Political History)
SADFAA	South African Department of Foreign Affairs Archive
SANDFA	South African National Defense Forces Archive
SAPMO-BArch	*Stiftung Archiv der Parteien und Massenorganisationen der DDR—Bundesarchiv* (Archive of the Parties and Mass Organizations of the GDR in the Federal Archives, Germany)

Introduction

1. Quoted in Heikal, *The Cairo Documents*, 349.

2. Ibid., 344.

3. See Louro, "Rethinking Nehru's Internationalism."

4. See, for example, Aydin, *The Politics of Anti-Westernism in Asia*; Mishra, *From the Ruins of Empire: The Intellectuals Who Remade Asia*; Lake and Reynolds, *Drawing the Global Color Line*.

5. Manela, *The Wilsonian Moment*, 224.

6. Nkrumah, *Neocolonialism: The Last Stage of Imperialism*, 256.

7. For the most recent work on the Sino-Soviet split, see Luthi, *The Sino-Soviet Split*, and Radchenko, *Two Suns in the Heavens*. For a post-Soviet Russian take, see Kulik, *Sovetsko-Kitaiskiĭ Raskol*. For a good summary of the Cold War–era scholarship, see Ellison, ed., *The Sino-Soviet Conflict*.

8. Westad, *Brothers in Arms*, 30.

9. Brutents, *Tridtsat' Let na Staroĭ Ploshchadi*, 140.

10. See for example Ulam, *In the Name of the People: Prophets and Conspirators in Prerevolutionary Russia*; and Wolfe, *Three Who Made a Revolution*.

11. Quoted in Martin, *Affirmative Action Empire*, 6.

12. Ulam, *Expansion and Coexistence*, 52–53.

13. Quoted in Ulam, *Expansion and Coexistence*, 121.

14. Karl Radek, Address to the Baku Congress of the Peoples of the East, September 2, 1920, http://www.marxists.org/history/international/comintern/baku/ch02.htm.

15. Lazitch and Drachovitch, *Lenin and the Comintern*, 376.

16. "Theses on the Eastern Question," Fourth Congress of the Communist International, December 5, 1922, http://www.marxists.org/history/international/comintern/4th-congress/eastern-question.htm.

17. Quoted in Karl, *Staging the World: Chinese Nationalism at the Turn of the Twentieth Century*, 195.

18. Meisner, *Li Ta-Chao and the Origins of Chinese Marxism*, 99.

19. Hunt, *The Genesis of Chinese Communist Foreign Policy*, 214.

20. At least one scholar does think that, despite the public image, Mao secretly thought that a Japanese victory would be the best thing for the Chinese revolution. See Sheng, *Battling Western Imperialism*.

21. See Cheng, *Creating the New Man*, 50–55.

22. Meisner, *Mao Zedong*, 110.

23. Quoted in Schram, *The Thought of Mao Tse-tung*, 123.

24. Burlatskii, *Mao Tse-tung*, 227.

25. Meisner, *Mao Zedong*, 77.

26. See, for example, Li, *Village China under Socialism and Reform*, 18, and Levine and Pantsov, *Mao*, 395–96.

27. Levine and Pantsov, *Mao*, 392.

28. Vogel, *Canton under Communism*, 95.

29. Conquest, *Harvest of Sorrow*, 261.

30. Li, *Village China under Socialism and Reform*, 338.

31. Levine and Pantsov, *Mao,* 421.

32. See Dikötter, *The Tragedy of Liberation,* 84–102, 155–63.

33. Vogel, *Canton under Communism,* 134.

34. Quoted in Schram, *The Thought of Mao Tse-tung,* 112.

35. Dikötter, *The Tragedy of Liberation,* 171.

36. Quoted in Vogel, *Canton under Communism,* 170.

37. For an extensive, well-documented narrative of the Comintern's Chinese episode, see Pantsov, *The Bolsheviks and the Chinese Revolution 1919–1927.*

38. See Caballero, *Latin America and the Comintern, 1919–1943,* 65.

39. Ibid., 85–93.

40. Quoted in Mazov, *A Distant Front in the Cold War,* 12.

41. Quoted in Claudin, *The Communist Movement,* 580.

42. For more on the "intermediate zone" see Chen, *China's Road to the Korean War,* 17–23.

43. See ibid., 18–19. Also see Chen, "China and the Bandung Conference: Changing Perceptions and Representations," 132–35.

44. Interview of author with Karen Brutents, March 13, 2008, in Moscow.

45. See Brutents, *Tridtsat' Let na Staroĭ Ploshchadi,* 164.

46. See for example Leonov, *Likholet'e,* 98–99, 112.

47. See, for example, Brutents, *Tridtsat' Let na Staroĭ Ploshchadi,* 145.

48. See Leonov, *Likholet'e,* 112, and Brutents, *Tridtsat' Let na Staroĭ Ploshchadi,* 165.

49. Brutents, *Tridtsat' Let na Staroĭ Ploshchadi,* 166.

50. Ibid., 170.

51. Ibid., 167–69.

52. Eran, *Mezhdunarodniki,* 130.

53. See Mazov, *A Distant Front in the Cold War,* 26–28.

54. At its foundation in 1950–1951 its mandate was even more specific, as its primary responsibility was to maintain contacts with Asian Communist parties. See Shen and Xia, "Leadership Transfer in the Asian Revolution: Mao Zedong and the Asian Cominform," 12.

55. See chapter 4 and Ma, *The Cultural Revolution in the Foreign Ministry of China.*

56. See, for example, Golan, *The Soviet Union and National Liberation Movements in the Third World;* Hough, *The Struggle for the Third World;* Katz, *The Third World in Soviet Military Thought;* and *The USSR and Marxist Revolutions in the Third World;* Light, ed., *Troubled Friendships;* MacFarlane, *Superpower Rivalry and Third World Radicalism;* Rubinstein, *Moscow's Third World Strategy;* Saivetz and Woodby, *Soviet–Third World Relations;* Wheelan and Dixon, *The Soviet Union in the Third World.*

57. See, for example, Gaiduk, *The Soviet Union and the Vietnam War;* Gleijeses, *Conflicting Missions;* Mazov, *A Distant Front in the Cold War.*

58. Olsen, *Soviet-Vietnam Relations and the Role of China, 1949–1964,* xix.

59. Ross, *Re-examining the Cold War,* 2.

60. Chai, *Choosing an Identity,* 144.

61. The question may be raised where those ideological beliefs came from, which would require a deeper story about the formation of ideological beliefs, but for our

current purposes it is sufficient that, by the time someone is in a position to affect a state's foreign policy, certain ideological beliefs may already be in place.

62. Gourevitch, *Politics in Hard Times*, 62–63.

63. Westad, in *The Global Cold War*, writes: "In the early 1980s, Soviet Marxists still preferred to view the emergence of political Islam as being in its "main trends" "objectively" allied to Western imperialism. Eventually, most policy makers in Moscow believed, regimes such the Iranian would end up in bed with the Americans, because of their shared anti-Communism" (299).

64. Khrushchev speech at Party Plenum, December 13, 1963, RGANI f.2 0.1 d.679, 126.

Chapter One

1. "20th Congress of the Communist Party of the Soviet Union, Stenographic Report," Vol. 1, March 1956, 25, quoted in *"O Tvorcheskom Primenenii Marksistsko-Leninskoĭ Teorii v Issledovanii Problem Vostokovedeniia," Problemy Vostokovedeniia* 3 (1959): 10.

2. For more on the reasons for disbandment of the Cominform, see Brzezinski, *The Soviet Bloc: Unity and Conflict.* For Nehru's comment that the existence of the Cominform would not be compatible with peaceful coexistence, see van Eekelen, *Indian Foreign Policy and the Border Dispute with China*, 58.

3. Quoted in Claudin, *The Communist Movement*, 591.

4. A. M. Diakov and G. Z. Sorkin, *"Natsional'no-Kolonial'nyĭ Vopros v Resheniiakh Kongressov Kommunisticheskogo Internatsionala,"Problemy Vostokovedeniia* 2 (1959): 64.

5. For more information on Chinese foreign policy and Sino-Soviet cooperation in Asia in the early 1950s, see Chen, *China's Road to the Korean War*; Westad, ed., *Brothers in Arms*; Zhai, *China and the Vietnam Wars, 1950–1975.*

6. Van Eekelen, *Indian Foreign Policy and the Border Dispute with China*, 56–57.

7. See, for example, Sun Peijun, "亚非国家经济发展的前景" (Prospects for Afro-Asian Countries' Economic Development), *Shijie ZhiShi* 2 (1958): 7–9.

8. Quoted in Zhai, *China and the Vietnam Wars*, 21–22.

9. Luthi, *The Sino-Soviet Split*, 77.

10. Shen, ed., 中苏关系史纲 (Historical Outline of Sino-Soviet Relations), 153–61.

11. Quoted in Armah, *Ghana's Foreign Policy, 1957–1966*, 4.

12. Conversion based on rate in Chinese Foreign Ministry Report "Soviet Economic and Military 'Aid' to Asian and African Nationalist Countries," January 18, 1965, Chinese Foreign Ministry Archive (CFMA), doc. 109-03652-03, 1.

13. See Report from State Committee on External Economic Ties (GKES) to Secretary of the Central Committee N. Mukhitdinov, June 3, 1961, Russian State Archive of Contemporary History (RGANI) f.5 0.30 d.371, 40–139, CFMA doc. 109-03652-03, 1; Report of GKES on aid to "Underdeveloped Capitalist Countries," August 16, 1957, Russian State Archive of the Economy (RGAE) f.365 0.2 d.88, 1–10.

14. Chinese embassy in Moscow to MFA, "Situation of Post-war Soviet Foreign Economic Aid," 12/6/1961, CFMA doc. 109-03022-04, 1.

15. See M. Lavrichenko, *"Ekonomicheskaia Pomoshch' SSSR Slaborazvitym Stranam,"* *Kommunist* 15 (1959): 110–17.

16. Report of Commission on Travel Abroad to General Department of the Central Committee (CC), March 4, 1959, RGANI f.5 0.14 d.19, 12–14.

17. Ibid., 14.

18. Brutents, *Tridtsat' let na Staroĭ Ploshchadi,* 197–98.

19. Soviet Foreign Ministry report on economic connections of PRC with underdeveloped countries of Asia and Africa, February 2, 1961, Foreign Policy Archive of the Russian Federation (AVPRF) f.100 0.48 papka 203 d.37, 95–97. For Algeria, see Chinese Foreign Ministry West Asia/Africa Division report for 1958 and plan for 1959, CFMA doc. 108-00060-01, 4.

20. For more information on the Liaison Department, see Wu Xiuquan, 回忆与怀念, 320–99. Wu was a member of the Liaison Department from 1958 to 1966 and his memoir indicates a department focused almost exclusively on issues within the Communist bloc.

21. Letter from MFA to State Council and Xinhua, September 20, 1956, CFMA doc. 102-00026-01, 5.

22. Chinese MFA report on creating Second Asia Division, October 23, 1958, CFMA doc. 102-00033-01, 4.

23. Chinese MFA to all embassies, foreign trade representatives, consulates, December 18, 1957, CFMA doc. 108-00004-07, 16–23.

24. Report of State Committee on Cultural Ties (GKKS) to General Department CC, March 22, 1958, RGANI f.5 0.30 d.272, 43–45.

25. Ibid.

26. Chinese MFA to all embassies, March 17, 1958, CFMA doc. 108-00004-07, 20–23.

27. Report by Liu Ningyi to socialist countries' ambassadors in China on AAPSO Conference, January 20, 1958, CFMA doc. 109-00822-01, 5–7.

28. Report by Liu Ningyi to CC CCP from First AAPSO Conference, January 5, 1958, CFMA doc. 108-00004-07, 7.

29. MFA letter to all embassies on First AAPSO Conference, March 17, 1958, CFMA doc. 108-00004-07, 23.

30. Quoted in *"XXI S'ezd i zadachi Vostokovedeniia," Problemy Vostokovedeniia* 1 (1959): 19.

31. Ibid., 20.

32. Ibid., 24.

33. Proposals for the development of economic ties between the USSR and developing countries for a conference of the Economic Section of Orientalists, October 29–November 1, 1958, RGANI f.5 0.30 d.272, 176.

34. RGAE f.365 0.2 v.1, XI–XII in the introduction of the opus.

35. Ibid., 220.

36. Report on the participation of the state and private sectors in Afro-Asian trade with USSR, to N. A. Mukhitdinov, secretary of the CC, June 15, 1961, RGANI f.5 0.30 d.371, 147–50.

37. Report of GKES to N. A. Mukhitdinov, secretary of the CC, August 21, 1961, RGANI f.5 o.30 d.371, 227–36.

38. M. Lavrichenko, *"Ekonomicheskaia' Pomoshch' SSSR Slaborazvitym Stranam,"* 116.

39. MFA report on the situation in French-controlled Africa, December 1, 1958, CFMA doc. 110-00833-01, 1–31.

40. MFA West Asia/Africa Division report for 1958 and plan for 1959, CFMA doc. 108-00060-01, 1–8.

41. Report on events in West Asia/Africa and tendencies for development, Central Committee Investigations Department Research Office circular, January 25, 1959, CFMA doc. 108-00060-02, 1–37.

42. Ibid., 21–22.

43. MFA report on Africa to all embassies and consulates, January 9, 1959, CFMA doc. 108-00145-04, 1–3.

44. MFA West Asia/Africa Division report for 1958 and plan for 1959, CFMA doc. 108-00060-01, 21.

45. Letter from Union of the Peoples of Cameroon to the Chinese Committee of Afro-Asian Solidarity, August 3, 1958, CFMA doc. 108-00120-12, 11.

46. Letter from embassy Rabat to MFA on Cameroonian aid request, July 10, 1959; Letter from embassy Cairo to MFA on Senegalese request for aid, July 6, 1959, CFMA doc. 108-00134-02, 1–7; Report from embassy Prague to MFA, October 8, 1959, CFMA doc. 108-00134-04, 1.

47. MFA report on Africa to all embassies and consulates, January 9, 1959, CFMA doc. 108-00145-04, 3.

48. Report of GKKS to General Department of the CC on meeting with Chinese delegation, May 15, 1959, RGANI f.5 o.30 d.307, 12–16.

49. See, for example, the cautious Soviet approach on Vietnam at this time as evidenced in Asselin, *Hanoi's Road to the Vietnam War, 1954–1965,* 63.

50. MFA report to CC CPSU on China and question of peaceful coexistence, July 2, 1960, AVPRF f.100 o.47 Papka 197 d.45, 207.

51. For the different approaches of the USSR and the PRC to the issue of normalization of relations with Yugoslavia, see Kulik, *Sovetsko-Kitaiskiĭ Raskol: Prichiny i Posledstviia,* 318–22.

52. Stenogram of speech of head of Chinese delegation in meeting with Soviet GKKS, April 24, 1959, RGANI f.5 o.30 d.307, 19.

53. Brzezinski, *The Soviet Bloc: Unity and Conflict,* 336. For an excellent discussion of the Yugoslav issue at the time, see the entire chapter, 309–37.

54. Hai Nan, "印度对维护世界和平的贡献" (India's Contribution to the Preservation of World Peace), *Shijie Zhishi* 2 (1958): 23–24.

55. Report from MFA Division of USSR/Eastern Europe on Yugoslav-Indian relations, 1959, CFMA doc. 109-01432-01, 14.

56. Neuhauser, *Third World Politics: China and the Afro-Asian People's Solidarity Organization,* 13.

57. Letter from embassy Cairo to Chinese Peace Committee, January 20, 1959, CFMA doc. 108-00146-01, 5.

58. Letter from embassy Cairo to Chinese Peace Committee, February 14, 1959, ibid., 10.

59. Letter from Chinese Peace Committee to embassy Cairo, June 9, 1959, ibid., 32.

60. Luthi, *The Sino-Soviet Split*, 144.

61. Ibid., 145. Luthi cites *Pravda*, September 10, 1959, 3.

62. Kulik, *Sovetsko-Kitaiskiĭ Raskol*, 293–94. Kulik cites conversations between Chen Yi and the Soviet chargé d'affaires N. G. Sudarikov from the Foreign Policy Archive of the Russian Federation (AVPRF).

63. Luthi, *The Sino-Soviet Split*, 149.

64. Mikhail Suslov, report at CC CPSU Party plenum, December 12, 1959, RGANI f.2 o.1 d.415, 19–44.

65. Quoted in Luthi, *The Sino-Soviet Split*, 144.

66. Letter from embassy Cairo to MFA and Chinese Peace Committee, August 30, 1959, CFMA doc. 108-00146-01, 51–55.

67. Letter from embassy Cairo to MFA and Chinese Peace Committee, November 5, 1959, ibid., 97–102.

68. Report from Zhu Ziqi, Chinese representative at AAPSO secretariat in Cairo to Chinese Peace Committee, March 24, 1960, CFMA doc. 108-00106-01, 21. Also see Gott, Major, and Warner, eds., *Documents on International Affairs 1960*.

69. Stenogram of Session of Presidium of Soviet Committee of Solidarity with the Countries of Asia and Africa (SKSSAA), January 8, 1960, State Archive of the Russian Federation (GARF) f.9540 o.1 d.60, 35.

70. Ibid., 39.

71. Zhu Ziqi to Chinese Peace Committee, March 10, 1960, CFMA doc. 108-00106-01, 8.

72. Zhu Ziqi to Chinese Peace Committee, March 23, 1960, ibid., 15.

73. Embassy Cairo to Chinese Peace Committee and Politburo CC CCP, report on preparatory work for Second AAPSO Conference, March 6, 1960, ibid., 4.

74. Ibid., 4 and 15.

75. Zhu Ziqi to Chinese Peace Committee, March 24, 1960, ibid., 20.

76. Chinese Peace Committee to CC CCP, report on Second AAPSO Conference, June 22, 1960, ibid., 57.

77. Liu Dingyi and Liao Chengzhi to Zhou Enlai, Chen Yi, Liaison Department, Chinese Peace Committee, report from Second AAPSO Conference, April 10, 1960, ibid., 43.

78. Ibid.

79. Ibid., 46.

80. Ibid., 47–48.

81. Chinese Peace Committee to CC CCP, report on Second AAPSO Conference, June 22, 1960, ibid., 59.

82. Zhu Ziqi to Chinese Peace Committee, March 10, 1960, ibid., 8.

83. Conversation of Sekou Touré with Chinese Afro-Asian Solidarity Committee delegation, April 18, 1960, CFMA doc. 108-00106-03, 3.

84. Report of Soviet delegation on visit to Ghana, June 28–July 10, 1960, RGANI f.5 o.30 d.336, 96–107.

85. Stenogram of SCSCAA Presidium session, February 12, 1960, GARF f.9540 o.1 d.62, 16.

86. Report of deputy head of Ministry of Higher Education to CC "On Measures for Strengthening Aid of USSR to Underdeveloped Countries in the Area of Higher and Middle Specialized Education," 1961, RGANI f.5 o.14 d.20, 27–28.

87. Report on fulfillment of CC CPSU resolution of January 29, 1960, on improving Soviet radio propaganda overseas, RGANI f.5 o.33 d.175, 82–87.

88. For discussion on the relationship between SCSCAA and *Aziia i Afrika Segodnia,* see, for example, GARF f.9540 o.1 d.80, 49.

89. Letter from the Cultural Office of PRC embassy Moscow to MFA, February 16, 1960, CFMA doc. 109-02099-01, 1–2, and report from embassy Moscow to MFA, April 5, 1960, ibid., 18.

90. Ibid., 2–3.

91. Embassy Moscow to MFA, November 18, 1960, ibid., 5–6.

92. PRC Committee on Foreign Cultural Ties to MFA, May 9, 1960, CFMA doc. 108-00223-04, 2–4.

93. Ibid., 4.

94. Ibid.

95. Liaison Department, distributing "Report to CC on Black African Personnel Coming to China to Study Revolutionary Experience," October 6, 1960, CFMA doc. 108-00223-06, 2.

96. Ibid., 1–3.

97. Report from Committee on Foreign Cultural Ties, March 25, 1960, CFMA doc. 108-00213-04, 1–3.

98. Reports on Xinhua delegation to Latin America, April 23–June 25, 1959, CFMA doc. 111-00274-01, 1–14.

99. Quoted in Li Anshan, "African Studies in China in the Twentieth Century: A Historiographical Survey," *African Studies Review* 48. 1 (April 2005): 62.

100. Ibid., 63.

101. Mark Sidel, "Latin American Studies in the People's Republic of China," *Latin American Research Review* 18.1 (1983): 143–53.

102. Quoted in Luthi, *The Sino-Soviet Split,* 161–62.

103. Ibid., 163.

104. Report of Frol Kozlov at CC CPSU plenum, July 7, 1960, RGANI f.2 o.1 d.458, 12.

105. Ibid., 13.

106. Ibid., 65.

107. Report from CC Propaganda Department on propaganda of African liberation movements, August 22, 1960, CFMA doc. 108-00214-02, 5.

108. Letter from MFA to PRC embassy in London, June 27, 1960, CFMA doc. 108-00218-01, 8–9.

109. Letter from PRC embassy in Switzerland to CC, August 6, 1960, CFMA doc. 108-00171-02, 4.

110. Report of Youth League to Liaison Department on visiting African student delegation, August 1960, CFMA doc. 108-00223-09, 6.

111. Ibid.

112. Ibid., 7.

113. Report from Youth League to Liaison Department, November 9, 1960, ibid., 31.

114. See MFA report on Angola, January 7, 1963, AVPRF f.658 o.3 papka 1 d.1 pp.38, for the USSR and SAPMO-BArch DY 30/IV 2/20/416, *"Aktenvermerk über die Aussprache mit Herrn da Cruz, Führer der nationalen Angolas Volksbefreiungsbewegung am 1.10.1960,"* 3, for East Germany.

115. Letter of MFA to party committees of Shenyang, Harbin, and Changchun on upcoming visit of delegation led by Viriato da Cruz and Amilcar Cabral, August 1960, CFMA doc. 108-00098-01, 27.

116. Letter of Zhu Ziqi and Liao Chengzhi to Liu Ningyi on aid to MPLA and PAIGC, September 9, 1960, CFMA doc. 108-00209-02, 3, 8–9.

117. Report from Beijing City State College, September 30, 1960, CFMA doc. 108-00150-05, 5–7.

118. SCSCAA Presidium Session, April 25, 1960, GARF f.9540 o.1 d.60, 117.

119. KGB to General Department CC CPSU, July 19, 1961, RGANI f.5 o.30 d.369, 105.

120. SCSCAA Presidium Session, January 8, 1962, GARF f.9540 o.1 d.109, 97–98.

121. MFA report on situation in black Africa, July 13, 1960, CFMA doc. 108-00025-02, 2.

122. Ibid., 3.

123. Ibid., 4.

124. MFA Report on British and formerly British Africa, December 12, 1960, CFMA doc. 108-00108-01, 3.

125. Ibid., 4.

126. See Luthi, *The Sino-Soviet Split*, 182–91.

127. Report by M. Suslov on 1960 Moscow meeting to CPSU plenum, January 8, 1961, RGANI f.2 o.1 d.510, 19.

128. Ibid., 20.

129. MFA circular to all embassies and representatives abroad, December 6, 1960, CFMA doc. 109-00936-01, 1.

130. Ibid., 5.

131. Ibid., 9.

132. Embassy Moscow to MFA, December 9, 1960, CFMA doc. 109-02064-06, 1–4.

Chapter Two

1. N. S. Khrushchev, *"Za Novye Pobedy Mirovogo Kommunisticheskogo Dvizheniia,"* *Kommunist*, 28.

2. Quoted in Michael E. Latham, *Modernization as Ideology*, 3.

3. Ibid., 56.

4. Kenneth Lieberthal, "The Great Leap Forward and the Split in the Yan'an leadership, 1958–1965," in *The Politics of China*, ed. Roderick Macfarquhar, 114.

5. Ibid., 112.

6. See, for example, Lorenz Luthi, *The Sino-Soviet Split*, 213, 237.

7. See Arthur Jay Klinghoffer, *Soviet Perspectives on African Socialism*, 196–97.

8. Letter of MFA to all representatives abroad, December 9, 1960, CFMA doc. 109-00936-01, 1.

9. Embassy London report on British and former British Africa, December 2, 1960, CFMA doc. 108-00108-01, 16.

10. Zhu Ziqi (PRC representative in AAPSO secretariat) to the Liaison Dept., January 15, 1961, CFMA doc. 108-00269-03, 7.

11. Bao Erhan (vice chairman, Chinese Committee on Afro-Asian Solidarity) to Liaison Department, January 19, 1961, ibid., 10.

12. Bao Erhan to Liaison Department, January 23, 1961, ibid., 13–15.

13. For more on Soviet policy in the Congo in this period, see Sergey Mazov, *A Distant Front in the Cold War,* 77–129, 159–81.

14. Conversation between PRC deputy MFA Zhang Hanfu and Soviet ambassador in Beijing Chervonenko, February 23, 1961, CFMA doc. 109-02267-01, 3–4.

15. SCSCAA Presidium session, May 8, 1961, GARF f.9540 o.1 d.81, 17–18.

16. Embassy Cairo to PRC Peace Committee, January 14, 1961, CFMA doc. 108-00269-03, 2.

17. Liu Ningyi (head of CC CCP Propaganda Department) to CC and Liaison Department, April 21, 1961, CFMA doc. 108-00269-05, 4.

18. SCSCAA Presidium session, April 15, 1961, GARF f.9540 o.1 d.81, 26.

19. Zhu Ziqi to Liu Ningyi, March 24, 1961, CFMA doc. 108-00269-01, 23–25.

20. Zhu Ziqi to Chinese Peace Committee, March 8, 1961, ibid., 3.

21. Zhu Ziqi to Liaison Department, December 24, 1961, CFMA doc. 108-00269-06, 7.

22. SCSCAA Presidium session, April 25, 1961, GARF f.9540 o.1 d.81, 12.

23. Liaison Dept to Liu Ningyi, April 8, 1961, CFMA doc. 108-00269-01, 39–41.

24. Liu Ningyi to CC and Liaison Department, April 21, 1961, CFMA doc. 108-00269-05, 4–6.

25. Ibid., 8.

26. Embassy Moscow to MFA, September 13, 1961, CFMA doc. 109-03037-01, 4–5.

27. Embassy Moscow to MFA, June 5, 1961, ibid., 10–11.

28. See, for example, John K. Cooley, *East Wind over Africa,* 210–20, Bruce Larkin, *China and Africa, 1949–1970,* 43–44, Phillip Snow, *The Star Raft,* 117.

29. Charles Neuhauser, *Third World Politics,* 36.

30. Embassy Moscow to MFA, August 29, 1961, CFMA doc. 109-00936-091, 1.

31. *"Proekt Programmy KPSS i Nekotorye Problemy Natsional'no-Osvoboditel'nogo Dvizheniia Narodov Azii i Afriki," Narodii Azii i Afriki* 5 (1961): 8. See also G. Mirskii, *"Tvorcheskii Marksizm i Problemy Natsional'no-Osvoboditel'nykh Revoliutsii," Mirovaia Ekonomika i Mezhdunarodnye Otnosheniia* 2 (February 1963): 66–67.

32. Quoted in Klinghoffer, *Soviet Perspectives on African Socialism,* 20.

33. Quoted in S. Ogurtsov, *"Razvivaiushchiesia Strany i Sotsial'nyi Progress," Aziia i Afrika Segodnia* 7 (July, 1963): 2.

34. G. Mirskii and V. Tiagunenko, *"Tendentsii i Perspektivy Natsional'no-Osvoboditel'nykh Revoliutsii," Mirovaia Ekonomika i Mezhdunarodnye Otnosheniia* 11 (1961): 30, *"Proekt Programmy KPSS i Nekotorye Problemy Natsional'no-Osvoboditel'nogo*

Dvizheniia Narodov Azii i Afriki," *Narody Azii i Afriki* 5 (1961): 11, *"Nekotorye Problemy Afrikanistov v Svete Reshenii XXII S'ezda KPSS,"* *Narody Azii i Afriki* 1 (1962): 15.

35. For a more extensive discussion of African socialism see Klinghoffer, *Soviet Perspectives on African Socialism,* 15–39.

36. Mirskii and Tiagunenko, *"Tendentsii i Perspektivy Natsional'no-Osvoboditel'nykh Revoliutsii,"* 30.

37. Paper of M. Suslov to CPSU Plenum, January 18, 1961, RGANI f.2 o.1 d.510, 20.

38. Quoted in V. I. Pavlov and I. B. Red'ko, *"Gosudarstvo Natsional'noi Demokratii i Perekhod k Nekapitalisticheskomu Razvitiiu,"* *Narody Azii i Afriki* 1 (1963): 30.

39. See V. Pavlov, *"Soiuz Rabochego Klassa i Krest'ianstva i Sotsial'nye Preobra- zovaniia na Vostoke,"* *Aziia i Afrika Segodnia* 10 (October 1961): 10, G. Kotovskii, *"Sel'skokhoziastvennyi Proletariat v Stranakh Azii i Afriki,"* *Aziia i Afrika Segodnia* 5 (May 1962): 16–18, G. Kim, *"O Gosudartsve Natsional'noi Demokratii,"* *Aziia i Afrika Segodnia* 10 (October 1962): 2–5, Mirskii and Tiagunenko, *"Tendentsii i Perspektivy Natsional'no-Osvoboditel'nykh Revoliutsii,"* 27.

40. See I. Potekhin, *"Afrika: Itogi i Perspektivy Antiimperialisticheskoi Revoliutsii,"* *Aziia i Afrika Segodnia* 10 (October 1962): 14–15, and G. Kim, *"O Gosudarstve Natsiona'noi Demokratii."*

41. V. Li, *"Dva Litsa Odnogo Klassa,"* *Aziia i Afrika Segodnia* 3 (March 1962): 6–9.

42. G. Kim, *"O Gosudarstve Natsional'noi Demokratii,"* 5.

43. V. Li, *"O Nekapitalisticheskom Puti Razvitiia,"* *Aziia i Afrika Segodnia* 11 (November 1961): 13.

44. V. Pavlov, *"Soiuz Rabochego Klassa i Krest'ianstvo i Sotsial'nye Preobrazovaniia na Vostoke,"* 10.

45. See above chapter 1, 57–58.

46. G. Mirskii, *"Tvorcheskii Marksizm i Problemy Natsional'no-Osvobiditel'nykh Revoliutsii,"* *Mirovaia Ekonomika i Mezhdunarodnye Otnosheniia* 2 (1963): 68.

47. Boris Ponomarev, *"O Gosudarstve Natsional'noi Demokratii,"* *Kommunist* 8 (May 1961): 45.

48. Ibid., 44.

49. See, for example, Ponomarev, *"O Gosudarstve Natsional'noi Demokratii,"* 34.

50. V. Pavlov, *"Soiuz Rabochego Klassa i Krest'ianstvo i Sotsial'nye Preobrazovaniia na Vostoke,"* 12.

51. V. Li, *"O Nekapitalisticheskom puti Razvitiia,"* 10; G. Kim, *"O Gosudarstve Natsional'noi Demokratii,"* 2.

52. R. Avakov and G. Mirskii, *"O Klassovoi Strukturv Slaborazvitykh Stranakh,"* *Mirovaia Ekonomika i Mezhdunarodnye Otnosheniia* 4 (1962): 78.

53. Conversation of March 22, 1955, quoted in Boden, *Die Grenzen der Weltmacht,* 185, footnote 206.

54. Letter of ambassador of USSR in Indonesia D. Zhukov to member of MFA collegium S. K. Tsarapkin, December 15, 1955, AVPRF f.91 o.8 papka 4 d.9, 33.

55. Letter of ambassador USSR in Indonesia Zhukov to deputy MFA Kuznetsov, June 18, 1956, AVPRF f.91 o.9 papka 5 d.16, 182.

56. Ragna Boden, *Die Grenzen der Weltmacht,* 179.

57. Report on the economy of the Republic of Indonesia, economic attaché, Soviet embassy Jakarta, A. Ivanov, July 23, 1956, AVPRF f.91 o.9 papka 5 d.17, 52.

58. Political letter of Soviet embassy Jakarta, "On the Visit of the Chairman of the Council of Ministers of the USSR Comrade N. S. Khrushchev to Indonesia," March 6, 1960, AVPRF f.091 o.16 papka 18 d.2, 8.

59. Report on the "Eight-Year Plan for General Development of Indonesia," first secretary Soviet embassy Jakarta, V. Vlasov, June 17, 1961, AVPRF f.91 o.14 papka 15 d.14, 119.

60. Report on "The State Sector in the Indonesian Economy," Soviet embassy Jakarta, first secretary V. Vlasov, August 19, 1961, AVPRF f.91 o.14 papka 15 d.14, 164.

61. Report of V. I. Likhachev, head of the Southeast Asia Division of MFA, on "The Contemporary Domestic and Foreign Political Situation in Indonesia," December 30, 1960, AVPRF f.091 o.16 papka 20 d.19, 226.

62. Report on Indonesian socialism, third secretary, Soviet embassy Jakarta, V. Sigaev, April 25, 1961, AVPRF f.91 o.14 papka 15 d.14, 50.

63. Report to head SE Asia Division GKES E. P. Volkov, October 25, 1963, RGAE f.365 o.2 d.2097, 19.

64. R. Avakov and G. Mirskii, "*O Klassovoĭ Strukture v Slaborazvitykh Stranakh,*" *Mirovaia Ekonomika i Mezhdunarodnye Otnosheniia* 4 (1962): 73.

65. Report to CC on visit of Soviet delegation led by deputy chair of Gosplan to India, February 1957, RGANI f.5 o.28 d.499, 13.

66. P. Baratovskii, Soviet embassy Jakarta, adviser on economic cooperation to G. M. Prokhorov, acting head of division of underdeveloped capitalist countries, State Committee on Foreign Economic Ties, March 17, 1958, RGAE f.365 o.2 d.1960, 14.

67. R. Avakov and G. Mirskii, "*O Klassovoĭ Strukturv Slaborazvitykh Stranakh,*" *Mirovaia Ekonomika i Mezhdunarodnye Otnosheniia* 4 (1962): 77.

68. Angela Stent, "Soviet Aid to Guinea and Nigeria: From Politics to Profit," in *Chinese and Soviet Aid to Africa,* ed. Warren Weinstein, 151.

69. Samir Amin, *Trois expériences africaines de développement,* 143.

70. Charles Bettelheim, "China's Economic Growth," in *China Shakes the World Again,* 10.

71. Keita N'Famara, "*Sozdanie Ekonomicheskikh Osnov Nezavisimoĭ Gvineĭ,*" *Narody Azii i Afriki* 2 (1961): 53–61.

72. Ibid., 54.

73. Ibid., 56.

74. PRC embassy Conakry to MFA, March 21, 1963, CFMA doc. 108-00905-02, 15, CFMA doc. 108-00897-01, 2.

75. Letter of CC CCP to Liaison Department on Soviet policy in Guinea and Mali, August 21, 1963, CFMA doc. 108-00897-01, 2.

76. CFMA doc. 108-00905-02, 15.

77. CFMA doc. 108-00897-01, 3. Sergey Mazov puts the total number of advisers, technicians, and teachers in Guinea at the beginning of 1962 at 1,500 (see Mazov, *A Distant Front in the Cold War,* 191).

78. Angela Stent, "Soviet Aid to Guinea and Nigeria: From Politics to Profit," 151, and Christopher Andrew and Vasili Mitrokhin, *The World Was Going Our Way,* 438.

Andrew claims that a British academic saw snow ploughs rusting at the end of a runway in Conakry.

79. Angela Stent, "Soviet Aid to Guinea and Nigeria: From Politics to Profit," 151.

80. Campbell and Trapp, "Guinea's Economic Performance under Structural Adjustment," 2–6.

81. Y. Bochkaryov, "The Guinean Experiment," *New Times* (1960), 29.

82 Boris Ponamarev, "*O Gosudarstve Natsional'noĭ Demokratii,*" 42.

83. PRC MFA Report, "On Materials of Revisionists on Guinea Question," February 16, 1962, CFMA doc. 108-00301-05, 1.

84. Ibid.

85. Ibid.

86. See Mazov, *A Distant Front in the Cold War,* 183–86.

87. See ibid., 187–89 for more detail on events surrounding the so-called Teacher's Plot.

88. Letter from B. Burkov (chairman of Novosti) to CC, passing on report of Novosti correspondent in Conakry, December 23, 1961, RGANI f.5 0.30 d.369, 111–13.

89. CC CCP Letter to Liaison Department on Soviet policy in Guinea and Mali, August 21, 1963, CFMA doc. 108-00897-01, 4–5.

90. Mazov, *A Distant Front in the Cold War,* 189.

91. PRC embassy Conakry to MFA, March 21, 1963, CFMA doc. 108-00905-02, 16.

92. CFMA doc. 108-00897-01, 6.

93. Ibid., 9.

94. PRC embassy Accra to MFA, March 23, 1963, CFMA doc. 108-00927-01, 5–6.

95. CFMA doc. 108-00897-01, 12–13.

96. PRC embassy Conakry to MFA, July 9, 1962, CFMA doc. 108-00811-05, 3.

97. V. I. Pavlov and I. B. Red'ko, "*Gosudarstvo Natsional'noĭ Demokratii i Perekhod k Nekapitalisticheskomu Razvitiiu,*" *Narody Azii i Afriki* 1 (1963): 36.

98. *Current Digest of the Soviet Press* 14 20, July 13, 1962, 7.

99. Quoted in Mazov, *A Distant Front in the Cold War,* 222.

100. Ibid., 218.

101. PRC embassy Moscow to MFA, June 2, 1962, CFMA doc. 109-03220-03, 5.

102. CFMA doc. 108-00897-01, 1.

103. PRC embassy Accra to MFA, March 23, 1963, CFMA doc. 108-00927-01, 5.

104. Ibid., 7.

105. CFMA doc. 108-00897-01, 9.

106. See, for example, daily reports on Cuban delegation to PRC led by Che Guevara, November 1960, CFMA doc. 204-00098-05.

107. See, for example, Instructions from Liaison Department to Youth League on visit of student delegation from black Africa, August 1960, CFMA doc. 108-00223-09, 7–8; report by Youth League CC Department of Foreign Ties on reaction of African student delegation after return to Czechoslovakia, November 9, 1960, ibid., 31–34; State Committee on Foreign Cultural Ties to MFA, Peace Committee, Youth League, May 9, 1960, doc. 108-00223-04, 3; Peace Committee daily report on visit of Senegalese delegation, February 26, 1960, CFMA doc. 108-00190-01, 19–20.

108. Quoted in Neuhauser, *Third World Politics,* 30.

109. CFMA doc. 108-00897-01, 9–10.

110. See, for example, Ma Zhidan, "马里见闻," *Shijie Zhishi* 17 (1961): 18–20, Zhuang Mulan, "加纳见闻," *Shijie Zhishi* 16 (1961): 16–18.

111. Report from Soviet embassy Kathmandu on trip of Nepalese prime minister Bishvesvar Prasad Koirala to PRC, March 1960, AVPRF f.100 o.47 papka 197 d.45, 21–22, quoting the Nepalese paper *Svatantra Samachar*, March 27, 1960.

112. PRC embassy Conakry to MFA, July 4, 1963, CFMA doc. 108-00905-02, 61–62, CFMA doc. 108-00897-01, 12–13.

113. Report from Institute of the Peoples of Asia to deputy MFA V. V. Kuznetsov on "Development of Economic Ties of the PRC with the Countries of Asia, Africa, and Latin America," June 28, 1961, AVPRF f.100 o.48 papka 203 d.37, 201.

114. PRC embassy Conakry to MFA, March 21, 1963, CFMA doc. 108-00905-02, 12.

115. *"Proekt Programmy KPSS i Nekotorye Problemy Natsional'no-Osvoboditel'nogo Dvizheniia Narodov Azii i Afriki," Narody Azii i Afriki* 5 (1961): 8.

116. Wu Lengxi, 十年论战*1956–1966*中苏关系回忆录, 468.

117. Ibid., 460.

118. Ibid., 468.

119. Luthi, *The Sino-Soviet Split*, 206–7.

120. Luthi, *The Sino-Soviet Split*, 207–8.

121. PRC embassy Bamako to MFA, November 23, 1961, CFMA doc. 108-00708-01, 2–3, CFMA doc. 108-00719-07, 1–2.

122. PRC embassy Bamako Party Committee to MFA and Zhonglianbu, November 18, 1961, and December 1, 1961, CFMA doc. 108-00708-01, 1, 4–6.

123. PRC embassy Hanoi to MFA, January 4, 1962, CFMA doc. 106-00661-06, 1–2.

124. PRC embassy Havana to MFA, December 11, 1961, CFMA doc. 111-00346-03, 1.

125. PRC embassy Havana to MFA and Zhonglianbu, December 20, 1961, CFMA doc. 111-00329-02, 1.

126. PRC embassy Conakry to MFA, December 12, 1961, CFMA doc. 108-00719-07, 4, PRC embassy Bamako to MFA, November 23, 1961, CFMA doc. 108-00708-01, 3.

127. Circular, PRC MFA and Zhonglianbu to embassies India, Indonesia, Pakistan, Ceylon, Nepal, Afghanistan, Burma, UAR, Iraq, Ghana, Mali, January 30, 1962, CFMA doc. 109-03215-01, 1–2.

128. PRC embassy Moscow to MFA, February 12, 1962, CFMA doc. 109-03215-01, 3–8.

129. CFMA doc. 109-03215-01, 4–5.

130. Report of Safronov on AAPSO session in Gaza to SCSCAA Presidium, January 8, 1962, GARF f.9540 o.1 d.109, 52.

131. Ibid., 54.

132. Ibid., 103.

133. Report of Tursun-Zade on Second Afro-Asian Writers' Conference in Cairo to SCSCAA Presidium, February 22, 1962, GARF f.9540 o.1 d.110, 3–4.

134. Ibid., 5–7.

135. Ibid., 12.

136. Report of Tursun-Zade on visit of SCSCAA delegation to Latin America to SCSCAA Presidium, February 22, 1962, ibid., 31.

137. SCSCAA Presidium session, January 8, 1962, GARF f.9540 o.1 d.109, 73, 83.

138. Report of deputy chairman of APN S. I. Belgin to CC on trip to Morocco, Mali, Guinea, Ghana, Togo, Ethiopia, UAR, Tunisia, December 22, 1961, RGANI f.5 o.33 d.181, 116.

139. Recommendations of APN Chairman B. Burkov based on CC on trip of S. I. Belgin to Africa, January 11, 1962, RGANI f.5 o.33 d.208, 20.

140. GARF f.9540 o.1 d.109, 56.

141. Report to CC on strengthening Soviet radio propaganda in Africa by head of radio administration in Ministry of Communications, A. Badalov, and head of technical administration of State Committee on Radio and Television M. Yegorov, March 7, 1961, RGANI f.5 o.33 d.177, 64.

142. KGB to CC, February 28, 1962, RGANI f.5 o.33 d.207, 6.

143. KGB proposal to CC, January 11, 1961, RGANI f.5 o.33 d.177, 2, and deputy head of Agitprop Department A. Romanov and deputy head of international department D. Shevliagin to CC, March 3, 1961, RGANI f.5 o.33 d.177, 11.

144. Letter of A. Rumyantsev to F. Kozlov, CC secretary, July 3, 1961, RGANI f.5 o.33 d.164, 113–21.

145. GARF f.9540 o.1 d.109, 84.

146. SCSCAA Presidium session, November 21, 1961, GARF f.9540 o.1 d.82, 17.

147. SCSCAA Presidium session, April 26, 1962, GARF f.9540 o.1 d.110, 40.

148. PRC embassy Moscow to MFA, top secret report on Soviet policy in Asia, Africa, Latin America after 22nd Congress, August 31, 1962, CFMA doc. 109-03215-01, 15–21.

149. Ibid., 18.

150. See Chen Jian, *Mao's China and the Cold War*, 83, and Luthi, *The Sino-Soviet Split*, 219–45.

151. Luthi, *The Sino-Soviet Split*, 211.

152. Ibid., 213.

153. For additional discussion on this issue, see Niu Jun, "1962: The Eve of the Left Turn in China's Foreign Policy," Cold War International History Project, Working Paper 48, October 2005, 28–30.

154. Luthi, *The Sino-Soviet Split*, 220–22.

155. Ibid., 223.

156. Bruce Larkin, *China and Africa, 1949–1970*, 54.

157. MFA background on Che Guevara, November 13, 1960, CFMA doc. 204-00680-01, 5. See also Chinese Foreign Ministry documents on Cuba published and translated in *Cold War International History Project Bulletin* 17–18 (Fall 2012): 21–116.

158. Zhou Enlai report to meeting of State Council, December 7, 1959, CFMA doc. 111-00209-01, 4.

159. Chinese ambassador in UAR to CC and MFA, January 20, 1960, CFMA doc. 111-00301-03, 6–7.

160. State Council Foreign Affairs Office to Chen Yi, Zhou Enlai, CC, March 3, 1960, CFMA doc. 111-00209-01, 13–14.

161. PRC representative in Norway to MFA, Chen Yi, CC, report on conversation with Mikoyan on way back from Cuba, February 16, 1960, CFMA doc. 109-02095-01, 3–4.

162. See documents on Cuba, July 24–September 19, 1960, CFMA doc. 111-00301-04, and documents on USSR and Cuba, July 13–November 25, 1960, CFMA doc. 109-02095-02.

163. PRC representative in Cuba to Zhonglianbu and MFA, July 24, 1960, CFMA doc. 111-00301-04, 2.

164. Conversation between Mao and Che Guevara, November 19, 1960, CFMA doc. 111-00163-02.

165. PRC representative in Cuba to Zhonglianbu, September 17, 1960; Zhonglianbu response, September 19, 1960, CFMA doc. 111-00301-04, 5–8.

166. For details on Soviet propaganda efforts in Cuba in this period, see the report of the Soviet embassy in Havana to Gromyko, July 1, 1961, RGANI f.5 0.33 d.164, 122–36.

167. GARF f.9540 0.1 d.110, 29.

168. Conversation between Che Guevara and PRC ambassador in Cuba, October 13, 1962, CFMA doc. 111-00362-03, 4–7.

169. PRC embassy Cuba to MFA, November 6, 1962, CFMA doc. 109-03218-05, 5. For Che's apology, see PRC embassy Cuba to MFA, Zhonglianbu, December 4, 1962, CFMA doc. 109-03218-05, 20.

170. PRC embassy Cuba to MFA, November 12, 1962, ibid., 11–12.

171. See "Documents on Soviet-Cuban Relations after Soviet Removal of Missiles from Cuba and Our Actions," November 1–12, 1962, CFMA doc. 111-00601-05, and "Documents on Cuban Reaction to Soviet Military Retreat," October 30–December 7, 1962, CFMA doc. 109-03218-05.

172. Protocol of Presidium session December 3, 1962, in *Arkhivy Kremlia: Prezidium TsK KPSS, 1954–1964*, 663.

173. Quoted in Sergey Radchenko, *Two Suns in the Heavens,* 26.

174. Protocol of Presidium session October 14, 1962, in *Arkhivy Kremlia: Prezidium TsK KPSS, 1954–1964*, 616.

175. Radchenko, *Two Suns in the Heavens,* 29–30.

176. Protocol of Presidium session December 3, 1962, in *Arkhivy Kremlia: Prezidium TsK KPSS, 1954–1964*, 663.

177. November 19–23, 1962, Plenum, RGANI f.2 0.1 d.632, 103, cited in Luthi, *The Sino-Soviet Split,* 227.

178. Report of APN chairman B. Burkov to CC on situation of Soviet propaganda in Cuba, April 17, 1963, RGANI f.5 0.55 d.58, 73.

179. Luthi, *The Sino-Soviet Split,* 237–38.

180. Report from consultant of International Division of journal *Kommunist* Yu. Shirovskii to CC on trip to UAR, Lebanon, Algeria, April 15, 1963, RGANI f.5 0.55 d.54, 62.

181. See RGANI f.5 0.55 d.54, 61–62 for North Africa, conversation of A. Rumyantsev with Idris Cox of Communist Party of Great Britain, sent to CC, March 20, 1964, RGANI f.5 0.55 d.116, 26–27 for East Africa; notes from diary of G. Sazhenev on conversation with Deputy Head of International Ties Division, Cuban Ministry of Armed Forces, Major Rio, May 9, 1963, AVPRF f.104 0.18 papka 13 d.4, 102.

182. Head of Press Division MFA L. Zamiatin to CC Secretary L. F. Il'ichev, report responding to Il'ichev's request for information on Soviet propaganda in Africa, collected from embassies, March 7, 1963, RGANI f.5 0.55 d.54, 39.

183. Peace Committee to embassies UAR, Tanganyika, Algeria, Ghana, Guinea, Mali, Morocco, Somalia, DPRK, DRV, Ceylon, Indonesia, Burma, Cambodia, Laos, Nepal, Iraq, Syria, India, Pakistan, Cuba, December 21, 1962, CFMA doc. 108-00320-03, 4–5. The same line was repeated in Peace Committee report to Liu Ningyi, Liao Chenzhi, MFA, December 13, 1962, CFMA doc. 108-00415-01, 2.

184. Ibid.

185. SCSCAA Presidium session, August 20, 1962, GARF f.9540 o.1 d.110, 82, CFMA doc. 108-00415-01, 2.

186. Report of Tursun-Zade on Third AAPSO Conference to SCSCAA Presidium, February 18, 1963, GARF f.9540 o.1 d.129, 28.

187. Documents on discussion of Tricontinental at Third AAPSO Conference, December 17–February 23, 1963, CFMA doc. 111-00375-04.

188. Report of Liu Ningyi to CC on Third AAPSO Conference, February 8, 1963, CFMA doc. 108-00320-02, 10.

189. Report of CC on Third AAPSO Conference to PRC representatives abroad, written by Liu Ningyi, February 17, 1963, CFMA doc. 108-00415-01, 6–7.

190. Report of A. Safronov on Third AAPSO Conference to SCSCAA Presidium, February 18, 1963, GARF f.9540 o.1 d.129, 38.

191. PRC representative at AAPSO headquarters in Cairo Zhu Ziqi to Peace Committee, September 29, 1962, CFMA doc. 108-00833-01, 9.

192. PRC embassy Moscow to MFA, top secret report on Soviet activity in Asia, Africa, and Latin America after Twenty-Second Congress, August 31, 1962, CFMA doc. 109-03215-01, 20.

193. PRC embassy Tanganyika to MFA, March 20, 1963, CFMA doc. 108-00336-02, 3.

194. PRC ambassador in Moscow to MFA, May 29, 1963, CFMA doc. 111-00616-09, 22.

195. See above chapter 1.

196. PRC embassy Tanganyika to MFA and Peace Committee, December 14, 1962, CFMA doc. 108-00834-03, 8.

197. Ibid.

Chapter Three

1. See Lorenz Luthi, *The Sino-Soviet Split*, 228–36.

2. Nikita Khrushchev, *Khrushchev Remembers*, 504.

3. Luthi, *The Sino-Soviet Split*, 238.

4. Sergey Radchenko, *Two Suns in the Heavens*, 46.

5. Wu Lengxi, 十年论战 *1956–1966* 中苏关系回忆录, 556–57, quoted in Luthi, *The Sino-Soviet Split*, 240.

6. For the full text of the letter, see http://ia341238.us.archive.org/1/items/AProposalC oncerningTheGeneralLineOfTheInternationalCommunistMovement/MicrosoftWord -Document1.pdf (accessed September 24, 2014).

7. Luthi, *The Sino-Soviet Split*, 243.

8. Stenogram of Presidium session June 7, 1963, in *Arkhivy Kremlia: Prezidium TsK KPSS, 1954–1964*, 722.

9. Report on Soviet-Vietnamese relations, Second Secretary Southeast Asia Department MFA G. Zverev, December 30, 1963, AVPRF f.079 o.19 papka 44 d.28, 8–28.

10. Report of deputy head Ideological Department CC V. Spastin to CC on "Questions Posed in Plenums of Party Committees, Party Gatherings and Meetings of Ideological Workers on Disagreements between CCP and CPSU and Whole World Communist Movement," July 6, 1963, RGANI f.5 o.55 d.1, 135.

11. Stenogram of Presidium session September 10, 1963, in *Arkhivy Kremlia: Prezidium TsK KPSS, 1954–1964,* 759.

12. Ibid.

13. Quoted in Radchenko, *Two Suns in the Heavens,* 35.

14. See PRC Peace Committee to ambassador in UAR, December 18, 1962, CFMA doc. 108-00834-03, 15, PRC embassy Guinea to MFA, March 21, 1963, doc. 108-00905-02, 17, ambassador UAR to Peace Committee, January 8, 1963, doc. 108-00833-02, 23.

15. Report of deputy chairman of APN to CC on anti-Chinese activity of APN, September 16, 1963, RGANI f.5 o.55 d.58, 118.

16. Ibid., 124.

17. Chairman APN B. Burkov to CC, November 13, 1963, ibid., 155.

18. Soviet ambassador in India to CC, November 29, 1963, RGANI f.5 o.55 d.54, 346–53.

19. See, for example, MFA to CC, forwarding report from embassy Pakistan, February 6, 1964, RGANI f.5 o.55 d.116, 2–4; Soviet embassy Ghana to Ideological Department CC, June 24, 1964, f.5 o.55 d.116, 304–16; Soviet ambassador in Ceylon to CC, June 25, 1964, f.5 o.55 d.116, 321–25; Soviet embassy DRV to CC, June 18, 1964, f.5 o.55 d.116, 337–48; Soviet embassy Burma to CC, July 24, 1964, f.5 o.55 d.116, 442–43; Soviet embassy Indonesia to CC, August 2, 1964, f.5 o.55 d.116, 453–73.

20. RGANI f.5 o.55 d.116, 316.

21. Ibid., 12 and 324.

22. Speech of Mikhail Suslov at Communist Party plenum, February 14, 1964, RGANI f.2 o.1 d.720, 116, 126–27.

23. Khrushchev could not bear to let the Chinese charges of Soviet failure to support armed struggle go unchallenged, even when they came out of the mouth of Suslov. He interrupted Suslov's speech to list the types of weapons the Soviets had provided to Indonesia during the course of the West Irian crisis as well as the arms they were currently providing covertly in support of the Egyptian effort in Yemen, declaring curiously, "You see, we are the true, so to speak, Christians, who observe the commandments of Christ." Needless to say, this part was not included in the versions of Suslov's speech that were exported. Ibid., 67–69.

24. Ibid., 18.

25. Ibid., 57.

26. Ibid., 63.

27. Letter of A. Rumyantsev to Khrushchev, January 25, 1964, RGANI f.5 o.30 d.435, 47.

28. "*Vazhneishaia Zadacha,*" *Aziia i Afrika Segodnia* (September 1963): 3.

29. "*Ideologicheskaia Bor'ba i Zadachi Sovetskikh Vostokovedov,*" *Narody Azii i Afriki* 5 (1963): 9.

30. G. Kim, *"Natsional'naia Nezavisimost' i Sotsial'nyĭ Progress,"* *Aziia i Afrika Segodnia* (October 1964): 4–7.

31. Ibid., 6.

32. See, for example, V. Kiselev, *"Rabochiĭ Klass i Natsional'no-Osvoboditel'nye Revoliutsii,"* *Mirovaia Ekonomika i Mezhdunarodnye Otnosheniia* 10 (1963): 93–98.

33. E. Alekseev, *"Natsional'no-Osvoboditel'noe Dvizhenie—Sostavnaia Chast' Mirovogo Revoliutsionnogo Protsessa,"* *Aziia i Afrika Segodnia* (December 1963): 3.

34. Chairman Presidium All-Union Chamber of Commerce to Mikoyan, RGANI f.5 0.30 d.307, 85.

35. SCSCAA Presidium session, January 8, 1962, GARF f.9540 0.1 d.109, 85.

36. See SCSCAA Presidium sessions, April 8, 1964, and June 9, 1964, GARF f.9540 0.1 d.154, 13 and 55.

37. Deputy chairman GKKS to Ideological Department CC, June 18, 1964, RGANI f.5 0.55 d.115, 134.

38. See, for example, MFA Intelligence Report on Khrushchev's visit to UAR, May 30, 1964, CFMA doc. 109-03526-07, 6, and PRC embassy Indonesia to MFA, report on visit of Mikoyan to Indonesia, July 8, 1964, doc. 109-03525-02, 25.

39. E. Alekseev, *"Natsional'no-Osvoboditel'noe Dvizhenie—Sostavnaia Chast' Mirovogo Revoliutsionnogo Protsessa,"* 4.

40. GARF f.9540 0.1 d.154, 16–20.

41. Quoted in Jeffrey James Byrne, "Our Own Special Brand of Socialism," 9.

42. See Joseph Chinyong Liow, *The Politics of Indonesia-Malaysia Relations,* 54–56.

43. V. Tuagunenko, *"Sotsialisticheskie Doktriny Obshchestvennogo Razvitiia Osvobodivshikhsia Stran,"* *Mirovaia Ekonomika i Mezhdunarodnye Otnosheniia* 8 (1965): 84.

44. Ragna Boden, *Die Grenzen der Weltmacht,* 290.

45. Documents on Soviet attendance at Afro-Asian Islamic Conference, December 13, 1964–January 5, 1965, CFMA doc. 105-01329-04 and SCSCAA Presidium session, October 13, 1964, GARF f.9540 0.1 d.155, 19–20.

46. Boden, *Die Grenzen der Weltmacht,* 294–95.

47. SCSCAA Presidium session, September 24, 1963, GARF f.9540 0.1 d.129, 49.

48. Quoted in Charles Neuhauser, *Third World Politics,* 51.

49. See MFA intelligence report on Khrushchev's visit to UAR, May 30, 1964, and PRC embassy Moscow to MFA, May 27, 1964, CFMA doc. 109-03526-07, 1–10.

50. KGB report on World Youth Forum to CC, September 19, 1964, RGANI f.5 0.30 d.456, 51.

51. KGB report on World Youth Forum to CC, September 22, 1964, ibid., 58.

52. Report of embassy DRV to MFA "On Activity of CCP Leadership to Expand Its Influence over VWP and DRV and the Submission of the VWP to Its Schismatic Course," July 29, 1964, AVPRF f.079 0.19 papka 44 d.30, 60.

53. Report from Southeast Asia Division MFA on Sino-Vietnamese relations, January 9, 1964, AVPRF f.079 0.19 papka 44 d.28, 237.

54. Notes from conversation of Soviet ambassador in DRV with Cuban ambassador in DRV, December 25, 1963, AVPRF f.079 0.19 papka 44 d.28, 171.

55. Report from embassy DRV "On Relations of the Embassy with the Government of the DRV and Vietnamese Administrative Organs and on Relations toward Soviet Specialists and Soviet Citizens Working in the DRV," June 4, 1964, AVPRF f.079 0.19 papka 43 d.26, 37.

56. Report of embassy DRV to MFA "On Activity of CCP Leadership to Expand Its Influence over VWP and DRV and the Submission of the VWP to Its Schismatic Course," July 29, 1964, AVPRF f.079 0.19 papka 44 d.30, 83.

57. See ambassador in Guinea to MFA, July 23, 1963, CFMA doc. 109-03342-03, 9, and PRC embassy Algeria to MFA, July 23, 1963, CFMA doc. 109-03342-09, 10.

58. PRC embassy Algeria to MFA, July 29, 1963, CFMA doc. 109-03342-09, 17.

59. PRC embassy Guinea to MFA, August 29, 1963, CFMA doc. 109-03342-03, 23.

60. PRC embassy Indonesia to MFA, July 23, 1963, CFMA doc. 109-03342-01, 1.

61. PRC embassy Algeria to MFA, July 29, 1963, CFMA doc. 109-03342-09, 18.

62. PRC embassy Guinea to MFA, November 22, 1963, CFMA doc. 108-00905-02, 107.

63. Ibid., 111.

64. Ibid., 110.

65. See Jeremi Suri, *Power and Protest*, 71–87.

66. Alaba Ogunsanwo, *China's Policy in Africa*, 115–19.

67. Ibid., 269.

68. PRC embassy Burma to MFA, August 27, 1963, CFMA doc. 109-03342-02, 1.

69. Ogunsanwo, *China's Policy in Africa*, 124.

70. The principles are listed in "周恩来总理的非洲之行" ("Prime Minister Zhou Enlai's Trip to Africa"), *Shijie Zhishi* 4 (1964): 7.

71. See above chapter 2.

72. "周恩来总理的非洲之行," *Shijie Zhishi* 4 (1964): 5.

73. Yong Longgui, "亚非人民争取彻底的经济独立的道路" ("Afro-Asian People's Path to Achieving Complete Economic Independence"), *Shijie Zhishi* 12 (1965): 9–11.

74. Ibid., 11.

75. Ogunsanwo, *China's Policy in Africa*, 276.

76. Ibid., 139–40, 154.

77. Ibid., 272. Ogunsanwo cites the UN Economic Commission for Africa—Foreign Trade Statistics of Africa Series A.

78. Martin Bailey, *Freedom Railway*, 41–42.

79. Richard Hall and Hugh Peyman, *The Great Uhuru Railway*, 15.

80. Ibid., 71.

81. Ogunsanwo, *China's Policy in Africa*, 139–40.

82. Huang Hua, *Huang Hua Memoirs*, 187–88.

83. PRC MFA to embassy Congo (Brazzaville) and embassy Burundi, July 9, 1964, CFMA doc. 108-00493-02, 1–2.

84. Report of first secretary embassy Guinea on "First Conference of National Organizations of Portuguese Colonies," May 24, 1961, AVPRF f.658 0.1 papka 1 d.1, 36; MFA background report *"Zur Lage in Angola,"* April 17, 1961, SAPMO-BArch DY 30/IV 2/20/416, 8.

85. Background on Holden Roberto from adviser, First African Department MFA, December 24, 1963, AVPRF f.658 0.3 papka 1 d.1, 74.

86. Deputy permanent representative of USSR at UN to deputy MFA V. A. Zorin, August 22, 1963, ibid., 2.

87. MFA to embassy UAR, January 11, 1964, CFMA doc. 108-01384-01, 6.

88. PRC embassy Congo (Brazzaville) to MFA, May 11, 1964, CFMA doc. 108-01384-03, 9.

89. PRC embassy Congo (Brazzaville) to MFA, June 30, 1964, and MFA to embassies UAR, Tanzania, Kenya, Congo (Brazzaville), Algeria, July 17, 1964, ibid., 1–2, 28.

90. MFA to embassies UAR, Algeria, July 31, 1964; embassy UAR to MFA, August 1, 1964, ibid., 30–31.

91. Report "FNLA," MFA (Portugal) to PIDE (International Police for External Defense), October 7, 1966, IAN/TT (Torre do Tombo), PIDE/DGS SC Serie SR No de Proc 882/61 No sas unidades 3079, 29.

92. Report from Institute of the Economy of the World Socialist System to CC Secretary P. N. Demychev, May 24, 1965, RGANI f.5 0.30 d.481, 1–7.

93. Ibid., 3.

94. Ibid., 7.

95. MFA report "Soviet Economic and Military 'Aid' to Nationalist Countries of Asia and Africa," CFMA doc. 109-03652-03, 1.

96. See, for example, Luthi, *The Sino-Soviet Split*, 287; Radchenko, *Two Suns in the Heavens*, 127–29.

97. KGB to CC, November 2, 1964, RGANI f.5 0.30 d.456, 75.

98. Deputy head of Ideological Department to CC, forwarding Report on conversations of head of sector of Ideological Department with Luis Corvalan and Salvador Allende, October 31, 1964, RGANI f.5 0.55 d.115, 174–75.

99. Quoted in Luthi, *The Sino-Soviet Split*, 289.

100. Speech of Brezhnev to Communist Party plenum, November 16, 1964, RGANI f.2 0.1 d.762, 117.

101. Ibid., 113.

102. Report of Soviet-East European Department of MFA on foreign policy of new Soviet leadership, February 15, 1965, CFMA doc. 109-03652-01, 14.

103. Report of European and American Department of MFA on policy of new Soviet leadership in Latin America, February 11, 1965, CFMA doc. 109-03652-07, 2.

104. Zhonglianbu to MFA, January 3, 1965, CFMA doc. 111-00403-01, 1–8.

105. Secret report of Afro-Asian Department MFA, February 12, 1965, CFMA doc. 109-03652-05, 4.

106. Secret report from Africa Department MFA, January 30, 1965, CFMA doc. 109-03652-04, 4.

107. Speech of Suslov at Communist Party plenum, March 26, 1965, RGANI f.2 0.1 d.782, 89.

108. Secret report of Afro-Asian Department MFA, February 12, 1965, CFMA doc. 109-03652-05, 1.

109. MFA report on "Soviet Economic and Military Aid to Nationalist Countries of Asia and Africa," CFMA doc. 109-03652-03, 16. Also see Jesse Ferris, "Egypt, the Cold War, and the Civil War in Yemen, 1962–1966," 182–85.

110. Secret report of American and European Department, Soviet–East European Department MFA on actions of new Soviet leadership in Africa and Asia, March 31, 1965, CFMA doc. 109-03652-02, 45.

111. Ibid., 40–41.

112. Ibid., 44. For Egypt, see Ferris, "Egypt, the Cold War, and the Civil War in Yemen, 1962–1966," 209.

113. CFMA doc. 109-03652-02, 44.

114. V. Solodvnikov, "*Puti Ekonomicheskogo Progressa Razvivaiushchikhsia Stran,*" *Mirovaia Ekonomika i Mezhdunarodnye Otnosheniia* 6 (1965): 19.

115. CFMA doc. 109-03652-02, 47.

116. SCSCAA Presidium session, February 5, 1965, GARF f.9540 o.1 d.188, 12.

117. CFMA doc. 109-03652-02, 37.

118. Ibid., 38–39.

119. CFMA doc. 109-03652-01, 10.

120. Soviet ambassador in DRV to MFA Gromyko and Yuri Andropov, forwarding excerpts of conversations Czechoslovak ambassador in DRV with Hoang Van Hoan and Le Duc Tho, November 27, 1964, AVPRF f.079 o.19 papka 44 d.30, 287.

121. Ilya Gaiduk, *The Soviet Union and the Vietnam War*, 19.

122. PRC embassy Moscow to MFA, Zhonglianbu, December 1, 1964, CFMA doc. 109-03520-04, 3.

123. CFMA doc. 109-03652-01, 8, and Gaiduk, *The Soviet Union and the Vietnam War*, 20.

124. Report of embassy DRV on "Celebration in DRV of 47th Anniversary of October Revolution," December 17, 1964, AVPRF f.079 o.19 papka 43 d.26, 169–74.

125. CFMA doc. 109-03652-02, 36, and report of embassy DRV on "International Conference of Solidarity with Vietnamese People against Aggression of U.S. Imperialism in Defense of Peace, in Hanoi 11/25–29/1964," December 17, 1964, AVPRF f.079 o.19 papka 44 d.30, 315–22.

126. Gaiduk, *The Soviet Union and the Vietnam War*, 30.

127. MFA News Department report on Soviet military aid to DRV, March 3, 1965, CFMA doc. 109-02850-01, 1–2.

128. Gaiduk, *The Soviet Union and the Vietnam War*, 19.

129. Ibid., 31.

130. CFMA doc. 109-02850-01, 2.

131. Radchenko, *Two Suns in the Heavens*, 144–48.

132. Ibid., 141–43.

133. Report of embassy DRV "On PRC Relations to Vietnamese Problem," October 20, 1965, AVPRF f.079 o.20 papka 49 d.26, 32.

134. PRC embassy Moscow to MFA, secret report on activities of new Soviet leadership in half year in Asia and Africa, May 26, 1965, CFMA doc. 109-03652-02, 58.

135. CFMA doc. 109-03652-01, 6.

136. PRC embassy Moscow to MFA, May 26, 1965, CFMA doc. 109-03652-02, 60.

137. Ibid., 65.

138. Ibid.

139. PRC embassy Guinea to MFA, February 8, 1965, CFMA doc. 109-03652-04, 9–10.

140. MFA Report "Soviet Economic and Military 'Aid' to Nationalist Countries of Asia and Africa," January 18, 1965, CFMA doc. 109-03652-03, 1.

141. Ibid., 3.

142. General director of TASS to Suslov, forwarding report of TASS correspondent in Damascus, October 26, 1959, RGANI f.5 0.30 d.290, 119–20.

143. Boris Ponomarev, *"O Gosudarstve Natsional'noĭ Demokratii," Kommunist* 8 (1961): 44.

144. Chairman GKKS G. Zhukov to N. A. Mukhitdinov, CC secretary, report on Soviet propaganda recently banned in Egypt, July 3, 1959, RGANI f.5 0.30 d.290, 83–86.

145. See Ferris, "Egypt, the Cold War, and the Civil War in Yemen, 1962–1966," 39–41.

146. Ogunsanwo, *China's Policy in Africa,* 161.

147. See Jesse Ferris, "Egypt, the Cold War, and the Civil War in Yemen, 1962–1966," 132–80.

148. PRC ambassador in UAR to MFA, June 22, 1965, CFMA doc. 109-03645-01, 17.

149. PRC embassy UAR to MFA, July 22, 1965, ibid., 22.

150. PRC embassy UAR to MFA and Xinhua, July 12, 1965, ibid., 20.

151. Ferris, "Egypt, the Cold War, and the Civil War in Yemen, 1962–1966," 207–8.

152. PRC embassy Moscow to MFA, September 4, 1965, CFMA doc. 109-03645-01, 28, and Report West Asia/North Africa Department MFA, September 18, 1965, ibid., 55.

153. Ibid., 59.

154. Sha He, "阿尔及利亚在前进" ("Algeria Is Advancing"), *Shijie Zhishi* 1 (1963): 21.

155. See I. Genin, *"Ekonomicheskie Meropriiatie Alzhirskogo Pravitel'stva," Mirovaia Ekonomika i Mezhdunarodnye Otnosheniia* 11 (1963): 116, and Byrne, "Our Own Special Brand of Socialism," 432.

156. Quoted in R. G. Landa, *"Nekapitalisticheskiĭ Put' Razvitii Alzhira," Narody Azii i Afriki* 5 (1964): 19.

157. Quoted in Piero Gleijeses, *Conflicting Missions,* 39.

158. See, for example, Vladimir Shubin, *ANC: A View From Moscow,* 30, and Shao He, "建设中的阿尔及利亚" ("Algeria in the Midst of Construction"), *Shijie Zhishi* 24 (1963): 15.

159. Gleijeses, *Conflicting Missions,* 52.

160. Sha Chu, "前进中的阿尔及利亚" (Algeria in the Process of Advancement"), *Shijie Zhishi* 20 (1964): 10.

161. PRC embassy Algeria to MFA, July 29, 1963, CFMA doc. 109-03342-09, 18.

162. Shao He, "建设中的阿尔及利亚," 14–15.

163. Sha Chu, "前进中的阿尔及利亚," 10–11.

164. Ogunsanwo, *China's Policy in Africa,* 154.

165. Ibid. and Shao He, "建设中的阿尔及利亚," 15.

166. Ibid., 15.

167. Byrne, "Our Own Special Brand of Socialism," 440.

168. I. Genin, *"Ekonomicheskie Meropriiatie Alzhirskogo Pravitel'stva,"* 120.

169. Y. Potemkin, *"Alzhirskaia Revoliutsiia: Sversheniia i Perspektivy,"* *Mirovaia Ekonomika i Mezhdunarodnye Otnosheniia* 10 (1964): 29–30.

170. Ibid., 32.

171. Ibid.

172. Ibid., 34.

173. PRC embassy USSR to MFA, January 2, 1964, CFMA doc. 109-03526-08, 2.

174. Ibid., 1–3.

175. MFA intelligence report to CC on Ben Bella's visit to USSR, May 9, 1964, ibid., 5–7.

176. PRC embassy Algeria to MFA, report on Ben Bella's visit to USSR, May 19, 1964, ibid., 14–17.

177. PRC embassy Algeria to MFA, May 11, 1965, CFMA doc. 109-03645-02, 5–6.

178. Ibid., 9.

179. Ibid., 10.

180. Conversation of Brezhnev with Houari Boumedienne, April 27, 1965, RGANI f.5 0.30 d.479, 32.

181. Report from Soviet–East European MFA Department on Soviet attitude and actions toward Algerian coup, June 25, 1965, CFMA doc. 109-03645-02, 17.

182. Ibid., 17 and 20.

183. Report from Soviet–East European MFA Department on Soviet attitude and actions toward Algerian coup, July 8, 1965, ibid., 32 and embassy Algeria to MFA, August 1, 1965, ibid., 40–42.

184. Embassy Algeria to MFA, December 14, 1965, ibid., 53–55.

185. Report from Soviet-East European MFA Department on Soviet attitude and actions toward Algerian coup, July 8, 1965, ibid., 30.

186. Boden, *Die Grenzen der Weltmacht,* 90.

187. Ibid., 214.

188. Ibid., 164–65.

189. David Mozingo, *Chinese Policy towards Indonesia, 1949–1967,* 158.

190. Ibid., 178–79. See also Taomo Zhou, "Ambivalent Alliance," 11–16.

191. Ibid., 186.

192. See, for example, report of second secretary embassy Indonesia O. Kinkadze "On the Question of Economic Policies of the Political Parties of Indonesia," July 6, 1963, AVPRF f.91 0.16 papka 18 d.13, 95–111.

193. Boden, *Die Grenzen der Weltmacht,* 107.

194. See Sheldon W. Simon, *The Broken Triangle,* 49–72.

195. See Liow, *The Politics of Indonesia-Malaysia Relations,* 98–100.

196. Simon, *The Broken Triangle,* 78–79.

197. *Pravda* editor P. A. Sativkov to CC secretary L. F. Il'ichev, head International Department CC B. Ponomarev, report on visit to Indonesia, April 4, 1963, RGANI f.5 0.55 d.56, 153.

198. Embassy Indonesia to CC, report on certain questions of ideological work in Indonesia, August 2, 1964, RGANI f.5 0.55 d.116, 453.

199. Intelligence report from First Asia Department MFA on Mikoyan's visit to Indonesia, July 7, 1964, CFMA doc. 109-03525-02, 36.

200. PRC embassy Indonesia to MFA, March 30, 1964, CFMA doc. 109-03481-01, 32, and PRC embassy Indonesia to MFA and Zhonglianbu, July 11, 1964, CFMA doc. 105-01231-02, 3.

201. Ibid., 1–2, and PRC embassy Moscow to MFA on Subandrio's visit to USSR, July 17, 1964, CFMA doc. 109-03525-02, 18–20.

202. RGANI f.5 0.55 d.116 p.459.

203. PRC embassy Indonesia to MFA and Zhonglianbu, top secret, October 16, 1964, and PRC embassy Indonesia to Zhonglianbu, top secret, December 19, 1964, CFMA doc. 105-01606-01, 1–5.

204. MFA International Department report on Soviet attitude toward Indonesia leaving UN, April 1, 1965, CFMA doc. 109-03641-02, 4–5.

205. Report of ambassador in Indonesia to CC on Soviet-Indonesian relations, April 1965, AVPRF f.091 0.21 papka 33 d.1, 4.

206. For Chen Yi, see ibid., 19. For Mao's quote, see Taomo Zhou, "Ambivalent Alliance," 19.

207. Bradley R. Simpson, *Economists with Guns,* 167. Cambodia was not thrilled with its inclusion: see Simon, *The Broken Triangle,* 108.

208. Quoted in Simon, *The Broken Triangle,* 82.

209. Ibid., 83–86.

210. Ibid., 107–8, and Mozingo, *Chinese Policy toward Indonesia,* 223–24.

211. Ibid., 225.

212. Report of *Pravda* correspondent in Indonesia V. Shurygin to Brezhnev, Suslov, Demychev, Andropov, Ponomarev on situation in Indonesia after events of September 30 and October 16, 1965, RGANI f.5 0.30 d.480, 134–40.

213. Abridged version of top secret report of ambassador in Indonesia to Gromyko on events of September 30 and Soviet-Indonesian relations, November 18, 1965, AVPRF f.091 0.21 papka 33 d.1, 150.

214. See secret report of News Department MFA on Soviet actions since Indonesian coup, October 22, 1965, CFMA doc. 109-03641-02, 33, and Brezhnev speech to Communist Party plenum, March 26, 1966, RGANI f.2 0.1 d.820, 12.

215. Boden, *Die Grenzen der Weltmacht,* 338–39.

216. See Soviet embassy Indonesia to CC, report on certain questions of ideological work in Indonesia, August 2, 1964, RGANI f.5 0.55 d.116, 473, and Boden, *Die Grenzen der Weltmacht,* 318.

217. See RGANI f.5 0.30 d.480, 79–92 for information on a CPSU Central Committee resolution directing Soviet embassies around the world to talk to their host countries about the Soviet desire to attend the conference as well as Soviet attitudes about its projected agenda, June 18, 1965.

218. See letters of Gromyko to Suslov, June 5, 1965, June 17, 1965, June 18, 1965, RGANI f.5 0.30 d.480, 94–126, Gromyko to CC Foreign Policy Commission on directive to Soviet delegation at second Bandung Conference, October 28, 1965, ibid., 142–67. Deputy MFA V. Kuznetsov to Suslov, Andropov, Ponomarev on question of Soviet participation in Second Bandung, October 19, 1965, ibid., 191–95.

219. RGANI f.5 0.30 d.480, 94–95.

220. RGANI f.5 0.30 d.480, 142–67.

Chapter Four

1. Quoted in S. Bulygin, "Mir i Natsional'noe Osvobozhdenie," *Aziia i Afrika Segodnia* 8 (1966): 3.

2. SCSCAA Presidium session, March 15, 1967, GARF f.9540 o.1 d.225, 14–15.

3. See Lien-Hang Nguyen, *Hanoi's War*, 96–97.

4. Che Guevara, "Message to the Tricontinental," April 16, 1967, Workers' Web ASCII Pamphlet Project, 1997, 2nd (HTML) ed., 1998. http://www.rcgfrfi.easynet.co .uk/ww/guevara/1967-mtt.htm (accessed on September 24, 2014).

5. See Piero Gleijeses, *Conflicting Missions*, 169–72.

6. Brezhnev speech to Communist Party plenum, December 12, 1966, RGANI f.2 o.3 d.45, 104–5.

7. Barbara Barnouin and Yu Changgen, *Chinese Foreign Policy during the Cultural Revolution*, 4–5.

8. Ibid., 12.

9. Jisen Ma, *The Cultural Revolution in the Foreign Ministry of China*, 73–74.

10. According to Huang Hua, some individuals in the Chinese embassy in Cairo wanted to send him back as well, but Zhou prevented it, arguing that China needed someone to represent itself abroad, especially in the wake of the June 1967 war. See Huang Hua, *Huang Hua Memoirs*, 197.

11. Barnouin and Yu, *Chinese Foreign Policy during the Cultural Revolution*, 13–14.

12. Ibid., 14, and Ma, *The Cultural Revolution in the Foreign Ministry of China*, 77–81.

13. Ma, *The Cultural Revolution in the Foreign Ministry of China*, 57–60.

14. Ibid., 55.

15. Ibid., 118.

16. Barnouin and Yu, *Chinese Foreign Policy during the Cultural Revolution*, 22–23.

17. Ibid., 24.

18. Ma, *The Cultural Revolution in the Foreign Ministry of China*, 201–3.

19. Barnouin and Yu, *Chinese Foreign Policy during the Cultural Revolution*, 25.

20. Ma, *The Cultural Revolution in the Foreign Ministry of China*, 214–26.

21. Ibid., 218.

22. Ibid., 155.

23. Quoted in Alaba Ogunsanwo, *China's Policy in Africa*, 191–92.

24. Ibid., 195.

25. Report of embassy Uganda on reaction to internal political situation in China, March 3, 1967, AVPRF f.100 o.54 papka 231 d.30, 47.

26. Report of embassy Uganda on Ugandan-Chinese relations, May 8, 1969, AVPRF f.100 o.56 papka 240 d.36, 43.

27. Conversation of O. V. Kvasov, advisor embassy Havana, with VP Cuban Academy of Sciences Julio Le Riverend, October 6, 1966, AVPRF f.104 o.21 papka 17 d.4, 65.

28. Boris T. Kulik, *Sovietsko-Kitaiskii Raskol*, 444.

29. Embassy Beijing, report on Chinese press, June 14, 1967, AVPRF f.100 o.54 papka 231 d.30, 71.

30. Embassy Beijing, report on preparation in Beijing for "Solidarity Conference of Afro-Asian Writers and Journalists," September 14, 1967, ibid., 105.

31. Martin Meredith, *The Fate of Africa*, 250–59.

32. Phillip Snow, *The Star Raft*, 101–2.

33. See above chapter 3.

34. For an outline of a contemporary Soviet dissertation from the Moscow State Institute of International Relations on Chinese policy in Latin America during this period, see AVPRF f.100 o.54 papka231 d.30, 56–69.

35. Archivo del Ministerio de Relaciones Exteriores de Chile (AMREC) 1966 Embajada de Chile en Rusia: Oficios confidenciales no.1, Conf. no.18, February 3, 1966.

36. AMREC 1966 Embajada de Chile en Rusia: Oficios confidenciales no.1, Conf. no.21, February 12, 1966.

37. Brezhnev Speech at Communist Party plenum, December 12, 1966, RGANI f.2 o.3 d.45, 69.

38. Brezhnev Speech at Communist Party plenum, June 20, 1967, RGANI f.2 o.3 d.65, 55–57.

39. Ibid., 57.

40. See Jorge G. Castañeda, *Compañero*, 380–84.

41. Report to CC on meeting of group of chief editors and leading workers of organs of central committees of other Communist Parties by invitation of *Pravda* editorial board, Moscow November 3–15, 1967, December 8, 1967, RGANI f.5 o.59 d.26, 228–29.

42. See above chapter 3. For Soviet-Palestinian relations, see Brezhnev speech at Communist Party plenum, June 20, 1967, RGANI f.2 o.3 d.65, 54; SCSCAA Presidium session, February 18, 1969, GARF f.9540 o.1 d.255, 68; SCSCAA Presidium session, September 5, 1967, GARF f.9540 o.1 d.227, 16; and Christopher Andrew and Vasili Mitrokhin, *The World Was Going Our Way*, 246–59. See also Huang, *Huang Hua Memoirs*, 199–200.

43. Scholars engage in debate as to whether or not the Soviets did anything to stoke tensions in the region, in particular in order to divert American attention from Vietnam. Isabella Ginor, Gideon Remez, and Judith Klinghoffer argue that that was the case, pointing to a supposedly mistaken intelligence report passed by Moscow to Cairo in early May detailing an Israeli troop buildup on the Syrian border. According to Tom Segev, this interpretation was even discussed within the Israeli cabinet in the weeks leading up to the war. Segev, Galia Golan, and Uri Bar-Noi maintain, however, that the intelligence report, mistaken or not, does not prove a Soviet desire to start a war, and Segev in particular dismisses the possible significance of the report given the sheer quantity of belligerent Israeli statements and actions at the time. Nevertheless, both sides agree that as the month went on and it became clear to Moscow that the United States was going to let Israel fend for itself, the Soviets tried, unsuccessfully, behind the scenes to prevent war from breaking out. For more information, see *The Cold War in the Middle East*, ed. Nigel J. Ashton, and Klinghoffer, "The 1967 Middle East Crisis: A Second Vietnam," in *International Perspectives on Vietnam*, ed. Lloyd C. Gardner and Ted Gittinger, 204–24; Tom Segev, *1967*, 230–31.

44. Brezhnev speech at Communist Party plenum, June 20, 1967, RGANI f.2 o.3 d.65, 15.

45. Quoted in Klinghoffer, "The 1967 Middle East Crisis: A Second Vietnam," 212.

46. Brezhnev speech at Communist Party plenum, June 20, 1967, RGANI f.2 o.3 d.65, 20.

47. Ibid., 21.

48. Ibid., 53.

49. Ibid., 51.

50. Ibid., 46.

51. Ibid., 65.

52. Ibid., 70–73.

53. Brezhnev speech at Communist Party plenum, April 9–10, 1968, RGANI f.2 o.3 d.95, 49. See also Craig Daigle, *The Limits of Détente*, 15.

54. *"Armiia i Osvoboditel'noe Dvizhenie," Aziia i Afrika Segodnia* (September 1966): 2–4.

55. See V. Iordanskii, *"O Kharaktere Voennykh Diktatur v Tropicheskoĭ Afrike," Narody Azii i Afriki* 4 (1967): 22–37; G. Mirskii, *"Politicheskaia Rol' Armii v Stranakh Azii i Afriki," Narody Azii i Afriki* 6 (1968): 3–14; I. Symbatian, *"Armiia v Politicheskoi Sisteme Natsional'noĭ Demokratii," Narody Azii i Afriki* 4 (1969): 34–38.

56. G. Mirskii, *"Politicheskaia Rol' Armii v Stranakh Azii i Afriki,"* 14.

57. V. Iordanskii, *"Tropicheskaia Afrika: O Prirode Mezhetnicheskikh Konfliktov," Mirovaia Ekonomikia i Mezhdunarodnye Otnosheniia* 1 (1967): 47–56.

58. See, for example, I. Pronichev, *"Nekapitasticheskiĭ Put' Razvitii i ego Mesto v Istoricheskom Protsesse," Mirovaia Ekonomika i Mezhdunarodnye Otnosheniia* 12 (1966): 6, and R. Andeasian, *"Revoliutsionnye Demokratii Azii i Afriki," Aziia i Afrika Segodnia* (October 1966): 3.

59. I. Pronichev, *"Nekapitasticheskiĭ Put' Razvitii i ego Mesto v Istoricheskom Protsesse,"* 11.

60. K. Brutents, *"O Revoliutsionnoĭ Demokratii," Mirovaia Ekonomika i Mezhdunarodnye Otnosheniia* 4 (1968): 28.

61. See for example A. Letnev, *"Afrikanskie Partii i ikh Problemy," Mirovaia Ekonomika i Mezhdunarodnye Otnosheniia* 6 (1969): 50–59.

62. O. V. Martyshin, *"Klassy i Klassovaia Bor'ba v Ideologii Natsional'noĭ Demokratii," Narody Azii i Afriki* 5 (1967): 48–58.

63. I. Pronichev, *"Nekapitalisticheskiĭ Put' Razvitii i ego Mesto v Istoricheskom Protsesse,"* 5.

64. Brutents, *"O Revoliutsionnoĭ Demokratii,"* 32.

65. Fedor Burlatskiĭ, *Maoizm ili Marksizm*, 122.

66. R. Ul'ianovskiĭ, *"Nauchnyĭ Sotsializm i Osvobodivshiesia Strani," Kommunist* 4 (1968): 93–102.

67. Fedoseev speech at Communist Party plenum, June 26, 1969, RGANI f.2 o.3 d.159, 97–100.

68. Brezhnev speech at Communist Party plenum, December 12, 1966, RGANI f.2 o.3 d.45, 112.

69. GDR SED Department of International Ties (AIV) proposal to Politburo, *"Beratung über Probleme der Politik der gegenwärtigen Führungsgruppe der KP Chinas vom 14-21.12.1967 in Moksau,"* November 30, 1967, SAPMO-BArch DY 30/IV A 2/20 1132.

70. SCSCAA Presidium session, February 18, 1969, GARF f.9540 o.1 d.255, 14.

71. Report of Far Eastern and Southeast Asia Departments MFA to Gromyko, Andropov, Shelepin, Ustinov, et al. on PRC-DRV relations, December 22, 1965, AVPRF f.079 o.20 papka 49 d.26, 144.

72. Ilya Gaiduk, *The Soviet Union and the Vietnam War*, 72.

73. Embassy PRC to MFA, "On the Perspectives of the Development of the Situation in Indochina in Connection with the Particular Course of the Chinese Leadership," January 13, 1966, AVPRF f.079 o.21 papka 55 d.29, 14.

74. Embassy PRC, chronicle of Chinese press on Vietnam, March 9, 1967, AVPRF f.100 0.54 papka 231 d.29, 2.

75. Embassy DRV, report titled "Relations of DRV with the Countries of Africa," August 16, 1966, AVPRF f.079 o.21 papka 55 d.30, 22.

76. Ibid., 17–42.

77. Ibid., 24.

78. See, for example, Gaiduk, *The Soviet Union and the Vietnam War*, 79–80. In fact, most of the book is devoted to various Soviet attempts to encourage peace negotiations behind the scenes. See also James Hershberg, *Marigold: The Lost Chance for Peace in Vietnam*.

79. See, for example, report of Far Eastern and Southeast Asia Departments MFA to Gromyko, Andropov, Shelepin, Ustinov, et al. on PRC-DRV relations, December 22, 1965, AVPRF f.079 o.20 papka 49 d.26, 143, and report of embassy PRC "On the PRC Position on the Vietnam Question," February 25, 1967, AVPRF f.079 o.22 papka 60 d.27, 8, and report on Soviet awareness of the Chinese desire to damage Soviet-American relations and embassy PRC to MFA, "On the Perspectives of the Development of the Situation in Indochina in Connection with the Particular Course of the Chinese Leadership," January 13, 1966, AVPRF f.079 o.21 papka 55 d.29, 20, for Soviet fears of a Sino-American rapprochement.

80. Soviet military attaché in DRV to CC, October 6, 1965, RGANI f.5 o.30 d.479, 133.

81. "Note on a Conversation between Tarka, Jurgas, and Milc at the Soviet Embassy in Hanoi, 10 September 1964," in Lorenz Luthi, "Twenty Four Soviet-Bloc Documents on Vietnam and the Sino-Soviet Split, 1964–1966," 371.

82. SCSCAA Presidium session, December 22, 1966, GARF f.9540 o.1 d.208, 3.

83. See, for example, Gaiduk, *The Soviet Union and the Vietnam War*, 108–10.

84. Ibid., 58. For statistical information on Soviet aid to the DRV, see Gaiduk, *The Soviet Union and the Vietnam War*, 58–59, and Xiaoming Zhang, "Communist Powers Divided: China, the Soviet Union, and the Vietnam War," in *International Perspectives on Vietnam*, ed. Gardner and Gittinger, 92. For statistical information on Chinese aid to the DRV, see Zhang, "Communist Powers Divided," 91, and Zhai Qiang, *China and the Vietnam Wars, 1950–1975*, 136. However, Harish C. Mehta has claimed that new evidence from North Vietnamese archives shows that, despite a wealth of earlier reports and studies, Chinese economic aid to the DRV in 1967–68 still exceeded Soviet economic aid, though the latter had become the primary provider of sophisticated military equipment. See Mehta, "Soviet Biscuit Factories and Chinese Financial Grants: North Vietnam's Economic Diplomacy in 1967 and 1968."

85. Qiang, *China and the Vietnam Wars*, 135.

86. Report of Southeast Asia Department MFA "On the Question of Vietnamese Presentations in Connection with the Transit of Weapons through China," January 28, 1967, AVPRF f.079 0.22 papka 60 d.27, 10.

87. Report of Soviet embassy DRV "On Relations between PRC and DRV," September 20, 1967, ibid., 220.

88. Report of Soviet embassy PRC "On the PRC Position on the Vietnam Question," February 25, 1967, ibid., 18.

89. Report of Soviet embassy PRC "On the Relations of the PRC to the Vietnam Question," June 2, 1966, AVPRF f.079 0.21 papka 55 d.29, 137.

90. Conversation among Zhou Enlai, Deng Xiaoping, Kang Sheng, Le Duan, and Nguyen Duy Trinh, April 13, 1966, in Westad, Chen, Tonnesson, Nguyen, and Hershberg, eds., "77 Conversations between Chinese and Foreign Leaders on the Wars in Indochina, 1964–1977," 94.

91. Ibid.

92. Ibid., 188.

93. Report of Soviet embassy DRV "On Relations between PRC and DRV," September 20, 1967, AVPRF f.079 0.22 papka 60 d.27, 229.

94. Report of Southeast Asia Department "Relations of the DRV and VWP Leadership to the 'Cultural Revolution' in China," October 11, 1966, AVPRF f.079 0.21 papka 55 d.30, vol. II, 125.

95. Ibid.

96. Ibid., 126–29.

97. Report of Soviet embassy DRV on attitude of VWP toward question of calling new meeting of international communist movement, March 25, 1967, AVPRF f.079 0.22 papka 60 d.27, 88.

98. See Report of Soviet embassy DRV on Sino-Vietnamese Relations, August 8, 1966, AVPRF f.079 0.21 papka 55 d.29, 244; Report of Soviet embassy DRV "On the Activity of the Chinese in Vietnam and the Measures of the Soviet Embassy," March 16, 1967, AVPRF f.079 0.22 papka 60 d.27, 57. Also see Qiang, *China and the Vietnam Wars,* 157–75.

99. See Nguyen, "The War Politburo: North Vietnam's Diplomatic and Political Road to the Tet Offensive," 29–30.

100. Ibid.

101. Conversation of Zhou Enlai and Pham Van Dong, April 13, 1968, in "77 Conversations," 122.

102. Qiang, *China and the Vietnam Wars,* 172.

103. Ibid., 179.

104. For the lack of Soviet attention to the student movements in the West before this time, see Klaus Mehnert, *Moscow and the New Left,* 9–17.

105. For more on Soviet youth in this period, see Serghei I. Zhuk, *Rock and Roll in the Rocket City,* and Gleb Tsipursky, "Pleasure, Power, and the Pursuit of Communism: Soviet Youth and State-Sponsored Popular Culture during the Early Cold War, 1945–1968."

106. KBG to CC, May 12, 1965, RGANI f.5 0.30 d.480, 53–55.

107 "Brezhnev Addresses Moscow City Party Conference," *Pravda*, March 29, 1968, p1+. *Current Digest of the Soviet Press*, (CDSP), vol. 20.

108. Georgi Arbatov, *The System*, 172–73.

109. Brezhnev speech at Communist Party plenum, April 9, 1968, RGANI f.2 o.3 d.95, 26–35.

110. T. Shmeleva, "The Idea of the Unity of Democratic Forces," *Pravda*, October 3, 1968, 3, in *CDSP*, vol. 20.

111. N. Molchanov, "Students Rebel in the West: The Meaning, Causes, and Goals," *Literaturnaia Gazeta* 45 (November 6, 1968): 13, in *CDSP*, vol. 20.

112. Ibid. and R. Kosolapov, "Socialism and Young People," *Pravda*, March 17, 1969, p3+, in *CDSP*, vol. 21.

113. E. Gnedin, *"Masshtabyi i Kharakteryi," Novyi Mir* 10 (1968): 234.

114. KBG to CC, RGANI f.5 o.60 d.48, 120–53. I thank Amir Weiner of Stanford University for providing me with this document.

115. Ibid., 146.

116. *Peking Review* 21 (May 24, 1968): 18–19, as quoted in Klaus Mehnert, *Peking and the New Left*, 62.

117. Mehnert, *Peking and the New Left*, 62.

118. *Peking Review* 22 (May 31, 1968): 9–10, as quoted in Mehnert, *Peking and the New Left*, 63.

119. Chairman Council of Ministers Committee on Press N. Mikhailov to CC, April 20, 1969, RGANI f.5 o.61 d.41, 109–10.

120. Meeting of International Departments Communist Parties of Bulgaria, Hungary, East Germany, Czechoslovakia, Poland, Mongolia, and USSR on China in Berlin, January 28–31, 1969, SAPMO-BArch DY 30/11929, 46.

121. Ibid., 47–48.

122. Brezhnev speech at Communist Party plenum, June 26, 1969, RGANI f.2 o.3 d.159, 20.

123. The Soviet press during this time spent a great deal of time and energy attacking Marcuse in particular in the harshest possible terms. See Mehnert, *Moscow and the New Left*, 58–70.

124. SCSCAA Presidium session, February 18, 1969, GARF f.9540 o.1 d.255, 68.

125. Andrew and Mitrokhin, *The World Was Going Our Way*, 246.

126. Ibid., 250–51.

127. SCSCAA Presidium session, February 18, 1969, GARF f.9540 o.1 d.255, 58–62.

128. Brezhnev speech at Communist Party plenum, June 26, 1969, RGANI f.2 o.3 d.159, 6–7.

129. Ibid., 12.

130. Ibid., 30.

131. Ibid., 25.

132. Ibid., 56.

133. Brutents, *Tridtsat' Let na Staroĭ Ploshchadi*, 142–43.

134. Ibid., 141.

135. Barnouin and Yu, *Chinese Foreign Policy during the Cultural Revolution*, 78. See also Ma, *The Cultural Revolution in the Foreign Ministry of China*, 309–13.

136. Report from Institute of Far East to MFA Far East Department on "Activization of Foreign Policy of Mao Clique in Africa in 1968," June 20, 1968, AVPRF f.100 o.55 papka 234 d.16, 80–88.

137. Ogunsanwo, *China's Policy in Africa*, 216.

138. Excerpts of the report in Barnouin and Yu, *Chinese Foreign Policy during the Cultural Revolution* 139–42. See also Ma, *The Cultural Revolution in the Foreign Ministry of China*, 292–301.

139. Ibid., 94–95.

140. Ma, *The Cultural Revolution in the Foreign Ministry of China*, 319.

141. Ibid., 320.

Chapter Five

1. Karen Brutents, *Tridtsat' Let na Staroĭ Ploshchadi*, 142.

2. Zhai Qiang, *China and the Vietnam Wars*, 136–37.

3. See Alvin Z. Rubinstein, *Red Star on the Nile*, 103–21, and Karen Dawisha, *Soviet Foreign Policy towards Egypt*, 51.

4. Anatoly Dobrynin, *In Confidence*, 176.

5. Brezhnev speech to Communist Party plenum, December 15, 1969, RGANI f.2 o.3 d.171, 160.

6. Cited in V. G. Solodovnikov, "*Vneshneekonomicheskie Sviazi SSSR s Razvivaiushchimsia Stranami,*" *Narody Azii i Afriki* 5 (1971): 6–9.

7. Martin Meredith, *The Fate of Africa*, 276–81.

8. A. I. Dinkevich, "*Nekotorye Voprosy Ekonomicheskogo Razvitiia Stran 'Tret'ego Mira,*'" *Narody Azii i Afriki* 1 (1971): 3–16.

9. Quoted in Peter Willetts, *The Non-aligned Movement*, 28.

10. Quoted in Gwyneth Williams, *Third World Political Organizations*, 31.

11. Soviet scholars were aware of the dangers of dependency theory and alternative theories and ideologies then current. See for example Karen Brutents, *National Liberation Revolutions Today: Part II*, 57–79.

12. Brezhnev speech at Communist Party plenum, March 22, 1971, RGANI f.2 o.3 d.230, 6.

13. See L. Leont'ev, "*Mezhdunarodnoe Znachenie XXIV S'ezda KPSS,*" *Mirovaia Ekonomika i Mezhdunarodnye Otnosheniia* 5 (1971): 4–17, and "*XXIV S'ezd KPSS i Problemy Natsional'no-Osvoboditel'nogo Dvizheniia,*" *Narody Azii i Afriki* 3 (1971): 3–14.

14. "*XXIV S'ezd KPSS i Problemy Natsional'no-Osvoboditel'nogo Dvizheniia,*" 7.

15. Ibid., 9.

16. Ponomarev, "Under the Banner of Marxism-Leninism and Proletarian Internationalism," 13.

17. A. Gavrilov, "*Programma Bor'by za Mira i Bezopasnost' Narodov,*" *Mirovaia Ekonomika i Mezhdunarodnye Otnosheniia* 7 (1971): 3–11.

18. Samuel S. Kim, *China, the United Nations, and World Order*, 170.

19. Brezhnev speech at Communist Party plenum, December 10, 1973, RGANI f.2 0.3 d.317, 84.

20. Conversation of Nicolae Ceaușescu with PRC government and party delegation led by Li Xiannian, August 25, 1974, Arhivele Naționale Istorice Centrale din România (ANIC), RCP CC Foreign Relations Section, Dosar 187/1974, 42.

21. Brezhnev speech at Communist Party plenum, November 22, 1971, RGANI f.2 0.3 d.251, 44–48.

22. Dawisha, *Soviet Foreign Policy towards Egypt*, 59–63.

23. Craig Daigle, *The Limits of Détente*, 230. See Isabella Ginor and Gideon Remez, "The Origins of a Misnomer: The 'Expulsion of Soviet Advisers' from Egypt in 1972," in *The Cold War in the Middle East*, ed. Nigel J. Ashton, 136–63. Also see Daigle, *The Limits of Détente*, 212–20, 228–37.

24. For Soviet cultivation of Indira Gandhi, see Christopher Andrew and Vasili Mitrokhin, *The World Was Going Our Way*, 316–19.

25. Brezhnev speech to Communist Party plenum, November 22, 1971, RGANI f.2 0.3 d.251, 53.

26. Quoted in Andrew and Mitrokhin, *The World Was Going Our Way*, 321.

27. Ibid. For more on Soviet-Indian relations in this period, see also Bhatia, *Indira Gandhi and Indo-Soviet Relations*.

28. See Lien-Hang Nguyen, "Between the Storms," 200–215.

29. Brezhnev speech to Communist Party plenum, May 19, 1972, RGANI f.2 0.3 d.270, 46.

30. Qiang, *China and the Vietnam Wars*, 200.

31. Nguyen, "Between the Storms," 216–18.

32. See ibid., 239, Dobrynin, *In Confidence,* 243–50, Ilya Gaiduk, *The Soviet Union and the Vietnam War*, 233–38.

33. Nguyen, "Between the Storms," 258.

34. Brezhnev speech to Communist Party plenum, April 26, 1973, RGANI f.2 0.3 d.292, 10.

35. R. Ul'ianovskii, *"O Edinom Antiimperialisticheskom Fronte Progressivnykh Sil v Osvobodivshikhsia Stranakh," Mirovaia Ekonomika i Mezhdunarodnye Otnosheniia* 9 (1972): 80–82.

36. Karen Brutents, *"Praviashchaia Revoliutsionnaia Demokratiia: Nekotorye Cherty Prakticheskoĭ Deiatel'nosti," Mirovaia Ekonomika i Mezhdunarodnye Otnosheniia* 12 (1972): 117.

37. R. Ul'ianovskii, *"O Edinom Antiimperialisticheskom Fronte Progressivnykh Sil v Osvobodivshikhsia Stranakh,"* 84.

38. Brutents, *"Praviashchaia Revoliutsionnaia Demokratiia: Nekotorye Cherty Prakticheskoi Deiatel'nosti,"* 112.

39. For Syria and Iraq, see, for example, G. Akopian, *"Ob Antiimperialisticheskoĭ Napravlennosti Natsionalizma Razvivaiushchikhsia Stran," Mirovaia Ekonomika i Mezhdunarodnye Otnosheniia* 9 (1975): 77–87; A. S. Kaufman, *"O Roli Rabochego Klassa i ego Partii v Stranakh Sotsialisticheskoĭ Orientatsii," Narody Azii i Afriki* 4 (1976): 3–17; for the PDRY, see, for example, G. I. Shitarev, *"Nekotorye Problemy Evoliutsii*

Revoliutsionno-Demokraticheskikh Organizatsii v Napravlenii Partii-Avangarda," *Narody Azii i Afriki* 2 (1976): 33–46; for Soviet instruction in Marxism-Leninism and party formation in the Republic of Congo, see report of embassy Congo (Brazzaville) to CC on work of group of Soviet consultants for party enlightenment, July 1, 1972, RGANI f.5 o.64 d.94, 112–18, report of embassy Congo (Brazzaville) to CC on informational-propaganda work of embassy, June 30, 1974, RGANI f.5 o.67 d.134, 213–21; for Benin see report of embassy Benin to CC "On the Question of Soviet Ideological Influence in Benin," July 22, 1976, RGANI f.5 o.69 d.482, 2–10; for Angola see report from Department of Socialist Economic Planning to CC SED secretariat, *"Reise einer Lektorengruppe in die VR Angola zur Durchführung eines Lehrganges zur Qualifizierung von Leitern für die Wirtschaft,"* March 16, 1977, SAPMO-BArch DY 30/J IV 2/3J 2182.

40. Brezhnev speech to Communist Party plenum, March 22, 1971, RGANI F.2 O.3 d.230, 9.

41. Carlos Altamirano, *Informe al Pleno Nacional, Partido Socialista*, 18.

42. CC SED secretariat protocol, report *"Zur Lage in Chile und Unterstützung der Kommunistischen Partei Chiles,"* August 20, 1973, SAPMO-BArch DY 30/J IV 2/3A 2381, 103. See also report of AIV, *"Vermerk über ein Gespräch des Genossen Paul Verner mit dem Generalsekretär der Sozialistischen Partei Chiles, Genosse Altamirano, am 4.1.1972 in Santiago,"* SAPMO-BArch DY 30/IV B 2/20 354.

43. Leonov, "Soviet Intelligence in Latin America during the 'Cold War,'" 24–25.

44. Report AIV, *"Bericht über eine Konsultation mit dem stellvertretenden Leiter der Internationalen Abteilung im ZK der KPdSU, Mitglied der ZRK, Genossen J. I. Kuskow, zu den Ereignissen in Chile,"* September 20, 1973, SAPMO-BArch DY 30/IV B 2/20 437, 6.

45. Andre Gunder Frank, "The Development of Underdevelopment."

46. See Richard Peet and Elaine Hartwick, *Theories of Development*, 168.

47. S. Tiul'panov, *"K Voprosu o Sotsial'noĭ Strategii Razvivaiushchikhsia Stran,"* *Mirovaia Ekonomika i Mezhdunarodnye Otnosheniia* 7 (1970): 37–46.

48. Ibid., 45.

49. Brutents, *"Praviashchaia Revoliutsionnaia Demokratiia: Nekotorye Cherty Prakticheskoi Deiatel'nosti,"* 112.

50. A. I. Dinkevich, *"Nekotorye Voprosy Ekonomicheskogo Razvitiia Stran 'Tret'ego Mira,'"* *Narody Azii i Afriki* 1 (1971): 3–16.

51. See Richard B. Remnek, *Soviet Scholars and Soviet Foreign Policy*, 244–56.

52. I. Ivanov, *"Problemy Torgovli i Razvitiia na Rubezhe 70-kh godov,"* *Mirovaia Ekonomika i Mezhdunarodnye Otnosheniia* 8 (1972): 28.

53. Ibid., 29.

54. S. Tiul'panov, *"K Voprosu o Sotsal'noi Strategii Razvivaiushchikhsia Stran,"* 46.

55. Jisen Ma, *The Cultural Revolution in the Foreign Ministry of China*, 321.

56. Odd Arne Westad et al., eds., "77 Conversations," 166.

57. Cited in Boris T. Kulik, *Sovetsko-Kitaiskii Raskol*, 455.

58. See Jian Chen, *Mao's China and the Cold War*, 238–45.

59. SCSCAA Presidium session August 10, 1971, GARF f.9540 o.1 d.287, 4.

60. Ibid., 37.

61. Ibid., 31–34.

62. Ma, *The Cultural Revolution in the Foreign Ministry of China*, 330–31.

63. Entire speech contained in Barbara Barnouin and Yu Changgen, *Chinese Foreign Policy during the Cultural Revolution*, 162–69.

64. For an analysis of the content of Chinese speeches at the UN 1971–76, see Kim, *China, the United Nations, and World Order*, 118–19.

65. See Kim, *China, the United Nations, and World Order,* 167, and SCSCAA Presidium session, February 11, 1971, GARF f.9540 o.1 d.286, 10.

66. Report of embassy Kenya to MFA on East African press coverage of PRC foreign policy, January 26, 1972, AVPRF f.100 0.59 papka 255 d.22, 61.

67. Soviet Defense Minister Grechko speech at Communist Party plenum, November 23, 1971, RGANI f.2 o.3 d.252, 89.

68. SCSCAA Presidium session December 17, 1971, GARF f.9540 o.1 d.288, 16.

69. Ibid., 19.

70. SCSCAA Presidium session February 3, 1972, GARF f.9540 o.1 d.318, 11–20.

71. Report of embassy Kenya on East African press coverage of Chinese foreign policy, May 20, 1972, AVPRF f.100 0.59 papka 255 d.22, 182.

72. Ibid., 183.

73. Barnouin and Yu, *Chinese Foreign Policy during the Cultural Revolution*, 169.

74. George T. Yu, "Sino-Soviet Rivalry in Africa," in *Communism in Africa*, ed. David E. Albright, 170–71. Yu relies on sources from the U.S. State Department and CIA.

75. Warren Weinstein, ed., *Chinese and Soviet Aid to Africa*, 281.

76. Report of Soviet representative at UN to MFA on PRC aid to developing countries, March 13, 1972, AVPRF f.100 0.59 papka 255 d.22, 108.

77. Report of Soviet representative at UN in Geneva to MFA on Chinese aid to developing countries, 1954–1972, October 3, 1973, AVPRF f.100 0.60 papka 258 d.21, 250.

78. Soviet embassy Ethiopia to MFA, translation from Amharic of interview of Zhou Enlai with Ethiopian paper *Addis Zemen*, December 15, 1972, AVPRF f.100 0.59 papka 255 d.22, 305.

79. Ma, *The Cultural Revolution in the Foreign Ministry of China*, 343.

80. See report from permanent Soviet representative at international organizations in Vienna to MFA, "On the Attempts of the PRC to Gain Recognition as a Developing Country Belonging to the Third World," May 27, 1975, AVPRF f.100 0.62 papka 265 d.11, 41–42, for a general treatment of the strategy, and Soviet embassy Mauretania to MFA, May 1972, AVPRF f.100 0.59 papka 255 d.22, 168, for a specific example in Mauretania.

81. See report of Soviet embassy Mexico to MFA on visit of President Echeverria to PRC, May 31, 1973, AVPRF f.100 0.60 papka 258 d.21, 123–26, and Kim, *China, the United Nations and the World Order,* 168.

82. See report of embassy UK to MFA on visit of MFA PRC to Iran based on British press, June 26, 1973, AVPRF f.100 0.60 papka 258 d.21, 165, for Iran, and Soviet embassy Argentina to MFA, report on Sino-Argentine relations, August 1973, ibid., 227–31, for Argentina.

83. Ibid., 228–29.

84. Soviet embassy Senegal to First African Department MFA, translation of article in Senegalese paper *Soleil* on visit of President Senghor to PRC, May 6, 1974, AVPRF f.100 0.61 papka 263 d.26, 83.

85. Soviet embassy Rwanda to MFA, report on showing of Chinese films in PRC embassy in Kigali, November 20, 1973, AVPRF f.100 0.60 papka 258 d.21, 316–17.

86. See, for example, report of Institute of Far East to MFA, translation of article on Chinese Communist activity in neutral Afro-Asian countries from Taiwanese journal, 1970, AVPRF f.100 0.59 papka 255 d.22, 32–33; Soviet embassy Malaysia to MFA, translation of White Book of Malaysian government "Threat of Militant Communism in Sarawaka," February 1972, ibid., 111–15; report of Soviet embassy PRC to MFA on relations between PRC and Southeast Asia, April 12, 1972, ibid., 139–141; report of Soviet embassy Cambodia on "Intrigues of Maoists in Southeast Asia," May 1972, ibid., 164–67; Soviet embassy Cambodia to head of Southeast Asian Department MFA S. S. Nemchina, translation of article from journal *Realité Cambodienne*, "Foreign Policy of China Loses Its Aggressiveness," April 7, 1973, AVPRF f.100 0.60 papka 258 d.21,93, details how each of those Communist Parties conducted radio broadcasts from Chinese territory. Also see Westad et al., eds., "77 Conversations," 169. For more on Thailand and American support in fighting Communist guerrillas during the Vietnam War, see Arne Kislenko, "Bamboo in the Shadows: Relations between the United States and Thailand during the Vietnam War," in *America, the Vietnam War, and the World*, ed. Andreas Daum, Lloyd C. Gardner, and Wilfried Mausbach, 197–220.

87. See Soviet embassy Malaysia to MFA, translation of article from Malaysian newspaper *Utusan Malaysia* on secret negotiations between Malaysian and PRC leaders, November 21, 1972, AVPRF f.100 0.59 papka 255 d.22, 284; and report of Soviet embassy Burma to MFA on visit of Burmese journalists to PRC, April 4, 1973, AVPRF f.100 papka 258 d.21, 75; Soviet embassy Cambodia to head of Southeast Asian Department MFA S. S. Nemchina, translation of article from journal *Realité Cambodienne*, "Foreign Policy of China Loses Its Aggressiveness," April 7, 1973, ibid., 89–92.

88. See Soviet ambassador in Bangladesh to Deputy MFA N. D. Firiubin, January 15, 1975, AVPRF f.100 0.62 papka 267 d.25, 1–5.

89. Westad et al., eds., "77 Conversations," 176.

90. See conversation between RCP Politburo member Ilie Verdet with CCP Politburo member Qi Denggui, September 6–7, 1975, ANIC, RCP CC Foreign Relations Section, Dosar 276/1975, 22, and conversation in Beijing between RCP delegation led by Emil Bodnaras and CCP delegation led by Zhou Enlai, September 5–7, 1973, Dosar 174/1973, 23.

91. Soviet ambassador in Sri Lanka to Head Department of Ties with Socialist Countries CC O. Rakhmanin, May 4, 1975, AVPRF f.100 0.62 papka 267 d.25, 71–79.

92. Report of permanent Soviet representative at UN to MFA on policy of Beijing in Latin America, using sources from Taiwanese press, August 21, 1973, AVPRF f.100 0.60 papka 258 d.21, 198.

93. Embassy France, translation of article "Interpol Diplomacy" from French newspaper *Le Monde*, June 27, 1973, ibid., 172.

94. See AIV Report, *"Beratung sozialistischer Länder über die gemeinsame Chinaforschung,"* on meeting of Soviet bloc Sinologists in Moscow, June 6–11, 1973,

SAPMO-BArch DY 30/J IV 2/3A 2361, 100, for Interkit, and DY 30/13929 for a December 12, 1972, report from the CC CPSU to the SED on Chinese foreign policy. See also, for example, Brezhnev speech to Communist Party plenum, April 26, 1973, RGANI f.2 o.3 d.292, 20; Podgornyi speech to Communist Party plenum, April 26, 1973, RGANI f.2 o.3 d.295, 10–16; and T. Deich, *"Novyi Kurs Pekina v Afrike,"* *Mirovaia Ekonomika i Mezhdunarodnye Otnosheniia* 2 (1974): 39–49.

95. Suslov speech to Communist Party plenum, April 26, 1973, RGANI f.2 o.3 d.296, 11.

96. See report of Soviet embassy Kenya to MFA on increasing activity of Maoists in East Africa, 1972, AVPRF f.100 o.59 papka 255 d.22, 198; and report of Soviet embassy Kenya to MFA on reception of Chinese propaganda in Africa, April 14, 1973, AVPRF f.100 o.60 papka 258 d.21, 48.

97. Report of Soviet embassy Kenya to MFA on "Anti-Sovietism of Maoists in the Service of Imperialism," August 17, 1973, AVPRF f.100 o.60 papka 258 d.21, 187.

98. Director of Institute of Latin America to CC Department of Agitprop, report on "Schismatic Activity of Maoists in Latin American Revolutionary and Communist Movements," December 22, 1972, RGANI f.5 o.64 d.98, 77.

99. Roderick MacFarquhar and Michael Schoenals, *Mao's Last Revolution.*

100. See above chapter 3.

101. See Nguyen, "The Sino-Vietnamese Split and the Indochina War, 1968–1975," in *The Third Indochina War*, ed. Odd Arne Westad and Sophie Quinn-Judge, 18–27.

102. Brezhnev speech at Communist Party plenum, 4/26/1973, RGANI F.2 O.3 d.292, 50.

103. Embassy West Germany to MFA, report on West German reaction to NAM conference in Algiers, September 24, 1973, AVPRF f.100 o.60 papka 258 d.21, 239.

104. Conversation of attaché Soviet general consulate in Santiago de Cuba A. N. Shananin with member of Commission of Revolutionary Orientation (COR) of the Regional Committee of CP Cuba in Santiago Orlando Larente, September 24, 1973, AVPRF f.104 o.25 papka24 d.3, 165–66.

105. I. I. Kovalenko and R. A. Tuzmukhamedov, eds., *The Non-aligned Movement*, 181–98.

106. Conversation in Beijing between RCP delegation led by Emil Bodnaras and CCP delegation led by Zhou Enlai, September 5–7, 1973, ANIC RCP CC Foreign Relations Section, Dosar 174/1973, 7.

107. Soviet embassy West Germany to MFA, report on West German reaction to NAM conference in Algiers, September 24, 1973, AVPRF f.100 o.60 papka 258 d.21, 239.

108. *En Estrecha y Eterna Amistad*, 145.

109. Latin American Department MFA Report on Cuba, July 13, 1970, AVPRF f.104 o.25 papka 21 d.9, 128–29.

110. Brezhnev speech to Communist Party plenum, November 22, 1971, RGANI f.2 o.3 d.251, 87. See also Brezhnev speech to Communist Party plenum, April 26, 1973, RGANI f.2 o.3 d.292, 14, and Brezhnev speech to Communist Party plenum, December 10, 1973, RGANI f.2 o.3 d.317, 77.

111. MFA report on Cuban press coverage of visit of MFA Roa to Chile, August 30, 1971, AVPRF f.104 o.26 papka 22 d.9, 6–9.

112. Conversation of third secretary Soviet embassy Cuba D. Atabekov with head MFA Cuba Department of International Organizations A. Moreno, February 10, 1972, AVPRF f.104 o.27 papka 23 d.4, 24–25.

113. Soviet embassy Cuba to MFA, report on Cuba in international organizations, December 23, 1972, AVPRF f.104 o.27 papka 23 d.7, 223–25.

114. See Edward George, *The Cuban Intervention in Angola*, 43 and 260.

115. See Conversation of official of Soviet embassy Cuba V. A. Gurenko with cultural attaché Algerian embassy in Cuba M. Benasilla, April 29, 1974, AVPRF f.0104 o.29 papka 25 d.3, 85–86.

116. Deputy permanent representative at UN to head Far East Department MFA M. S. Kapitsa, report on Chinese position at Geneva session of Third Conference on International Law of the Sea, July 25, 1975, AVPRF f.100 o.62 papka 265 d.11, 53–54.

117. SCSCAA Presidium session January 5, 1973, GARF f.9540 o.1 d.351, 134.

118. Quoted in Williams, *Third World Political Organizations*, 74.

119. "Speech by Chairman of the Delegation of the People's Republic of China, Teng Hsiao-ping, at the Special Session of the UN General Assembly (April 10, 1974)," in *Chinese Foreign Policy during the Cultural Revolution*, by Barnouin and Yu, 214–26.

120. SCSCAA Presidium session, December 7, 1972, GARF f.9540 o.1 d.318, 184–93.

121. I. Ivanov and K. Olegvasov, *"OON i Problemy 'Tret'ego Mira," Mirovaia Ekonomika i Mezhdunarodnye Otnosheniia* 7 (1974): 30–39.

122. Permanent representative at UN to MFA, report on "Position of PRC at Seventh Special Session GA UN on Development and International Economic Cooperation," October 29, 1975, AVPRF f.100 o.62 papka 265 d.11, 104–7.

123. Quoted in I. Ivanov, *"'Tret'ii Mir' v Bor'be za Spravedlivost' i Ravnopravie," Mirovaia Ekonomika i Mezhdunarodnye Otnosheniia*, 1976, no. 9, 115–16.

124. Ibid., 114.

125. Ibid., 115.

126. Ibid., 111.

127. Ibid., 112.

128. L. D. Iablochkov, *"Razvivaiushcheisia Strany i Perestroika Mezhdunarodnykh Otnoshenii," Narody Azii i Afriki* 1 (1977): 23–29.

129. Soviet embassy Kenya to MFA, report on reaction of East African press to PRC actions in international organizations, June 15, 1973, AVPRF f.100 o.60 papka 258 d.21, 157.

130. Soviet embassy Kenya to MFA, report on reaction of East African press to PRC domestic and foreign policy, January 30, 1975, AVPRF f.100 o.61 papka 263 d.26, 17–18, 27–28. See also V. Voronin, *"Pekinskaia Diplomatiia v OON," Mirovaia Ekonomika i Mezhdunarodnye Otnosheniia* 6 (1974): 76–82.

131. Head administration APN to CC, report on propaganda work of APN in Latin America, December 14, 1973, RGANI f.5 o.66 d.166, 171.

132. Report from permanent Soviet representative at international organizations in Vienna to MFA, "On the Attempts of the PRC to Gain Recognition as a Developing Country Belonging to the Third World," May 27, 1975, AVPRF f.100 o.62 papka 265 d.11 43–44.

133. Ibid.

134. Deputy permanent representative at UN to head Far East Department MFA M. S. Kapitsa, report on Chinese position at Geneva session of Third Conference on International Law of the Sea, July 25, 1975, ibid., 53–55; permanent representative at UN to MFA, report on "Position of PRC at Seventh Special Session GA UN on Development and International Economic Cooperation," October 29, 1975, ibid., 104–7.

135. Letter of SCSCAA on "Question of Extraordinary International Solidarity Conference with People's Republic of Angola," January 1976, GARF f.9540 o.1 d.405d, 5.

136. Report of SCSCAA delegation to Extraordinary International Solidarity Conference with Struggle of People of Angola in Luanda, February 2–4, 1976, GARF f.9540 o.1 d.405a, 9.

137. Soviet embassy Guinea-Bissau to MFA, report on relations of Guinea-Bissau with PRC, October 17, 1976, AVPRF f.100 o.63 papka 274 d.29, 145–47.

138. "*Vermerk über ein Gespräch mit Genossen Kirejew stellvertretender Leiter der 1 Fernost-Abteilung des MID, am 24.5.1977,*" SAPMO-BArch DY 30/IV B 2/20 126, 7.

139. See MacFarquhar and Schoenals, *Mao's Last Revolution*, 379–95. See also B. Koloskov, "*Vnutreniaia i Vneshnaia Politika Maoizma: Priiamye i Obratnye Sviazi,*" *Mirovaia Ekonomika i Mezhdunarodnye Otonsheniia* 7 (1976): 34–45.

140. Ma, *The Cultural Revolution in the Foreign Ministry of China*, 347.

141. See Chen Jian, "China's Changing Policies toward the Third World and the End of the Global Cold War," in *The End of the Cold War and the Third World*, edited by Radchenko and Kalinovsky, 111–14.

142. Quoted in G. F. Kim and A. S. Kaufman, "*XXV S'ezda KPSS i Problemy Natsional'no-Osvoboditel'nykh Revoliutsiiuakh,*" *Narody Azii i Afriki* 3 (1976): 3.

143. See ibid., 7–8, and meeting of SCSCAA *aktiv*, April 6, 1976, GARF f.9540 o.1 d.400, 22.

144. A. S. Kaufman, "*O Roli Rabochego Klassa i ego Partii v Stranakh Sotsialist-icheskoi Orientatsii,*" *Narody Azii i Afriki* 4 (1976): 17.

145. Brutents, *Tridtsat' Let na Staroĭ Ploshchadi*, 143.

146. Kulik, *Sovetsko-Kitaiskii Raskol*, 464.

Conclusion

1. Quoted in Sergey Radchenko, *Two Suns in the Heavens*, 59.

2. See Karen Brutents, *Tridtsat' Let na Staroĭ Ploshchadi*, 143, and Anatoly S. Chernyaev, *My Six Years with Gorbachev*, 146–50.

3. Quoted in Stephen Kotkin and Jan T. Gross, *Uncivil Society*, 50.

4. Margot Light, "Introduction: The Evolution of Soviet Policy in the Third World," in *Troubled Friendships*, 21.

5. Nikolai Leonov, *Likholet'e*, 114.

6. Report from Soviet embassy Benin to CC, "On Question of Soviet Ideological Influence in Benin," July 22, 1976, RGANI f.5 o.69 d.482, 2–10.

7. Quoted in Robert D. English, *Russia and the Idea of the West*, 176.

8. Chernyaev, *My Six Years with Gorbachev*, 52.

9. See English, *Russia and the Idea of the West*, 205, and Odd Arne Westad, *The Global Cold War*, 365.

10. Chernyaev, *My Six Years with Gorbachev*, 51.

11. Edward George, *The Cuban Intervention in Angola*, 195.

12. Westad, *The Global Cold War*, 365.

13. English, *Russia and the Idea of the West*, 207.

14. Quoted in Westad, *The Global Cold War*, 384–85.

15. Quoted in ibid.

16. Vladimir Shubin, *ANC: A View from Moscow*, 306.

17. Light, *Troubled Friendships*, 21.

18. Quoted in David Shambaugh, *China's Communist Party*, 43.

19. Quoted in ibid., 44.

20. Quoted in ibid., 59.

21. Ibid., 64.

22. Jialin Zhang, *China's Response to the Downfall of Communism in Eastern Europe and the Soviet Union*, 20–21.

23. Quoted in Shambaugh, *China's Communist Party*, 85.

24. Ibid., 169.

25. Ibid.

26. Quoted in Robert B. Rakove, *Kennedy, Johnson, and the Nonaligned World*, 255.

27. Quoted in Ilya Gaiduk, *The Soviet Union and the Vietnam War*, 87.

28. Samuel P. Huntington, "The Clash of Civilizations?," 45.

29. Westad, *The Global Cold War*, 5.

Bibliography

Archives

CHILE

Archivo Histórico del Ministerio de Relaciones Exteriores (Historical Archive of the
Ministry of Foreign Relations)

CHINA

中国外交部开放档案 (*Zhongguo Waijiaobu kaifang dang'an*—[Declassified] Chinese
Foreign Ministry Archive)

GERMANY

Stiftung Archiv der Parteien und Massenorganisationen der DDR—Bundesarchiv
(Archive of the Parties and Mass Organizations of the GDR in the Federal
Archives)

MOZAMBIQUE

Arquivo Histórico de Moçambique (Historical Archive of Mozambique)

PORTUGAL

Instituto dos Arquivos Nacionais da Torre do Tombo (Institute of National Archives
of the Torre do Tombo)

ROMANIA

Arhive Diplomatice ale Ministerul Afacerilor Externe (Diplomatic Archive of the
Ministry of Foreign Affairs)

Arhivele Naționale Istorice Centrale din România (National Historical Archive of
Romania)

RUSSIA

Arkhiv Vneshneĭ Politikoĭ Rossisskoĭ Federatsii (Archive of the Foreign Policy of
the Russian Federation)

Gosudarstvennyĭ Arkhiv Rossisskoĭ Federatsii (State Archive of the Russian
Federation)

Rossisskiĭ Gosudarstvennyĭ Arkhiv Ekonomiki (Russian State Archive of the
Economy)

Rossisskiĭ Gosudarstvennyĭ Arkhiv Noveisheĭ Istorii (Russian State Archive of
    Contemporary History)
Rossisskiĭ Gosudarstvennyĭ Arkhiv Sotsial'no-Politicheskoĭ Istorii (Russian State
    Archive of Socio-Political History)

SERBIA
Arhiv Jugoslavije (Archive of Yugoslavia)

SOUTH AFRICA
South African Department of Foreign Affairs Archive
South African National Defense Forces Archive

UNITED STATES
Hoover Institution Library and Archives

Newspapers, Journals, and Magazines

CHINESE LANGUAGE
Hongqi
Renmin Ribao
Shijie Zhishi

ENGLISH LANGUAGE
Current Digest of the Soviet Press
The New Times
World Marxist Review

RUSSIAN LANGUAGE
Aziia i Afrika Segodnia
Izvestiia
Komsomol'skaia Pravda
Latinskaia Amerika
Literaturnaia Gazeta
Mirovaia Ekonomika i Mezhdunarodnye Otnosheniia
Narody Azii i Afriki
Pravda
Problemy Vostokovedeniia
Sovremennyi Vostok

SPANISH LANGUAGE
El Mercurio
Punto Final
Ultima Hora

Published Primary Sources

Altamirano, Carlos. *Informe al Pleno Nacional, Partido Socialista* (Speech to the
    National Plenum of the Socialist Party). Santiago, Chile: Prensa
    Latinoamericana, 1971.

Brutents, Karen. *National Liberation Revolutions Today*. 2 vols. Moscow: Progress Publishers, 1977.

Burlatskiĭ, Fedor. *Maoizm ili Marksizm* (Maoism or Marxism). Moscow: Izdatel'stvo Politicheskoi Literaturyi, 1967.

Burr, William, ed. *The Kissinger Transcripts: The Top-Secret Talks with Beijing and Moscow*. New York: New Press, 1998.

"Chile en los Archivos de la URSS, 1959–1973" ("Chile in the Archives of the USSR, 1959–1973"). *Estudios Publicos* 72 (1998): 391–476.

China and the Asian-African Conference: Documents. Beijing: Foreign Languages Press, 1955.

Debray, Régis. *The Chilean Revolution: Conversations with Allende*. New York: Pantheon Books, 1971.

"Documentos Clave de la Izquierda Chilena, 1969–1973" ("Key Documents of the Chilean Left, 1969–1973"). *Estudios Publicos* 91 (2003): 311–90.

En Estrecha y Eterna Amistad: Visita a Cuba del compañero Leonid I. Brezhnev, secretario general del Comité Central del Partido Comunista de la Unión Soviética (In close and eternal friendship: Visit to Cuba of comrade Leonid I. Brezhnev, general secretary of the Central Committee of the Communist Party of the Soviet Union). Havana: Editorial de Ciencas Sociales, 1974.

Fanon, Frantz. *The Wretched of the Earth*. New York: Grove Weidenfeld, 1991.

Fursenko, A. A., ed. *Arkhivy Kremlia: Prezidium TsK KPSS, 1954–1964* (Kremlin Archives: Presidium CC CPSU, 1954–1964). Moscow: ROSSPEN, 2004.

Gittings, John. *The Sino-Soviet Dispute: A Commentary and Extracts from the Recent Polemics, 1963–1967*. London: Oxford University Press, 1968.

Gott, Richard, John Major, and Geoffrey Warner, eds. *Documents on International Affairs 1960*. London: Oxford University Press, 1964.

Guevara, Che. "Message to the Tricontinental," April 16, 1967. Workers' Web ASCII Pamphlet Project, 1997, 2d (HTML) edition 1998. http://www.rcgfrfi.easynet.co.uk/ww/guevara/1967-mtt.htm. September 26, 2014.

Guevara, Ernesto Che. *Che Guevara Reader: Writings by Ernesto Che Guevara on Guerrilla Strategy, Politics, and Revolution*. New York: Ocean Press, 1997.

Hacia la conquista de un gobierno popular: Documentos del XII Congresso Nacional del Partido Comunista de Chile (Toward the conquest of a popular government: Documents of the 12th National Congress of the Chilean Communist Party). Santiago, Chile: Impresora Horizonte, 1962.

Lenin, Vladimir. *Imperialism, the highest Stage of Capitalism: A Popular Outline*. New York: International Publishers, 1939.

Luthi, Lorenz. "Twenty-Four Soviet-Bloc Documents on Vietnam and the Sino-Soviet Split, 1964–1966." *Cold War International History Project Bulletin* 16 (Fall 2007–Winter 2008).

Marcuse, Herbert. *Counterrevolution and Revolt*. Boston: Beacon Press, 1972.

———. *Eros and Civilization*. Boston: Beacon Press, 1955.

Nasser, Gamal Abdel. *On Non-alignment*. Cairo: Information Administration, 1966.

———. *The Philosophy of Revolution*. Cairo: National Publication House Press, 1966.

Nkrumah, Kwame. *Neocolonialism: The Last Stage of Imperialism.* New York: International Publishers, 1965.

Nyerere, Julius K. *Ujamaa: Essays on Socialism.* London: Oxford University Press, 1968.

Ponomarev, Boris. "Under the Banner of Marxism-Leninism and Proletarian Internationalism." *World Marxist Review* 14.6 (1971).

"Proposal Concerning the General Line of the International Communist Movement." http://ia341238.us.archive.org/1/items/AProposalConcerningTheGen eralLineOfTheInternationalCommunistMovement/MicrosoftWord-Document1 .pdf. September 26, 2014.

Radek, Karl. "Address to the Baku Congress of the Peoples of the East, September 2, 1920." http://www.marxists.org/history/international/comintern/baku/ch02 .htm. September 26, 2014.

Rostow, Walt W. *The Stages of Economic Growth.* London: Cambridge University Press, 1960.

Soekarno, Ahmed. Translated by Karel H. Warouw and Peter D. Weldon. *Nationalism, Islam, and Marxism.* Ithaca, NY: Modern Indonesia Project, Southeast Asia Program, Department of Asian Studies, Cornell University, 1970.

"Theses on the Eastern Question." Fourth Congress of the Communist International, December 5, 1922. http://www.marxists.org/history/international /comintern/4th-congress/eastern-question.htm. September 26, 2014.

Tito, Josip Broz. *The Essential Tito.* New York: St. Martin's Press, 1970.

Uroki Chili (Lessons of Chile). Moscow: Nauka, 1977.

Westad, Odd Arne, Chen Jian, Stein Tonnesson, Nguyen Vu Tang, and James G. Hershberg, eds. "77 Conversations between Chinese and Foreign Leaders on the Wars in Indochina, 1964–1977." Cold War International History Project Working Paper 22. Washington, DC: Woodrow Wilson Center Press, 1998.

Memoirs

Aleksandrov-Agentov, A. M. *Ot Kollontai do Gorbacheva: Vospominania diplomata, sovetnika A.A. Gromyko, pomoshchnika L.I. Brezhneva, Iu. V. Andropova, K.U. Chernenko i M.S. Gorbacheva* (From Kollontai to Gorbachev: Recollections of a diplomat, adviser of A.A. Gromyko, aide of L. I. Brezhnev, Yu. V. Andropov, K. U. Chernenko, and M. S. Gorbachev). Moscow: Mezhdunarodnye Otnosheniia, 1994.

Arbatov, Georgi. *The System: An Insider's Life in Soviet Politics.* New York: Random House, 1992.

Brezhnev, A. A. *Kitai: Ternistyi put' k dobrososedstvu: Vospominaniia i razmyshleniia* (China: Thorny path to neighborliness: Recollection and contemplation). Moscow: Mezhdunarodnye Otnosheniia, 1998.

Brutents, Karen. *Tridtsat' Let na Staroi Ploshchadi* (Thirty years on Old Square). Moscow: Mezhdunarodnye Otnosheniia, 1998.

Cherniaev, A. S. *Moia Zhizn' i Moe Vremia* (My life and my time). Moscow: Mezhdunarodnye Otnosheniia, 1995.

Chernyaev, Anatoly S. Translated by Robert English and Elizabeth Tucker. *My Six Years with Gorbachev*. University Park: Pennsylvania State University Press, 2000.

Corvalan, Luis. *De lo vivido y lo peleado* (What I have lived and fought for). Santiago: LOM Ediciones, 1997.

Davis, Nathaniel. *Last Two Years of Salvador Allende*. Ithaca, NY: Cornell University Press, 1985.

Dobrynin, Anatoly. *In Confidence: Moscow's Ambassador to America's Six Cold War Presidents*. Seattle: University of Washington Press, 1995.

Gromyko, Andrei. Translated by Harold Shukman. *Memoirs*. New York: Doubleday, 1989.

Heikal, Mohammed Hassanein. *The Cairo Documents: The Inside Story of Nasser and His Relationship with World Leaders, Rebels, and Statesmen*. New York: Doubleday, 1973.

Huang, Hua. *Huang Hua Memoirs*. Beijing: Foreign Languages Press, 2008.

Khrushchev, Nikita. Translated by Strobe Talbott. *Khrushchev Remembers*. Boston: Little, Brown, 1970.

Kissinger, Henry. *The White House Years*. Boston: Little, Brown, 1979.

Kornienko, G. M. *Kholodnaia Voina: Svidetel'stvo ee uchastnika* (Cold War: Testimony of a participant). Moscow: Mezhdunarodnye Otnosheniia, 1995.

Leonov, Nikolaĭ. *Likholet'e* (Hard times). Moscow: Russkiĭ Dom, 2003.

Nixon, Richard Milhous. *RN: The Memoirs of Richard Nixon*. New York: Grosset & Dunlap, 1978.

Shebarshin, V. L. *Iz zhizni nachal'nika razvedki* (From the life of a boss of espionage). Moscow: Mezhdunarodnye Otnosheniia, 1994.

———. *Ruka Moskvy: Zapiski nachal'nika sovetskoi razvedki* (The arm of Moscow: Notes of a boss of Soviet espionage). Moscow: Tsentr-100, 1992.

Shi, Zhe. 毛泽东的翻译师哲眼中的高层人物 (High-level people through the eyes of Mao Zedong's translator Shi Zhe). Beijing: Renmin Chubanshe, 2005.

Stockwell, John. *In Search of Enemies: A CIA Story*. New York: Norton, 1978.

Wu, Lengxi. 十年论战 *1956–1966* 中苏关系回忆录 (Ten years of polemic war, 1956–1966: Record of Sino-Soviet relations). Beijing: Zhongyang Wenxian Chubanshe, 1999.

Wu, Xiuquan. 回忆与怀念 (Memories and nostalgia). Beijing: Chinese Communist Party Central School Press, 1991.

Zhisui, Li. Translated by Tai Hung-chao. *The Private Life of Chairman Mao: The Memoirs of Mao's Personal Physician*. New York: Random House, 1994.

Secondary Literature

Albright, David E. *Vanguard Parties and Revolutionary Change in the Third World*. Berkeley: University of California Press, 1990.

———, ed. *Communism in Africa*. Bloomington: Indiana University Press, 1980.

Ali, Tariq. *1968 and After: Inside the Revolution*. London: Blond and Briggs, 1978.

Almeyda, Clodomiro. *Pensando a Chile* (Thinking of Chile). Santiago, Chile: Terranova Editores, 1986.

Amin, Samir. *Trois expériences africaines de développement: Le Mali, La Guinée et le Ghana* (Three African experiences of development: Mali, Guinea, and Ghana). Paris: Presses Universitaires de France, 1965.

Andrew, Christopher, and Vasili Mitrokhin. *The Sword and the Shield: The Mitrokhin Archive.* New York: Basic Books, 1999.

———. *The World Was Going Our Way: The KGB and the Battle for the Third World.* New York: Basic Books, 2005.

Ang, Cheng Guan. *Vietnamese Communists and China, 1956–1962.* London: McFarland, 1997.

———. *Ending the Vietnam War.* London: RoutledgeCurzon, 2004.

Armah, Kwesi. *Ghana's Foreign Policy, 1957–1966.* Accra: Ghana Universities Press, 2004.

Armstrong, J. D. *Revolutionary Diplomacy: Chinese Foreign Policy and the United Front Doctrine.* Berkeley: University of California Press, 1977.

Ashton, Nigel J., ed. *The Cold War in the Middle East: Regional Conflict and the Superpowers, 1967–73.* London: Routledge, 2007.

Asselin, Pierre. *Hanoi's Road to the Vietnam War, 1954–1965.* Berkeley: University of California Press, 2013.

Aydin, Cemil. *The Politics of Anti-Westernism in Asia: Visions of World Order in Pan-Islamic and Pan-Asian Thought.* New York: Columbia University Press, 2007.

Baer, W., and J. Love, eds. *Liberalization and Its Consequences: A Comparative Perspective on Latin America and Eastern Europe.* Cheltenham, UK: Elgar, 2000.

Bailey, Martin. *Freedom Railway: China and the Tanzania-Zambia Link.* London: Rex Collings, 1976.

Barnett, Thomas P. M. *Romanian and East German Policies in the Third World: Comparing the Strategies of Ceausescu and Honecker.* Westport, CT: Praeger, 1992.

Barnouin, Barbara, and Yu Changgen. *Chinese Foreign Policy during the Cultural Revolution.* New York: Kegan Paul International, 1998.

———. *Ten Years of Turbulence: The Chinese Cultural Revolution.* London: Kegan Paul International, 1993.

Bernstein, Thomas P., and Hua-yu Li, eds. *China Learns from the Soviet Union, 1949–Present.* Lanham, MD: Lexington Books, 2010.

Bettelheim, Charles. *China Shakes the World Again.* New York: Monthly Review Press, 1959.

Bhatia, Vinod. *Indira Gandhi and Indo-Soviet Relations.* New Delhi: Panchsheel Publishers, 1987.

Bianco, Lucien. *Origins of the Chinese Revolution, 1915–1949.* Stanford, CA: Stanford University Press, 1971.

Biberaj, Elez. *Albania and China: A Study of an Unequal Alliance.* Boulder, CO: Westview, 1986.

Birmingham, David. *The Decolonisation of Africa.* Athens: Ohio University Press, 1995.

Boden, Ragna. *Die Grenzen der Weltmacht: Sowjetische Indonesienpolitik von Stalin bis Breznev* (The limits of a global power: Soviet Indonesia policy from Stalin to Brezhnev). Stuttgart: Franz Steiner Verlag, 2006.

Boorstein, Edward. *Allende's Chile*. New York: International Publishers, 1977.

Borstelmann, Thomas. *The Cold War and the Color Line: American Race Relations in the Global Arena*. Cambridge, MA: Harvard University Press, 2001.

Botha, Pierre du T. *Soviet Perspectives on National Liberation Revolutions in Africa: Theoretical Aspects, 1960–1990*. Pretoria: Africa Institute of South Africa, 1999.

Bradley, Mark Phillip. *Imagining Vietnam & America: The Making of Postcolonial Vietnam, 1919–1950*. Chapel Hill: University of North Carolina Press, 2000.

Bradley, Mark Phillip, and Robert K. Brigham. "Vietnamese Archives and Scholarship on the Cold War Period: Two Reports." Cold War International History Project Working Paper 7 (1993).

Breslauer, George W. *Khrushchev and Brezhnev as Leaders: Building Authority in Soviet Politics*. London: George Allen & Unwin, 1982.

———. "Review: Ideology and Learning in Soviet Third World Policy." *World Politics* 39.3 (1987): 429–48.

Brigham, Robert K. *Guerrilla Diplomacy: The NLF's Foreign Policy and Viet Nam War*. Ithaca, NY: Cornell University Press, 1999.

Brudny, Yitzchak M. *Reinventing Russia: Russian Nationalism and the Soviet State, 1953–1991*. Cambridge, MA: Harvard University Press, 1998.

Brzezinski, Zbigniew K. *The Soviet Bloc: Unity and Conflict*. Cambridge, MA: Harvard University Press, 1967.

Burlatskiĭ, Fedor. *Mao Tse-tung: An Ideological and Psychological Portrait*. Moscow: Progress Publishers, 1976.

Byrne, Jeffrey James. "Our Own Special Brand of Socialism: Algeria and the Contest of Modernities in the 1960s." *Diplomatic History* 33.3 (2009): 427–47.

Caballero, Manuel. *Latin America and the Comintern, 1919–1943*. New York: Cambridge University Press, 1986.

Campbell, Bonnie, and Jennifer Trapp. "Guinea's Economic Performance under Structural Adjustment." *Journal of Modern African Studies* 33.3 (1995): 425–49.

Castañeda, Jorge G. *Compañero: The Life and Death of Che Guevara*. New York: Alfred A. Knopf, 1997.

Cavoski, Jovan. "Arming Nonalignment: Yugoslavia's Relations with Burma and the Cold War in Asia (1950–1955)." Cold War International History Project Working Paper 61 (2010).

Chai, Sun-Ki. *Choosing an Identity: A General Model of Preference and Belief Formation*. Ann Arbor: University of Michigan Press, 2001.

Chaliand, Gerard. *Revolution in the Third World*. New York: Viking Penguin, 1989.

Chen, Jian. "China and the Bandung Conference: Changing Perceptions and Representations." In *Bandung Revisited: The Legacy of the 1955 Afro-Asian Conference for International Order*, edited by See Sang Tan and Amitav Acharya, 132–59. Singapore: NUS Press, 2008.

———. *China's Road to the Korean War: The Making of the Sino-American Confrontation*. New York: Columbia University Press, 1994.

———. *Mao's China and the Cold War*. Chapel Hill: University of North Carolina Press, 2001.

Cheng, Yinghong. *Creating the New Man: From Enlightenment Ideals to Socialist Realities.* Honolulu: University of Hawaii Press, 2009.

Christensen, Thomas J. "Worse than a Monolith: Disorganization and Rivalry within Asian Communist Alliances and U.S. Containment Challenges, 1949–69." *Asian Security* 1.1 (2005): 80–127.

"Clark Amendment article." http://academic.brooklyn.cuny.edu/history/johnson/clark.htm. September 26, 2014.

Claudin, Fernando. *The Communist Movement: From Comintern to Cominform: Part Two, the Zenith of Stalinism.* New York: Monthly Review Press, 1975.

Conquest, Robert. *Harvest of Sorrow: Soviet Collectivization and the Terror-Famine.* New York: Oxford University Press, 1987.

Contee, Clarence G. "Du Bois, the NAACP, and the Pan-African Congress of 1919." *Journal of Negro History* 57.1 (1972) 13–28.

Cooley, John K. *East Wind over Africa: Red China's African Offensive.* New York: Walker & Company, 1965.

Corvalan, Luis. *El gobierno de Salvador Allende* (The government of Salvador Allende). Santiago, Chile: LOM Ediciones, 2003.

Cumings, Bruce. "The Political Economy of Chinese Foreign Policy." *Modern China* 5.4 (1979): 411–61.

Daigle, Craig. *The Limits of Détente: The United States, the Soviet Union, and the Arab-Israeli Conflict, 1969–1973.* New Haven, CT: Yale University Press, 2012.

Dawisha, Karen. *The Kremlin and the Prague Spring.* Berkeley: University of California Press, 1984.

———. *Soviet Foreign Policy towards Egypt.* London: Macmillan, 1979.

Dikötter, Frank. *Mao's Great Famine: The History of China's Most Devastating Catastrophe, 1958–1962.* New York: Walker and Company, 2010.

———. *The Tragedy of Liberation: A History of the Chinese Revolution, 1945–57.* New York: Bloomsbury, 2013.

Dudziak, Mary L. *Cold War Civil Rights: Race and the Image of American Democracy.* Princeton, NJ: Princeton University Press, 2000.

Duffy, James. *Portuguese Africa.* Cambridge, MA: Harvard University Press, 1959.

Dziak, John J. "*The Soviet Union and National Liberation Movements: An Examination of the Development of a Revolutionary Strategy.*" Ph.D. diss., Georgetown University, 1971.

Easterly, William. *The Elusive Quest for Growth: Economists' Adventures and Misadventures in the Tropics.* Cambridge, MA: MIT Press, 2001.

Ellison, Herbert J., ed. *The Sino-Soviet Conflict: A Global Perspective.* Seattle: University of Washington Press, 1982.

English, Robert D. *Russia and the Idea of the West: Gorbachev, Intellectuals, and the End of the Cold War.* New York: Columbia University Press, 2000.

Eran, Oded. *Mezhdunarodniki: An Assessment of Professional Expertise in the Making of Soviet Foreign Policy.* Ramat Gan, Israel: Turtledove Publishing, 1979.

Falcoff, Mark. *Modern Chile, 1970–1989: A Critical History.* London: Transaction Publishers, 1989.

Fermandois, Joaquin. *Chile y el Mundo, 1970–1973: La politica exterior del gobierno de la Unidad Popular y el sistema internacional* (Chile and the World, 1970–1973: The Foreign Policy of the Unidad Popular Government and the International System). Santiago, Chile: Ediciones Universidad Catolica de Chile, 1985.

———. "Pawn or Player? Chile in the Cold War." *Estudios Publicos* 72 (1998): 1–23.

Ferris, Jesse. "Egypt, the Cold War, and the Civil War in Yemen, 1962–1966." Ph.D. diss., Princeton University, 2008.

Fink, Carol, Phillip Gassert, and Detlef Junker, eds. *1968: The World Transformed.* Washington, DC: Cambridge University Press, 1998.

Fleet, Michael. *The Rise and Fall of Chilean Christian Democracy.* Princeton, NJ: Princeton University Press, 1985.

Frank, Andre Gunder. "The Development of Underdevelopment." *Monthly Review* 18 (1966).

Fukuyama, Francis. *The End of History and the Last Man.* New York: Free Press, 1992.

Furet, Francois. *The Passing of an Illusion: The Idea of Communism in the Twentieth Century.* Chicago: University of Chicago Press, 1999.

Gaddis, John Lewis. *We Now Know.* New York: Oxford University Press, 1997.

Gaiduk, Ilya. *Confronting Vietnam.* Stanford, CA: Stanford University Press, 2003.

———. *The Soviet Union and the Vietnam War.* Chicago: Ivan R. Dee, 1996.

Gardner, Lloyd C., and Ted Gittinger, eds. *International Perspectives on Vietnam.* College Station: Texas A&M University Press, 2000.

———. *The Search for Peace in Vietnam, 1964–1968.* College Station: Texas A&M University Press, 2004.

Garver, John W. *Foreign Relations of the PRC.* Englewood Cliffs, NJ: Prentice Hall, 1993.

George, Edward. *The Cuban Intervention in Angola, 1965–1991: From Che Guevara to Cuito Cuanavale.* New York: Frank Cass, 2005.

Gil, Frederico G., Ricardo E. Lagos, and Henry A. Lansberger, eds. *Chile at the Turning Point: Lessons of the Socialist Years, 1970–1973.* Philadelphia: Institute for the Study of Human Issues, Inc., 1979.

Gilks, Anne. *The Breakdown of Sino-Vietnamese Alliance, 1970–1979.* Berkeley: University of California Press, 1992.

Ginor, Isabella, and Gideon Remez. "The Origins of a Misnomer: The 'Expulsion of Soviet Advisers' from Egypt in 1972." In *The Cold War in the Middle East,* edited by Nigel J. Ashton, 136–63. London: Routledge, 2007.

Gleijeses, Piero. *Conflicting Missions: Havana, Washington, and Africa, 1959–1976.* Chapel Hill: University of North Carolina Press, 2002.

Golan, Galia. *The Soviet Union and National Liberation Movements in the Third World.* Boston: Allen & Unwin, 1988.

Gourevitch, Peter. *Politics in Hard Times: Comparative Responses to International Economic Crises.* Ithaca, NY: Cornell University Press, 1986.

Grandin, Greg. *The Last Colonial Massacre: Latin America in the Cold War.* Chicago: University of Chicago Press, 2004.

Griffith, William E. *The Sino-Soviet Rift.* Cambridge, MA: MIT Press, 1964.

Guimarães, Fernando Andresen. *The Origins of the Angolan Civil War: Foreign Intervention and Domestic Political Conflict*. New York: St. Martin's Press, 2001.

Gurley, John G. "The Dialectics of Development: The USSR versus China." *Modern China* 4.2 (1978): 123–156.

Hall, Richard, and Hugh Peyman. *The Great Uhuru Railway: China's Showpiece in Africa*. London: Victor Gollancz, 1976.

Harris, Lillian Craig. *China's Foreign Policy toward the Third World*. New York: Praeger, 1985.

Harris, Lillian Craig, and Robert Worden, eds. *China and the Third World*. Dover, MA: Auburn House Publishing, 1986.

Harvey, David. *A Brief History of Neoliberalism*. New York: Oxford University Press, 2005.

Haslam, Jonathan. *The Nixon Administration and the Death of Allende's Chile*. London: Verso, 2005.

Henderson, Lawrence W. *Angola: Five Centuries of Conflict*. Ithaca, NY: Cornell University Press, 1979.

Hershberg, James. *Marigold: The Lost Chance for Peace in Vietnam*. Stanford, CA: Stanford University Press, 2012.

Horne, Alistair. *Small Earthquake in Chile*. New York: Viking Press, 1972.

Hough, Jerry F. *The Struggle for the Third World: Soviet Debates and American Options*. Washington, DC: Brookings Institution, 1986.

Hunt, Michael. *The Genesis of Chinese Communist Foreign Policy*. New York: Columbia University Press, 1996.

Huntington, Samuel P. "The Clash of Civilizations?" *Foreign Affairs* 72.3 (September 1993): 22–49.

———. *The Clash of Civilizations and the Remaking of the World Order*. New York: Simon & Schuster, 1996.

Hutchinson, Alan. *China's African Revolution*. London: Hutchinson, 1975.

Irwin, Ryan. *Gordian Knot: Apartheid and the Unmaking of the Liberal World Order*. New York: Oxford University Press, 2012.

Issawi, Charles. "The 1973 Oil Crisis and After." *Journal of Post-Keynesian Economics* 1.2 (1978–79): 3–26.

Jackson, Steven F. "China's Third World Foreign Policy: The Case of Angola and Mozambique, 1961–93." *The China Quarterly* 142 (1995): 388–422.

James, W. Martin, III. *A Political History of the Civil War in Angola, 1974–1990*. New Brunswick, NJ: Transaction Publishers, 1992.

Jinadu, L. Adele, and Ibbo Mandaza. *African Perspectives on the Non-aligned Movement*. Harare, Zimbabwe: African Association of Political Science, 1986.

Johnson, Chalmers. *Peasant Nationalism and Communist Power: The Emergence of Revolutionary China*. Stanford, CA: Stanford University Press, 1962.

Johnson, R. W. *South Africa: The First Man, the Last Nation*. London: Wiedenfeld & Nicolson, 2004.

Johnston, Alastair Iain, and Robert S. Ross, eds. *New Directions in the Study of China's Foreign Policy*. Stanford, CA: Stanford University Press, 2006.

Judt, Tony. *Marxism and the French Left*. New York: Oxford University Press, 1986.

Jun, Niu. "1962: The Eve of the Left Turn in China's Foreign Policy." Cold War
International History Project Working Paper 48. Washington, DC: Woodrow
Wilson Center Press, October 2005.

Kalyvas, Stathis. *The Rise of Christian Democracy in Europe.* Ithaca, NY: Cornell
University Press, 1996.

Kapuscinski, Ryszard. Translated by William R. Brand and Katarzyna
Mroczkowska. *Another Day of Life.* New York: Harcourt Brace Jovanovich, 1987.

Karl, Rebecca. *Staging the World: Chinese Nationalism at the Turn of the Twentieth
Century.* Durham, NC: Duke University Press, 2002.

Katsikas, Suzanne Jolicoeur. *The Arc of Socialist Revolution: From Angola to
Afghanistan.* Cambridge, MA: Schenkman, 1982.

Katz, Mark N. *The Third World in Soviet Military Thought.* Baltimore: Johns
Hopkins University Press, 1982.

———. *The USSR and Marxist Revolutions in the Third World.* Cambridge, UK:
Cambridge University Press, 1990.

Kaufman, Edy. *Crisis in Allende's Chile: New Perspectives.* New York: Praeger, 1987.

Keller, Edmond J., and Donald Rothschild, eds. *Afro-Marxist Regimes.* Boulder, CO:
Lynne Rienner, 1987.

Kempton, Daniel R. *Soviet Strategy toward Southern Africa: The National Liberation
Movement Connection.* New York: Praeger, 1989.

Kim, Samuel S. *China, the United Nations, and World Order.* Princeton, NJ:
Princeton University Press, 1979.

Kislenko, Arne. "Bamboo in the Shadows: Relations between the United States and
Thailand during the Vietnam War." In *America, the Vietnam War, and the
World,* edited by Andreas W. Daum, Lloyd C. Gardner, and Wilfried Mausbach,
197–220. Cambridge, UK: Cambridge University Press, 2003.

Klinghoffer, Arthur Jay. *The Angolan War: A Study in Soviet Policy in the Third
World.* Boulder, CO: Westview, 1980.

Klinghoffer, David. *Soviet Perspectives on African Socialism.* Teaneck, NJ: Farleigh
Dickinson University Press, 1969.

Klinghoffer, Judith. "The 1967 Middle East Crisis: A Second Vietnam." In
International Perspectives on Vietnam, edited by Lloyd C. Gardner and Ted
Gittinger, 204–24. College Station: Texas A&M University Press, 2000.

Kolinsky, Martin, and William E. Paterson, eds. *Social and Political Movements in
Western Europe.* London: Croom Helm, 1976.

Kotkin, Stephen. *Armageddon Averted: the Soviet Collapse, 1970–2000.* New York:
Oxford University Press, 2001.

———. "The Kiss of the Debt." In *The Shock of the Global: The 1970s in Perspective,*
edited by N. Ferguson et al., 80–90. Cambridge, MA: Harvard University Press,
2010.

Kotkin, Stephen, and Jan T. Gross. *Uncivil Society: 1989 and the Implosion of the
Communist Establishment.* New York: Modern Library, 2009.

Kovalenko, I. I., and R. A. Tuzmukhamedov, eds. *The Non-aligned Movement.*
Moscow: Progress Publishers, 1988.

———. *The Non-aligned Movement: The Soviet View.* New Delhi: Sterling, 1987.

Kulik, Boris T. *Sovetsko-Kitaiskii Raskol: Prichiny i Posledstviia* (The Sino-Soviet schism: Reasons and consequences). Moscow: Russian Academy of Sciences, 2000.

Lake, Marilyn, and Henry Reynolds. *Drawing the Global Color Line: White Men's Countries and the International Challenge of Racial Equality.* Cambridge, UK: Cambridge University Press, 2008.

Larkin, Bruce. *China and Africa, 1949–1970.* Berkeley: University of California Press, 1971.

Latham, Michael E. *Modernization as Ideology: American Social Science and "Nation Building" in the Kennedy Era.* Chapel Hill: University of North Carolina Press, 2000.

Lawson, Eugene K. *The Sino-Vietnamese Conflict.* New York: Praeger, 1984.

Lazitch, Branko, and Milorad M. Drachovitch. *Lenin and the Comintern. Vol. 1.* Stanford, CA: Hoover Institution Press, 1972.

Leatt, James, Theo Kneifel, and Klaus Nuernburger. *Contending Ideologies in South Africa.* Cape Town: David Phillip Publisher, 1986.

Legum, Colin, and Tony Hodges. *After Angola: The War over Southern Africa.* New York: Africana, 1976.

Leonhard, Wolfgang. *Three Faces of Marxism: The Political Concepts of Soviet Ideology, Maoism, and Humanist Marxism.* New York: Holt, Rinehart & Winston, 1974.

Leonov, Nikolai. Translated by Tim Ennis. "Soviet Intelligence in Latin America during the 'Cold War.'" *Estudios Publicos* 73 (1999): 1–32.

Leonov, Nikolai, Eugenia Fediakova, and Joaquin Fermandois. Translated by Tim Ennis. "General Nikolai Leonov at the CEP." *Estudios Publicos* 73 (1999): 1–37.

Levine, Steven I., and Alexander V. Pantsov. *Mao: The Real Story.* New York: Simon & Schuster, 2012.

Li, Anshan. "African Studies in China in the Twentieth Century: A Historiographical Survey." *African Studies Review* 48.1 (2005): 59–87.

Li, Huayin. *Village China under Socialism and Reform: A Micro History, 1948–2008.* Stanford, CA: Stanford University Press, 2009.

Light, Margot, ed. *Troubled Friendships: Moscow's Third World Ventures.* London: British Academic Press, 1993.

Liow, Joseph Chinyong. *The Politics of Indonesia-Malaysia Relations: One Kin, Two Nations.* New York: Routledge Curzon, 2005.

Louro, Michele. "Rethinking Nehru's Internationalism: The League against Imperialism and Anti-imperial Networks, 1927–1936." *Third Frame: Literature, Culture, and Society* 2.3 (September 2009): 79–94.

Low, Alfred D. *The Sino-Soviet Dispute.* Cranbury, NJ: Associated University Presses, 1976.

Lukin, Aleksander. *The Bear Watches the Dragon: Russia's Perceptions of China and the Evolution of Russian-Chinese Relations since the Eighteenth Century.* London: M. E. Sharpe, 2003.

Luthi, Lorenz. *The Sino-Soviet Split: Cold War in the Communist World.* Princeton, NJ: Princeton University Press, 2008.

Ma, Jisen. *The Cultural Revolution in the Foreign Ministry of China*. Hong Kong: Chinese University Press, 2004.

Mabeko-Tali, Jean-Michel. *Dissidências e Poder de Estado: O MPLA perante si próprio (1962–1977)*. 2 vols. (Dissent and state power: The MPLA before itself (1962–1977). Luanda, Angola: Editorial Nzila, 2001.

MacFarlane, Neil S. *Superpower Rivalry and Third World Radicalism*. Baltimore: Johns Hopkins University Press, 1985.

Macfarquhar, Roderick. *The Origins of the Cultural Revolution. Vol. 3, The Coming of the Cataclysm, 1961–1966*. Oxford: Oxford University Press, 1997.

———, ed. *The Politics of China: The Eras of Mao and Deng. 2d ed*. Cambridge, UK: Cambridge University Press, 1997.

Macfarquhar, Roderick, and Michael Schoenals. *Mao's Last Revolution*. Cambridge, MA: Belknap Press of Harvard University Press, 2006.

Manela, Erez. *The Wilsonian Moment: Self-Determination and the International Origins of Anticolonial Nationalism*. New York: Oxford University Press, 2007.

Marcum, John. *The Angolan Revolution: Exile Politics and Guerilla Warfare, 1962–1976. Vol. 2*. Cambridge, MA: MIT Press, 1978.

———. *The Angolan Revolution: The Anatomy of an Explosion, 1950–1962*. Baltimore: Port City Press, 1969.

Martin, Terry. *The Affirmative Action Empire: Nations and Nationalism in the Soviet Union, 1923–1939*. Ithaca, NY: Cornell University Press, 2001.

Mateus, Dalila Cabrita. A PIDE/DGS na Guerra Colonial, 1961–1974 (PIDE/DGS in the colonial war, 1961–1974). Lisbon: Terramar, 2004.

Mazov, Sergey. *A Distant Front in the Cold War: The USSR in West Africa and the Congo, 1956–1964*. Stanford, CA: Stanford University Press, 2010.

Mehnert, Klaus. *Moscow and the New Left*. Translated by Helmut Fischer and Luther Wilson. Berkeley: University of California Press, 1975.

———. *Peking and the New Left: At Home and Abroad*. Berkeley: University of California Press, 1969.

Mehta, Harish C. "Soviet Biscuit Factories and Chinese Financial Grants: North Vietnam's Economic Diplomacy in 1967 and 1968." *Diplomatic History* 36.2 (April 2012): 301–35.

Meisner, Maurice. *Li Ta-Chao and the Origins of Chinese Marxism*. Cambridge, MA: Harvard University Press, 1967.

———. *Mao Zedong: A Political and Intellectual Portrait*. Cambridge, UK: Polity Press, 2007.

Meredith, Martin. *The Fate of Africa: A History of Fifty Years of Independence*. New York: Public Affairs, 2005.

Minter, William. *Apartheid's Contras*. Johannesburg: Witwatersrand University Press, 1994.

Mishra, Pankaj. *From the Ruins of Empire: The Intellectuals Who Remade Asia*. London: Allen Lane, 2012.

Monson, Jamie. *Africa's Freedom Railway: How a Chinese Development Project Changed Lives and Livelihoods in Tanzania*. Bloomington: Indiana University Press, 2011.

Mozingo, David. *Chinese Policy towards Indonesia, 1949–1967.* Ithaca, NY: Cornell University Press, 1976.

Müller, Joachim W., and Karl P. Sauvant. *Chronology, Bibliography, and Index for the Group of 77 and the Non-aligned Movement.* New York: Oceana Publishers, 1993.

Murphy, Craig N. "What the Third World Wants: An Interpretation of the Development and Meaning of the New International Economic Order Ideology." *International Studies Quarterly* 27.1 (1983): 55–76.

Neuhauser, Charles. *Third World Politics: China and the Afro-Asian People's Solidarity Organization.* Cambridge, MA: Harvard University Press, 1968.

Nguyen, Lien-Hang. *Hanoi's War: An International History of the Struggle for Peace in Vietnam.* Chapel Hill: University of North Carolina Press, 2012.

———. "Between the Storms: North Vietnam's Strategy during the Second Indochina War (1955–1973)." Ph.D. diss., Yale University, 2008.

———. "The Sino-Vietnamese Split and the Indochina War, 1968–1975." In *The Third Indochina War,* edited by Odd Arne Westad and Sophie Quinn-Judge, 12–32. New York: Routledge, 2006.

———. "The War Politburo: North Vietnam's Diplomatic and Political Road to the Tet Offensive." *Journal of Vietnamese Studies* 1.1–2 (2006): 4–58.

Odom, William E. *On Internal War: American and Soviet Approaches to Third World Clients and Insurgents.* Durham, NC: Duke University Press, 1992.

Ogunsanwo, Alaba. *China's Policy in Africa, 1958–1971.* Cambridge, UK: Cambridge University Press, 1974.

Olsen, Mari. *Soviet-Vietnam Relations and the Role of China, 1949–1964.* New York: Routledge, Taylor and Francis Group, 2006.

Pantsov, Alexander. *The Bolsheviks and the Chinese Revolution, 1919–1927.* Honolulu: University of Hawaii Press, 2000.

Peet, Richard, and Elaine Hartwick. *Theories of Development: Contentions, Arguments, Alternatives.* New York: Guilford, 2009.

Pike, Douglas. *Vietnam and the Soviet Union.* Boulder, CO: Westview, 1987.

Portyakov, Vladimir. *The People's Republic of China: Economic Policy of the 1990s.* Moscow: Russian Academy of Sciences, 1999.

Qiang, Zhai. *China and the Vietnam Wars, 1950–1975.* Chapel Hill: University of North Carolina Press, 2000.

Ra'anan, Uri. *The USSR Arms the Third World: Case Studies in Soviet Foreign Policy.* Cambridge, MA: MIT Press, 1969.

Radchenko, Sergey. *Two Suns in the Heavens: The Sino-Soviet Struggle for Supremacy, 1962–1967.* Stanford, CA: Stanford University Press, 2009.

Radchenko, Sergey, and Artemy Kalinovsky, eds. *The End of the Cold War and the Third World.* New York: Routledge, 2011.

Radu, Michael, and Arthur Jay Klinghoffer. *The Dynamics of Soviet Policy in Sub-Saharan Africa.* New York: Holmes and Meier, 1991.

Rakove, Robert B. *Kennedy, Johnson, and the Nonaligned World.* New York: Cambridge University Press, 2013.

Remnek, Richard B. *Soviet Scholars and Soviet Foreign Policy: A Case Study in Soviet Policy towards India.* Durham, NC: Carolina Academic Press, 1975.

Rodrik, Daniel. *In Search of Prosperity.* Princeton, NJ: Princeton University Press, 2003.

Ross, Robert S. *The Indochina Tangle: China's Vietnam Policy, 1975–1979.* New York: Columbia University Press, 1988.

———, ed. *China, the United States, and the Soviet Union: Tripolarity and Policy Making in the Cold War.* London: M. E. Sharpe, 1993.

Ross, Robert S., and Jiang Chagbin, eds. *Re-examining the Cold War: U.S.-China Diplomacy, 1954–1973.* Cambridge, MA: Harvard University Press, 2003.

Rothenberg, Morris. *Whither China: The View from the Kremlin.* Miami: University of Miami Press, 1977.

Rozman, Gilbert. *The Chinese Debate about Soviet Socialism, 1978–1985.* Princeton, NJ: Princeton University Press, 1987.

———. *A Mirror for Socialism: Soviet Criticisms of China.* Princeton, NJ: Princeton University Press, 1985.

Rubinstein, Alvin Z. *Red Star on the Nile: The Soviet-Egyptian Influence Relationship since the June War.* Princeton, NJ: Princeton University Press, 1977.

———. *Soviet and Chinese Influence in the Third World.* New York: Praeger, 1975.

Rubinstein, Arthur. *Moscow's Third World Strategy.* Princeton, NJ: Princeton University Press, 1988.

Saivetz, Carol R., and Sylvia Woodby. *Soviet Third-World Relations.* Boulder, CO: Westview, 1985.

Sanchez-Sibony, Oscar. *Red Globalization: The Political Economy of the Soviet Cold War from Stalin to Khrushchev.* Cambridge: Cambridge University Press, 2014.

Sanderson, Stephen K. *Revolutions: A Worldwide Introduction to Political and Social Change.* Boulder, CO: Paradigm Publishers, 2005.

Schmidt, Elizabeth. *Cold War and Decolonization in Guinea, 1946–1958.* Athens, Ohio: Ohio University Press, 2007.

Schram, Stuart. *The Thought of Mao Tse-tung.* Cambridge, UK: Cambridge University Press, 1989.

Segev, Tom. Translated by Jessica Cohen. *1967: Israel, the War, and the Year That Transformed the Middle East.* New York: Metropolitan Books, 2007.

Selden, Mark. *The Yenan Way in Revolutionary China.* Cambridge, MA: Harvard University Press, 1971.

Shambaugh, David. *China's Communist Party: Atrophy and Adaptation.* Washington, DC: Woodrow Wilson Center Press, 2008.

Shen, Zhihua, ed. 中苏关系史纲 (Historical outline of Sino-Soviet relations). Beijing: Xinhua Press, 2007.

Shen, Zhihua, and Xia Yafeng. "Leadership Transfer in the Asian Revolution: Mao Zedong and the Asian Cominform." *Cold War History* 14.2 (2014): 195–213.

Sheng, Michael M. *Battling Western Imperialism: Mao, Stalin, and the United States.* Princeton, NJ: Princeton University Press, 1997.

Shubin, Vladimir. *The Hot "Cold War": The USSR in Southern Africa.* London: Pluto Press, 2008.

———. *ANC: A View from Moscow.* Cape Town: Mayibuye Books, 1999.

Sidel, Mark. "Latin American Studies in the People's Republic of China." *Latin American Research Review* 18.1 (1983): 143–53.

Sigmund, Paul E. *The Overthrow of Allende and the Politics of Chile, 1964–1976.* Pittsburgh: University of Pittsburgh Press, 1977.

Simon, Sheldon W. *The Broken Triangle: Peking, Djakarta, and the PKI.* Baltimore: Johns Hopkins University Press, 1969.

Simpson, Bradley R. *Economists with Guns: Authoritarian Development and U.S.-Indonesian Relations, 1960–1968.* Stanford, CA: Stanford University Press, 2008.

Snow, Phillip. *The Star Raft: China's Encounter with Africa.* London: Weidenfeld & Nicolson, 1988.

Srivastava, Gyanendra N. *NAM and the Soviet Foreign Policy.* New Delhi: Indian Institute for Non-Aligned Studies, 1989.

Srivastava, R. *India and the Nonaligned Summits: Belgrade to Jakarta.* New Delhi: Northern Book Centre, 1995.

Stallings, Barbara. *Class Conflict and Economic Development in Chile, 1958–1973.* Stanford, CA: Stanford University Press, 1978.

Statler, Kathryn C., and Andrew L. Johns, eds. *The Eisenhower Administration, the Third World, and the Globalization of the Cold War.* Lanham, MD: Rowman & Littlefield, 2006.

Sturgill, Claude C. *The Military History of the Third World since 1945.* Westport, CT: Greenwood, 1994.

Suarez Bastidas, Jaime. *Allende: Vision de un militante* (Allende: Vision of a militant). Santiago, Chile: Salesianos Impresores, 2008.

Suri, Jeremi. *Power and Protest: Global Revolution and the Rise of Detente.* Cambridge, MA: Harvard University Press, 2003.

Talavera, Arturo Fontaine. "The United States and the Soviet Union in Chile." *Estudios Publicos* 72 (1998): 1–12.

Taylor, Ian. *China and Africa.* New York: Routledge, 2006.

Tsipursky, Gleb. "Pleasure, Power, and the Pursuit of Communism: Soviet Youth and State-Sponsored Popular Culture during the Early Cold War, 1945–1968." Ph.D. diss., University of North Carolina, 2011.

Ulam, Adam. *In the Name of the People: Prophets and Conspirators in Prerevolutionary Russia.* New York: Viking Press, 1977.

———. *Expansion and Coexistence: Soviet Foreign Policy, 1917–73.* New York: Praeger, 1974.

Ulianova, Olga. "Soviet Perceptions and Analyses of the Unidad Popular Government and the Military Coup in Chile." *Estudios Publicos* 79 (2000): 1–89.

Ulianova, Olga, and Eugenia Fediakova. "Aspects of Financial Aid to Chilean Communism from the USSR Communist Party during the Cold War." *Estudios Publicos* 72 (1998): 1–36.

van Eekelen, W. F. *Indian Foreign Policy and the Border Dispute with China.* The Hague: Martinus Nijhoff, 1964.

Vanneman, Peter, and W. Martin James III. *Soviet Foreign Policy in Southern Africa.* Pretoria: Africa Institute of South Africa, 1982.

van Ness, Peter. *Revolution and Chinese Foreign Policy: Peking's Support for Wars of National Liberation.* Berkeley: University of California Press, 1970.

Vogel, Ezra. *Canton under Communism: Programs and Politics in a Provincial Capital, 1949–1968.* Cambridge, MA: Harvard University Press, 1969.

———. *Deng Xiaoping and the Transformation of China.* Cambridge, MA: Belknap Press of Harvard University Press, 2013.

Walker, Ignacio. "Del Populismo al leninismo y la 'inevitabilidad del conflicto': El Partido Socialista de Chile (1933–1973)" ("From populism to Leninism and the 'inevitability of conflict': The Socialist Party of Chile (1933–1973)"). *Notas Tecnicas* 91 (1986).

Wedeman, Andrew Hall. *The East Wind Subsides: Chinese Foreign Policy and the Origins of the Cultural Revolution.* Washington, DC: Washington Institute Press, 1987.

Weinstein, Warren, ed. *Chinese and Soviet Aid to Africa.* New York: Praeger, 1975.

Westad, Odd Arne. "Moscow and the Angolan Crisis, 1974–1976: A New Pattern of Intervention." *Cold War International History Project Bulletin* 8–9 (1996): 21–37.

———. *The Global Cold War.* New York: Cambridge University Press, 2007.

———, ed. *Brothers in Arms: The Rise and Fall of the Sino-Soviet Alliance, 1945–1963.* Stanford, CA: Stanford University Press, 1998.

Westad, Odd Arne, and Sophie Quinn-Judge, eds. *The Third Indochina War: Conflict between China, Vietnam, and Cambodia, 1972–79.* New York: Routledge, 2006.

Wheelan, Joseph G., and Michael J. Dixon. *The Soviet Union in the Third World: Threat to World Peace?* New York: Pergamon-Brassey's, 1986.

Willets, Peter. *The Non-aligned Movement: The Origins of a Third World Alliance.* New York: Nicols, 1978.

Williams, Gwyneth. *Third World Political Organizations: A Review of Developments.* London: Macmillan, 1987.

Williams, Kieran. *The Prague Spring and Its Aftermath.* New York: Cambridge University Press, 1997.

Wolfe, Bertram D. *Three Who Made a Revolution.* New York: Dell, 1964.

Wu, Frederick W. Y. "From Self-Reliance to Interdependence? Developmental Strategy and Foreign Economic Policy in Post-Mao China." *Modern China* 7.4 (1981): 445–82.

Yang, Kuisong. "Changes in Mao Zedong's Attitude toward the Indochina War, 1949–1973." Cold War International History Project Working Paper 34 (2002).

Yu, George T. "Sino-Soviet Rivalry in Africa." In *Communism in Africa,* edited by David E. Albright, 168–88. Bloomington: Indiana University Press, 1980.

Zagoria, Donald. *The Sino-Soviet Conflict, 1956–1961.* Princeton, NJ: Princeton University Press, 1962.

———. *Vietnam Triangle: Moscow, Peking, Hanoi.* New York: Pegasus, 1967.

Zhang, Jialin. *China's Response to the Downfall of Communism in Eastern Europe and the Soviet Union.* Stanford, CA: Hoover Institution, 1994.

Zhang, Xiaoming. "Communist Powers Divided: China, the Soviet Union, and the Vietnam War." In *International Perspectives on Vietnam,* edited by Lloyd C.

Gardner and Ted Gittinger, 77–97. College Station: Texas A&M University Press, 2000.

Zhou, Taomo. "Ambivalent Alliance: Chinese Policy towards Indonesia, 1960–1965." Cold War International History Project Working Paper 67 (August 2013).

Zhuk, Sergei I. *Rock and Roll in the Rocket City: The West, Identity, and Ideology in Soviet Dniepropetrovsk, 1960–1985*. Baltimore: Johns Hopkins University Press, 2010.

Zubok, Vladislav, and Constantine Pleshakov. *Inside the Kremlin's Cold War: From Stalin to Khrushchev*. Cambridge, MA: Harvard University Press, 1996.

promoted in, 83–86; Soviet socialism building in, 69–83
—1963–1965: anti-Sovietism in, 115; autonomous independent economy model and, 118–19; intense Sino-Soviet competition in, 104–5; PRC aid program and, 117–20
—1966–1969: centralized political organization and, 161; economics and, 163; Maoism and nationalism and, 162; military coups and, 160–61
—1970–1976: China as aspiring leader in, 195–203; conclusions about, 214; countries of socialist orientation and, 189–91; Cuba as spokesman for Moscow, 205–6; decade of discontent and, 181–82; dependency theory and, 192–94; economic injustice and, 182–83; guerrilla warfare and, 200–201; Lusaka Declaration and, 182; Moscow fights for, 203–10; NIEO and, 207–8; PRC aid and, 198–99, 211; PRC diplomatic offensive in, 199–200; Soviet natural alliance with, 183–84; USSR as champion of, 208–9
Disarmament, 67; dividend, 206
DRV. *See* Democratic Republic of Vietnam

Economy: Africa, 181–82; autonomous independent model of, 118–19; "China's Economic Growth," 78; Chinese Revolution, 12–13; GKES, 35; NIEO, 207–8; Sino-Soviet split and, 217; United States and, 182–83
—developing world and: 1966–1969, 163; 1970–1976, 182–83
Egypt: friendship treaties and, 187; PRC and, 41–42, 43; Six-Day War and, 158–59; Soviet aid to, 181. *See also* United Arab Republic

Faure, Edgar, 116
First Non-Aligned Conference, 67–68
FLN (National Liberation Front), 135

FNLA (National Front for the Liberation of Angola), 121–22
Four Modernizations, 211
Fourth National People's Congress, 210–11
Fourth Non-Aligned Summit, 204–5
France, 135
Friendship treaties, 187–88

Gafurov, Babadjan, 17–18
Games of New Emerging Forces (GANEFO), 141–42
Gandhi, Indira, 187
GANEFO. *See* Games of New Emerging Forces
Ganovskii, Yuri, 76
Gao, Di, 222
Ghana, 29, 47, 77, 81, 82
GKES (State Committee on External Economic Ties), 35
GMD (Guomindang), 14
Gorbachev, Mikhail, 219, 220
Great Leap Forward, 62
Green Guards, 155
Gromyko, Andrei, 17, 145, 220
Guerrilla warfare, 200–201
Guevara, Che, 88, 94, 149; death of, 157; Mikoyan and, 95; Nasser and, 1
Guinea, 223; aid to, 77–78, 79; socialism and, 78–79; Soviet fallout with, 80–81; state of national democracy and, 77–81
Gulf of Tonkin, 113–14
Guomindang (GMD), 14

Ho Chi Minh, 88, 170
Huang Hua, 121, 151

Ideology: *Mezhdunarodniki* and, 22; policy and, 19–23; Westad on, 6
Il'inskii, Mikhail, 165
Imperialism, 215–16. *See also* Anti-imperialism, CCP; Anti-imperialism, USSR
India: aid to, 131; Brezhnev on treaty with, 187–88; friendship treaties and, 187–88; Kozlov on, 52; Sino-Indian

border conflict, 42–43, 68–69, 95–96;
Tito and, 41
Indonesia, 65, 128–29; aid to, 131–32;
Chinese living in, 141; coup in, 144;
PRC and Soviet relations with,
140–45; religion and, 110–11; state of
national democracy and, 74–76
Indonesian Communist Party (PKI):
antirevisionist rhetoric of, 142; armed
uprising by, 140; CCP and CPSU and,
142–43; coup and, 144; Sukarno and,
143–44
Intermediate zone, 16
International Department, 17, 18
Internationalists (*Mezhdunarodniki*),
18, 22
International Seminar on the 25th
anniversary of Mao's speech in
Yan'an on Literature and Art, 155
Islam, 110–11
Israel, 32, 129, 158–59, 181

Jiang Jieshi, 14

Kasavubu, Joseph, 46
Kaunda, Kenneth, 155
Kawawa, Rashidi, 120
Keita, Modibo, 77, 81–82, 177
Kennedy, John F., 60
Kennedy, Robert F., 223
Khartoum conference, 174, 175
Khrushchev, Nikita, 16; Algeria and, 136,
138, 140; Aswan High Dam and,
111–12; Castro and, 102; on Mao, 51; on
missile crisis, 101; Nasser and, 112; on
newly independent states, 30, 83; on
new possibilities, 60; noncapitalist
path and, 34; ouster of, 104; peaceful
coexistence pronouncement of, 25–26;
on Sino-Soviet split, 215; Sukarno
and, 140; on United States, 22; verbal
attack of China by, 105; World Forum
for Solidarity of Youth and Students
and, 112–13
Kim, G., 108

Kolosovskii, Andrei, 220–21
Kommunist (CPSU), 162
Kosygin, Alexei, 104, 124–25
Kouyate, Seydou Badian, 70
Kozlov, Frol, 52, 91

Land reform, 11–12
Latin America: 1964 conference of
Communist Parties in, 126; peaceful
coexistence and, 156–58; propaganda
and, 91; Zhou and, 94. *See also specific
countries*
Latinskaia Amerika (journal), 48
Le Duan, 168, 188
Lenin, Vladimir, 2; imperialism theory
of, 8; on nationalism, 7–8; noncapital-
ist path and, 26; Roy and, 14
Leonov, Nikolai, 48, 219
Liaison Department (*Zhonglianbu*),
18–19
Lianluozhan (liaison station), 152–53
Little red book (*Quotations from
Chairman Mao*), 154
Liu Ningyi, 33, 46
Liu Shaoqi, 12, 52, 93, 168
"Long Live Leninism" (Mao-inspired
polemic), 51
Lu Dingyi, 27
Lumumba, Patrice, 46, 61
Lusaka Declaration, 182

Mali, 77, 81–82
Malik, Yakov, 157
Maoism, 149, 150, 162–64, 173, 179, 201,
205, 219
"Maoism or Marxism" (Burlatskii), 162
Mao Zedong: business and economy
and, 12–13; class and, 10–11; death of,
211; Foreign Ministry and, 152–53;
Great Leap Forward end and, 62;
imperialism and, 9–10; intermediate
zone and, 16; International Seminar
on the 25th anniversary of Mao's
speech in Yan'an on Literature and
Art, 155; on knowledge of Africa, 51;

"Long Live Leninism" and, 51;
Quotations from Chairman Mao
and, 154; rhetoric change by, 196; on
Twenty-Second Congress, 87; Wang
Jiaxiang recommendations and,
92–93
Marxism, 4, 7, 9–10, 56, 111, 162, 172
Masyumi Party, 140
Mboya, Tom, 46
Mezhdunarodniki (Internationalists),
18, 22
Middle East: USSR and, 158–60; Zhou
and, 159. *See also specific countries*
Mikoyan, Anastas, 80–81, 94, 95, 142
Mirskii, G., 77
Modernization, 3–4
Monje, Manuel, 157
Moscow, 1969 international communist
movement meeting in, 175–76
Moscow Declaration, 63, 67, 71
Moshi conference, 97
MPLA (Popular Movement for the
Liberation of Angola), 54, 121, 122

Narody Azii i Afriki (journal), 108
Nasser, Gamal Abdel, 187; Guevara and,
1; Khrushchev and, 112; PRC and
Soviet relations with, 132–34; Soviet
anti-imperialism and, 158–59
National democracy, 57–58. *See also*
State of national democracy
National Front for the Liberation of
Angola (FNLA), 121–22
National independence, 83–84
Nationalism: Lenin on, 7–8; Maoism
and, 162
National Liberation Front (FLN), 135
Negritude, 200
Nehru, Jawaharlal, 67–68, 70
Nekolim, 65
Neocolonialism, 4, 65–66
*Neo-Colonialism: The Last Stage of
Imperialism* (Nkrumah), 4
Neto, Agostinho, 210
Ne Win, 117

New International Economic Order
(NIEO), 207–8
N'Famara, Keita, 78
NIEO. *See* New International Economic
Order
Nixon, Richard, 181, 186–87, 188–89
Nkrumah, Kwame, 4, 29, 77, 82, 121, 149
Non-Aligned Movement, 41, 67, 117, 182,
200, 204–7, 214
Noncapitalist path, 26; militant
working-class line and, 82–83; trials
and tribulations, 69–86; USSR and,
34–36, 62–63
Novosti press agency, 105–6
Nyerere, Julius, 120, 121, 155, 182

OAU. *See* Organization of African
Unity
Odinga, Oginga, 46
Organization of African Unity (OAU),
103, 121, 135

Palestine, 174–75
Partial Test Ban Treaty, 103
Patolichev, N. S., 208
Peaceful coexistence
—1956–1960: as Achilles' heel, 103;
Chinese criticism of, 83–84; Conakry
conference and, 44; conclusions
about, 58–59; India and, 43; Khrushchev's pronouncement of, 25–26;
noncapitalist path and, 26; People's
Friendship University and, 47–48;
PRC and, 26–28; racism and, 55–56;
scholarly and propaganda apparatus
supporting, 48–49; summary of
Soviet position regarding, 39
—1961–1963: conclusions about, 86;
Congo and, 64; disarmament and, 67;
Indonesia and, 65
—1966–1969: Brezhnev on, 148; Cuba
and, 156–58; Latin America and,
156–58
People's Friendship University, 47–48, 49
People's Liberation Army (PLA), 177

People's Republic of China (PRC):
AAPSO and, 196–97, 198; Africa,
diplomatic relations with, 116–17; aid
program, 117–20; aid to developing
world by, 31–32, 117–20, 198–99, 211;
Algerian relations with, 134–40;
Angola and, 209–10; anti-imperialism
and developing world and, 83–86;
anti-imperialism priority of, 2;
autonomous independent economy
model of, 118–19; competition and
adaptation and, 115–23; core visions
of, 222; decolonization and, 5–6;
developing world policy of, 29; DRV
and, 113–14, 130; Egypt and, 41–42, 43;
first conference of AAPSO and, 32–33;
foreign student complaints in, 55;
Fourth National People's Congress,
210–11; global revolution and, 4–5;
Great Leap Forward end in, 62;
Indian border conflict with, 42–44,
68–69, 95–96; Indonesian relations
with, 140–45; institutions of, 18–19;
international reemergence of, 176–77;
military involvement in Africa,
120–21; national independence and,
83–84; 1970 shift in rhetoric, 196;
Soviet scholarly and propaganda
apparatus and, 48–49; Tan-Zam
railway and, 120; theoretical evaluation of developing world by, 36–39; as
Third World aspiring new leader,
195–203; Tito and, 40–41; training
requests to, 50; Twenty-Second
Congress diplomacy and, 87–88; UAR
relations with, 132–34; UN and, 183,
197–98. *See also* Chinese Communist
Party; Chinese Revolution; Cultural
Revolution; Sino-Soviet split
Pham Van Dong, 129
PKI. *See* Indonesian Communist Party
PLA (People's Liberation Army), 177
Ponomarev, Boris, 17, 73, 79–80, 102, 220
Popular Movement for the Liberation of
Angola (MPLA), 54, 121, 122

Potekhin, I., 65–66
PRC. *See* People's Republic of China
Prebisch, Raúl, 182, 193
Problems of the Development of
Revolution and the Struggle for
Socialism in Liberated Countries, 161
Problemy Mira i Sotsializma (journal),
91, 107
Propaganda: anti-Chinese, 105–9;
Cuban Missile Crisis, 96–97;
following Twenty-Second Congress,
90–91; Latin America and, 91;
peaceful coexistence, 48–49
"Proposal Concerning the General Line
of the International Communist
Movement" (CCP), 102
PSI (Socialist Party), 140

Qiao Guanhua, 197
Quotations from Chairman Mao, 154

Racism: PRC and, 55; USSR and, 55–56
Radek, Karl, 8
Red Guards: criticism of, 154; Foreign
Ministry and, 152–53
Religion, 110–11
Revolutionary democracy, 156, 189–90
Revolutions: death of, 215–24; decoloni-
zation and, 5–6; global, 4–5; Guevara's
versus Nasser's, 1; institutions of,
16–19; modernization and, 3–4;
origins and trajectories, 6–13; tale of
two, 1–24. *See also* Chinese Revolu-
tion; Russian Revolution
Roberto, Holden, 121–22
Roy, M. N., 14
Rumyantsev, A., 107
Russian Revolution: anticapitalist
agenda of, 7–8; class and, 10–11;
developing world and, 13–16; land
reform and, 11–12

Al-Sadat, Anwar, 46, 187
Safronov, Anatoly, 44, 91
Schürer, Gerhard, 218

THE NEW COLD WAR HISTORY

SULMAAN WASIF KHAN, *Muslim, Trader, Nomad, Spy: China's Cold War and the Tibetan Borderlands* (2015).

JEREMY FRIEDMAN, *Shadow Cold War: The Sino-Soviet Competition for the Third World* (2015).

MARGARET PEACOCK, Innocent Weapons: *The Soviet and American Politics of Childhood in the Cold War* (2014).

AUSTIN JERSILD, *The Sino-Soviet Alliance: An International History* (2014).

PIERO GLEIJESES, *Visions of Freedom: Havana, Washington, Pretoria, and the Struggle for Southern Africa, 1976–1991* (2013).

LIEN-HANG T. NGUYEN, *Hanoi's War: An International History of the War for Peace in Vietnam* (2012).

TANYA HARMER, *Allende's Chile and the Inter-American Cold War, 1970–1973* (2011).

ALESSANDRO BROGI, *Confronting America: The Cold War between the United States and the Communists in France and Italy* (2011).

GREGG BRAZINSKY, *Nation Building in South Korea: Koreans, Americans, and the Making of a Democracy* (2007).

VLADISLAV M. ZUBOK, *A Failed Empire: The Soviet Union in the Cold War from Stalin to Gorbachev* (2007).

STEPHEN G. RABE, *U.S. Intervention in British Guiana: A Cold War Story* (2005).

CHRISTOPHER ENDY, *Cold War Holidays: American Tourism in France* (2004).

SALIM YAQUB, *Containing Arab Nationalism: The Eisenhower Doctrine and the Middle East* (2003).

FRANCIS J. GAVIN, *Gold, Dollars, and Power: The Politics of International Monetary Relations, 1958–1971* (2003).

WILLIAM GLENN GRAY, *Germany's Cold War: The Global Campaign to Isolate East Germany, 1949–1969* (2003).

MATTHEW J. OUIMET, *The Rise and Fall of the Brezhnev Doctrine in Soviet Foreign Policy* (2003).

PIERRE ASSELIN, *A Bitter Peace: Washington, Hanoi, and the Making of the Paris Agreement* (2002).

JEFFREY GLEN GIAUQUE, *Grand Designs and Visions of Unity: The Atlantic Powers and the Reorganization of Western Europe, 1955–1963* (2002).

CHEN JIAN, *Mao's China and the Cold War* (2001).

M. E. SAROTTE, *Dealing with the Devil: East Germany, Détente, and Ostpolitik, 1969–1973* (2001).

MARK PHILIP BRADLEY, *Imagining Vietnam and America: The Making of Postcolonial Vietnam, 1919–1950* (2000).

MICHAEL E. LATHAM, *Modernization as Ideology: American Social Science and "Nation Building" in the Kennedy Era* (2000).

QIANG ZHAI, *China and the Vietnam Wars, 1950–1975* (2000).

WILLIAM I. HITCHCOCK, *France Restored: Cold War Diplomacy and the Quest for Leadership in Europe, 1944–1954* (1998).

9 781469 645520